Tōkyō

Tōkyō Bay

Yokohama

Chigasaki

Ōiso

Kamakura

Yokosuka

Hayama

Miura
Peninsula

Sagami Bay

Japan
Suruga Bay to Tōkyō

0   10 MILES

J. Colman

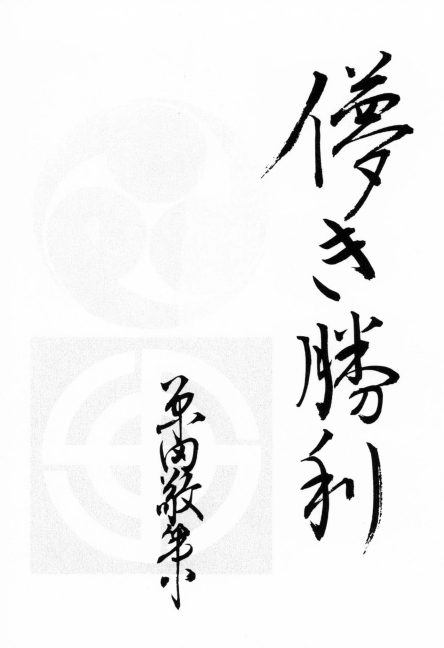

儚き勝利

原田敬策

Especially for this book Mr. Keisaku Harada,
the son of Baron Harada,
has graciously written and signed
this epigraph giving
a translation of the English title,
Fragile Victory
The Japanese is read as
Moroki Shōri.

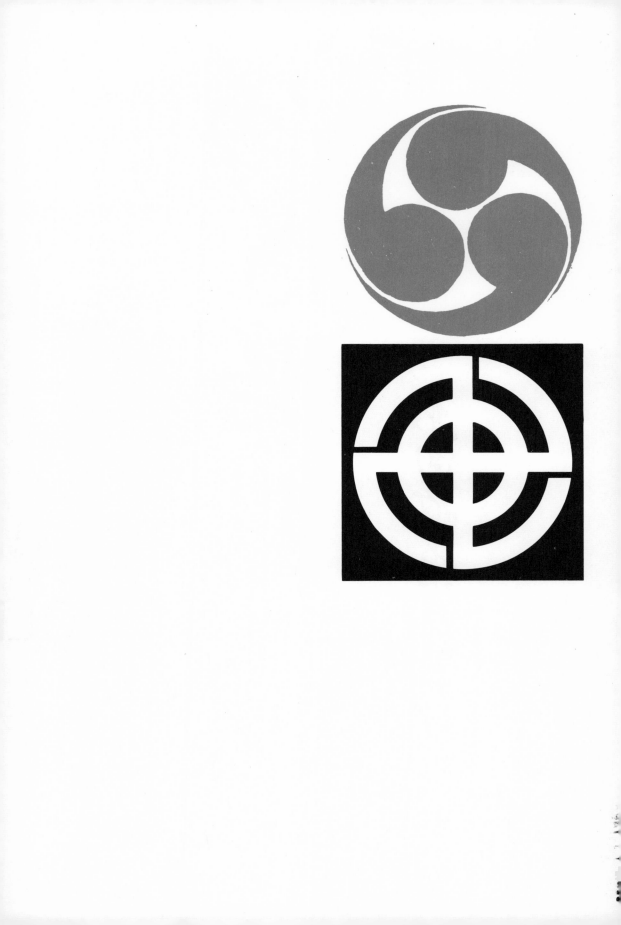

Saionji-Harada Memoirs

Fragile Victory

Prince Saionji and

the 1930 London Treaty Issue

from the Memoirs of

Baron Harada Kumao

Translated with an

Introduction and Annotations

by Thomas Francis Mayer-Oakes
WAYNE STATE UNIVERSITY

Wayne State University Press

Detroit 1968

Contents

In addition to his epigraph, Mr. Keisaku Harada has provided the portraits of his father and of Prince Saionji that appear on pages 43 and 17. Photographs of other persons used throughout this book (and they may be found by reference to the Index) were obtained by Mr. Kiyoaki Murata from the archives of the Kyōdō Tsūshin Photo Service, Tokyo, and date in most instances from the period of this narrative. The pictures of Prince Saionji's houses at Okitsu and Gotemba (pages 39 and 197) are the work of the architectural photographer, Mr. Kaneaki Monma.

The endpaper maps, designed by Mr. Richard Kinney, may be useful in locating the places recurrently visited and mentioned by Baron Harada in this narrative of his round of activities.

The seal impressions used as ornaments in chapter headings and elsewhere in this book are almost entirely from seals graven at various times by Prince Saionji for his own use, and usually bear one or another of his names.

On the dust jacket and cover are imprinted the heraldic family crests (or *mon*) of the house of Saionji (the triskelion design; in Japanese, *migi mitsu-domoe*) and of the Harada house (the modified swastika or gammadion).

Introduction

This work is a translation of the first volume of the memoirs written by Harada Kumao,[1] one of the most notable of many such works published in Japan since the end of World War II. Some, like the important Hara diary, are from more than a generation ago.[2] Some, such as the posthumous Konoe papers, are fragmentary apologia.[3] There are those by men who still had hopes for a political future.[4] Others, like those of Shidehara, Wakatsuki, Okada, and Ugaki,[5] are reflections in retirement, dictated to amanuenses—or ghost-written, and not always buttressed with much evidence beyond memory itself.

From all these the Harada papers differ in their size and detail and their contemporaneity with the events recorded, and for intrinsic reasons. Harada's documents deal with the inner background workings of Japanese politics, in the decade of the 1930s, as they concerned Prince Saionji Kimmochi. In his own person this venerable figure (he was eighty-two in 1930) expressed a singular para-

---

[1] Harada Kumao, *Saionji ko to seikyoku* [*Prince Saionji and the Political Situation*] (9 vols.; Tōkyō: Iwanami shoten, 1950-56). Throughout this introduction and in the following text Japanese names are given according to Japanese convention: family name is given first and personal name is second.

[2] Hara Keiichirō (ed.), *Hara Takashi nikki* [*The Diary of Hara Takashi*] (10 vols.; Tōkyō: Kengensha, 1950-51).

[3] Konoe Fumimaro, *Ushinawareshi seiji* [*The Policy That Failed*] (Tōkyō: Asahi Shimbunsha, n.d.).

[4] Shigemitsu Mamoru, *Shōwa no dōran* [*Upheavals of the Showa Period*] (2 vols.; Tōkyō: Chūō Kōronsha, 1952). Shigemitsu had survived conviction and imprisonment as a war criminal to become one of the foci of conservative opposition to the regime of Yoshida Shigeru, like him a former career diplomat under the old order, and Foreign Minister in the postwar Hatoyama Cabinet.

[5] Shidehara Kijūro, *Gaikō gojūnen* [*Diplomacy Through Fifty Years*] (Tōkyō: Yomiuri Shimbunsha, 1951); Wakatsuki Reijirō, *Kofūan kaikoroku* [*Memoirs of Kōfuan (Wakatsuki)*] (Tōkyō: Yomiuri Shimbunsha, 1950); Okada Keisuke, *Okada Keisuke kaikoroku* [*Memoirs of Okada Keisuke*] (Tōkyō: Mainichi Shimbunsha, 1950).

The title which General Ugaki Kazushige gave to his memoirs suggests the tone of many of these: *Shōrai seidan* [*Old Man's Talk 'Midst Sighing Pines*] (Tōkyō: Bungei Shunjū Shinsha, 1951).

dox: he was the last of the *genrō* and at the same time renowned as a "moderate" and even a "liberal." The *genrō*—Japan's unofficial but prepotent Elder Statesmen—had shaped and guided Japanese modernization as an authoritarian oligarchy. Since 1924 Saionji was the sole *genrō*, holding dearly his prerogative as "maker of cabinets." Yet at the same time he had hoped for and had fostered developments toward more responsible parliamentarism within Japan and supported cooperative policies internationally, especially in concert with Britain and the United States.

Harada's voluminous work is far less a memoir about Saionji, however, than it is a meticulously detailed report of the political intelligence he gathered for Saionji, and an accounting of his own sedulous political liaison activities on the old prince's behalf. The old prince, so extraordinary in the range of his experiences and interests, may have deserved a Boswell; but for such an undertaking Harada had neither purpose nor opportunity. In his last decade Saionji saw most of the "liberal" patterns he preferred dissolving before the plangent waves of rising nationalism, aggression abroad, and internal preparation for total war.

It is perhaps obvious to expect that the Harada papers, once available in the post-war period, have served many purposes since their first projection into the Tokyo War Crimes Trials. They have been a mother lode for miners in search for diverse ores. At least three general types of use can be discerned. One type might be called thematic studies, as in Storry's skilful study of pre-war ultra-nationalists or in Maxon's largely institutional review of how the Japanese military came to control the state's foreign policy.[6] Secondly, there have been analytic studies, often by iconoclastic younger Japanese scholars, such as Maruyama Masao, asking anew how the pathological political order they had suffered and survived might best be understood.[7] A third kind of use might be called episodic mining wherein segments of the Harada materials are used (and sometimes badly used) on particular episodes or on particular persons.[8]

---

[6] Richard Storry, *The Double Patriots: A Study of Japanese Nationalism* (London: Chatto and Windus, 1957); Yale Candee Maxon, *Control of Japanese Foreign Policy: A Study of Civil-Military Rivalry, 1930-1945* (Berkeley: University of California Press, 1957).

[7] Maruyama Masao, *Gendai seiji no shisō to kōdō* (2 vols.; Tōkyō: Mirai-sha, 1958). Nine of the eighteen essays of this work have been translated and published under the editorship of Ivan Morris as *Thought and Behaviour in Modern Japanese Politics* (London: Oxford University Press, 1963).

[8] Yoshihashi, Takehiko, *Conspiracy at Mukden: The Rise of the Jap-

It is equally obvious that such uses of the Harada materials merely as a kind of archive, as a source for data, may tend to disregard the work itself, its texture and testimony as an emanation from a particular segment of Japanese life. Before the war journalists and scholars alike, from outside Japan, were apt to dismiss (or to argue for the early obliteration of) the aristocratic and oligarchic aspects of modern Japan as being vestigial if not noxious archaic survivals. The soundest survey of Japan's government a generation ago, written as Harada was beginning his record, bemoaned the "prolonged influence of an ultra-conservative aristocracy beyond the epoch of history to which it belonged."[9] But "belonging" or not, the aristocracy was clearly and influentially there, and by no means functioning monolithically in ultra-conservative causes.

It seems probable that the "old liberal" in Saionji would today approve of the formal abolition of his class in the postwar period (as his own descendants have done);[10] and that in "the continuity of events" and "in the persistent growth . . . of a more open society" he would regard the military violence from 1931 to 1945 as a ghastly but temporary "interruption."[11] With his sense

---

anese Military (New Haven: Yale University Press, 1963); and Frank O. Miller, *Minobe Tatsukichi: Interpreter of Consitutionalism in Japan* (Berkeley: University of California Press, 1965).

[9] Harold S. Quigley, *Japanese Government and Politics* (New York: D. Appleton-Century, 1932), p. 64. In its context, of course, Quigley's phrase is not a mere cliché.

[10] A grandson has identified himself with the far left in *apure (après guerre)* politics. During the war he had been formally charged with involvement in the Sorge spy case and received a suspended sentence (See F. W. Deakin and G. R. Storry, *The Case of Richard Sorge* (New York: Harper & Row, 1966), pp. 290-94 *et passim*).

[11] The quoted phrases are from William W. Lockwood's essay "Economic and Political Modernization—Japan" in the symposium edited by Robert E. Ward and Dankwart A. Rustow, *Political Modernization In Japan and Turkey* (Princeton: Princeton University Press, 1964), pp. 117-45. They reflect the recently changing interests and interpretations of specialists in many disciplines in studying modern Japan in greater depth. The war and its causes (and its antipathies) are seen as less significant than the longer secular processes of change called modernization in which the Japanese continue to be so successful, and the possible relevance of the Japanese experience for understanding "development" generally. On the limited problem of assessing the nature of prewar parliamentary politics George O. Totten has assembled representative diverse views in his *Democracy in Prewar Japan: Groundwork or Façade?* (Boston: D. C. Heath and Co., 1965). The first of six planned volumes published for The Conference on Modern Japan of the Association for Asian Studies presents the broad conceptions and scope of this important collective study of Japan's modernization: Marius B. Jansen, ed., *Changing Japanese Attitudes Toward Modernization* (Princeton: Princeton University Press, 1965).

of history he would doubtless remind us that it took the survivors in 1945 of the "moderate" men he was depending upon in 1930—Suzuki, Okada, Wakatsuki, Kido, and Konoe, and even the Emperor himself—to end the holocaust the military men had made.[12] He might even remind us that although the imperial houses of Hapsburgs and Hohenzollerns whose courts he knew, of Romanovs and Ottomans and the House of Savoy are as dust today, the Shōwa Emperor in whose service Saionji died still reigns from "the Throne of a lineal succession unbroken for ages eternal."[13]

The part of the lengthy Harada corpus chosen for this translation is extensive enough to be a reasonable sample of the whole. It is not an anthology or group of selections epitomizing the whole. It was not re-worked by Harada's later literary editor. In conception and design it constitutes a topical unit in contrast with the more amorphous annalistic later portions. In subject matter this volume of the memoirs reveals much of what has been called "liberalism's last effort": the successful negotiation and ratification of the London Naval Treaty of 1930.[14] It is not basically concerned with details of the London Conference, or with the treaty terms *per se*, but chiefly with the repercussions in domestic power struggles in 1930. The treaty issue, perhaps more than any other before this time, provided the occasion for a sharp dislocation along the age-old fault line of Japanese social and political topography—the division of civil and military authority, a dislocation plain to all when within a year the invasion of Manchuria was undertaken.[15] It is at once an *ex parte* report on the liberals' efforts and a testimony that some of them, at least, sensed how fragile was their victory.

In this introduction an attempt is made to epitomize the story of Saionji's character and his role in Japanese public life, to identify the author's relationship to him, to note the origin and character of the memoirs themselves, to review certain problems they have presented as a text, and finally, to present criticisms and evaluations

---

[12] Robert J. C. Butow, *Japan's Decision to Surrender* (Stanford: Stanford University Press, 1954).

[13] From the preamble to the Meiji Constitution of 1889, in the translation of Count Itō Miyoji.

[14] Arthur Morgan Young, *Imperial Japan, 1926-1938* (New York: William Morrow and Co., 1938), pp. 48-62; a gossipy and shrewd report by a former editor of the *Japan Chronicle*.

[15] Takashi Oka uses principally the second volume of the Harada memoirs for his excellent review of "Saionji and the Manchurian Crisis," in *Papers on China from the Regional Studies Seminars*, VIII (Privately distributed, Committee on International and Regional Studies, Harvard University, 1954), 38-74.

that can be made of them. A brief discussion is also given of the institutional and political context in which the London Treaty issue came to assume the proportions of a crisis in 1930.

The Harada Diary and Its Relationship
to Prince Saionji

When the International Military Tribunal for the Far East convened on November 12, 1948, to give judgment and to sentence the Japanese charged and found guilty before it as major war criminals, it was concluding an inquiry that had been in progress for nearly two and a half years. The Transcript of its Proceedings and the formally accepted Exhibits before the Tribunal ran to more than seventy-five thousand pages of record. Oral testimony had been heard from 419 witnesses and depositions and affidavits had been received from 779 other witnesses. Its record reviewed not only the careers of the specific defendants in these Tokyo War Crimes Trials, but also virtually all aspects of Japan's political and diplomatic history in the two preceding decades, and particularly since 1931. In addition to this formal record of the Tribunal, there had been assembled a very large body of additional data of high presumptive significance for an historical analysis of modern Japan. Usually identified collectively as the "International Prosecution Section Documents," they did not as a whole become part of the formal record; parts of certain documents did appear through excerpts; others were rejected as irrelevant to the issues before the Tribunal.[16]

To the long drawn-out Tribunal proceedings the Western

---

[16] For a précis of the documentation produced by the International Military Tribunal, see Delmer M. Brown, "Recent Japanese Political and Historical Materials," *American Political Science Review*, XLIII (December 1949), 1010-17. Solis Horwitz' descriptive analysis of the Tokyo trial summarizes in an appendix the "historical materials" elicited for the court ("The Tokyo Trial," *International Conciliation*, No. 465 [November, 1950], pp. 473-584).

A "selection of 682 titles from the complete file of documentary evidence as it existed in the International Prosecution Section, GHQ, SCAP," is included in the more than two million pages of archival material microfilmed for the Library of Congress, under the auspices of the U.S. Department of State, between 1949 and 1951 (Cecil H. Uyehara and Edwin G. Beal [compilers], *Checklist of Archives in the Japanese Ministry of Foreign Affairs, Tokyo, Japan, 1868-1945* [Washington: Photoduplication Service, Library of Congress, 1954], p. ix). Hereafter, a document from this collection will be identified by citation, in addition to its own title, of the short form, "LC Microfilm Collection," plus the number or letter-and-number designation used on the actual microfilm itself and in the Uyehara *Checklist*.

world showed but an apathetic interest which was nearly matched
by the indifference of the Japanese public sated with the war's
woes and its aftermath. Yet a notable new interest was stimulated
for them when, in the rebuttal phase of its case, the Prosecution
Section introduced extensive excerpts from one group of these
"IPS documents." Generally referred to as "the Harada Diary"
(or latterly, as "the Saionji-Harada Memoirs"), this group of documents limned in great detail the kaleidoscopic patterns of personal
and group relationships among the higher echelons of the Japanese
government, court, and military establishments for the dozen years
before 1940. It was a truism that the plague of faction was endemic
in Japanese public life. Here, in the Harada documents, its ver-
miculation was depicted both in extraordinary detail and with
unusual if not unique authority.[17]

The "Harada Diary" was not precisely a diary; nor did its
authority stem from Harada. The late Baron Harada Kumao, who
had died early in the occupation period before the Tokyo Trials
had begun, had been relatively obscure, even to many politically
conscious Japanese. His importance and the authority of his memoirs derive solely from his long close association with Prince Saionji
whose political secretary he had been for fourteen years before the
Prince's death at ninety-two in 1940. For nearly two decades
Prince Saionji had been sole survivor of that curious self-appointed,
extra-constitutional, and extra-legal body known as the *genrō*, or
Elder Statesmen. In the *genrō* was concentrated a unique prestige;
for they were a projection into the twentieth century of the narrow
oligarchy that had directed Japan's transformation from a divided
feudal kingdom to a modern industrial state following the Meiji
Restoration of 1868, and for this reason they identified themselves
as uniquely representing the Emperor's will.

Harada's diary was more fittingly referred to before the Tribunal as the Saionji-Harada Memoirs.[18] Indeed, the memoirs had
been written as a record of the ideas and instructions of Saionji as
the Emperor's chief adviser, and of Harada's activities only as
Saionji's agent and representative. When Harada began to keep this
record in 1930, Saionji could be described as the most powerful

---

[17] The Harada documents had come into the hands of the Tribunal in
the form of a voluminous stenographic transcript, of more than ten thousand
pages, of Harada's dictation over a period of ten years.

[18] Under this title the complete English translation prepared for the
Tribunal, by many hands, totals 3,286 pages of typescript (LC Microfilm Collection, SP161). Certain aspects of this translation are discussed below.

Prince Saionji at an entrance to his
Tokyo residence at Surugadai. From a photograph
he inscribed as a birthday gift to his secretary,
Baron Harada, in 1929, the year before
this narrative begins.

single man in Japan. The Tribunal in its lengthy Judgment thus testifies to the weight it gave to the testimony from such a source:

> The special position of Prince Saionji as the last of the Genro provoked full and candid disclosure to him through his secretary Harada. Harada's long period of service to the Genro in this special task of obtaining information from the very highest functionaries of the Government and the Army and Navy is a test of his reliability and discretion. . . . As to the authenticity of the Saionji-Harada documents . . . the Tribunal is satisfied that these are the original memoranda as dictated by Harada and edited by Saionji. To the extent to which they are relevant the Tribunal considers them helpful and reliable contemporary evidence of the matters recorded.[19]

And similarly, even summary accounts of the Tokyo Trials echo this attention called to these particular documents.[20]

As the Tribunal was completing its task in the fall of 1948, the Harada documents were in process of being finally edited for publication in accordance with Harada's original plans for them.[21] In all, nine stout volumes were to be produced. But before the first volume appeared in August, 1950, the publishing house of Iwanami whetted public interest in further disclosures by publication in the new monthly journal *Sekai (World)* of extracted chapters on certain of the dramatic, bloody, and aborted coups d'etat of the 1930s, such as the "May 15th Incident"—the 1932 cold-blooded assassination of Prime Minister Inukai, and the "February 26th Incident"—the more serious mutiny in 1936 that sought to strike down civilian leaders in political and court circles and conservative military leaders as well.[22]

These advance disclosures at once reminded the Japanese public that Prince Saionji himself typified the "liberal" and "internationalist" policies against which the ultra-nationalists conspired,

---

[19] *Judgment of the International Military Tribunal for the Far East,* November 12, 1948, pp. 21-22.

[20] E.g., Brown; Horwitz, pp. 535, 577.

[21] The Harada documents had not come into the Tribunal's possession by confiscation or command, but had been "voluntarily" offered through the agency of Lieut. Colonel Paul Rusch, Chief of the Special Activities Branch of the Civil Intelligence Section of the American Army command in occupation. After being completely microfilmed for the court's use, the documents were returned to Harada's heirs.

[22] Harada Kumao, "Fuasshizumu no roka—Go jūgo jiken [The Signal of Fascism—the May 15th Incident]," *Sekai,* No. 49 (January, 1950), 59-69; Harada, "Ni niroku jiken—jōsōbu no ugoki [The February 26th Incident—Changes in the Elite]," *Ibid.,* No. 50 (February, 1950), 92-102. The journal, *Sekai,* is a publication of Iwanami Shoten.

his person had been recurrently the target of unsuccessful plots, and he had symbolized for the radicals of the right those elements "about the Throne" whom the terrorist wing of reaction sought to replace, by assassination if need be.[23]

The Role of the Genrō

Functionally, the *genrō's* power derived from the tradition, established since the late Meiji period, that the *genrō* alone were authorized to recommend a new Prime Minister to the Throne.[24]

---

[23] The compound word *sokkin* (about the Throne) is a characteristically Japanese ellipsis, of elastic meaning and usage. Narrowly it refers to the immediate circle of court functionaries attendant upon the person of the Emperor: the Lord Keeper of the Privy Seal, the Grand Chamberlain, the Imperial Household Minister, *et al.* Normally it was used to include high unofficial advisers as well, and specifically the *genrō.* But right-wing propagandists gave wide currency to a pejorative sense implying malign and corrupting influences which were conceived to be clouding the true Imperial effulgence. In this sense there was suggested the psychologically valuable catharsis of crusade, and a sense of historic mission to be fulfilled.

The long-established pattern of military dictatorship—the shogunate—through which Japan had been controlled from the twelfth to the mid-nineteenth centuries could be viewed as an illegitimate usurpation. Thus, the Meiji Restoration had swept away the intervening shogunal institution and "restored" direct Imperial rule. Hence, then, the need to accomplish a like mission for the Meiji Emperor's grandson. This was the general meaning of the phrase "Shōwa Restoration" given currency in the thirties. (Since 1868 the Japanese have employed a single regnal name for each Emperor's period: Mutsuhito's reign, 1868-1912, was the Meiji period; his son, Yoshihito, was denominated the Taishō Emperor; and his grandson, Hirohito, reigns in the Shōwa era, 1926 to the present.)

[24] The word *genrō* is the Japanese "reading" for two Chinese characters once used by ancient Chinese rulers as an accolade for meritorious ministers who achieved advanced age. In popular usage it means veteran or patriarch, reflecting at least a verbal nod to the gerontotropic values of traditional society; but it may simply designate the senior figures of whatever group—veteran business leaders, industrial magnates, or gang bosses, and thus may connote power as much as age. There is an apt psychological insight in such usage: the wilfulness of leadership must be accepted and deferred to much as is the wilfulness of the aged. Related words were institutionalized in the Tokugawa bureaucracy for the Council of State (*rōjū,* literally the council of elders) and the Regency (*tairō,* the great elder) and in the early Meiji period for the Senate (*genrōin*), one of the several transitional forms that preceded the constitutional regime.

Under the constitution the term was not institutionally stipulated or formally used. But in the nineties some seven survivors of the original Meiji oligarchy were so identified because of the real power of decision they yet wielded (whatever their official or retired roles might be). Three were former Chōshū clansmen: Itō Hirobumi, Yamagata Aritomo, and Inoue Kaoru; and four were former Satsuma *samurai:* Matsukata Masayoshi, Kuroda Kiyotaka, Ōyama Iwao, and Saigō Tsugumichi. They were not yet far advanced in age; in 1890 the youngest was forty-eight, the eldest, fifty-five.

As it originally developed, the informal council of the Elder Statesmen had been an effective device to palliate conflicts and to circumvent deadlocks among the several agencies which collectively exercised the executive authority in the Emperor's name. And from
the selection of Prime Ministers their authority extended outward
to all other important political matters. All of the original *genrō*
had begun their careers as low-ranking *samurai* from the two pre-
Meiji fiefdoms, Satsuma and Chōshū, which had nearly monop-
olized the leadership of Meiji Japan.[25] The Meiji Constitution,
promulgated in 1889, had left to the definition of practice the precise relationships to obtain among Cabinet, Privy Council, and the
agencies of the Supreme Command (the War and Navy Ministries
and the Army and Navy General Staffs); but each could assert a
wide autonomy if not independence of the others. In the unity provided by the collective counsel of the *genrō*, the fundamentally
schismatic character of Japanese governmental institutions was dis-
guised, and the system as a whole was given apparent and temporary
coordination. At that time the liberal scholar and publicist, Nakae
Chōmin, a friend of Saionji from Paris student days together,
scoffed at the new system as "a strange creature with one body and
many heads." But it seemed possible to some then (including
Saionji) as well as to recent students today that "the Meiji Constitution was not as illiberal and absolutist as some interpretations
assume. . . . and (in application would) allow for further development in the direction of democratic government."[26] Again and
again throughout his career Saionji made choices that were meant
to reinforce such liberal as against absolutist developments; but
he did so without projecting himself into a blatantly partisan role

---

Ōkuma Shigenobu of Hizen, once importantly involved within the
oligarchy but dissident and critical of his former colleagues since the early
eighties, was late in life accorded *genrō* status but always refused to function
as one. The only additions to this group were Katsura and Saionji.

It has become conventional to translate *genrō* into English as Elder
Statesman. The term *jūshin*, the term used for the later less prestigious group
of unofficial palace advisers, after Saionji's death, is usually translated as Senior
Statesmen. (See the annotations to the text: chap. ii, note 18; chap. iv, note 19;
and chap. vii, note 1.)

[25] The Japanese term for fiefdom (*han*) has usually been translated as
"clan," though it does not in general have the sociological significance of the
latter term in English. The term "clan politics" refers to the dominance of
cliques of Satsuma and Chōshū bureaucratic politicians in Meiji political
history and after. The former controlled the Navy; the latter, the Army; both
had wider ramifications.

[26] Joseph Pittau, S.J., *Political Thought in Early Meiji Japan* (Cambridge: Harvard Univ. Press, 1967), pp. 198f.

or (to state it somewhat negatively) without jeopardizing his life-long patrician aloofness and his sense of a special personal relation to the imperial institution, to the Throne. Clearly the existence of the *genrō* device as an extraconstitutional resolution of the pluralism in the power structure led to irresponsibility and irrationality. Yet if there were a theme or motive that pervaded Saionji's public undertakings, perhaps sharpened by his long and fondly-remembered years in France, it was to work for a greater rationality in the whole task of bringing Japan abreast of the best in the world.[27] In one sense, thus, he devoted himself conscientiously to being the *genrō* who would end Japan's need for *genrō*.

Much of Saionji's public career before 1930 is important enough to be epitomized and accessible, in outline at least, in a responsible textbook on modern Japan.[28] Even so a review here of some segments of his experience and aspects of his personality may illumine what is taken for granted by Harada and assumed by the persons in his book in their dealings with Saionji as the sole *genrō* in 1930.

When Saionji was co-opted to the original group after the death of the Meiji emperor,[29] only two of them remained politically active: Yamagata, who had built his personal authority largely by his control of the army; and Matsukata, the financial expert among the Meiji oligarchs.

---

[27] Other recent studies of the Meiji elite suggest a need to see a greater "rationality" in many of their undertakings. See Bernard S. Silberman and H. D. Harootunian, eds., *Modern Japanese Leadership: Transition and Change* (Tucson: Univ. of Arizona Press, 1966), especially Marlene Mayo, "Rationality in the Meiji Restoration," pp. 323-69.

[28] Such as John K. Fairbank, Edwin O. Reischauer, and Albert M. Craig, *East Asia: The Modern Transformation*, being Vol. II of *A History of East Asian Civilization* (Boston: Houghton Mifflin Co., 1965).

[29] A *genrō* was usually so designated by an imperial message requesting merely his continued "assistance." Such a message, regarded merely as the written version of an oral command (*chokugo*) thereby needed no countersignature by minister or adviser. Saionji received such a *chokugo* just after resigning the Prime Ministership for the second and last time in the midst of the "Taishō political crisis." Dated December 21, 1912, it is in the special language used only by and of an emperor. The English version in a biography by Saionji's one-time secretary gives some of the regal flavor and most of the opaque blandness of the original:

It is only a few days since We succeeded to the Throne. Upon you, who for many years served the late Emperor and personally enjoyed His Majesty's intimate commands, We depend much in future for counsel. In obedience to Our desire, exert yourself to assist and support Us.

Yoshisaburo Takekoshi, *Prince Saionji* (Kyōto: Ritsumeikan Univ., 1933), pp. 269-70; Japanese text in Andō Tokki, *Tōan kō eifū* [*Mementoes of Prince Tōan* (i.e., Saionji)] (Kyoto: Shinmi shoin, 1937), p. 137.

There was something paradoxical in Saionji's joining this group, for by antecedents and temperament he scarcely belonged to so bold and brash a company. Not that he, too, had not been a pioneer on new frontiers and a conscious innovator—with him these had been personal ventures. But the others were self-made men who had re-shaped their whole nation. When they died full of high honors and as princes of the realm, they held princedoms in a new peerage of their own creation.[30] In Saionji, however, there was nothing of the *arriviste*. Among the oligarchs he had been closest to, indeed was the political heir of the canniest and most flexible of them, Itō Hirobumi, Japan's first Prime Minister and "author" of the constitution. In origins the contrast between them could scarcely have been sharper. Both bore through life the names of adopted parents, but there the initial resemblance stopped.[31] Itō was born a peasant's son and was early adopted to carry on the name of a childless *samurai* family of lowly rank. Saionji's was the most patrician lineage in the land, of the ancient civil court nobility called the *kuge*, a few score families whose existence and duties had been attendant upon the person of the emperor and the ceremonies of his court in Kyoto for more than a thousand years.

Saionji was born in 1849 as the second son of Tokudaiji Kin-

---

[30] Modern Japan's peerage was designed to replace the traditional hierarchy by ascription (i.e., by birthright alone) with an aristocracy of achievement or merit. In fact the new order of nobles, created by imperial ordinance in 1884, was a hybrid like other Meiji institutions. It established five ranks as in most contemporary European monarchies—prince, marquis, count, viscount, and baron (using in Japanese, however, titles derived from the late Chou period in classical China), and appointed to these ranks some five hundred men, including former civil and military nobles plus a number of the "new men," the oligarchs themselves and their chief aides. Saionji was then made a marquis and was elevated to the rank of prince only in 1920. Itō was made a count and, like most of the other original *genrō*, was rapidly advanced to highest rank.

[31] In the closed endogamous society of the ancient Heian court, marital alliances and adoptions between collateral or similarly ranked families were the very stuff of politics, needed to preserve and advance, if possible, the all-important family lineage. The Saionji by tradition resorted frequently to adoption. The adoption system in several forms, thus once originated among the small elite of court nobles, came to be widely used in Japan by other classes, to preserve and revivify lineages, to maintain properties, or to transmit traditions in the arts and crafts (as by painters, potters, bankers, and actors) and even in academic and literary pursuits.

How widespread this system became is suggested by the fact that fully a quarter of the hundred and more men mentioned in this volume of Harada's memoirs for 1930 were adopted sons. These include the Prime Minister and four others of the cabinet, such personages as Count Makino, the Lord Privy Seal, Dr. Ikki, the Imperial Household Minister, and of course, Saionji himself and his own legal heir.

zumi, the head of a *kuge* house of second rank.[32] He was adopted in 1852 as a "real son *(jisshi)*" of the house of Saionji and soon became its "head," and was thenceforth named Kimmochi. His elder brother came to head the parental house, and as Prince Toku-daiji Sanenori held at various times between 1871 and his death in 1919 all the highest offices in the Imperial Court itself. A younger brother, sixth son of Kinzumi, was adopted to become the head of a commoner family, the Ōsaka merchant house of Sumitomo. As Sumitomo Kichizaemon he was subsequently created a baron, less because of his *kuge* origin than because he had presided over the remarkable growth of the Sumitomo interests into one of the great financial-industrial capital complexes called *zaibatsu*. As a matter of course Sumitomo met the financial needs of his elder brother,

---

[32] No definitive biography of Saionji exists, but his personality and career have been subject to great curiosity and frequent discussion. In his middle years the circle of his associates included many younger literary men and journalists, and some, not always with his approval, have published sketches of his earlier life. Saionji's one-time secretary, Takekoshi Yosaburō, a scholar-bureaucrat in his own right, wrote an anecdotal biography of his patron's life up to 1918 using Saionji's "studio name" as its title, *Tōan kō* (Tōkyō: Sōbunkaku, 1930), of which an English version exists, translated by Kozaki Nariaki as *Prince Saionji* (Kyōto: Ritsumeikan Univ., 1933). Another writer and lesser political figure once associated with Saionji, Koizumi Sakutarō (Sanshin), edited some of Saionji's earlier essays with other material under the title *Zuihitsu Saionji kō* (Tōkyō: Iwanami shoten, 1939), and some of Koizumi's material is used in Kimura Ki, *Saionji Kimmochi jiden* (Tōkyō: Kōdansha, 1949). Popular biographies exist in Shirayanagi Shūko, *Saionji Kimmochi den* (Tōkyō: Nihon hyōronsha, 1929) and Andō Tokki, *Saionji Kimmochi* (Tōkyō: Hakuyōsha, 1938); and Andō uses other materials in discussing Saionji's rela-tions with the important historian of China, Naitō Torajirō, whose "studio name" was Konan, *Saionji kō to Konan sensei* (Tōkyō: Genkai shobō, 1936). Andō also edited the volume of memorabila, *Tōan kō eifu*, mentioned above, note 29. Except that he has written more than a hundred other works the veteran journalist Kimura Ki would seem to have made a specialty of Saionji, writing at least four others than the one mentioned above: *Saionji Kimmochi*, a five-act play with sundry appended material (Tōkyō: Shomotsu tembōkai, 1933); *Saionji Kimmochi den* (Tōkyō: Denki kankōkai, 1937), *Saionji Kimmochi* (Tōkyō: Sara shobō, 1948); and *Saionji Kimmochi* (Tōkyō: Jiji tsūshinsha, 1958). In addition to Kimura's play there are at least two frankly fictionalized biog-raphies: Tanaka Kōtarō, *Saionji Kimmochi den* (Tōkyō: Kaizōsha, 1932); and in English, one by Bunji Omura, *The Last Genro: The Statesman Who Western-ized Japan* (Philadelphia: J. B. Lippincott Co., 1938).

By far the best critical appraisal, though only in the compass of a short essay, is the study by Oka Yoshitake in his *Kindai Nihon no seijika* [*Modern Japanese Statesmen*] (Tōkyō: Bungei shunjū shinsha, 1960), pp. 197-244.

In English, Jackson H. Bailey has studied his career up to the first World War in "Prince Saionji: A Study in Modern Japanese Political Leadership" (unpublished Ph. D. dissertation, Harvard University, 1959), and in the articles cited below in footnotes 38 and 39.

Saionji, paying for his various houses through the years—in Kyoto, Tokyo, Okitsu, and elsewhere, and arranging that Harada remain nominally (and financially) on the Sumitomo staff while devoting himself entirely to Saionji's service. Before Baron Sumitomo's death in 1926 his son Atsushi was married to Saionji's granddaughter Haruko.

The Saionji belonged to the same rank in the *kuge* hierarchy as the Tokudaiji.[33] Both were branches of the ramified Fujiwara clan that had been dominant in Japan before the rise of feudalism with its new warrior aristocracy (called the *buke* or *bushi*) and its creation of an hereditary military dictatorship known as the shogunate.

The Fujiwara were historically important both for subtle techniques of usurping rule while preserving the imperial institution as a puppetry to legitimize their system, and for their creation and perfection of the unique culture of the Heian period (from the mid-9th to the 12th centuries). The remarkable novel from this period, *The Tale of Genji* by Lady Murasaki, singularly evokes the "rule of taste," of refinement and esthetic sensibility that was a chief characteristic of Heian culture.[34] In turn, the once proud political and economic power of the *kuge* was usurped by the *buke;* but the other studied lineaments of their culture were nonetheless preserved, like bees in amber, with succeeding generations of their still closed small society oscillating about the throne, stressing canonized intellectual, literary, and artistic pursuits, the punctilious performance of traditional if empty imperial court protocol, and indulgence in gossip and such place-seeking as the parsimonious patrimony allowed them by the feudal overlords would permit.

However attenuated and remote from the modern world this culture of the *kuge* might have seemed in the mid-nineteenth century, it did still require of its young nobles the disciplined personal

---

[33] At the head of the *kuge* class were the *go-sekke,* the five families from which empresses and regents were chosen. Next stood the group of families called the *seika* (originally seven in number) whence came the chancellors and great ministers of left and right. The Saionji and the Tokudaiji were second and third in the *seika* group. The Konoe family belonged to the higher *go-sekke* group. Full genealogies of these families (and they were carefully preserved) show marital relationships with the Imperial house and with most other great houses of Japan's past, such as the Minamoto and the Oda.

[34] See Sir George B. Sansom's classic discussion in *A History of Japan* Vol. I, chs. viii and ix (Stanford: Stanford Univ. Press, 1958); Ivan Morris' deft special study, *The World of the Shining Prince* (New York: Alfred A. Knopf, 1964); and Arthur Waley's translation of *The Tale of Genji* (2 vols.; Boston: Houghton Mifflin, 1935).

acquisition of traditional skills, in classical literature, in Chinese, in calligraphy and its associated arts. It emphasized a sense of history and of personal relationship with the imperial institution. As a boy in this setting, Saionji's quick intelligence gave him a thorough grounding in this classical learning that was of life-long use. Some of his lessons were learned under the regent Konoe (with whose son's and grandson's careers he was to be later involved) and in company with a slightly younger Imperial prince who became the Meiji emperor.

In the fifteen years between Commodore Perry's arrival in 1853 and the collapse of the centuries-old shogunal system in 1868 the once placid court in Kyoto was aswirl with varied arguments about Japan's future and the possibility of an imperial restoration. As boy chamberlain to the Emperor Kōmei Saionji was alert to the intrigues and conspiracies against the established order that found their focus in Kyoto. He was nineteen when the breakthrough occurred and the restoration was proclaimed.

Already he had shocked his elders and welcomed what was new. He had learned to ride, though to *kuge* courtiers equestrian skills were the tabooed and demeaning mark of lower-ranking military orders. He was perhaps the first at court to read and discuss widely Fukuzawa's *Seiyō jijō (Conditions in the Western World)* which was both a travel account and a tract arguing for modernization. When he was assigned *pro forma*, as an available *kuge*, to be titular commander of loaned samurai troops in the Imperial cause for the brief war against the Shogun's partisans, he established an easy camaraderie with both samurai and village commoners recruited to the Imperial cause. Back at court, he spoke up strongly to urge that Kido, Ōkubo, and Gotō, brash young *samurai* from the outer baronies, should sit within the council chamber rather than grovel in the gravelled courtyard outside as protocol required.

He shocked them further when he cut his hair in the Western fashion, had his friend Itō acquire for him an elegant outfit of Western dress and was the first noble to appear in court in tight trousers and frock coat. He even said he thought of choosing a wife from the despised pariah class, the Eta. When the new emperor and his new government were transferred to the teeming city of Edo from which the shoguns had ruled Japan since 1600 but now newly named Tokyo (capital in the East), young Saionji turned down appointments to sinecure provincial posts. For a time he felt free to enjoy, under a pseudonym, the plebeian delights of teahouse life and the pleasure quarters in this, to him, new great city.

But it was really the more distant stranger world of Europe that he wanted to know. In favor with Iwakura, the leading *kuge* in the new oligarchy, and strongly urged by its younger members near his own age, Saionji went abroad to study.[35]

He arrived in Paris in 1871. There he studied, eventually took a law degree at the Sorbonne, and remained for a whole decade immersing himself in the new milieu. He was deeply affected by the renewed revolutionary tenets of the Third Republic and involved himself with radical intellectuals and journalists. And he joined in the literary as well as the political circles of the day.[36]

Back in Japan in the early eighties, he must have seemed like a deracinated man; for a reaction was setting in against the earlier avid adulation of Western ways. Or else he was a prime exemplar of *jiyū-shugi*—liberalism. He was drawn toward the group critical of "clan" politics in the government and clamorous for popular rights *(minken)* and a more liberal regime.[37] For a brief period in early 1881, joining with two young fellow Francophiles, Nakae Chōmin and Matsuda Masahisa, Saionji headed and wrote for the *Tōyō Jiyū Shimbun (Oriental Liberty News* or *Eastern Free Press)*, a journal to foster European liberal ideas and argue for representative and constitutional government.[38] At first he resisted attempts

---

[35] A year later in November 1871 the emperor himself addressed an assembly of nobles: "If we would benefit by the useful arts and sciences and conditions of Society prevailing among more enlightened nations, we must either study these at home as best we can, or send abroad an expedition of practical observers, to foreign lands, competent to acquire for us those things our people lack, which are best calculated to benefit this nation." And in another year Iwakura himself and half the ministers of the government would undertake a lengthy study tour abroad. See Marlene Mayo, "The Iwakura Mission to the United States and Europe, 1871-1873," *Researches in the Social Sciences on Japan*, No. 6 (Columbia University, East Asian Institute Studies, 1959), pp. 28-47.

[36] Clemenceau and Gautier are usually cited among his friends in Paris in this period. Much in Gautier's literary and esthetic theories was consonant with the traditions of Kyoto's culture. Clemenceau was later to record his impression of Saionji, after the Versailles Conference, as being of amiable and "quietly ironical disposition" (Georges Clemenceau, *Grandeur and Misery of Victory* [New York, 1930], p. 150).

[37] Sir George B. Sansom, *The Western World and Japan: A Study in the Interaction of European and Asiatic Cultures* (New York: Alfred A. Knopf, 1950), examines in rich detail the fluxion of new and old in this generation of Meiji Japan. Nobutake Ike has given a careful study to the political liberals of this period as typified in Nakae and Ueki Emori (*The Beginnings of Political Democracy in Japan* [Baltimore: The Johns Hopkins Press, 1950]).

[38] Nakae had translated Rousseau's *Social Contract* into the ponderous Chinese that was yet the language of sober literature. Matsuda, a close friend in Paris student days, was to join Saionji a quarter of a century later as Justice

by government leaders and his own elder brother, the Emperor's chamberlain, to dissuade him from this undertaking. It took a direct order from the Throne to force him to sever the connection as too radical and unseemly for a court noble. In accepting this order he nonetheless protested in a cogent strongly-worded letter addressed to the Emperor.

Before the year was out, however, the government had announced that a constitution with provision for a parliament would in fact be granted by 1890. This opened the door for Saionji, without compromise of principle, to accept official posts, first on the commission to draft a modern civil law code, then within a few months a more attractive role directly utilizing his experiences abroad.

Saionji was included in the entourage of Itō Hirobumi when that Chōshū leader, now the dominant figure in the oligarchy, in preparation for drafting the constitution made an extended tour of European capitals to examine models abroad. From this Saionji was given diplomatic assignments, first as minister to Vienna, then to Berlin and Belgium. When he finally returned to Japan in the early 1890s, he had been abroad for seventeen of the last twenty years. Japan had changed much from the halting beginnings of modernization he had left in 1870. A whole new constitutional and parliamentary form of government had come into being.

Itō was tussling with the task of making this new constitutional structure into a viable instrument of government. The unaccustomed feature of a parliament was far from easily amenable to control. Itō persuaded the rather diffident Westernized nobleman to accept appointment to the Privy Council, then to become Education Minister in his second cabinet in 1894. Saionji also served in Itō's two later cabinets during which he was brevetted to fill various temporary vacancies among the ministries—as Finance Minister *ad interim*, twice as Foreign Minister, and twice for Itō himself as Acting Prime Minister.

As Itō's successor Saionji became President of the Privy Council in 1900 when Itō decided to work with and through a parliamentary political party, the Seiyūkai, which he had just founded. This was a reflection of the key conflict in Japanese poli-

---

Minister in Saionji's two cabinets. On Nakae, see Hayashi Shigeru, *Kindai Nihon no shisōkatachi* [*Political Thinkers of Modern Japan*] (Tōkyō: Iwanami shinsho, 1958), pp. 7-69; and Pittau (cited above, n. 26), *passim*. On Saionji's role, see Jackson H. Bailey, "Prince Saionji and the Popular Rights Movement," *Journal of Asian Studies*, Vol. XXI, No. 1 (Nov. 1961), pp. 49-63.

tics of the nineties between Itō and Yamagata as leaders, respectively, of "civilian" and of "military" factions in the bureaucracy.

When Itō found his ambivalent role as *genrō* and as party leader impossible to maintain in the face of Yamagata's intrigues, the party presidency was turned over to Saionji in 1903. In the next decade the Itō-Yamagata contest was continued with Saionji and Katsura Tarō (of Chōshū) as the front figures. Till the end of the Meiji reign these two men alternated in the office of Prime Minister. Saionji formed his first government in 1906. Though the Seiyūkai held a majority in the lower house of the Diet, this was not yet a party government. Yet Saionji gave the two actual party leaders in the lower house, Hara Takashi and Matsuda Masahisa, the politically important Home and Justice Ministries.

As the constitution was interpreted in its first decade, the Supreme Command agencies (which had been created before the constitution was promulgated) continued to have the right of direct access to the Emperor *(iaku jōsō)*. And Yamagata had the canny foresight to establish by Imperial ordinances, by 1900, the requirement that the War and Navy ministries be headed only by officers of top rank from the active list.

It was Saionji's lot, more than a decade later, to face the consequences of such Supreme Command autonomy carried to its political extreme, the first crisis of its kind revealing the fault-line potentially dividing the civil and military elites. It has come to be known as the "Taishō political crisis *(Taishō seihen)*" because it occurred within a few months of the Taishō emperor's accession following the death of the Meiji emperor in July, 1912.[39] Saionji was in his second Prime Ministership. He and his whole cabinet had agreed on the necessity of a budget retrenchment. The Army, however, through the War Minister General Uehara wanted authorization to add two new divisions. Saionji and his cabinet refused. Uehara, backed by Yamagata, would not compromise, and under the claimed right of *iaku jōsō* presented his resignation directly to the emperor, not to Saionji. The Army refused to authorize any other general to replace him in Saionji's cabinet. Thus Saionji was forced to resign. That his party, the Seiyūkai, had a clear ma-

---

[39] The events, if not the consequences, of this crisis are detailed in two studies: Roger F. Hackett, "Yamagata and the Taisho Crisis, 1912-1913," and Jackson H. Bailey, "Prince Saionji and the Taisho Political Crisis," in Sidney Devere Brown, ed., *Studies on Asia, 1962* (Lincoln: Univ. of Nebraska, 1962), pp. 21-57.

jority in the lower house of the Diet seemed irrelevant. Initially the *genrō* resolved the impasse by sanctioning a third cabinet for Katsura, but this brought resistance from the Navy and more critically from a coalition of several parties in the Diet "to protect the constitution" and condemn the oligarchs. Protests and riots rocked the capital. Katsura sought to form a new party. It failed for his purpose. He obtained an imperial order to the Navy to assist him. Hence, Admiral Saitō reluctantly remained as Navy Minister. Katsura obtained a further imperial order to Saionji, as president of the majority party. Saionji carefully explained to the Seiyūkai Diet members why he must loyally obey such an order; but with equal care he refrained from arguing that they should be bound by it. To underscore his position he resigned from the party presidency. The Diet members remained intransigent in their opposition to Katsura and he resigned, and died soon after.

It was at this point that Saionji was himself first drawn into *genrō* consultations after refusing to take the reins of government again. The compromise whereby Admiral Yamamoto Gombei, of Satsuma, became Prime Minister resulted largely from Saionji's persuasions, working vis-à-vis Yamamoto through his friend Makino, also of Satsuma provenience. Although Yamamoto's government was based on oligarchic choice, as indeed had been all prior cabinets, yet paradoxically it brought an immediate increase in party power: virtually all his cabinet members were party men and legislation enacted under him was highly favorable to party growth and power.

For Saionji the whole brief episode underscored his revulsion at the blatant use of the power of the Throne for personal advantage, as Katsura had employed it; and he refused to use the same device. It underscored further the possibility that the Diet could and perhaps should increasingly become the focus of the nation's political life. When in 1930 a "Supreme Command controversy" once again became a gross political issue for the first time since 1912, Saionji must have reacted with a sense of *déja vue* as he clearly supported the civilian party Prime Minister against a segment of the Supreme Command.

From 1913 on, Saionji withdrew from the political front lines, even withdrawing from Tokyo to live at his villa in Kyoto. Ultimately the party accepted his resignation and Hara succeeded him as its president. Saionji accepted public official position only once again: on Hara's recommendation, he headed his emperor's dele-

gation to the Versailles Conference. The work of the conference
he left to younger ambitious men in his delegation. For him it was
a chance to see again the haunts of his youth, and a chance to have
his favorite daughter and her husband (whom he had adopted)
see them too.

As *genrō*, Prince Saionji seems to have used his influence from
the first to magnify the role of the political parties. It was to his
arguments that the other *genrō* finally gave assent when Hara, as
majority leader in the House of Representatives, and president of
the Seiyūkai, organized the celebrated first real party cabinet in
1918.[40] Or it would be more accurate to say that party activity had
gradually assumed certain functions performed earlier by the
genrō collectively—the harmonizing of bureaucratic and economic
pressures—and that to this development Saionji did not in general
dissent. Most party leaders were in fact bureaucrats who had transferred their operations to the media of party operations, and they
retained much of the personalism and factionalism of bureaucratic
groupings. The larger economic blocs usually known by the de-
preciatory epithet of *zaibatsu*—massive concentrations of commercial, industrial, and financial power operating as family holdings
under a handful of houses such as the Mitsui, Mitsubishi, Yasuda,
and Sumitomo—had learned to work increasingly with and through
party leaders. By the 1920s two fairly consistent party groupings
had emerged as contenders for dominance in the lower house, and
with increasing consistency the *genrō*'s recommendations chose the
Prime Ministers alternatively from the parties. In popular parlance
the ministries of the two postwar leaders Hara and Katō were
known as "Mitsui" and "Mitsubishi" cabinets, from the known
financial support they derived from these two largest family com-
bines. The corruption latently possible in this relationship was
frequently and blatantly present, but it was commonly assumed
that the Kenseikai (Minseitō) leadership was more "pure" than its
rival, the Seiyūkai.

If the conflicts between discordant elements in the Japanese
state were to be settled adequately and effectively in the parliamentary arena, then Japan would have evolved into that happy
liberal pattern which had so caught Saionji's enthusiasm in Europe
in the 1870s. Following Yamagata's death in 1922 and Matsukata's
in 1924, no other man was accorded *genrō* status along with Saionji.
If party rotation in office could become normal, there would little
longer be need for such a *deus ex machina* as the *genrō*. Saionji

---

[40] Hara Keiichirō, *Hara Takashi nikki*, VIII, 4-31.

might even contemplate the abolition of the *genrō* system altogether.[41]

Although the old Prince was inclined to let more and more political decisions be settled by "normal constitutional" processes (*kensei no jōdō*, a phrase given much currency in Japanese journalism in the twenties) his recommendations were yet crucial, and party and bureaucratic leaders still continually sought his "understanding." And he took with utmost seriousness his duty to advise, counsel, and protect the Throne. This he sought to do by special care in appointment and supervision of the major court officials. Whereas Yamagata had counted on the personal loyalty to himself from the military establishment which he had built up and controlled directly, and whereas Itō's power had been in large part a reflection of the civil bureaucracy, Saionji was content that the small group of those in direct continuous contact with the Emperor owe their positions to him. These posts, which nominally headed the entire bureaucracy, were staffed with men, like himself, who had studied or lived abroad and knew a wider world than Japan.

The three major court officials, the Lord Keeper of the Privy Seal, the Imperial Household Minister, and the Grand Chamberlain, were particularly important through controlling access to the person of the Emperor. They could prove a troublesome barrier to political opponents who might seek to give advice of which they did not approve, or alternatively they might themselves favor one petitioner against another. As this and later volumes of Harada's memoirs suggest, they were the principal fulcrum point in the Japanese governmental structure to which the *genrō* might most effectively apply pressure. Though titled "ministers" they were not members of the cabinet, but held office permanently, or until they desired to retire, and were considered to be above or outside "politics."[42]

---

[41] In the early 1920s young Prince Konoe, who had been a member of Saionji's suite at the Paris Conference, sometimes served Saionji in political liaison activities much as Harada did later. As the bureaucratic Kiyoura cabinet was tottering to its fall under attack of a second "Protect the Constitution" movement among the parties in 1924, Konoe issued a statement after several meetings with the *genrō* in Kyoto which had the general purport given here. Yabe Teiji, *Konoe Fumimaro* (2 vols.; Tōkyō: Kōbundō, 1952), Vol. I, pp. 129-30.

Yoshino Sakuzō, constitutional scholar and a leading liberal publicist, so also represented the *genrō*'s views, though unofficially yet without contradiction, in an article in the September 1926 number of the magazine *Chūō Kōron* [*The Central Review*] (*vide* paraphrase in Andō Tokki, *Saionji Kimmochi den*, pp. 29-31).

[42] See Appendices I B and II C below.

In the period of the London treaty crisis the Imperial Household Minister *(kunaidaijin)* was Dr. Ikki (or Ichiki) Kitokurō, a scholar and life-long bureaucrat. The younger brother of Privy Councillor Okada Ryōhei, a former Education Minister, Dr. Ikki had been educated in Germany and had himself been Education Minister and Home Minister in the second Ōkuma cabinet during World War I. After holding lesser posts in the Imperial Household Ministry he became *kunaidaijin* in 1925. His principal duties were essentially administrative and concerned the management of the vast properties owned by the Imperial Household and of the numerous members and branches of the Imperial Family—both matters quite outside the control or purview of any governmental agency. He was also a noted constitutional scholar who supported the so-called "liberal" theory, usually associated with Professor Minobe Tatsukichi (whose teacher he had once been), that regarded the Emperor as an "organ of state."[43] A few years later when Dr. Ikki was ill and wished to retire, this circumstance coincided with the retirement of the Privy Council President, Baron Kuratomi whom Saionji regarded as a nonentity. By normal procedure Kuratomi would be succeeded by the Council's Vice President, Baron Hiranuma. But Saionji had a profound distrust of Hiranuma's extreme right-wing views and a distaste for his political activism. Such was Saionji's view of Ikki's sense and moderation that he made one of his rare trips to the capital and to the Palace to dissuade Ikki from retirement and to persuade him to accept the Council's presidency. Though thus temporarily blocked Hiranuma continued to play the "off-stage menace" role that Harada gives him in this volume. With the assassination of Lord Privy Seal Saitō in 1936, Dr. Ikki took over this post as Saionji manoeuvered to keep right-wing personages from being intruded into inner court posts. Much of the ultra-conservative attack on Minobe in the 1930s was basically directed at Ikki, and through Ikki at Saionji.

The Grand Chamberlain *(jijūchō)*, Admiral Suzuki Kantarō, was the most recently appointed member of these "advisers close to the Throne." He had had a distinguished naval career and was particularly associated with the effective measures taken to cleanse the Navy after the "Siemens Affair," a scandal involving extensive bribery in the naval establishment disclosed in 1914—through his post as Navy Vice Minister in eight successive cabinets. He was

---

[43] Miller's *Minobe Tatsukichi* contains the first extensive English discussion of this school of thought.

made a Supreme War Councillor in 1924, and Chief of the Navy General Staff in 1925. Upon retirement from active duty in 1929, he was appointed Grand Chamberlain in succession to Viscount Chinda (who had been Saionji's colleague and second at the Paris Conference). Severely wounded by would-be assassins during the February Mutiny in 1936, Suzuki retired and was created a baron. Such was his reputation for soundness and probity (and remoteness from wartime politics) that the conference of senior statesmen *(jūshin kaigi)* chose him to head the government in the critical spring of 1945 for the implicit purpose of finding a way to end the war, a difficult task which he slowly, bunglingly accomplished.

Suzuki

In 1930 Saionji could accept some bungling on Suzuki's part, for he was then new to court circles and requirements. He had needed to be chided for his maladroit handling of Tanaka's last audience with the Emperor as his government fell in June-July, 1929. Saionji took pains to lead him to more correct judgments during this year of the London treaty issue. Though technically no longer in the naval service, Suzuki was clearly expected to work along with such other senior Navy figures as Saitō and Okada to ameliorate the impending crisis. This he did, notably in persuading Admiral Katō, the Chief of the Navy General Staff who was bitterly opposed to the treaty, to postpone his request for a "direct appeal to the Throne." He accomplished this as much because he was Katō's senior in the Navy and his predecessor as Chief of Staff, as because of his court position.[44]

Most important of these court offices was that of Lord Keeper of the Privy Seal *(naidaijin*, literally, "inner minister"), and its occupant in 1930 was the eldest and most experienced of the group. Count Makino Nobuaki (or Shinken) was the second son of Ōkubo Toshimichi, the able young Satsuma *samurai* who was the most influential single figure in the oligarchy at the time of his assassination in 1878. Makino had first gone abroad at an earlier age even than Saionji, for at twelve he had accompanied the Iwakura mission, of which his father was a member, as one of the large group of young men and boys sent abroad with the mission but to stay for longer periods of study and training. For Makino (who had been adopted by the family of an aunt) this meant a period of public schooling in the United States followed by a period of study in England where Saionji, on a trip from Paris, seems first to have met

[44] Aoki Tokuzō, *Taiheiyō senso zenshi* [*Historical Prelude to the Pacific War*] (Tōkyō: Sekai heiwa kensetsu kyōkai, 6 vols., 1950-51), Vol. I, pp. 15-19.

him as a clerk in the London legation. His long bureaucratic career included frequent close association with Saionji: as Vice Minister of Education when Saionji was Minister in the Itō cabinet of 1894, as Minister of Education and of Agriculture and Commerce in Saionji's two cabinets, as Foreign Minister in Admiral Yamamoto's first cabinet in 1913-14, and as a member (indeed the chief Japanese negotiator on the matter of the League Covenant) of the Saionji-led delegation to Versailles. He was prominent in the politics of the House of Peers as a kind of *genrō* for the powerful bloc of counts and viscounts. He was made Imperial Household Minister in 1921, transmitting this post to Dr. Ikki when he himself became Lord Privy Seal in 1925. Upon his resignation in 1935, Admiral Saitō was given the post. Like Saionji, Suzuki, Saitō (and even Harada) he was on the black list for assassination by the February, 1936 mutineers; but he escaped unharmed.

Despite an appearance that these court offices derived from ancient usage, they had in fact been established or redefined anew by the Meiji oligarchs and used by them for political manipulation. To Saionji there was nothing sacred in them and he moved in many ways to divest these offices of political significance and to dissuade the men holding them from direct involvement with governmental policy, beyond facilitating the "normal course of constitutional government." Usually Saionji communicated with them by oral messages that Harada carried back and forth. For matters of more consequence they went to see Saionji and Harada was seldom present nor, in most instances, informed of their interviews. Occasionally it is apparent to Harada that Saionji sharply criticizes even Count Makino if he appears to go beyond the bounds Saionji would have kept. In this London treaty year, he chided the Lord Privy Seal for suggesting it would be well for the Navy Minister to resign, "It ill becomes third parties to volunteer advice" on relations between a Prime Minister and his cabinet.[45] The nature of Saionji's relationship to this officer is clearer in a case occurring in mid-1931:

Saionji has heard that Makino has discussed or is about to discuss with the Prime Minister proposals that have been made to him about strengthening the Privy Council. Saionji called Harada with a message for Marquis Kido, then Makino's chief secretary. It was a curt, "Have Kido see me at once." Summoned by phone Kido went immediately to see the old prince at his summer house in Gotemba, where he was instructed, "If the Lord Privy Seal makes

---

[45] See chapter v, below, p. 195.

any direct suggestions to the government, I want you to come to inform me of it immediately!" Not surprisingly Makino himself shortly after went to Gotemba to talk with Saionji. Subsequently Saionji told Harada, "Kido gave him my message plainly enough and the Lord Privy Seal accepted and agreed. He said, 'I've never made any gratuitous or meddlesome suggestions to the government.'" Saionji's tone must have softened somewhat as he closed the subject saying to Makino, "Well, for people who hold such positions as yours and mine, since anything we may say to the government is bound to cause consternation among some of the officials, isn't it thus better for us, as far as possible, to restrain ourselves and to quietly keep our own counsel?"[46]

Makino

Perhaps using similar cajolery, Saionji was also careful to cultivate like-minded men, moderate, rational, and professional, for key posts in the military and naval establishments. Two such men were important in 1930: Admiral Saitō Makoto (his sometime Navy Minister) and Admiral Okada Keisuke. For understanding Saitō's role in 1930, the annotations in the text may suffice, except to note here his subsequent career. Partly because Saionji had judged him to be effective along with Okada in controlling Navy extremists on the London treaty issue, Saitō was designated to become Prime Minister in 1932. Then, in the wake of the Manchurian invasion and the assassinations of Prime Ministers of both parties (Hamaguchi and Inukai), Saionji was led to countenance a revival of national or "transcendental" cabinets. Saitō later succeeded Makino as Lord Privy Seal and was holding that post when assassinated in the 1936 mutiny.

Okada was much more continuingly involved with the London treaty matter, and his role exhibited the combination of personal and status pressures that Saionji and his circle could seek to employ. As Navy Minister in the Tanaka cabinet Okada was both a successor and a predecessor to Takarabe. He and Takarabe had been close friends since their naval academy days, both being graduated in 1889. Like Takarabe, Okada had gone up the Navy's ladder of commands, both ashore and afloat; and upon leaving the Navy Ministry he had become a Supreme War Councillor. Because he was the senior member of the Navy not in an actual administrative or command post, and perhaps also because he had a relationship with the opposition political party in the Diet, the pro-treaty forces (both Saionji and Hamaguchi) were careful to enlist his help in mollifying the Navy's intransigeants. He was both aware of his

---

[46] Harada, II, 28-39.

rather ambivalent role and played it with considerable skill and relish.

During Takarabe's absence in London, Hamaguchi had himself assumed the *ad interim* position of Acting Navy Minister but left all Ministry business in the hands of the Vice Minister, Vice Admiral Yamanashi Katsunoshin. Yamanashi, however able, could not assume the avuncular and counselling tone toward the choleric Katō that came naturally to Okada who was not only Katō's senior, but also came from the same small hamlet in Fukui-ken that was Katō's birthplace. Neither Katō nor Okada came from the Satsuma tradition that had predominated in the Navy since before the Restoration. Old Admiral Yamamoto Gombei, long an exemplar of this Satsuma tradition, was yet alive; and Takarabe, though native of another heath, was Yamamoto's son-in-law, thus at least nominally keeping the Satsuma tradition alive.

True, some of that generation of the bureaucracy nearer to Saionji's age than to his spirit were restive under the new day of parliamentary party ascendancy. They sought to make the Privy Council or the House of Peers into conservative counterweights. With such moves Saionji was in general quite unsympathetic, partly because of his conception of an historically possible evolution toward more democratic forms, and partly because of a personal antipathy toward most of the conservative spokesmen, such as Itō Miyoji and Hiranuma Kiichirō in the Privy Council. He was quite prepared to contemplate the curtailment of the Privy Council's powers to the merely honorific or ceremonial. So firmly, by the late twenties, did Japan's path seem to accord with Saionji's ideas of the proper development that after the "young Emperor" had been safely enthroned, Saionji's withdrawal seemed nearly complete.[47]

An amiable and diffident man, quite lacking in the driving energy and ambition of most other Meiji leaders, and with more than a dilettante's interest in literature and history, Saionji may have earned a reputation as a sybarite in his *jeunesse dorée*. He retained in maturity his full measure of aristocratic wilfulness and early iconoclasm and was perhaps less kindred psychologically to his Victorian contemporaries than to his image of the Age of Reason: a philosophical radical, hence an enlightened oligarch.

---

[47] Hirohito, the Shōwa emperor, was thus the fourth sovereign whom Saionji served. He had been regent since 1921 when his mentally incompetent father could no longer perform court ritual. Regnant in his own right since 1926, he was formally enthroned by ancient elaborate ceremony in the old court setting of Kyoto in 1928.

It was as heir to the patterns of *kuge* privilege (and the facilities of the adoption system) as well as, perhaps, of French libertarianism (and the indulgence of his personal tastes) that, though he never formally married, Saionji had not lacked feminine companionship and the concerns of parenthood. Upon returning from Europe he had taken into his household a spirited former *geisha* he had known before his years abroad. She became the mother of his elder daughter, Shinko, in 1887. Later she was succeeded by another former *geisha* who bore his second daughter, Sonoko, in 1904. With a new third mistress, Ohana, nearly fifty years his junior, who was included in the large suite accompanying him to the Paris Conference, the liaison was briefer and soon ended because of her indiscretions.

But now, in his old age, he took on more and more the characteristics of a withdrawn Taoist sage. Living neither in Kyoto, the ancient imperial capital and home of the *kuge*, nor in the new capital, Tokyo—though homes were maintained for him in both cities at the expense of his *zaibatsu* brother, Sumitomo—he preferred the simplicities of a small house of his own design in Kyoto style on the beach in the fishing town of Okitsu, some hundred miles from Tokyo. Except when summer's heat made his mountain retreat more suitable, in an ancient thatch-roofed farmer's house at Gotemba on the slopes of Mt. Fuji, it was in Okitsu that his last years were spent.[48]

Since it is in this setting that he is usually encountered throughout this volume of Harada's memoirs, it may be appropriate to quote a journalist's description of the Okitsu house:

The "estate" was sixty feet wide and one hundred and fifty feet long. The main house, a tile-roofed, two story frame structure, had two rooms

---

[48] The Taoist image is deliberate. Saionji had long used the "studio-name" (or pen-name) of Tōan, suggesting parallels with the attitudes of the great Chinese poet T'ao Ch'ien (or T'ao Yüan-ming, A.D. 376-427) who abandoned official life in Taoist fashion for quiet simplicities of his farm.

The little Okitsu house bore at its entrance a weathered board on which was carved in Chinese characters done by a vigorous hand the name "Zagyosō." The name and the name plaque had been given to Saionji by Viscount Watanabe Chifuyu (the son of a former Imperial Household Minister and adopted son of a colleague of Saionji in the Itō cabinets) as a kind of punning compliment. In the Chinese classics the great founders of the Chou dynasty (the culture heroes of Confucianism) had been aided by a legendary sage who mysteriously knew the workings of nature but spurned the use of his power and preferred simply to sit fishing at the water's edge. One of the sage's epithets is T'ai Kung Wang, written with the same characters that compose Saionji's personal name Kimmochi. "Zagyosō" literally means the "sitting fishing cottage." Watanabe was Justice Minister in Hamaguchi's cabinet.

on the second floor for visitors, and two eight-mat rooms on the ground floor; one of these was Saionji's study-bedroom, dining room and frequently infirmary, and the other was for the general use of his secretary, his steward, and Ohana. There were also a bathroom and kitchen, and four small rooms on the same floor for maids and servants. Beside this house, covering about two hundred and eighty square yards, were other small buildings for the stewards, house guards, and for storage.

No fences separated the property on the east and west from the fishermen's dwellings. On the north it was shut off from the highway and the town's main street by a modest teahouse-like wooden gate, and on the south, below a ten-foot stone [retaining] wall, lay the sandy beach of Suruga Bay.

The main house faced south. At the rear of the buildings was a small grove of evergreen trees and in front, a garden. In one corner of the garden were varieties of black and spotted bamboo bushes, and in another was a little mound of dwarfed pine trees and a miniature gray stone pagoda of thirteen stories. In front of these stood a pair of stone lanterns of the Nara style.[49]

To many of his contemporaries Saionji had seemed a puzzling sort of man whose contrary traits were somehow not at odds within his own makeup. One popular critic sought to sum up his personality in three English words, as exhibiting to an unusual degree the three "ins"—of intelligence, indolence, and indifference.[50] His patrician position gave him no reason to pursue place. His brother's generosity gave him no reason to pursue wealth. His preference for personal freedom gave him little pleasure in public office. His finely-honed intelligence gave him little hope his countrymen would soon or easily share his own rational attitudes.[51]

He had often been afflicted with ill health, and this may have

---

[49] Bunji Omura, *The Last Genro*, 354-55. This fictionalized biography, replete with imagined conversations, uses without acknowledgement some of the earlier published Japanese works cited above (note 32). This quotation is a simplified paraphrase of passages in Koizumi, *Zuihitsu*, 15-17, divested of Japanese descriptive details that have no English analogues. After Saionji's illness in 1930, an additional room in occidental style was added. On its burnished floor stood a small desk in Directoire style with chairs and a small settee upholstered in silk damask. The desk was beside an east window with leaded panes and had bookcases within easy reach. A glass-enclosed porch adjoined this room on the south, thus overlooking the garden and the sea beyond.

[50] Tokutomi Sohō (Iichirō), quoted in Andō, *Saionji Kimmochi*, 186.

[51] Saionji had a typical liberal's faith in education, and had helped several private schools; but he was aware that mass education by the state could propagate irrational shibboleths. Part of his contempt for Hiranuma stemmed from Hiranuma's untiring and effective sponsorship of mystical ultra-nationalism. See R. P. Dore, "Education, Japan," in Ward and Rustow, *Modernization*, 176-204. For Saionji's later pithy expression of his disappointment, see Harada, VII, 84, 93, 373; VIII, 49.

The Zagyosō

*Saionji's seaside
house at Okitsu*

39

contributed to the impression of indolence. After his severe illness in the spring of 1930, much attention was paid to the regimen for his health. Normally he devoted much of the day to reading—works in Chinese, Japanese, and French.[52] On warm windless afternoons he strolled in the garden facing across the bay to the then still pine-clad peninsula of Miho, the setting for the legend of Hagoromo, the heavenly maiden dancing in the feathered robe. After a siesta he would sometimes sit straight at his desk, playing with a deck of cards. He still took some pleasure in calligraphy, an art in which he preferred a "strong-boned" style to the "Konoe style" learned in his youth at court before the Restoration.[53] Better yet he was pleased with two other small and ancient arts: *bonsai*, the nurture and training of dwarfed plants and trees, and especially *tenkoku*, the carving of seals in stone and wood and ivory of many textures.[54] Habituated to tobacco and alcohol since his boyhood, he had now given up Havana cigars and limited himself to Egyptian cigarets. With his evening meal he was yet fond of the fine sake called *nadazake*. Once an Edwardian dandy in his Western dress, he nowadays more usually wore Japanese dress of sombre hue. His *tabi* (socks) invariably came from the Sanoya in Owari-chō, his *geta* (clogs) from the Anamiya in Ginza-nishi. For personal accoutrements with Western dress he liked things made of gold and touched with crimson. There were vestiges of his days in France a half century before: he always used Vichy water, imported for him by the Meijiya; his toiletries were by Houbigant. His gloves and wallets, too, were of French manufacture. Even at an advanced age Saionji did not lose the traces of a sophisticated man of fashion.[55]

Harada and Saionji

Though in ostensible retirement, Prince Saionji in fact kept in closer touch with contemporary politics than was commonly

---

[52] His taste in Chinese included not only poets and historians of the past, but newer studies of China by contemporary Japanese specialists. Harada's memo books include a list of French works, undoubtedly to be purchased for Saionji, mostly political biographies and memoirs: on Clemenceau, Benes, Trotsky, Bülow, Col. House, Churchill, and works on contemporary England, France, and Russia. Harada, IX, 161.

[53] His calligraphy was sufficiently admired for a volume of reproductions to be published in Kyoto in 1952.

[54] Most of the seals decorating this book were cut by Saionji.

[55] Oka uses the vernacular adjective *haikara*, a literal transcription of the English words "high collar," a Victorian vestige that still in Japanese connotes high fashion (see essay cited in n. 32, above).

known. His advice to the Throne must be informed, must depend on more than mere judgment of petitions received. Petitioners there might be, but only select and significant ones might reach him directly in his remote retreat.[56] It was in this life of retirement that the old Prince had need of effective, trustworthy, and continuing personal liaison with the capital and its currents. For this role he chose Baron Harada Kumao, a younger man of the generation of his own adopted heir and son-in-law, Saionji Hachirō, who was a member of the Imperial court entourage. For the last fourteen years of Saionji's life, Harada served as his agent, his alter ego, for virtually all of his responsibilities as the *genrō*.

There was an old connection between Harada's family and Saionji.[57] It was Harada's grandfather, an aide to Ōmura Masajirō —the key adviser to young General Saionji in the Imperial military camp against the Tokugawa—who had urged the young nobleman to study abroad just after the Restoration. While Saionji was in France in the seventies, Harada's father was sent to study geology in Germany. Saionji met him there while accompanying Itō to Europe in 1882. Though there were few professional interests in common, they were for some years "summer neighbors" at the beach resort of Ōiso on Sagami Bay, some forty miles southwest of Tokyo.

Harada Kumao was born in Tokyo on January 7, 1888, and was in his second year at the Imperial University of Kyoto when Saionji built his villa there called the "Seifuso." Young Harada was an occasional visitor; and his own father having recently died, he frequently turned to Saionji for avuncular counsel, for example, on the choice of a profession. He had hoped to accompany Saionji when the old prince headed the Japanese delegation to the Versailles Conference, but he deferred to his friend and fellow-student, Konoe Fumimaro, who had been anxious for this post.

After being graduated from the Kyoto Imperial University law faculty in 1915, Harada was on the staff of the Bank of Japan until 1922. Then for the next two years he undertook special

---

[56] The deliberateness with which Saionji chose his visitors is illustrated many times in these memoirs. Even an Imperial prince, if improperly importunate, was put off with a diplomatic illness (pp. 167-68).

[57] Data on the Harada-Saionji relationship has been derived from the "Preface" by Yamanouchi Hideo published in the first volume of these documents (Harada, I, "Shogen [Preface]," i-xiv). A writer better known by his nom de plume of Satomi Ton, Yamanouchi was a kinsman of Harada by marriage, and had been employed by Harada to edit his bulky memoirs. See also the essay by Hayashi Shigeru at the end of Harada, IX.

41

An example of Prince Saionji's calligraphy

assignments for the Imperial Household Ministry, in the course of which he travelled in Europe and America. When party government was resumed in 1924 with the appointment of Katō Kōmei to head a coalition cabinet, Harada became Katō's private secretary.[58] He continued in this official post as the Prime Minister's secretary in Katō's second cabinet and also (after Katō's death in office) in the successor cabinet of Wakatsuki Reijirō.

Thus in the decade before the events and relations described in this volume of the *Memoirs*, Harada had come to have personal knowledge and familiarity (albeit at a junior's level) with court personalities and procedures and also, as it happened, with the same political leaders in the cabinet who were once again, in 1930, the ministers of state. It is perhaps a mark of his self-effacing attitude toward his work that Harada's dictated diary nowhere touches on these experiences or suggests that they may have signally facilitated his ability to function skilfully as Saionji's principal means of liaison with the court and the current political leadership.

Harada resigned from this official position on the Prime Minister's staff in mid-1926 and joined the executive staff of the Sumitomo company. But this was not to return to the world of finance; for, as Harada's literary editor explains it,

> Saionji asked the then managing director of Sumitomo, Yukawa Kankichi, to give Harada leave from any official duties with the company and to assign him to such services as Saionji might have need. Before his death the late Baron Sumitomo, younger brother of Saionji, had arranged that such services and requests were to be met. Harada was, of course, happy to comply as well; and thereafter, until death ended the old prince's brilliant career at 92 on November 22 [*sic*], 1940, Harada devoted himself exclusively to Saionji's affairs.[59]

It did not indicate a diversion from Saionji's affairs or a search for a personal political career, but rather a seemly undertaking for a man of his rank and position, that in the by-election of January, 1931, Harada was elected from his baronial rank to the

---

[58] Katō had been Saionji's first Foreign Minister in his cabinet of 1906.

The supplemental volume (here called Volume IX) to the Iwanami edition of the Harada papers reproduces, among other auxiliary matters, some forty-three pocket diaries and memo books in which Harada kept daily jotted records of his appointments and interviews. These begin two days after his appointment as Katō's secretary in 1924 and thus deal with his activities some six years before he began to use these jottings as the principal raw material for his dictated *Memoirs*. (See Harada, IX, 3-341.)

[59] Yamanouchi, "Shogen," in Harada, I, vi-vii; see also Hayashi, "Atogaki," Harada, IX, 389-90.

Baron Harada

House of Peers and that he was re-elected in the regular elections of 1932 and 1939.

The Origin and Character of Harada's Memoirs

To Saionji's mind, Katō's adventitious death in office necessitated no government change, so that on Saionji's advice Wakatsuki Reijirō (Katō's Home Minister), who was chosen to follow him as Kenseikai president, was made his successor as Prime Minister as well. This first Wakatsuki cabinet was a continuation of the last Katō government in all ministerial posts. But multifaceted conservative opposition toppled this government in 1927. Saionji gave the opposition Seiyūkai leader, Tanaka Giichi, who stood well with the second generation of Chōshū leadership in the Army, his chance as successor. When Tanaka's domestic corruption and maladroit and aggressive foreign program lost both business and popular support, Saionji was not sorry to turn again, in 1929, to the men of the Kenseikai which had meanwhile reorganized as the Minseitō and had made Hamaguchi Yūkō (Katō's Finance Minister) its party president.[60]

It was this government which needed to deal with the increasingly severe repercussions in Japan of the world-wide depression, and which chose retrenchment, international cooperation, and disarmament as its key tools.[61] But these tools of the liberal arsenal were rejected in advance by many elements of the new generation which felt that all parties were mere holding companies of privilege.

---

[60] Hamaguchi, nicknamed "the Lion" by the Japanese press, displayed unusual vigor and acumen in quickly constructing his government, in introducing drastic economic measures (budget reforms, resumption of the gold standard), and in efforts to popularize his ten-point program by press and radio. His party managers produced a resounding victory in elections for the lower house in February, 1930. His government included no less than nine members of the House of Peers (four ministers and five of vice-ministerial rank) to minimize obstruction from that conservative body. His Finance Minister Inoue brought him significant support from the business community; and he early sought the benign support of the "Saionji circle." See the unique political study by Arthur E. Tiedemann, "The Hamaguchi Cabinet: First Phase, July 1929—February 1930," unpublished Ph.D. dissertation, Columbia University, 1959).

[61] Harada's purview does not lead him to inquire into the broad problem of the failure of the powers to establish a viable framework for international relations in the Far East after the first world war. Such a study is attempted by Akira Iriye in his *After Imperialism: The Search for a New Order in the Far East, 1921-1931* (Cambridge: Harvard Univ. Press, 1965), which notably comments on the limitations of the "Shidehara diplomacy" that Saionji admired.

The London Naval Conference, in particular, was an issue which released a barrage of vitriol and vituperation touching even the privileged precincts close to the Throne. Like the murder of Chang Tso-lin in 1928 which the Tanaka government had sought to hush,[62] but of wider significance, this response to the London Treaty issue gave evidence of an increasing disposition to cut adrift from the patterns evolving from the Meiji constitution that Saionji had fostered and approved.[63] Saionji had seen revolution at close hand in the Paris of 1870.[64] He knew well how shallow a growth was Japan's parliamentarism. He was determined to give stout support to Hamaguchi on the Treaty issue.

Particularly the "Supreme Command Issue" as raised in Japan by the London Conference and its treaty made plain to Saionji and his circle the precarious balance in the institutional structure of Japanese government. It focused on the threat, long latent but not previously so likely to be uncontrollable, that lay in the divided sovereignty in the constitutional pattern. It was an awareness of this episode and period as marking a crossroads for Japan that buttressed Harada's conviction that he should record for posterity what seemed to him Saionji's real role; at least it convinced him of his responsibility to make plain his patron's purposes in the face of a new kind of Japanese opinion which was distorting if it did not deliberately defame Saionji's role. Harada began the habit of dictating his memoirs, later to grow to such massive bulk, with the dictation on March 6, 1930, of the material with which this translation begins.[65] A decade later, a month before Saionji's

Hamaguchi

---

[62] Paul S. Dull uses material from Harada's memoirs to give a rounded story of this episode ("The Assassination of Chang Tso-lin," *The Far Eastern Quarterly*, XV [1952], 453-63). But he apparently did not have access to such Foreign Ministry memoranda as *Chō Sakurin bakushi jiken (The Assassination of Chang Tso-lin)*, June 1928-May 1932, LC Microfilm Collection, P VM 58; or to the translated *Documents Relating to the Circumstances surrounding the Death of Chang Tso-lin on June 4, 1928. . . . from the Files of Hatoyama Ichiro* (IPS Doc. Nos. 2316-22), LC Microfilm Collection, IMT 440. (Hatoyama had been Chief Secretary to the Tanaka Cabinet.)

[63] See James B. Crowley, *Japan's Quest for Autonomy, 1930-1938* (Princeton: Princeton Univ. Press, 1966), a somewhat revisionist study that treats of the London treaty issue as a first stage toward the formulation of new Japanese national security policies through articulating criticisms of the "Shidehara policies."

[64] Saionji's eye-witness account of the violence of the Paris Commune, a contemporary letter to a friend in Japan, is quoted in Andō Tokki, *Saionji kō to Konan sensei*, pp. 56-59.

[65] Only later did Harada dictate that brief record of the earlier episode— the imbroglio over Army responsibility in the assassination of Chang Tso-lin, and Saionji's reaction thereto—with which the memoirs chronologically begin (Harada, I, 3-13).

death, he was to dictate the story of why the memoirs had been undertaken and to describe how they were made.

This is from his dictation on October 23, 1940, as he records his request that Prince Takamatsu, the Emperor's younger brother, accept custody of his voluminous files:

On the same day [October 18] I went down to Okitsu and reported on the most recent developments. Then we [Saionji and Harada] discussed the prospect of requesting that his Imperial Highness Prince Takamatsu take custody of the documents which comprise this record, until they are to be transmitted to His Majesty, the Emperor. Prince Saionji agreed, saying that if it is acceptable to Prince Takamatsu, this should be a splendid arrangement. On the nineteenth I returned to Ōiso. The next morning, having learned that Prince Takamatsu had returned to his residence from his ship [At this time Takamatsu held the rank of Commander in the Navy], I telephoned and spoke with him directly. He suggested that I call on him at four that afternoon. I went to his Takanawa residence at the appointed time and spoke with him as follows:

"This record was begun from 1929. The basic reason for undertaking it, at the time of the London Treaty, was that in the atmosphere of distortion and falsehood then prevailing, little of the true situation was understood. In particular, His Majesty's attitude and the nature of the counsel given him by the *genrō*, by those about the throne, and by the Cabinet Ministers were subject to much falsification and misinterpretation. In consequence there arose very serious repercussions in the political world, and numerous problems were caused within the Army and the Navy as well.

"There was propaganda, malicious almost beyond belief, contemning His Majesty's moral character and intellectual discernment. I felt that this was highly regrettable. And since from my own position I was cognizant of the true facts, I deemed it essential to record them in written form. Thus I discussed this project with Konoe; and from that time on, with the assistance of the wife of Konoe's younger brother [Viscountess Konoe Yasuko] to whom I have dictated it, I have been compiling this record. By now it has grown to well over ten thousand pages.

"This record has come into being in the following way. Each week I see and report to Prince Saionji and subsequently my memoranda for such reports are dictated. I take the transcription of these notes to Prince Saionji. He reads the material personally, corrects mistakes, and adds such additional material as he deems pertinent. I receive this back from him at my next call on him, and then have a fresh clean copy made which is checked and then filed away.

"Since at present the press has occasionally hinted at the existence of such a record, and the fact that it is in the custody of the Sumitomo Trust Company has become known, it is possible that some rightist faction might seize an opportunity to destroy it. I have discussed this with Prince Saionji and would like to request that the whole record be kept in Your

Highness' custody until it is completed. When it is completed, the original manuscript with Prince Saionji's corrections and revisions will be presented to His Majesty. An edited version will be published at some suitable occasion—I should imagine not until some ten or fifteen years after Prince Saionji's death. In any case, the present circumstance is that I have asked Matsudaira [Yasumasa], the Chief Secretary to the Lord Keeper of the Privy Seal, to take charge of this matter in the future. Thus, so that Matsudaira may be conversant with our present arrangements, I would appreciate having Your Highness instruct a member of your household staff to maintain close relations with him on this matter."

Prince Takamatsu said: "I'm very happy to agree to this. I shall speak of it with my steward. Will you please follow through to make suitable arrangements with him?"

I expressed my appreciation to him for this, and then our talk turned to other topics.[66]

Problems of the Text

With Saionji's death on November 24, 1940, the dictation of these memoirs came to an end. But with Japan moving under more and more complete control of those whom Saionji opposed, it was quite uncertain when they might be published. Yet the obligation to publish them eventually was as firm as that to present the text with Saionji's corrections to the Emperor whom Saionji had served. Harada made no pretensions as a writer. He knew his dictation was rough and diffuse, the subject matter ill-organized. Much, he thought, must be done.

The whole file of his memoirs lay in three subject headings, quite disparate in size. He had begun with a section which he titled, "Prince Saionji and the Naval Conference." Before this section had been completed at the end of 1930, he had retrospectively dictated a much shorter section on the Chang Tso-lin murder: "Prince Saionji and the Grave Manchurian Incident."[67] From this point on, the one heading, "Prince Saionji and Disarmament," covered the entire matter dictated.

To tackle this huge editorial task he employed his kinsman, Yamanouchi Hideo, a writer better known by his nom de plume of Satomi Ton, who found that wartime Japan had little use for and offered little remuneration to the creative writer. He was sworn to

---

[66] Harada, VIII, 371-72.

[67] Such a phrase as "grave incident" used here and other similar terms were not invented by the Japanese ironically to minimize such outbreaks abroad or at home. They were euphemisms invented by journalists to circumvent the rigid censorship the government imposed in an effort to prevent public discussion.

absolute secrecy, and began his work in Harada's office at the Sumitomo headquarters. Yamanouchi seems to have applied himself to this task in a rather desultory fashion, even before the conditions of wartime life in Tokyo interrupted it completely. He began his editing with the huge third section, and at war's end had "corrected" only about one-sixth of it.

Harada, who had suffered a cerebral thrombosis in 1942 and remained an invalid until his death in February, 1946, had instructed Yamanouchi to have the Iwanami publishing house print the memoirs. When the documents "loaned" to the International Military Tribunal's Prosecution Section were returned to the Harada family, Yamanouchi, Matsudaira, and other Harada friends placed the materials in the custody of a publication committee consisting of Kobayashi Isamu, Nagato Mikio, and Yoshino Gensaburō as general editor. But the editorial task had been barely begun. Yamanouchi has written,

> Although as the one who knew wherein lay the ambiguities of the stenographic transcript I might cherish the hope of completing this editorial task, it was evident that a decade or more of unremitting work would not get me through the remaining revision—five-sixths of my task.[68]

Thus the Iwanami publication committee decided to turn over this task to Professor Maruyama Masao of Tokyo University, one of the country's best-known young historians specializing in the Shōwa period, with the suggestion that the editorial work should be begun *de novo*. Maruyama accepted this undertaking late in 1948 and elicited the help of Professor Hayashi Shigeru, also of Tokyo University. Under the direction of these two men a staff of five younger scholars from the Law department of the University began their work.[69]

In the "Postscript" to the first published volume, issued in August, 1950, Maruyama and Hayashi describe at some length the nature of the documents that had come into their hands, the process of collation and subdivision which they used, and the policy of revision which the group adopted. Since it is the text resulting from their work that has been used for the present translation, their comments are pertinent here.[70]

---

[68] Yamanouchi, Harada, I, p. xi.

[69] This staff included Imai Seiichi, Kamishiro Jirō, Fujiwara Hirotatsu, Matsumoto Sannosuke, and Waki Keibei.

[70] These comments are condensed from the joint Maruyama-Hayashi "Postscript [Atogaki]," (Harada, I, 295-305).

Prince Saionji's note to Harada upon
reading the original manuscript of this book:

Your fine manuscript has reached me. I have
read it again and again. How vividly you depict
my poor thoughts and your own cares and undertakings on my behalf! Later ages will not
exhaust their admiration of it as excellent
historical source material. I return it with
much appreciation. When next we meet we shall
indeed speak about it at greater length.
                    Cordially,
                    Kimmochi

May 25, 1931
His Excellency Harada

Much of the document had gone through some four phases of preparation: (a) Viscountess Konoe's transcription of Harada's dictation, (b) copy to which Harada had made corrections and additions, (c) copy to which Saionji had made additions and corrections, and (d) copy to which modifications had been made by Yamanouchi. Not all these steps were involved for the entire document. For some sections only the last form was available. The editors' general principle was to take the "Saionji corrected text" as the basis; when there were lacunae in this, to use the "Harada corrected version"; and to use the "Yamanouchi corrected version" only when no equivalent passages were available in the other two. This translation derives from a "Saionji-corrected text" without any of Yamanouchi's emendations.

Yamanouchi has written as follows of the editorial problem as he first faced it:

Even in conversation Harada had the habit of restlessly chattering on, taking much for granted, frequently omitting the subjects or objects of his sentences. In conversation one could clarify the matter by chiming in occasionally with a question or two. But he had dictated these documents, pocket notebook in hand, with no riposte or interjected query to his rapid speech—only the scratching of the stenographer's pencil. And he seldom added a word to it after.

Thus in the flood of his words the meaning (quite apart from matters of good or bad style) was frequently obscure. Knowing his way of speaking from our childhood together, I might guess at his meaning, and often I thought I could. But sometimes repeated re-reading and even guessing could not bring a fully satisfactory understanding. My revisions were not thoughtlessly made.

My task, then, was to rectify such confusion, to make the text readable and understandable by anyone, to put it into a plain and simple style, correcting time sequences and eliminating needless repetitions. Sometimes a missing meaning was supplied; illogical conjunctions were changed; or adjectives were weighed for aptness and precision. I little thought that this would take so much time! To resolve doubts that assailed me when I found passages in which there were two or even three possible meanings, I made it a point to waylay Harada on his infrequent visits to the office and would plague him with my problem until he would listen.[71]

The historian editors had a different approach from that of the creative writer:

The matter of greatest difficulty for us in preparing this work was the clarification and correction of its style and composition. On this par-

---

[71] Yamanouchi, Harada, I, p. ix.

ticular point Mr. Satomi [i.e., Yamanouchi] has testified to the difficulties which he encountered. Quite unlike Mr. Satomi with his close personal acquaintance with Harada and his knack for understanding the jist of Harada's way of speaking, we undertook this task wholly from the outside, as third parties. Consequently, in the matter of arranging the original text, we took utmost care whether a single character or a whole phrase seemed to need change. Even in cases where we might have ventured to make excisions, we most frequently left the text in its original form lest some nuance of the original be clouded. In the transcription of the original dictation, where we judged that Harada had not made his corrections, or where it seemed that drastic revision might be in order, even though the text seemed awkward and the relationship between its various parts seemed unclear, we left these passages as they stood; and we adopted the policy of leaving it to future historians to work out such interpretations as might be possible. . . . Certainly there is no doubt that the nature of the dictation text frequently gave us much trouble. Yet there were but few cases where grammatical confusion made the sense incomprehensible and interpretation might produce diametrically opposite meanings. Most instances are simply cases of bad style, and careful collation within the context may establish the essential meaning of the term or phrase for use in other contexts. Yet in cases where we had the slightest doubt, we refrained from any modification of meaning. . . .

Furthermore, in addition to having at hand Mr. Satomi's account of his experience . . ., we did not neglect to question Viscountess Konoe on Harada's habits of speech and his methods of dictation. Mr. Matsudaira Yasumasa, who had been closely associated with Harada, both personally and officially, was good enough to tell us much that was very useful, on the circumstances of the preparation of this work and on the character of Harada himself.[72]

If a Japanese novelist and a septet of Japanese historians have need to confess to some uncertainty when confronted with Harada's prose, an American translator may bespeak occasional obstacles to an effective Englishing of it, outside his own insufficient and bookish knowledge of the Japanese tongue. As historian he heartily approves of his Japanese confreres' approach to the text. And he must also speak gratefully of the careful footnote identifications[73] by full name of all persons mentioned in the text, and of the detailed and pertinent reference materials they have assembled. Both of these adjuncts he has translated: the footnotes in full and with additions (marked by square brackets) which he thought helpful; the appendices with some omissions. Since a number of the laws and ordinances given in the appended materials had been

---

[72] Maruyama and Hayashi, "Postscript," Harada, I, pp. 300, and 303. (The ellipsis marks enclose a passage from the latter page which has been intruded into the main comment from page 300.)

[73] These are, literally, "headnotes" in the Japanese text.

translated for the International Military Tribunal for the Far East, he has compared them with the Japanese text—then made his own translation of them.

The material in this volume, as translated for the Tokyo Court, appeared as "Supplement A" of the undated "Special Report: Saionji-Harada Memoirs."[74] In its originally "classified" condition this version was unavailable when the present translation was made from the Iwanami edition. Since its more recent "declassification" the present translator has compared it with his own prior work and has found no notable discrepancies in the subject matter of the Army version and the Iwanami text.

But as a translation the Army version has many limitations. Produced by Army personnel with some assistance from Japanese civilians employed for the purpose, it has been somewhat charitably characterized by a member of the Tribunal staff as "not wholly satisfactory."[75] It contains some egregious (though explicable) errors, many inept passages, and some that are nearly incomprehensible.[76] Yamanouchi Hideo, in his preface to the Iwanami edition, makes this relevant comment:

> If I may write as one who offered some slight assistance in the task of translating these documents, in the haste of producing an English version for the Court a number of errors was probably unavoidable. The majority of the Nisei [Japanese-American] translators had but a slight knowledge of Japan; and some, in truth, could not even read Viscountess Konoe's transcription.[77]

There is a further and perhaps minor point to which the translator would draw attention in a discussion of the Harada text. Impressed with Harada's ability to record in the quiet of his study lengthy conversations he may have heard days before (for which he may well have had in hand notes and sundry jottings), the translator was led to observe a certain sense of drama—perhaps contrivance—in his otherwise quite "unliterary" author, an effort to play a certain *leitmotif* upon the entry and re-entry of certain characters in his story. This may even be noticeable in the English translation, say, when Admiral Katō Kanji first appears or the Privy Council's chief secretary, Futagami.

---

[74] The full imprimatur reads, "Civil Intelligence Section, Military Intelligence Section, General Staff, Far East Command General Headquarters."

[75] Horwitz, p. 577; cf. also pp. 538 *et seq.* for a discussion of the formidable linguistic and other difficulties of an international tribunal such as this.

[76] Cf. Oka (as cited in note 15 above), p. 70, n. 1, for a parallel estimate of the work of these Army translators.

[77] Yamanouchi, Harada, I, p. xii.

He noted also that Harada was closely attendant upon the spoken word. Some of the persons quoted recurrently throughout the text have clearly distinguishable mannerisms; one can almost note a difference of timbre from speaker to speaker. Such distinctions are not always possible to transfer into another tongue. At best, the translator has tried to give that simulacrum of spontaneity which he occasionally finds in the Harada text. In part, this feature of the text may result less from effort or contrivance on Harada's part than from the nature of Japanese speech habits in general. His Japanese editors, both Satomi the literary man and Maruyama the academic scholar, felt required to comment for their Japanese reading public on the personal idiosyncrasies of Harada's language. But they leave quite unmentioned, however, certain idiosyncrasies of the Japanese language itself (assumed by and familiar to such a public) that may reflect something of the texture of Japanese culture and the nuances of behavior expected within it.

In speech the Japanese language exhibits an extreme sensitivity to levels of usage and a reluctance to make direct personal references. It normally employs a variety of forms (honorific, polite, ordinary, abrupt, or humble) for a single basic meaning but differing in vocabulary, grammar, and syntax in order to denote differing social positions. That is, Japanese has a far greater number of gradations and of fixed devices for conveying different levels of politeness and familiarity than can be found in so egalitarian a language as English.[78] Since Harada's memoirs deal almost exclusively with his face-to-face encounters, they show him to have been adept in reproducing and in selecting from alternative "levels" according to the requirements of his various encounters.

A single illustration will both give an example of such different levels of usage and also show Harada's adroitness in functioning to "translate" as well as to "transmit" Saionji's messages. His pocket diaries served him mainly as appointment books and usually have only the most laconic details. Occasionally, however, he jotted in them on the spot the precise words or phrases Saionji (and sometimes others) used in giving him messages to be orally delivered. But speech that was natural for Saionji, who made a habit, almost a fetish, of plain speech and whose rank in any case was such that there were few in the land to whom he need pay deference—such

---

[78] "The variables in any given situation are the relative hierarchical positions occupied by the speaker, by the person or persons spoken to, and by the person or persons spoken of." See Joseph K. Yamagiwa, "Language as an Expression of Japanese Culture," in John Whitney Hall and Richard K. Beardsley, *Twelve Doors to Japan* (New York: McGraw-Hill Book Co., 1965), pp. 186-221.

speech would be quite incorrect coming from Harada's lips. Later, in dictating the memoirs, Harada may give the message *as he delivered it*, not changed in basic meaning but given at a more polite, and perhaps more palatable, level suitable *for him* to use vis-à-vis the recipient of the message—usually his senior in years and rank. Thus, when Ugaki, the War Minister, hinted he wanted to resign in June, 1930, at a time that could seriously embarrass the government, Saionji sent him an urgent message to deflect him from this purpose. The pocket memo version (presumably his *ipsissima verba*) is so plain as to be virtually a command; the version Harada dictated into his memoirs is much more polite:

Pocket memo version	*Memoirs version*
Gobyōki ni sukoburu godōjō suru ga *yametai* to iu koto wo kiita ga dōka godōjō suru ga sō iu koto wa *yamete kure* . . .	Gobyōki ni tsuite wa sukoburu godōjō ni taenai ga konnichi *oto-dome ni naritai* to iu okangae wa zehi *omoitodomatte itadakitai* . . .
For your illness I have much sympathy but I've heard talk *you want to quit*. Though I know how you feel, *do quit* this talk . . .	While I am deeply concerned and sympathize with you in your illness, *I hope* very much *that you will give up* any thought that you may have of *resigning* at this juncture . . .

It will be observed that the operable verb forms (italicized) are quite different as words, and that Harada's are compound polysyllabic involutions (one mark of more deferential style) in contrast with the crisp punning imperative Saionji used.[79]

Such variance in usage is, perhaps, the familiar persiflage of status-consciousness in whatever culture, part of a gamesmanship only a little more exaggerated than, say, an American junior executive's need to know when to use and when to avoid the personal names of his superiors. But there is another aspect, notable both in classical and in modern times.

Japanese speech habits ofttimes exhibit such sensitivity and obliqueness toward second and third persons that the hearer can only intuit the real intention of the speaker behind the limited (or even contrary) meaning of the words spoken. This was a pronounced feature of the language of the ancient court nobility. Among the *kuge* aristocracy it was assumed that its members' experiences and values were so similar and "so familiar that any sys-

---

[79] See chapter iii, p. 152 below; Harada, I, 82; IX, 92; and for Ugaki's version, *Ugaki nikki* [*The Ugaki Diary*] (Tōkyō: Asahi shimbunsha, 1954), p. 137.

tematic exposition of one's thought was regarded as otiose, even boorish; and language became a sort of shorthand, immediately understood by those who were 'in,' vague and slightly mysterious to the outsider."[80] Much must be "read into" communications among members of a closed hierarchic society if the meanings are not to remain quite opaque. Yet from outside the culture this may be risky. Certainly in this book Prince Saionji's apparently bland messages to "do one's best for the country," to "act decisively," to "move towards greater rationality" can be read as more than vacuous encouragements. In the full span of the story the context gives such shorthand expressions more lucid and specific meaning.

Of course it is possible, perhaps even especially easy for one versed in both languages, to search for and find arcane "Japanese nuances" where there may be none. Thus, a recent study assumes that in dissuading Ugaki from resigning in mid-summer of 1930 Saionji virtually promised him a future premiership, and hence is explained why Ugaki, some nine months later, would have no part in a conspiracy that might make him a dictator. This interpretation is wholly derived from asserting of Saionji's message that "the language . . . in Japanese" is "solicitous," "replete with political significance," and "almost unbecoming a man of Saionji's eminence."[81] The assertion derives, of course, from Harada's "polite" version that Ugaki certainly heard. But if Saionji's actual bluntness was inappropriate for Harada, then Harada's language might indeed be odd "for a man of Saionji's eminence." Yet there is no real evidence, indeed it seems quite improbable, that Ugaki (who had known Harada and his canny courtliness for many years) would confuse the two and understand more from the message than either version explicitly stated.

Just how close the obliqueness of Japanese speech may come to hypocrisy or downright deception may defy easy analysis. In this volume, for example, Admiral Okada plainly admits to Harada that he must talk as if he were one of the Navy "diehards." Admiral Katō is prevented from seeing the Emperor "because His Majesty's calendar is already filled." Harada denies to an opposition politician that he or Saionji have moved to block Katō's manoeuvers. The Grand Chamberlain will not admit he took any stance against the Navy "stalwarts" despite his many undertakings apparently in just that direction. The Prime Minister insists that there is no

---

[80] Morris, *Shining Prince*, 280.
[81] Yoshihashi, *Conspiracy at Mukden*, 86.

constitutional issue involved in his handling of the treaty matter.[82]

It is not only in Japan that politics requires practice in the art of bluffing. But it is interesting to note how often and easily the major actors, on the political scene that Harada reports, use so naturally a terminology derived from that other craft of dissembling, of willing suspension of unbelief—from the make-believe of the theater. Ugaki feels himself to be out of things, "in the deafman's (spot in the) gallery;" Okada must "don the mask" of the opposition; Makino likens himself to a "sideman" in the wings, with no words of his own; Harada cannot reveal "what goes on behind the scenes." And Saionji himself, in a later context, decries and fears right-wing fanatics for they may treat the Emperor as a puppet acrobat who may be hauled down and replaced if his performance fails to please them.[83]

Just as politics is a kind of performance, so too its real creative work—the resolution of conflicts, the making of decisions—takes place beforehand, ere the curtain is raised. Thus again and again in Japanese public life, the councils and conferences, the cabinet and the Diet sessions, all tend to become less and less the occasions for debate and confrontation on issues, and more and more the ceremonial, almost ritual, ratification of consensus previously achieved.[84] No decision not unanimous seems to be truly valid; and once ritually validated may not easily be questioned. The last thing wanted, once the curtain goes up, is any show of discord. The show's the thing. The masque goes on.

Criticisms of the Harada Papers

Since the Harada papers were made public for the first time through excerpts introduced by the prosecution at the Tokyo War Crimes Trials, it was natural that the defendants and their counsel should seek to question and discredit their reliability and that of their author. The historian-editors of the Iwanami edition are at pains to examine these criticisms:[85]

---

[82] There is, of course, an old Japanese word—*haragei*—for such dissembling behavior, saying one thing and meaning another. Butow is fascinated by the possibility this "culture trait" must be appealed to in explaining why the leaders in 1945 stumbled through tortuous weeks not admitting to each other their common knowledge of defeat nor finding verbal formulae to voice it. See his *Japan's Decision to Surrender.*

[83] May, 1937, Harada, V, 320.

[84] See chapter v below, for an illustration of this process.

[85] The following is a paraphrased translation of a portion of the Maruyama-Hayashi "Postscript," Harada, I, pp. 301-4.

The Defense sought generally to give a very low valuation to Harada's reports. For example, Tōjō Hideki called Harada "just a high class information broker [gossip monger]."[86] Kidō Kōichi said that for keeping records of this sort Harada was by temperament quite untrustworthy and prone to exaggeration, that he was "incapable of recognizing accuracy." [87] Araki Sadao complained that Harada "would drop by from time to time, and without saying anything, would listen to chance conversation of the moment and go on his way. Not once did he so much as ask, 'What are your views—or—what do you think of such and such.' "[88] Itagaki Seishirō was wholly critical of him.[89] The defense attorneys also entered strongly adverse criticisms.

These criticisms may be summarized under the following headings:

(1) that Harada had no important role himself, either in the cabinet or the Privy Council, but was merely one member of the House of Peers; and that, consequently, whatever he had to report was only hearsay testimony;

(2) that these documents were replete with his own personal, and irresponsible, views and judgments;

(3) that he wrote from memory after a considerable lapse of time;

(4) that the documents had gone through the hands of several persons in the process of editing;

(5) that, by nature of the language used, the text is frequently difficult to understand;

(6) that Harada's ill-health in his later years raises serious question of his competence and capabilities.

Without entering into the pros and cons of these arguments as they bore upon court proceedings, we would note that the matter of the reliability of these materials as documentary evidence before a court and as historical materials are two quite separate questions. The historical value of this work stands quite apart from its technical evidentiary character before a court of law, but is to be judged wholly from the standards of historical scholarship. Final assessment of the value of these documents must be left to future historians. We merely put forward the following points.

In the first instance, the matter dictated and recorded in these documents, even those portions which are based on hearsay, were obtained generally from the persons most directly involved, and moreover from participants on both sides of actual events. Certainly Harada might have been only one member of the House of Peers; yet his fourteen years' service with Saionji found him charged with the specific and unique

---

[86] International Military Tribunal for the Far East, "Proceedings," and "Documents Collection" (hereafter cited as IMTFE), January 5, 1948; Doc. No. 347, p. 3.

[87] *Ibid.*, October 22, 1947; Doc. No. 298, pp. 10f.

[88] *Ibid.*, September 12, 1947; Doc. No. 270, p. 4.

[89] *Ibid.*, October 10, 1947; Doc. No. 290, p. 4.

responsibility of maintaining liaison with and collecting reports from the highest circles of the political world on behalf of the aged *genrō*. Even so, in these same highest political circles he had many close acquaintances of his own through the years—such men as Konoe Fumimaro and Kido; and his circle extended to include military men and business men as well. Kido himself has testified in court to the excellence of his political perceptions and to his energy as special traits of which Saionji made appreciative use.[90]

In the second place, to the contention that Harada's dictation was given some time after the events concerned, one must note that with only a very few exceptions these dictations were made within a month of the events. And various kinds of memos and notes from which the dictation was made were in almost all instances written virtually on the spot; immediately after his interviews and conferences, in his car on his home-ward trips from such meetings.

When it comes to the question of Harada's attitude toward his dictation, it is clear that he sought earnestly to avoid intruding his purely personal views. Only infrequently do we find evidence of what he himself thought or believed. Naturally, there may be instances of confusing his own evaluations with objective circumstance; and the bent of his own personality may be discernible in his judgments of men and events. Such considerations, however, are intrinsic in historical materials of this type and will be the basis for discriminating judgments to be made by historians to come.

One point of some significance for the historian, among those raised before the court, concerns the processes of editorial preparation and the muddiness of grammar and style of language. These we have already discussed.[91]

Going beyond these points, we must note that this is practically a unique document with respect to Saionji Kimmochi's last years. Such biographies as exist are mostly partial, fragmentary, and second-hand. We are told that it was Saionji's custom to destroy all documents by burning when his use of them was ended. Thus, apart from a few scattered materials, this must remain a prime source. True, Saionji is seen only through the screen which was Harada Kumao; yet apart from the *genrō* himself, none could be a more suitable or reliable witness to his thought and action. Yet this work is not limited to discussion of Saionji and the sector of relationships directly involving him. For Harada, from his unique position, can relate in considerable detail the political and social movements caught in his widely ramified intelligence network.

From first to last, however, it reflects the perspective and at-mosphere of the *genrō*'s position; and it must not be forgotten that it is conditioned basically by this viewpoint. Yet in Japan, where crucial political decisions are normally effected "behind the screen" and where, furthermore, the special personal relationships obtaining among the members of the upper levels of the political world take on decisive importance, this conditioned viewpoint enhances its value for history. We know

---

[90] *Ibid.*, October 22, 1947; Doc. No. 298, p. 10.
[91] See pp. 50-51, above.

of few records of the highly confused movements in the background of our political scene, and of the words and deeds of the participants therein, that are made in such detail, and with such sensitive, almost stubborn, faithfulness. Readers who want a single, swift, and simple story may feel annoyed at what seems too much trifling detail. Others may feel caught in confusing labyrinthine digressions. If these attitudes can be avoided, the attentive reader will have a rewarding sense of the various internal elements that were conducive to the swift collapse of the Japanese Empire.

To one who reads Harada's memoirs from outside the Japanese milieu, it will be apparent that Kidō's criticisms, to a certain extent, have a ring of truth when he seems to suggest that Harada had not the intellectual acumen to understand fully the matters it was his duty to record.[92] It will be clear that Harada's was not an analytic mind, and that it was not as elaborately furnished with the apparatus of historical knowledge or political commitment that one might expect to associate with his position.[93] There was no false humility in the man who wrote of himself as Saionji's "errand boy."[94] As such he did not ask or expect to be fully the confidant and collaborator of the old Prince. More than once there is a suggestion in his memoirs that he may not have been fully aware of the import of the data he recorded.[95] Another year beyond the events recorded in this volume will have elapsed before he can proudly note that Saionji has asked for his own

---

[92] An exchange in the limping language of the court-room may be of interest here; Kidō is being examined on his views about Harada's papers:

"*Question:* And was Harada a scholarly man?

"*Answer:* No. Harada was a very active man, and he had a very good political sense. However, from his student days he was very poor at going about his studies systematically, in an organized manner. His scholastic standing at school was not very good. . . . And if I may be permitted to give my comment, the recording of such matters in his diary was a matter which may be said to—correction—insofar as the recording of the diary is concerned, if I may be permitted to make my comment, he was extremely a poor hand.

"*Q.:* What about Prince Saionji? Did he have a disorganized mind, and was he quite a bit of a politician, too?

"*A.:* No. Prince Saionji was an entirely different man. He was an eminent and a very erudite statesman and a very fastidious reader." (IMTFE, "Proceedings," pp. 31, 540ff, October 22, 1947.)

[93] Note, for example, that Harada seems to come upon Minobe and his constitutional views quite *de novo* and at Saionji's instance in the course of assembling data on the treaty issue; and yet the "liberal *vs.* conservative" constitutional interpretations had been argued extensively from the period of Harada's university days before the first World War, by Minobe and others (pp. 112-15, below).

[94] Quoted by Yamanouchi, Harada, I, p. vii.

[95] E.g., Chapter vi, n. 31.

opinion on a crucial matter.[96] Clearly, what Saionji valued in Harada was the detail and accuracy of his reporting rather than the shrewdness of his judgments.

The translator may note here that he first turned to the Harada papers as simply one of many newly available and important sources on recent Japanese history. But before he had finished scanning this first volume, and before he had read Maruyama's evaluation of it, he was impressed with the vividness, the immediacy, and the range of its picture of Japanese political institutions in their actual operations.

There remains a general question about such a work as this: Are there significant gaps, unconscious or deliberate, in Harada's narrative, and what may be said of such lacunae? For this first volume, at least, it was not Harada's purpose to record totally Saionji's interests and activities in the political arena, but principally his relationship to the London treaty's acceptance and ratification. Any references to politics, finance, or diplomacy are in terms of relevance to this central theme. Harada's pocket diary notes show him to have had talks with many men on other subjects throughout the year that are not included in his dictated memoirs.

Thus it is probably not from inattention but by deliberate exclusion that he does not deal directly with two extremely serious issues confronting Japan's government in 1930: one, a new stage of the "China problem" as a new xenophobic nationalist government was just emerging with prospects of asserting itself throughout all China as no regime had done since the collapse of the old Manchu monarchy; the other, the severe economic, political, and social dislocations within Japan in the wake of the Great Depression. Indeed, Harada may perhaps be said to invoke these issues symbolically if indirectly: for he brackets this volume with references to the "China problem" in both the opening and the closing chapters; and he notes more than once Saionji's humanist concern for the indigent and the distressed. For such omitted but important topics one must turn to other sources.

Omitted, too, is any direct report of the visits made to Saionji by cabinet members and other important personages that must have borne directly on issues of strategy for handling the treaty matter. Some important such conferences preceded the March dic-

---

[96] On the matter of a successor to Wakatsuki in December, 1931: "For the first time, in five changes of cabinet since I've been associated with him, he asked my opinion" (Harada, II, 154).

tation by Harada with which the book opens; others are mentioned in the text. Harada was usually not present and the old prince seems seldom to have reviewed such interviews with him, or to have chosen to add anything to Harada's manuscript to fill this gap, as he might have done. Indeed it might be argued that since the book is deliberately an *ex parte* statement, an attempt to provide posterity with rebuttal of conservative and right-wing charges of undue collusion by Saionji and the court circle in support of Hamaguchi, thus it would follow that Harada carefully avoids such details as might lend credence to the charges. But circumspection is also a tool of persuasion. For instance, Hamaguchi saw Saionji on January 15, and on January 29 Admiral Okada had also "gone to Okitsu."

In the first chapter Harada mentions Okada's visit, that it was arranged by Hamaguchi, but that it was a perfunctory courtesy call. From Okada's diary, however, one gets a slightly different slant. Without any mention of Hamaguchi, Okada recalls,

> I met Count Makino and talked with him on the matter of disarmament, and the Lord Privy Seal said, "For Japan any disruption or failure of this conference will be most distressing." This I understood to be the attitude of His Majesty's entourage. And when I called on Prince Saionji to ask for his views he said he expected me to do my utmost to bring about the successful conclusion of a treaty.[97]

In his own eyes Okada was enlisted to support the treaty by the *genrō* and the court, not by a party politician. Clearly Saionji understood and accepted Okada's conceit, though not always without irritation, for he also understood that the War and Navy Ministers might be similarly motivated, as Harada's narrative makes apparent.

Still other omissions concern the accustomed workings of Japanese political institutions and the relationships of individuals within the elite groups. These Harada simply assumes. For these the annotations accompanying the text, however cumbersome as a gloss, may nonetheless provide a more adequate sense of context for Harada's various conferences and confidences.

The "perspective" and the "conditioned viewpoint" to which Maruyama and Hayashi refer would imply for the informed Japanese reader a number of themes that may not be immediately apparent to a non-Japanese. Moreover, these themes emerge clearly as basic problems in the text to follow, and some discussion of them

---

[97] Okada, *Kaikōroku*, 44.

in the rest of this introduction seems called for. To mention these themes is to suggest something of the "atmosphere" of the world in which Harada's record was made, and it may be useful to summarize certain of these themes: among them, the character of the Imperial institution, the nature of the Supreme Command issue, the role of the Privy Council, the undercurrents of chauvinism and of political terrorism, and the role of the London Treaty issue as a catalyst uniting ideological and political forces in an environment of economic depression eventually to destroy the edifice of Meiji parliamentarism that Saionji viewed so hopefully.

To outside observers Japan's *volte face* from the liberal parliamentary decade of the twenties to the warfare in China and fascist-like reconstruction at home in the thirties and forties may be best marked by the Manchurian invasion of 1931, and internally associated with the recrudescent assassinations and terrorism thereafter—notably the May 15th Incident (1932) in which not only civilian extremists but officers of the armed services undertook violent revolutionary "direct action" against the established order —which brought an end to party cabinets.[98] To the Japanese, however, the first overt steps toward fascism are associated with the reactions to the Hamaguchi government's apparent success in obtaining ratification of the London Treaty despite the opposition of important elements in the naval establishment and in the Privy Council.[99]

---

[98] This is essentially the position taken by the Prosecution at the International Military Tribunal for the Far East.

[99] The detailed quasi-documentary work of Aoki Tokuzō on the causes of the war begins with the topic of the London Treaty and the militarists' opposition to it. Aoki, I, 1-103.

The group of historians of the Rekishigaku Kenkyūkai (Society for Historical Research), within a generally Marxian frame, find the same topic a key episode in the immediate background of the Manchurian invasion. *Taiheiyō sensō shi* [*A History of the Pacific War*] (4 vols.; Tōkyō: Tōyō Keizai Shimpōsha, 1953-54), I, sect. ii, chap. ii.

An evaluation such as Shigemitsu's study of the "upheavals of Shōwa" likewise takes its departure from the repercussions of the disarmament issue (*op. cit.*, I, 9-73). A most recent work of significant Japanese scholarship is the so-called "Asahi history," edited for the Japan Association of International Relations, Committee to Study the Origins of the War: Tsunoda Jun (gen. ed.), *Taiheiyō sensō e no michi: Kaisen gaikōshi* [*The Road to the Pacific War: A Diplomatic History Before the War*] (7 vols.; Tōkyō: Asahi shimbunsha, 1962-63). This work, to which fourteen scholars contribute, also makes the subject of naval affairs its topical point of departure. Like the topically more limited recent studies by Butow, Crowley, and Iriye, it seeks a more adequate revision of the standard views popularized by the War Crimes trials; and an English translation is in process in this country.

The Imperial Institution

Modern Japan's revolutionary changes after the Meiji Restoration of 1868 were carried out by direct and continuing appeal to the image of the Emperor and his court, the most ancient and traditional symbols of Japanese identity. Theories and attitudes about the imperial institution were not full-blown and complete at the Restoration but were modulated of many elements, native and European, until a codification of formal structure and supporting theory was proclaimed with the constitution of 1889.[100] No other non-European society has succeeded in a program of modernization while using similar sanctions from its past. Indeed, within the European world itself, only Britain has retained and reinterpreted monarchic institutions of like antiquity. Saionji's Anglophile propensities were partly based on his view of power politics in his maturing years, and partly expressed his hope and expectation that Japan might have similar practical success in preserving the Throne while becoming technologically developed in a competing international order.

Only outwardly was the Emperor "restored" to direct rule. The Meiji oligarchs did not envisage that an Emperor, as an autocrat, should personally and directly exercise any of the vast prerogatives attributed to the Throne. This was a view fully acceptable to Saionji, though he had been absent from Japan in the critical years when orthodox attitudes were crystallizing; for while preserving the institution, he saw the possibility of pragmatic progressive measures to make Japan a more modern open society. For those who saw only absolutism and deification of the ruler in the ambiguities of the Meiji constitution or who would cultivate a mindless mystical adulation by the people, he had a rationalist's contempt.

Yet paradoxically his own strongest political sentiment was undoubtedly his sense of personal attachment to and affiliation with the imperial institution. He once told Admiral Yamamoto, "As far as politics are concerned, my family has had an abiding duty for a thousand years. I am the head of my family, and thus, as long as I live I cannot forswear my sense of duty publically to serve His Majesty."[101] This notion of a duty peculiarly incumbent upon him

---

[100] In addition to the Pittau study cited in note 26 above, see also Herschel Webb, "The Development of an Orthodox Attitude Toward the Imperial Institution in the Nineteenth Century," in Jansen, *Attitudes Toward Modernization*, pp. 163-191.

[101] Koizumi, *Zuihitsu*, 234.

was no doubt reinforced rather than diminished by his facile personal familiarity with his sovereign. He had known the Meiji emperor since their boyhood in Kyoto; as Prime Minister, apart from official functions, he chatted with the Emperor as a friend, and it shocked his Finance Minister (who chanced to overhear) that such camaraderie was possible.[102]

Even so, in playing the role of the sole *genrō* to the Meiji emperor's grandson, Saionji can be seen as retaining, protecting, even magnifying this mystical element in the Japanese state to the detriment of the liberalism he professed. To whatever extent the Meiji leaders used the Imperial institution simply to permit and shield their own autocracy, they perfected a series of devices both in doctrine and in institutions whereby the parliamentarism preferred by the last *genrō* could be destroyed.

A cardinal point of post-Meiji political doctrine was the untouchability, that is, the lack of any personal responsibility of the Throne and its occupant.[103] No less than the modern British sovereign, the Japanese *tennō* must never rule. But this was not because the system represented a resolution of a struggle historically waged between sovereign and subjects, or because a new personal intervention by an Emperor was to be avoided as a violation of the constitution or the people's rights. Rather, he must never have to be accountable for those errors in judgment or action inevitable in the secular order which, if attributable to an Emperor personally, might permit a revolutionary antithesis to emerge between the sanctified sovereign and his people.

It appears in the total Harada record, from the data on Saionji's responses to the graver crises of the years after 1930, that far more fundamental than Saionji's desire to perfect a parliamentary tradition was his wish to protect the Imperial institution, to preserve its politically transcendent and charismatic character.[104]

---

[102] Koizumi, *Zuihitsu*, 230.

[103] Cf. Colegrove, "The Japanese Emperor" (see Bibliography).

[104] The Harada papers, and the Kidō diary, for later periods make it plain that Hirohito was personally minded more than once, especially after the Manchurian invasion, to take a stronger stand against the militarists who had a growing sense of his antipathy to them; but Saionji and the Saionji-approved court officials purposely deflected the Emperor from such personal involvement: e.g., at the time of the movement of troops from Korea to Manchuria without Cabinet or Imperial sanction (Harada, II, 69).

In Saionji's young years the argument of court officials that it was unseemly in the Emperor's eyes for him to be associated with the radical paper, *Tōyō Jiyū Shimbun*, had dissuaded him from that venture. And later, when his second cabinet collapsed in 1912, he refrained from involving the Throne directly to gain immediate political ends, though both Katsura and Yamagata flagrantly resorted to this device.

In this first volume the issue appears in several forms: obliquely, as when there seems to be a danger that the Emperor's cousin, the Admiral Prince Fushimi, may be induced to take an unfortunate political stand;[105] and more directly, through the admonition of Admiral Okada who expostulates with certain Navy die-hards, "If the views of the advisers differ, how can His Majesty make a decision? Thus irresponsibly to seek the Emperor's judgment, vexing his mind in this way, is a matter about which we must be extremely careful."[106] The voice is Okada's but the words might be Saionji's.

But in 1930 compromises to the detriment of parliamentarism to preserve the Emperor's position yet lay in the future. In this year, instead, it seemed that one more step might be taken to make Japan a more modern state, to keep abreast of Britian and the United States as leaders of the international order;[107] and to set a needful precedent for the ascendancy of a party cabinet over other executive agents in the state. The London Treaty was the issue, and Hamaguchi the man with sufficient political courage (and a parliamentary majority) to be the instrument. And of courage he would have more than modest need.

The Meiji leaders had not only refurbished the doctrine of transcendent Imperial sovereignty. They had also furnished the Throne with such a plenitude of advisers responsible only to the Throne that the question yet remained: Where does ultimate authority for decision rest? Who is the final adviser?

The Supreme Command

Nowhere did this question arise more sharply than with respect to military matters. Before he had promulgated the constitution and created the Diet, the Meiji emperor had declared himself to be *Taigensui*—Generalissimo—and thus the sole head of the nation's military establishment.[108] The Cabinet, the General Staffs, and the Privy Council had also come into existence before the Diet.[109]

---

[105] See below, pp. 105, 138, 141-42, 177.

[106] See below, p. 144.

[107] Cf. below, pp. 84-86, 158 f.

[108] By Imperial rescript of January 4, 1882 (*Genkō Hōrei Shūran* [*Compilation of Laws and Ordinances in Force*] [Tōkyō, 1931], I, bk. i, chap. viii, p. 63).

[109] For good recent succinct statements on the formation and policies of the Meiji military establishment, see James B. Crowley, "From Closed Door to Empire," in Silberman and Harootunian, *Leadership*, pp. 261-87; and Roger F. Hackett, "The Military—Japan," in Ward and Rustow, *Political Modernization*, pp. 328-51.

In terms of the constitution the age-old bifurcation of civil and military right (Emperor and Shōgun, *kuge* and *buke*) was both obliterated and preserved through ambiguous terms which conditioned Japanese constitutional jurisprudence for the next fifty-five years. In popular parlance the Emperor exercised a right of military command (*gunrei*) by virtue of one article of the constitution, and by yet another he exercised the right of military administration (*gunsei*). Together, *gunsei* and *gunrei* might be combined and seen as *tōsui*—Supreme Command.[110] The distinction may seem academic since all sovereignty was the Emperor's. But a crucial issue is immediately faced at the echelon below the Throne. His Majesty's advisers in his exercise of the rights of *gunsei* and of *gunrei* were not one and the same. *Gunsei* could be viewed as but one aspect of the Emperor's general right to administer all state affairs, in which he was counselled by Ministers of State,[111] who were the members of the Cabinet. Thus the War Minister and the Navy Minister, for their separate sectors of the military establishment, were top advisers on *gunsei*. Distinct from the ministries and created by Imperial ordinance rather than constitutional stipulation were the two staffs, each with its chief, which were deemed His Majesty's chief advisers with respect of his right of *gunrei*, each chief possessing a right of direct access to the Emperor, independent of the Cabinet.[112]

Technically the Chief of the (Army) General Staff and the Chief of the Naval General Staff were not subordinate to the respective Ministers. Before the first decade's experience under the new constitution was completed, Yamagata, essentially to insure the continued dominance of his own Chōshū clique in the Army, had obtained in 1898 an Imperial ordinance requiring that the War Minister be a general or lieutenant-general on the active list; and

---

For the ordinances in force in 1930, see Appendix. Western students of these subjects are grateful to Kenneth Colegrove and his Japanese collaborators for charting the way to succinct summaries of the pertinent administrative and juristic literature. In addition to the articles cited in the Bibliography, attention should be called to his *Militarism in Japan* (Boston: World Peace Foundation, 1936).

[110] A more precise statement of this issue is found in chap. ii, below; see notes 9 and 10.

[111] See pp. 298-300, below. Note that there is no constitutional doctrine of cabinet unanimity explicit in Art. LV.

[112] This separation, while not expressly created by the Constitution, could depend upon the distinctions marked by Arts. XI and XII. Note that while administrative ordinances require ministerial countersignature (Art. LV), military (i.e. command) ordinances did not. The ordinances governing these staff agencies are given in Appendix II (pp. 306-07, below).

a similar subsequent order in 1900 stipulated that the Navy Minister must be an admiral or vice-admiral on the active list.[113] Thus the Ministers and the Chiefs would belong to one guild, the professionals of their services, and possible dissent was minimized. But it was this very area of possible dissent within the *tōsui* agencies, at the echelon just below the Throne, that could be and was used by an astute politician like Hamaguchi in his handling of the London Treaty issue, as is revealed in the following text.

But in addition to these two groups of advisers with respect to the military establishment, two other agencies had also been brought into being. The first and more important was the Supreme War Council, created in 1887, an advisory group in no way subordinate to the Ministries or Staffs and composed of the Field Marshals and Admirals of the Fleet, the Ministers of War and Navy, the two Chiefs of Staff, and such general officers of the Army and flag officers of the Navy as were especially appointed to be Supreme War Councillors. It was clearly a device to preclude discord with respect to advice on *gunsei* and *gunrei;* to be, so to speak, the ultimate adviser on *tōsui.* The second, created largely for honorific purposes after Japan's first modern war had distended the previously highest ranks, established the rank of *gensui* (translatable as Field Marshal for Army officers and as Fleet Admiral for Naval officers) whose holders constituted the *gensuifu,* or Board of Field Marshals and Fleet Admirals.[114] That the *gensuifu* was not necessarily purely honorific but could be, on occasion, *the* adviser on *tōsui* is evident from its use at the time of ratification of the Washington Treaties.[115]

In practice, the relationship between ministries and staffs seemed not to be one of subordination. The staffs exercised a wide measure of what would seem ministerial administrative responsibility.[116] But together through this group of military agencies the

---

[113] These ordinances, No. 314 of 1898 and No. 194 of 1900, are both given in the 1907 edition of *Genkō Hōrei Shūran,* bk. iii. pp. 49, 62. The modification of these ordinances, under the first Yamamoto ministry, to permit designation of War and Navy Ministers from officers on the reserve list, did not in fact change the relationships here discussed; for no reserve officers were ever assigned to these posts. But the possibility doubtless heightened the Army's sensitivity to a "threat" of increasing civilian authority. Cf. Yamagata's stand at the time of the Washington Conference mentioned below, p. li.

[114] See below, pp. 297, 305-06.

[115] See below, pp. 174-75, n. 21.

[116] "In Japan, the general staffs have carried on much of the administration that strictly speaking belongs to the ministers of war and of the navy. Thus, many details of the recruitment, training and discipline of the personnel

professional services could claim in theory and exercise in practice a very large measure of autonomy. To the Japanese this was *nijū seifu*—dual government, something very close in essential spirit to the long centuries of the shogunal regime. That such fissures were not earlier disruptive of the state's apparent unity under the Emperor can be attributed to many factors, not the least being the spirit of defensive and collective compromise which animated much of Meiji institution-building and also the essential homogeneity of the total Meiji elite group whether in military or civilian affairs.

For the purposes of the narrative given in this first volume of Harada's memoirs, it should be noted that, apart from the generally parallel structure for the Army and Navy outlined above, the two services diverged in several ways. For one thing, "administrative" and "staff" distinctions were perhaps sharper in the Navy than in the Army. Training programs, for example, in the Army came under an Inspector-General of Military Education, technically subordinate to the Chief of Staff rather than to the War Minister. This Inspector-General came to have sufficient autonomy in practice to rank with these other two officers as one of the "Big Three" of the Army. In the Navy, however, similar responsibilities were administered under the Navy Minister. At another level it should be noted that the Army was senior to, and more important than, the Navy. Whereas the Army was the modern version of an old important Japanese institution and could employ the *samurai* tradition for public support and personnel indoctrination, the Navy was quite lacking in a discrete Japanese tradition and was a new creation of westernizing Japan after Perry. Scalapino has aptly phrased another well-known difference between the two services (in reference to a slightly later period):

Although the navy was not without its extremists and although it certainly was not vitally concerned with the protection of representative government, it was destined by its very nature to be a more moderate force. Not only does a navy operate primarily away from the homeland, but also it is more elitist and much smaller in personnel, and thus it does not have the same capacity for, or interest in, a social revolutionary

---

of the army and navy, as well as manoeuvres and the disposal of the armed forces are handled by the general staffs. This is in addition to their duty to prepare plans for the land and naval defense of the Empire. Important questions of defense are referred to the Supreme War Council and even to the Board of Marshals and Fleet Admirals. At the end of such a meeting the Imperial will is signified and a command issued to the minister in charge" (Colegrove, *Militarism in Japan*, pp. 20-21).

movement or an authoritarianism based upon mass power. Moreover, the Japanese navy received little glory in continental expansion, and it had great respect for Anglo-American sea power. Indeed, the choice of navy men to head the two cabinets which followed the Inukai ministry after the May 15th Incident was prompted by this consideration.[117]

As it was the goal of proponents of representative government to establish the practice that cabinets reflect majorities in the Diet and as this came to seem accustomed practice in the 1920s, so it was the liberals' hope to utilize opportuntiies for maximizing the areas of governmental affairs in which cabinet advice took precedence over other executive agency advice.

The Japanese Context of the London Treaty Issue

That this was not entirely a forlorn hope may be seen in two developments of the preceding decade, the one internal to the military establishment, the other in the diplomatic field. As the political scene *per se* had seen a shift from the relatively simple Meiji clan politics to the less clearly-visaged business-related party politics of the twenties, so too there had developed more complexity in the military arena. The constitutional and institutional distinction between "administration" and "command" had in fact tended to produce two kinds of career in both military services. The earlier homogeneity of the officer corps leadership tended to break down under the same forces that were transforming the whole Japanese elite from a few to a multiplicity of groups.

In both the Army and Navy there emerged the figure of the high administrative officer, the Army or Navy bureaucrat with close affiliations outside his service—with court civilians, with the newly important party political leaders. In the longer story which includes the 1940s as well as the 1920s, such a figure may seem to have been briefly transitional. Soon a military leadership that was quite contemptuous of any contestant would resume command in the military establishment and in the state as well.

Edwin Reischauer's uniquely adroit brief account of the transition from "liberal democracy" in Japan to "nationalistic militaristic reaction" notes these changes as in part reflection of a widely ramifying contest of generations.[118] "Older generals and admirals were often men of broad outlook, who from long and

---

[117] Scalapino, p. 379 and n. 49 (see Bibliography).
[118] Edwin O. Reischauer, *Japan, Past and Present* (3d ed.; New York: Alfred A. Knopf, 1964), especially chaps. x-xii.

intimate association with business leaders had come to accept much of the business man's point of view, but the younger officers were mostly of a different breed."[119] In 1930, at the time of the London Conference, General Ugaki Kazushige and Admiral Takarabe Takeshi, the War and Navy Ministers, typified this "older" generation. Both exemplified "administrative" as against "command" traditions.

The Yamagata clique's dominance of the earlier army had not been without opposition within that service, from groups usually associated with men from other than Chōshū clan lineage—notably the so-called Saga group. But clan lines had become increasingly blurred as other distinctions arose. Lacking adequate new blood of strictly Chōshū lineage, the older Chōshū group had co-opted men of ability from other backgrounds. Ugaki was such a co-opted man as was his Chief of Staff, General Kanaya Hanzō, and some important slightly junior officers such as Minami Jirō.[120] However much they might be "Chōshū men" by a kind of adoption, their own generation's skills and alliances were distinctive and are important to be understood. General Ugaki, for example, was relatively unique among high Army figures at the end of the twenties. Early in his career he had served as an attaché in Europe; he had been assigned to Hirohito's staff when the Emperor was yet Crown Prince; he had had experience in several key staff offices. Except for the period of the Tanaka cabinet (1927-29), furthermore, he had been War Minister since January, 1924, and was rich in administrative experience and in readiness to maintain "understandings," as the Japanese say, with his cabinet colleagues. The greater part of his War Ministry leadership had been in Kenseikai-dominated or Minseitō-controlled governments. Though he would be quick to insist that as a military man he had no party allegiance, his service to party causes was notable: viz., in the earlier Kenseikai retrenchment[121] and in this London Treaty period. He could easily come to be represented as a politicians' general, or more critically

---

[119] *Ibid.*, p. 159.

[120] Ugaki was from Okayama, Kanaya and Minami from Ōita; these modern prefectures were essentially the feudal daimyates, respectively, of Bizen and Bungo. Harada, it will be noted, was of Okayama family background.

[121] See below, chapter i, n. 3. It expressed this notion of independence of party (shared by Navy Ministers too) that Ugaki did not think of himself as having served five times as War Minister. In the first four cabinets he succeeded himself in this post; and this constituted one "tour of duty." With the Hamaguchi cabinet he entered upon his "second" term as War Minister. See Ugaki, *Nikki*, pp. 122-42.

as a *zaibatsu* general; and a rising younger Army officer generation, of Saga group lineage, was eventually to make this criticism its own.[122]

Admiral Takarabe was Ugaki's analogue in the Navy. The Satsuma clique's dominance of the older smaller Navy had been less contested from within. Takarabe had a tincture of the Satsuma tradition by marriage.[123] His career as Navy Minister had begun in the cabinet of Admiral Baron Katō Tomosaburō in May, 1923; and when he returned to that post under Hamaguchi, it was the sixth cabinet in which he had served as Navy Minister. He had been the protégé of Katō Tomosaburō, "father of the modern Japanese Navy," on whom he continued to model himself and his position throughout this period. But he did not hold the same unquestioned leadership that had been Katō's.

Katō, as Navy Minister (1918-23) in the Hara government, had been given an almost completely free hand in the negotiation of the Five Power Naval Treaty as head of the Japanese delegation at the Washington Conference. Following that Conference he had been made Prime Minister (1923) prior to the final ratification of that first treaty of naval limitation. While he had been absent from the country at the Conference he had acquiesced in Hara's assumption of the role of Navy Minister pro tem, the first instance of a civilian thus, even obliquely, heading the Navy Ministry. At that time old Marshal Yamagata, then in his last year, took vigorous but unsuccessful exception to this possible precedent for establishing civilian control of the Army and Navy portfolios.[124]

It is clear that in 1929-30 Hamaguchi had a reasonable expectation of success in carrying through Japan's participation in the London Naval Conference. A worsening economic situation made a retrenchment program urgently necessary, in the Minseitō view. A reduction of naval expenditures could be made only with some assurance that the Navy's relative position vis-à-vis competitive navies would not also worsen. There was the precedent of the Washington Treaty under which the principle of naval limitation by international agreement had been accepted. Takarabe was

---

[122] Such was the antipathy to him after his retirement that the new Army leadership refused to permit him to form a cabinet in 1937, despite an Imperial order recommended by Saionji that he become the Prime Minister after the collapse of the Hirota government. He did subsequently serve as Foreign Minister in the first Konoe cabinet until forced out of that post by disagreement with the Army leadership. Cf. Ugaki; Harada, V, 235-46.

[123] See above, p. 37.

[124] Cf. Takeuchi, chap. xx (see **Bibliography**).

Navy Minister and, like Katō before him, would not only be a delegate but had accepted that Hamaguchi act in his absence as Navy Minister pro tem, as Hara had done. The Navy was inclined to preen itself as exhibiting better discipline and less faction than the Army,[125] and within his service generally, the Navy Minister was probably a more potent figure than the War Minister in the Army establishment as a whole.

The Washington Conference pattern had been economically and strategically advantageous to Japan, leaving her in a naval sense clearly preponderant in the western Pacific area. The Five Power treaty, in which Japan joined with Britain, the United States, France, and Italy, had provided for: a ten-year holiday in capital ship construction; the scrapping of certain specific vessels (with the United States and Britain thus scrapping more than Japan); the limitation of capital ship tonnage to 35,000 and 27,000 respectively for battleships and aircraft carriers, and of their maximum gun caliber to 16 inches and 8 inches respectively. In total tonnage for such vessels, Japan had accepted the ratio of 3:5:5 in proportion to the American and British fleets.[126]

Despite the patent advantages for Japan, the inferior ratio rankled deeply. And by the time of the Geneva Conference, which met in 1927, the Japanese Navy's position was that it needed a more favorable ratio of 70 per cent. The Geneva Conference efforts to extend the limitation pattern of Washington to other categories of vessels foundered principally because the British and Americans could not come to terms. But the Japanese position then was the one the Navy was prepared to argue at the London Conference.[127]

The economic background of the "London Treaty issue" is only dimly glimpsed in Harada's record, in the words of the scores

---

[125] Cf. Admiral Tochinai's remarks, p. 147, below.

[126] The best recent statement on the Japanese position at the Washington and London conferences is found in Crowley, *Japan's Quest for Autonomy*, pp. 3-82.

For the Washington, Geneva, and London conferences in general, see the apt summaries in Harley F. MacNair and Donald F. Lach, *Modern Far Eastern International Relations* (New York: D. Van Nostrand Company, 1950), pp. 226-30, 285-88; Paul Hibbert Clyde, *The Far East* (2d ed.; New York: Prentice-Hall, Inc., 1952), pp. 441-61, 569-71; A. Whitney Griswold, *The Far Eastern Policy of the United States* (New York: Harcourt, Brace and Co., 1938), pp. 305-32; and such fuller studies as Yamato Ichihashi, *The Washington Conference and After* (Stanford University Press, 1928), and Merze Tate, *The United States and Disarmament* (Cambridge, Mass.: Harvard University Press, 1948), pp. 121-198. Raymond Leslie Buell, *The Washington Conference* (New York, 1922).

[127] See pp. 94 f., n. 30; 246, n. 17, below.

of persons he consults; but it clearly burdened the minds of the more responsible statesmen. Japan had felt a foretaste of depression in the financial crisis of 1927. The Minseitō prescription from 1929 on was a policy of deflation. But the remedies of Hamaguchi (himself a financial expert) and his Finance Minister Inoue were confounded by the depth of the world-wide depression and the unprecedented effect, socially and politically, within Japan especially on the rural population. There was a precipitate decline in prices in general.[128] The movement of rice and silk prices resulted in unusual distress. The collapse of the American market for silk plummeted the raw silk price from 1,420 yen (per 100 *kin*) in April, 1929, to 540 yen in October, 1930. Rice (of which there had been four successive unusually heavy harvests in Japan and Korea from 1927 on) fell from an average, per *koku*, of 29 yen in 1929 to 17 yen in November, 1930. Both rice and silk tend to be characterized by inelasticity of supply in response to falling prices.[129] It has been estimated that in the half-decade, 1925-30, the net income of agricultural households declined by one-half or more.[130]

Of the expected political opposition to the treaty Hamaguchi and his advisers could make a fairly accurate prognosis and prepare careful positions for defense against the opposition's attack. If Takarabe negotiated the treaty, he and his senior contemporaries such as Admiral Okada and Admiral Saitō—exemplars of the administrative bureaucracy in the Navy—might be expected to see it through vis-à-vis strictly internal naval opposition.[131] If the complaisant Ugaki could be dissuaded from using an actual illness as excuse for resigning from the War Ministry, the top Army leadership which was similarly oriented to prefer harmonious solutions would probably not make common cause with the naval dissidents on the grounds of the "supreme command issue."[132] In the Diet the

---

[128] Wholesale prices, on an index with 1929 averages as 100, fell 30 points in 1931; retail prices, with 1926 as 100, fell to 68 points in 1931. Cf. William W. Lockwood, *The Economic Development of Japan* (Princeton: Princeton University Press, 1954), p. 131.

[129] George Cyril Allen, *A Short Economic History of Japan* (London: George Allen & Unwin, Ltd., 1946), pp. 97f; Lockwood, p. 57.

[130] Lockwood, p. 63, quoting official surveys. Cf. Harold G. Moulton, *Japan, An Economic and Financial Appraisal* (Washington: The Brookings Institution, 1931); John E. Orchard, *Japan's Economic Position: The Progress of Industrialization* (New York: McGraw-Hill Book Co., 1930).

[131] Such opposition first appeared in the naval advisory staff attached to the delegation to London which was largely by-passed by the civilian negotiators. Cf. Wakatsuki, pp. 356-59; Okada, p. 50; Takeuchi, pp. 292-93.

[132] Saionji and Harada were especially used to effect this neutralization of the Army, as a large part of this volume here translated reveals.

opposition Seiyūkai party was torn by intensely rivalrous factions. Inukai, its new president, however, was an ancient parliamentarian long famed for opposition to clan and militarist politics. Even if the more avidly nationalist elements of his party should push him to extreme condemnation of the Hamaguchi government, the Prime Minister could face critical Seiyūkai interpellations in the Diet with a certain equanimity, for his own somewhat better disciplined party had a clear majority,[133] and he need not accept debate on a constitutional issue that could become embarrassing with the Supreme War Council and the Privy Council.[134] This latter agency, "the Emperor's highest resort of counsel on administrative and legislative matters,"[135] was certain to be troublesome, indeed, but in common with other recent Prime Ministers of both parties, Hamaguchi could offer it a certain condescension based on his assurance of ultimate support from the *genrō* and the high court officials.[136]

In one sense the treaty's final formal ratification by the Emperor on October 2, 1930, was a signal victory for Hamaguchi, an apparent milestone toward bringing Japan to accept the executive leadership of parliamentary politics. Had he not won the support of such crucially placed military figures as the Navy Minister, the War Minister, and Admiral Okada? Had they really acted to "help Hamaguchi?" Or did their actions and decisions respond primarily to requests from Saionji and the court circle? Was it *vox populi* or *vox dei* that commanded their allegiance?

These are the "behind the scenes" elements of Harada's narrative telling how the expected opposition was frustrated. They played across the same stage on which Harada himself had a useful role.

The Chauvinists' Opportunity

But there were other levels, below the lights of Harada's intelligence network, down in the pit amongst the people whence

---

[133] At the 17th general election for the lower house, in February 1930, out of 466 seats the Minseitō won 273; the Seiyūkai, 174; six other parties, 14; and independents, 5. Cf. Harada, I, 259-60; Quigley, pp. 227-28.

[134] By precedent and practice, if not by constitutional stipulation, the treaty must successfully pass the scrutiny of these executive agencies before ratification could be achieved.

[135] Article VIII, Imperial Ordinance on the Privy Council, p. 302, below.

[136] Chaps. vi-vii, pp. 202-50, below, are largely devoted to this problem, its background and development.

a new generation of actors with other lines was soon to climb onto center stage. In this yet murky realm where economic distress was more corrosive of the established order there were rapidly maturing movements of which Harada, the Japanese public, and the world at large were still ill-informed. At this level "below the scenes" were several distinct groups for which the London Treaty issue provided in unusual measure the verbal formulae focussing a variety of discontents into a chorus of common antagonism to the premises and personalities associated with the liberal capitalist order. Three phases marked the developments producing a New Order within Japan: the proliferation of popular anti-liberal, anti-Western societies; the coalescence of civilian and military forces moving rapidly to the right; and the rising readiness of such forces to use direct action and terrorism. The London Treaty issue assisted in the crucial second stage in bringing together exponents of expansion, of extreme chauvinism, and of radical social and political reform. It provided an entree for professional civilian patrioteers to disseminate their anti-parliamentary and anti-capitalist ideas among receptive military men; and gave them an opportunity to associate semi-anarchic, largely agrarian, reform movements with a military leadership in an avowed effort to constitute a mass base for a purely Japanese variety of the fascist way.[137]

This volume of Harada's records scarcely lifts the curtain on these developments. The imprecise caption, "the young officers' movement," had not yet come to have wide currency.[138] But named so or not, the reality is noted however obliquely. Many officers of both services, especially junior officers, had been trained and

---

[137] Yanaga devotes a chapter to cataloging key nationalist and so-called secret societies and the acts by which they gave most public evidence of their growth in and after this period (chap. xxxii, pp. 489-518), as does Colegrove from earlier assembled, less complete data (*Militarism in Japan*, pp. 27-41). Hugh Byas, in his *Government by Assassination* (New York: Alfred A. Knopf, 1942), is most concerned with the third phase and adds important descriptive details from a contemporary journalist's files. A most effective, but selectively partial analysis of the historical and functional role of this movement is Scalapino's preface to his chapter on "The Militarist Era and Party Collapse" (pp. 346-65). Well-known in the very extensive Japanese literature on this subject, in addition to the work of Kada and Hattori listed in the Bibliography, is Kinoshita Hanji, *Nihon fuasshizumu shi* [*A History of Japanese Fascism*] (3 vols.; Tōkyō: Iwanami Shoten, 1949) and Tanaka Sōgorō, *Nihon fuasshizumu no genryū* [*Origins of Japanese Fascism*] (Tōkyō: Hakuyōsha, 1949).

[138] A study of the ideology and actions of this movement between 1925 and 1937 has been made by Royal Wald, "The Young Officers' Movement" (Unpublished Ph.D. dissertation, University of California, 1949). and is, of course, part of Storry's *Double Patriots* and similar studies.

were caught in the irrationalism of the myth of the Emperor-led people.[139] Some were restive at their obviously diminishing professional prospects as today the Navy was cut back and tomorrow, of a surety, it would be the Army. In the Army, particularly, many were inchoately resonant to the distress of the countryside as well as critical of their apparently compromising seniors. Glimpses of this development are found in the anti-Takarabe movement which Harada notes, and in the oft-iterated theme of a "need for reorganization" in the mouths of the administrators with whom Harada consorts.

Nowhere is Saionji's awareness of the dangers of these days—when the "pattern of politics by political parties may be destroyed" by the military—better conveyed than in the percipient advice the old prince sends to the Lord Privy Seal, via Harada, in the period of uncertainty after Hamaguchi was struck down by an assassin's bullet in mid-November, 1930.[140] The temporary (or was it to be the final?) removal of "Lion" Hamaguchi's stubborn leadership revealed quickly the rivalries within his own party. So serious were they that there was every expectation of a typically "transcendent" solution being called for; even to the point of calling on the "non-party" General Ugaki to assume both Minseitō presidency and the Prime Ministership.[141]

Ugaki's ambivalent role at this time, and especially in the the so-called "March Affair" less than four months after the close of this year (1930) of Harada's narrative, justifies in part the otherwise perhaps surprisingly cynical attitude of Saionji toward the general who first seemed a trusted friend but is last glimpsed in this volume as merely a useful chessman, an instrument—a piece capable of being taken easily by the opposition.[142]

---

[139] Note the use of this absolutist concept, under which the Meiji Restoration leaders had justified their actions, as an argument by those who would revolt against the contemporary form of Meiji institutions, e.g. as spoken by Admiral Katō Kanji (see below, p. 121).

[140] See p. 285, below.

[141] See chap. ix, pp. 272-91, below. A certain precedent for such a move on Ugaki's part could be found for ardent party men in General Tanaka Giichi's assumption of the Seiyūkai presidency after his retirement.

[142] See p. 285, below. The "March Affair" of 1931 seems to have been such an effort to "capture" Ugaki, a coup d'etat which planned to establish military rule by an Ugaki-headed cabinet that would discard Diet, parties, and politicians. It was immediately hushed at the time it was halted, two days short of its "D-Day," and was soon to be overshadowed by more effective coups. Though it is beyond the chronologic limits of this volume, it suggests how the treaty issue could serve as catalyst to produce the temper and readiness for direct action from this time on.

The publishers of Harada's diary in Japan have likened the work to Stendhal's *La Chartreuse de Parme.* The parallel, of course,

---

During September, 1930, as the Hamaguchi government successfully faced down the last opposition to treaty ratification, in the Privy Council, there was organized around a group of younger officers in the War Ministry and the General Staff a society which came to call itself the Sakurakai (Cherry Society). Originally including about a score of active duty officers of the rank of lieutenant-colonel or below, of whom Lt. Col. Hashimoto Kingorō was the key figure, its membership rapidly expanded. Hashimoto had just been transferred from the post of attaché in Turkey (where he deeply admired the military-led renovation by Kemal) to head the General Staff's "Russian desk." He functioned as an ardent proponent of the ideas of such civilian rightists as Ōkawa Shumei, enlisting the attention of such seniors as the Generals Koiso, Tatekawa, and Ninomiya (the latter the newly appointed Vice Chief of Staff, the others heads of Staff sections) and others including Tōjō Hideki. A paraphrased partial translation from the prospectus of the Sakurakai reveals how the turgid prose of civilian chauvinists had been adopted, albeit unofficially, to reflect the ideas of an important wing of the Army in the fall of 1930:

"To say how our country has come to its present parlous plight, we cannot but point to the very heavy responsibility of those 'statesmen' who ought to be the very nucleus of our national life. Consider how these presumed exemplars before the people soften the national policy. Despite the responsibility they bear toward His Majesty, they lack the courage to carry out national policy and, instead, destroy its very basis. In their indifference they give no consideration to the spiritual problems basic to the people's welfare. They are merely absorbed in lust for political power and materialism. They mask the Imperial effulgence above them; they deceive those below them. The flooding corruption of the political world has reached its climax. . . . There is no means to sweep aside the dark clouds, no way to call forth that courage and determination to slash through the root of the nation's evils. . . . Even now, in their ultimate degeneracy, that these party politicians have been able to strike a foul blow at the military establishment can be clearly seen in the London treaty. Yet the military establishment is paralyzed, lacks courage to come forward against this decadent politics, and can do no better than depend on the Privy Council, doddering old men of a past generation. . . . It is clear that the foul blows which the party politicians have recently struck at the Navy will be turned next on the Army." (Translated from Aoki, I, 121-26, *passim.*)

The March plot, set for the twentieth, was devised by members of the Sakurakai with the assistance of outsiders such as Ōkawa who talked to and sought to persuade Ugaki to step forward as leader. Weapons had been stockpiled, private funds collected, and rioters recruited. But at the last minute the whole affair seems to have been called off by advice of the senior officers involved. Little was publicly known of the plot until after the war. Harada, for example, did not get wind of it till August, 1931, nearly five months later, from Prince Higashi-Kuni. Affidavits from a number of the participants, including Ugaki, are part of the War Crimes Trial record. Ugaki insisted then, as he had earlier to Harada, that he had indignantly rejected overtures to head a revolt. Cf. Harada, II, 21-34, 120-24; Kinoshita, I, 101-14; Tanaka, pp. 313-19; IMTFE document collections, Docs. No. 11517 (Exhibit No. 157), No. 11514 (Exhibit No. 158), No. 11516 (Ugaki's affidavit, Exhibit No. 163), Defense Doc. No. 2231 (Hashimoto's affidavit, Exhibit No. 3195). Evidence of this plot was included in the charges against Okawa, Koiso, Hashimoto, and Tōjō before the Tokyo War Crimes trial.

recalls Beyle's literary method: *The Charterhouse of Parma* begins with a famous description of Waterloo, not in terms of the grand scheme and significance of the battle as a whole but in the precisely detailed, limited, partial view of a single actual observer. The parallel no doubt evokes recollections of Saionji's francophile and literary propensities, and at the same time stigmatizes the absolutist character of Japan's pre-war politics. Parliamentary democracy had clearly not sunk sufficiently sturdy roots into the sub-soil of Japanese society, nor in the minds of the few who yet made crucial decisions in the brief period of party ascendancy. It is as testimony to the shallowness of this footing in a rockily repellent soil that Harada's volume, herewith translated, may in part be valued. Like Stendhal's observer at Waterloo Harada is eyewitness to large events. He could view, and report, the inner workings of the last effective parliamentary government in Japan from a privileged position, yet a position of limited horizons.

Fragile
Victory

CHAPTER I

The London Treaty:
From Discussion of Disarmament
to Treaty Signature

Translator's Note: Harada began his whole voluminous record of his activities on Prince Saionji's behalf with his dictation on March 6, 1930, of the material that begins this chapter.[1] At this time the Minseitō ministry of Hamaguchi Yūkō had been in office for less than a year.[2] But Hamaguchi and his colleagues now at the helm of the Japanese government were neither strangers to that task, nor unknown quantities to Saionji.

Retrospectively, Harada goes back to the appointment, late in the previous year, of Japan's plenipotentiaries to the London Conference—Wakatsuki, a former Prime Minister and a senior figure in the recently organized Minseitō, and Admiral Takarabe, the Navy Minister—and begins with Prince Saionji's concern that they have a proper understanding of their roles as negotiators and of the need to conclude a treaty.

Like Hamaguchi, Wakatsuki had entered politics from the ranks of the bureaucracy just prior to World War I through joining the Dōshikai, the party by which Prime Minister Prince Katsura had hoped to counter the opposition of older party groups. Since university graduation Wakatsuki had been a Finance Ministry official and had risen to become Vice Minister in 1907 in Saionji's

---

[1] Harada's own statement of how this record came to be kept is set forth in the Introduction. Henceforth, brackets are used to indicate my additions, except where they are used in the body of the text to mark off the date on which Harada dictated the material which follows the said date.

[2] See Appendix I A for a list of the principal members of the Hamaguchi cabinet.

first cabinet. His "entry into politics" was as Finance Minister in Katsura's third cabinet in 1912; and throughout his subsequent career he had the name of being a finance expert rather than a persuasive political leader. Finance Minister again in the second Ōkuma cabinet during World War I, Wakatsuki resigned with two other ministers at least partly in criticism of the corruptionist activities of some of his colleagues in the election of March 25, 1915. Like Hamaguchi, he became a stalwart subaltern of Katō Kōmei (Takaakira), and was Home Minister in that Kenseikai leader's cabinets, 1924-26, in which Hamaguchi was Finance Minister, and Shidehara, Foreign Minister. When Katō died in office in January, 1926, Wakatsuki succeeded him as president of the Kenseikai, and (on Saionji's nomination) also as Prime Minister. Admiral Takarabe and General Ugaki were, respectively, Navy and War Ministers in each of these last three cabinets. Hamaguchi became Home Minister and Shidehara continued as Foreign Minister in the first Wakatsuki cabinet. But growing militarist antagonism to Shidehara, a bank crisis, and intransigent opposition of part of the higher bureaucracy, especially as led by Count Itō Miyoji in the Privy Council, toppled this cabinet in April, 1927.

These "Kenseikai cabinets" (actually based on coalitions in the lower house of the Imperial Diet) were identified with a conciliatory policy toward China (Shidehara); with economy and fiscal retrenchment touching even the military establishment;[3] and with parliamentary liberalism (e.g., in the adoption in 1925 of universal manhood suffrage). They were popularly labelled "Mitsubishi cabinets" because both Katō and Shidehara were sons-in-law of Baron Iwasaki,[4] the head of the huge Mitsubishi commercial and industrial interests, and because these policies pleased neither military, bureaucratic, landed, nor Mitsui-related interests predominant in the opposition Seiyūkai.

When this opposition, under retired General Tanaka Giichi's opportunistic leadership, followed Wakatsuki's first cabinet in the Seiyūkai cabinet of 1927-29, it was burned by its own fires of a

---

[3] Four Army divisions were disbanded. The following figures show the shrinking allocation in these years to the military in terms of percentages of the total national budget:

1920: 48%	1922: 42%	1925: 29%
1921: 49%	1923: 33%	1927: 28%

Imanaka Tsugimaro, *Nihon seijishi shinkō (New Materials on Japanese Political History)* (Tōkyō: 1928), II, 441.

[4] And Hamaguchi's birthplace was in the former Tosa, the original home of Iwasaki.

more *"positive"* policy on the continent—the *"Tsinan Incident,"* the *"Grave Manchurian Affair"* (i.e., the murder of Chang Tso-lin) —and open to the charge of lèse majesté *in concluding the Pact of Paris. It fell in the early summer of 1929, a denouement that Prince Saionji approved and facilitated.*

The former Kenseikai now had become reorganized as the Minseitō with Hamaguchi as party president replacing Wakatsuki, who was denominated by that term used for senior party notables, "counsellor (komon)." In the Hamaguchi cabinet, organized to succeed Tanaka in July, 1929, Shidehara returned to the Foreign Office, Ugaki to the War Ministry, and Takarabe to the Navy Ministry. Having dissolved the Diet, this Minseitō cabinet campaigned in the ensuing elections for purification of politics, reform of China policy, disarmament, economy, and removal of the gold embargo. It won a handy majority, and proceeded with some vigor to implement its program. It was quickly receptive to the formal invitation to the Conference on Limitation of Naval Armaments sent by the British government in October; partly, of course, because it was known that the Britain and the United States had come to some preliminary understanding.[5]

Wakatsuki was initially inclined to demur at appointment as chief Japanese delegate; for he lacked language skill for negotiation and felt himself to be too much a layman to argue naval matters cogently, if he were not unacceptable to the naval establishment. On this latter point he was reassured when Hamaguchi arranged a conference with chief figures of the Navy: Tōgō and Yamamoto Gombei, the "elders" of the service, and a dozen other bigwigs; and they voiced no notable objection. That he was persona non grata *to political right-wing groups he was well aware. Indeed, almost up to his departure for London, he was under pressure from such figures as that doyen of the patriotic societies, Tōyama Mitsuru, to resign from his plenipotentiary role.*[6]

---

[5] Japan, Ministry of Foreign Affairs, *Ei-bei jumbi kōshō kankei (Documents concerning British-U.S. Preliminary Negotiations),* June-October, 1929, in *Rondon kaigun kaigi ikken (Documents Relating to the London Naval Conference)* (LC Microfilm Collection, S 2.12.0.0-5). Hereafter this large group— exceeding 18,000 pages—will be cited as *Rondon ikken.* Needless to say, only a small portion of these documents are immediately pertinent to an appreciation of Baron Harada's diary.

[6] Wakatsuki Reijirō, *Kōfuan keikō roku—Wakatsuki Reijirō jiden* [*Memoirs of Kōfuan—The Autobiography of Wakatsuki Reijirō*] (Tōkyō: Yomiuri shimbunsha, 1950), pp. 332-339.

Accessible reviews of the political history here epitomized can be found in general works such as Robert A. Scalapino, *Democracy and the Party Move-*

> *Prince Saionji's Views on the Disarmament*
> *Conference—Wakatsuki and Takarabe*
> *Appointed as Chief Delegates—The*
> *Prince's Anecdotes—Diet Demands for a*
> *70 per cent Ratio.*

[Dictated March 6, 1930]

When the London Naval Conference opened, the press was busily discussing the strategy to be employed against hypothetical enemies and even naming states which might be regarded as potential enemies.[7]

Prince Saionji said,

"From the standpoint of international courtesy, no civilized

---

ment in Japan: The Failure of the First Attempt (Berkeley: University of California Press, 1953), especially chap. vi, "The Evolution of Political Parties in Japanese Institutional Structure and Theory, 1913-1932," and those listed in the Bibliography below, by Hugh Borton, Harold Quigley, Robert Reischauer, and Chitoshi Yanaga. Arthur E. Tiedemann gives an adroit summary of the institutional setting and political traditions to preface his unique study of the Hamaguchi cabinet which has thus far dealt only with its first eight months ("The Hamaguchi Cabinet: First Phase July 1929—February 1930: A Study in Japanese Parliamentary Government," unpublished Ph.D. dissertation, History Dept., Columbia University, 1959).

I have found the following Japanese shorter studies helpful: Rōyama Masamichi, *Seiji-shi* [*Political History*] ("Gendai Nihon bummei shi [A History of Contemporary Japanese Civilization]," Vol. II; Tōkyō: Toyo Keizai shimposha, 1940); Hayashi Shigeru (ed.), *Gendai shi* [*Modern History*] (Tōykō: Mainichi shimbunsha, 1957); Shiraki Masayuki, *Nihon seitō shi: Shōwa hen* [*A History of Japanese Political Parties: The Shōwa Period*] (Tōkyō: Chūō Kōronsha, 1949); Tōyama Shigeki (*et al.*), *Shōwa shi* [*History of the Shōwa Period*] (Tōkyō: Iwanami shoten, 1955).

Informed commentary and anecdotal vignettes of many of this volume's *dramatis personae* are to be found in the several collections of Baba Tsunego's contemporary criticisms: *Gendai jimbutsu hyōron* [*Contemporary Personalities*] (Tōkyō: Chūō Kōrensha, 1930); *Seikai jimbutsu fūkei* [*Men on the Political Scene*] (Tōkyō: Chūō Kōronsha, 1931); and *Gikai seijiron* [*A Critique of Parliamentary Politics*] (Tōkyō: Chūō Kōronsha, 1933).

A significant, somewhat "revisionist" Japanese historiography has recently appeared, a notable example being the collaborative work edited by Tsunoda Jun, *Taiheiyō sensō e no michi* [*The Road to the Pacific War*] (7 vols.; Tōkyō: Asahi shimbunsha, 1962-63), to the first volume of which Kobayashi Tatsuo contributes a discussion of naval affairs, 1921-36.

[7] [An epitome of press opinion throughout this period is given in Tatsuji Takeuchi, *War and Diplomacy in the Japanese Empire* (Garden City, New York: Doubleday, Doran and Co., 1935), pp. 283-336.

[The Japanese Foreign Ministry maintained an exhaustive file on press opinion. See the more than 4700 pages of such material under headings, *Yoron narabi ni shimbun ronchō (Public Opinion and Press Comments)*, and *Shimbun no kirinuki (Press Clippings)* in *Rondon ikken* (LC Microfilm Collection, S 2.12.0.0-6 and S 2.12.0.0-7.]

nation would allow its press openly and boldly to name other nations as potential enemies, as the great papers of Japan are now doing. I feel that it would be much better, for the sake of international morality, for the Home Ministry to be mindful of this and to guard against it.[8] Of course it's proper and fitting to hope that our delegates to the naval conference will bring back the best possible results; but for Navy partisans to insist on a 70 per cent ratio and to clamor that our delegates should kick over their seats, leave the conference, and come home if there is the slightest diminution of the 70 per cent ratio; this would be a most serious mistake. The Navy must, naturally, stand on its own ground; but when the matter is judged from the wider viewpoints of politics and diplomacy, it cannot hope for complete victory no matter how loud the clamor; and this, of course makes it even harder for them to talk of national strength.

"After all, a nation's military preparedness, its ability to maintain its strength in time, depends in the first instance upon its financial policies. The strength that derives from reckless plans and emergency *ad hoc* preparations is virtually no strength at all. Especially now, in order to produce a successful result at the conference, Japan should lead other nations to recognize her earnest promotion of international peace by voluntarily accepting 60 per cent. Japan will greatly increase her future international role if she takes a leading part in bringing this conference to a successful conclusion.

"Take Bismarck,[9] for instance, who firmly believed that it was Germany's future to expand. He was strongly determined to realize this belief. Yet he was well aware that such expansion was not immediately possible because his state lacked the essential power. Hence, while he seemed to pay unnecessary deference to Disraeli in London and Napoleon III in Paris, he was actually an astute statesman and a realistic diplomatist. Or more recently, after the Sino-Japanese war, when Japan brooked insult and complied with the advice on the retrocession of the Liaotung Peninsula, it was because she wanted the empire to expand in the future.[10] One

---

[8] [Japan's rigorous press control laws were administered under the Home Ministry.]

[9] [Saionji, the "expert on Europe" among late Meiji statesmen, was wont to illustrate his points from his own experiences and acquaintances in the period of his European sojourns from 1870 to 1892. As Minister to Germany, he had signed with Bismarck in Berlin in 1889 the revised treaty eliminating the previously humiliating extraterritoriality clauses.]

[10] [Saionji and Harada occasionally indulge in elliptical comment of which

could cite other similar examples from recent Japanese diplomatic history. In other words, would not Japan be able to assume, with Britain and America, a commanding position? France and Italy would be placed in the position of following this lead. For Japan to jeopardize its opportunity of playing such a role, simply because of insistence on the 70 per cent ratio, will leave it in a situation like that of France and Italy. Can there be any question of what course will be advantageous and of what course will be disadvantageous for Japan's future?

"I am convinced it would be extremely impolitic for the future of our country if we were to forego the privileges Japan has enjoyed, up to the present, of close ties with Britain and America. It is in fact by acting in concert with Britain and America in this instance that Japan will bring about the most suitable benefits to itself. What can be the advantage of throwing away this opportunity?"

I called on Wakatsuki[11] after he had been appointed a Chief Delegate to the London Conference. "It's a quite difficult situation I find myself in," he said. "Takarabe, the Navy Minister, has been to see me to say that, since it would be bad form for a military man like himself to urge Japan's claims and to insist on the 70 per cent ratio, he hopes that I, as a politician, will say what he would

---

the purport may not be directly apparent. The Sino-Japanese War ended in 1895 with the cession by China to Japan of Formosa and the adjacent Pescadores Islands and also of the Liaotung Peninsula in southern Manchuria. Eight days after the treaty was signed, the German, French, and Russian ministers in Tokyo, in what is known as the "Triple Intervention," jointly "recommended" the retrocession of Liaotung; and the Japanese government (of which Saionji was a member) was constrained to yield. The crowning blow to the humiliation of this Triple Intervention came when Russia took control of the same territory some three years later.

[Here Saionji doubtless means that by brooking this insult (the Japanese says, literally, "swallowing one's tears"), Japan was preparing to profit in the developments of the next decades: in alliance with Britain (1902), successful war with Russia (1904-05), absorption of Korea (1908-10), and participation on the winning side in World War I. Saionji's oft-noted pro-British propensities are here seen in a more realistic and less sentimental guise than is usually given them.

[This "insult" or "humiliation" was deeply felt and remembered. In August, 1945, when the Emperor sought to direct his ministers to accept the Allied surrender terms to end World War II, he more than once likened himself to his grandfather, the Meiji Emperor, who at the time of the Triple Intervention had had "to swallow his tears" and to "endure the unendurable." (Japan, Ministry of Foreign Affairs, *Shusen shiroku* [*Historical Records of the Termination of the War*] Tōkyō: Shimbun gekkansha, 1952), pp. 592, 701.]

[11] Wakatsuki Reijirō (1866-1949), member of the House of Peers, former Prime Minister, counsellor to the Minseitō. [Cf. "Translator's Note," above.]

want to say. To this I could only reply it would be difficult and that I would consider the matter after consulting with both the Foreign Minister and with Prime Minister Hamaguchi. For myself, however, I believe it is best to effect an agreement at whatever level is possible: if not at the 70 per cent ratio, then at 65 per cent or perhaps 67 per cent. But with the Navy so insistently clamoring for 70 per cent, any such flexibility is going to be very difficult to maintain. In any case, I don't want to depart on this mission without an opportunity to discuss this matter thoroughly with Prince Saionji."

It was after this that I met with Navy Minister Takarabe, who told me that he was about to pay his respects at the Grand Shrine at Ise.[12] "Then I hope," he said, "to join Mr. Wakatsuki at Kyoto and proceed together with him to call on Prince Saionji." But I had a letter from Mr. Wakatsuki who wrote, "Although the Navy Minister has expressed a wish to join with me in calling on Prince Saionji, I would prefer to meet with the Prince alone. Could you arrange that a message from the Prince might indicate his preference to meet with us separately?"

I went to Kyoto[13] to report on this matter to the Prince. "I prefer it that way too," he said. "When you've returned to Tokyo, tell the two Chief Delegates that it is Saionji's clear wish not to see them together, but rather to have a leisurely conference with each one individually."

The following day I saw both Chief Delegates together, as they were in conference at the Navy Ministry, and conveyed this request. Thus it came about that Wakatsuki and Takarabe finally met the Prince in separate conferences.

The Prince himself expressed some concern for the success of the disarmament conference.

Wakatsuki

---

[12] [One of the chief centers of the dynastic Shinto cult, sacred to the Sun Goddess, Amaterasu-ōmikami, (officially the divine progenitrix of the Imperial family) from prehistoric times. In modern times this state cult was particularly elaborated with such required ceremony as this; for Takarabe was not only the Emperor's Navy Minister, he must needs also announce to the Grand Shrine his added responsibilities as plenipotentiary to the London Conference. Cf. Daniel C. Holtom, *The Political Philosophy of Modern Shinto* ("Transactions of the Asiatic Society of Japan," Vol. XLIX, Part II; Tōkyō: Keio University, 1922), *The National Faith of Japan: A Study of Modern Shinto* (London: Kegan Paul, Trench, Trubner and Co., 1938), *Modern Japan and Shinto Nationalism: A Study in Present-day Trends in Japanese Religion* (Chicago: University of Chicago Press, 1943); and also John Paul Reed, "Kokutai: A Study of Certain Sacred and Secular Aspects of Japanese Nationalism" (Unpublished Ph.D. dissertation, Dept. of Sociology, University of Chicago, 1937), pp. 22-54.]

[13] [The old Saionji residence, "Seifuso," in Tanaka, formerly the northeastern outskirts of Kyoto and now within the city, was rarely visited by Saionji in his later years.]

"If only Saburi[14] were yet alive! He was indeed a man skilled in international conferences. If the Navy is going to be so clamorous that it threatens to make Japan bear responsibility for disrupting the conference, this could be disastrous; and in such a case I want to see Wakatsuki act decisively, send the other delegates home and act wholly on his own in order to bring the conference to an agreement. I want at least this much assurance.

"When I attended the Paris Peace Conference, and the Shantung question was so troublesome,[15] I made up my mind to send the rest of the delegation home if they were intransigent, and to stay behind alone to settle the matter."

This reminiscence of the Prince brought to mind what I had once heard from Saburi himself. When the Shantung issue was most difficult at Paris and all the Japanese delegation were saying the flag should be struck and they should leave the conference, the Prince had called them all together and addressed them.

"What's this you're saying? Don't you realize that there are far weightier international issues than this Shantung question? If you're so wrapped up in lesser issues like this Shantung question that you disregard the whole matter of the League of Nations and leave the conference, is this not a very foolish thing? If you are going home, then go ahead and leave. I shall remain here by myself. The rest of you may leave now."

And I was reminded of another story Saburi had told about Saionji. "This was some time ago during the Hara Ministry;[16] the

---

[14] Saburi Sadao [(1879-1929), a career diplomat who was the newly appointed Minister to China at the time of his death, presumably by suicide, in the preceding November. Saburi had been a member of the Saionji-led delegation to the Paris Peace Conference and had also represented Japan at the Washington Conference and at the Peking Tariff Conference (1928). His death meant the loss of a skilled negotiator and instrument for Shidehara's conciliatory foreign policy. See Shidehara Kijūrō, *Gaikō gojūnen (Fifty Years of Diplomacy)* (Tōkyō: Yomiuri shimbunsha, 1951), pp. 52-54, 92-96; Takehiko Yoshihashi, *Conspiracy at Mukden: The Rise of the Japanese Military* (New Haven: Yale University Press, 1963), pp. 119-21].

[15] [The question of the transfer to Japan of German rights in the Shantung Province of China threatened for a time to disrupt the Paris Conference. Makino and Chinda, rather than Saionji the head of the Japanese delegation, conducted a successful insistence on Japan's position in the Council of Ten and before the Supreme Council. Cf. Chitoshi Yanaga, *Japan Since Perry* (New York: McGraw-Hill Book Co. 1949), pp. 367-72; Russell H. Fifield, *Woodrow Wilson and the Far East: The Diplomacy of the Shantung Question* (New York: Thomas Y. Crowell Co., 1952).]

[16] From September, 1918 to November, 1921. [The first commoner and leader of a majority party in the lower house of the Japanese Diet to become Prime Minister, Hara Takashi (Kei) owed his appointment largely to Saionji's insistence in *genrō* circles. Hara had served as Home Minister in Saionji's

---

Paris Conference was over and Prince Saionji had gone to the Prime Minister's residence to conclude some matters that had remained. Admiral Saitō had just become Governor-General of Korea, and a farewell party was being held for him given by the Prime Minister. Since the Prince had thus chanced to call at the Prime Minister's residence, he joined in the festivities. After the usual greetings had been exchanged and when there was a sudden lull in the conversation, Prince Saionji raised his glass and in a loud voice addressed the Governor-General. 'May Your Excellency have an enlightened and civilized administration!' "[17]

At present the Navy's propaganda is increasingly assiduous.[18] In both Houses of the Diet[19] there is a movement to make an official announcement that "the 70 per cent ratio is the national policy." And the Foreign Minister, Shidehara, observed, "If the wording can be softened somewhat, since they want to issue such a statement, it will be unavoidable."

---

cabinets before World War I, and was Saionji's successor as president of the Seiyūkai. It was Hara, as Prime Minister, who was responsible for designating Saionji to head Japan's delegation at the Paris Conference. He was assassinated on November 12, 1921. Cf. Hara Takashi, *Hara Takashi nikki* [*The Diary of Hara Takashi*], ed. Hara Keiichiro (Tōkyō: Kengensha, 1950-51).]

[17] [This innocuous story of Saionji's toast a dozen years before may take on a little more meaning if its context is understood. Japan's overseas possessions, acquired through wars, were first ruled through purely military administrations with army officers as governors. One of Hara's reforms sought to change this system. He made the necessary legal changes to separate the military and civilian aspects of colonial government and ultimately civilians were assigned to the lesser posts; but he faced such intense criticism that, as a compromise, he nominated Admiral Saitō Makoto (1858-1936) to be Governor-General of Korea. Saitō, however, was both a Navy man and retired, and might be called a member of the "Saionji circle." He had served as Navy Minister in Saionji's first cabinet and continued in that post through the next four ministries. His long administration in Korea from 1919 to 1927 was widely regarded as a melioration of the previously army-dominated regimes, won him elevation to a viscountcy (1925) and appointment to the Privy Council (1927), and confirmed Saionji's expectations.

[At the time of Saburi's conversation, which Harada recalls from the preceding fall, Saitō has again become Governor-General of Korea, nominated by Hamaguchi to replace General Yamanashi Hanzō. Yamanashi, though his administration was shot through with corruption, had refused to resign when the Tanaka cabinet fell. Hamaguchi had needed Saionji's help and a direct Imperial order to bring about his resignation. Thus, Saitō will be expected again to give "enlightened and civilized" service not only in Korea, perhaps also in connection with the forthcoming new naval treaty; for along with the prestige of his seniority in the naval service, he had been delegate to the last international naval conference, in Geneva in 1927.]

[18] [A brief epitome of this propaganda campaign is given in Takeuchi, pp. 303-5.]

[19] The special session of the Fifty-eighth Diet was to open on April 25, 1930.

This left me quite concerned; for regardless of whether this wording was to be weak or strong, I believed that it could serve no good political purpose to create and foster such an atmosphere. When the Prince heard of the matter, he too said, "This sort of thing is quite inexcusable. There must be someone in the House of Peers—perhaps Konoe[20]—to take the initiative in stopping this foolishness." I relayed this to Konoe and through his efforts it was ended. This, of course, pleased the Prince and relieved his anxiety considerably.

> *Ambassador Castle and the Right-Wing* Rōnin—
> *Conference Progress and Governor-General*
> *Saitō's Views—The Atmosphere in the Navy*
> *Ministry—Admiral Okada's Visit with Prince*
> *Saionji.*

[Dictated March 10, 1930]

To assure the success of the Naval Conference, the United States decided to have an influential man in the American Embassy in Tokyo especially during the conference. William R. Castle was the man appointed. Some of the stupid right-wing elements in

---

[20] Prince Konoe Fumimaro [1891-1945]; member of the House of Peers. [Descendant of the ancient court *(kuge)* aristocracy like Saionji, though of higher family rank, Konoe was especially useful to Saionji, as in this instance, in dealing with the upper house in which body he had recently taken a leading role in organizing the bloc of princes and marquises called the Tuesday Society *(Kayōkai)*. Saionji had an old connection with him and his family and long held higher hopes for him.

[In 1930 Konoe had not yet been projected fully into the curiously ambivalent public career by which he was to be well known later in the decade (President of the House of Peers and thrice Prime Minister): a protégé of Saionji yet also *persona grata* to those who would reshape Japan's course on totalitarian lines that Saionji opposed.

[Apologia of sorts were left by Konoe when he committed suicide early in the post-war occupation period: *Ushinawareshi seiji* [*The Policy that Failed*] (Tōkyō: Asahi shimbunsha, n.d.), and *Heiwa e no dōryoku* [*Efforts Towards Peace*] (Tōkyō: Nihon dempō tsūshinsha, 1946). See also Yabe Teiji, *Konoe Fumimarō* (2 vols., Tōkyō: Kōbundō, 1952), and Arima Yoriyasu, *Yūjin Konoe* [*My Friend Konoe*] (Tōkyō: Kōbundō, 1948). The English historian, G. R. Storry, has written a deft characterization of the tragedy of Konoe's public life in "Konoye Fumimaro, 'Last of the Fujiwara'," in *St. Antony's Papers, No. 7: Far Eastern Affairs, No. 2,* ed. G. F. Hudson (London: Chatto and Windus, Ltd., 1960).

[Aspects of his later career are reviewed in such works as Herbert Feis, *The Road to Pearl Harbor: The Coming of the War Between the United States and Japan* (Princeton: Princeton University Press, 1950), Robert J. C. Butow, *Tojo and The Coming of the War* (Princeton: Princeton University Press, 1961), and in the general works cited in note 6 above.]

Tokyo had no sooner learned of this appointment than they asserted, "Ambassador Castle has come to woo Japan with gold." There was even talk that some were planning violence, so that the Metropolitan Police Board was concerned and took special precautionary measures when the Ambassador disembarked at Yokohama. No incident occurred.

After Ambassador Castle had assumed his new post, some followers of Ioki,[21] a *rōnin* of the same stripe as Uchida Ryōhei, head of the Kokuryūkai, pushed their way in to see and question the Ambassador. The Ambassador talked with them calmly and at some length about the mission of the disarmament conference and explained his wish for mutual cooperation to foster better relations with Japan, for world peace, and the welfare of mankind. The *rōnin* were so deeply impressed with his sincerity and earnestness that they broke out into tears of joy before taking their departure. And they widely praised the character of the Ambassador: "He's truly a great man!"[22] The Prince was quite pleased when I told him

Konoe

[21] Ioki Ryōzō [(1870-1937)], a member of the Seikyōsha. [Many members of so-called patriotic societies such as this one were recruited from bravoes and gangsters used as strong-arm squads (*ingaidan*, "lobbyists") by the political parties. They often deliberately evoked the outlaw *rōnin* tradition from feudal society and its use in the Meiji period, and were burgeoning anew in this period, as is discussed in the Introduction. Storry's *The Double Patriots: A Study of Japanese Nationalism* (London: Chatto and Windus, 1957) is perhaps the best general narrative account of such societies in English. Masao Maruyama's brilliant analysis of this aspect of what he calls Japan's "political pathology" is recently available to English readers in the selection of his essays published as *Thought and Behaviour in Modern Japanese Politics* (London: Oxford University Press, 1963).

[The Seikyōsha, itself, had been originally founded in 1888, an incidental product of the traditionalist and zenophobic reaction of the period. It opposed Westernization and urged maintenance of the "national essence" through its journal, *Nihonjin (The Japanese)*—later renamed *Nihon oyobi Nihonjin (Japan and the Japanese)*. The organization's name, Seikyōsha, is usually translated as "Society for Political Education." In Japanese, however, like many other terms in the favored language of right-wing organizations, it implies a mystic fusion of politics and religion. See below, p. 276; and cf. Sir George B. Sansom, *The Western World and Japan: A Study in the Interaction of European and Asiatic Cultures* (New York: Alfred A. Knopf, 1950), pp. 190-92, 348, 361; 371f, and also Harry Emerson Wildes, *Japan in Crisis* (New York: The Macmillan Co., 1934) chap, iv, "Ronin and Reaction," pp. 37-47.]

[22] ["Sincerity" and the general terms Harada here attributes to Castle in his remarks were part of the stock-in-trade of such professional nationalist patrioteers as Uchida Ryōhei, Ōkawa Shumei, and the like, and had strong compulsive force with many sectors of the Japanese public. The Kokuryūkai (Amur River Society, or more popularly, Black Dragon Society), founded by Uchida at the turn of the century, not only included in its program a zenophobic "let's lead Asia" line with intense chauvinistic criticism of domestic politics and leadership, but also urged the "harmonization" of Eastern and

of this incident; and he was reminded to speak of the time when, during his first Prime Ministership, William Howard Taft had visited Japan. The Prince spoke of his impression gained from several talks with Taft. "At that time there were many foreigners, apart from the diplomatic corps, coming to visit Japan; and Taft clearly left an impression of being without peer among them all. The new American ambassador seems indeed to have made much the same impression."[23]

On March 2, I went to Okitsu.[24] The Prince said with some concern, "I'm not very conversant with the London conference situation; but it's time there may be a change. Just how are attitudes changing? Just what is going to happen?"

Several days before this I had visited with Governor-General Saitō. He, too, had been quite concerned for the success of the conference, and voiced the same views as the Prince. I had heard

Western cultures. Cf. Kinoshita Hanji, *Nihon fuasshizumushi* [*A History of Japanese Fascism*] (Tōkyō: Iwasaki shoten, 1949), I, 7-10; or the society's own history, *Kokuryūkai yonjūnenchū reki* [*A History of the Kokuryūkai during the Past Forty Years*], 1940 |LC Microfilm Collection, IMT 478).
[The episode and behavior Harada here reports may be taken as a modest illustration of the amuletic use of such words by chauvinists. See I(van) I. Morris, *Nationalism and the Right Wing in Japan: A Study of Post-War Trends* (London: Oxford University Press, 1960), Appendix I.]

[23] [It is clear why Castle's favorable impression on the *rōnin* should remind Saionji of a possible parallel with the impression left by Taft a quarter of a century before. Six months before Saionji's first ministry, Taft as Theodore Roosevelt's Secretary of War had signed a secret "agreed memorandum" with Prime Minister Katsura approving in advance Japan's suzerainty over Korea. "The sentiments it bestowed on Anglo-Japanese-American cooperation 'for the maintenance of peace in the Far East' merely ornamented the material bargain it struck. Japan understood it as American assent to the protectorate over Korea, which speedily followed without protest from Washington" (A. Whitney Griswold, *The Far Eastern Policy of the United States* [New York: Harcourt, Brace and Co., 1938], p. 125). Cf. Alfred Vagts, *Deutschland und die Vereinigten Staaten in der Weltpolitik* (New York: The Macmillan Co., 1935), II, 1122-1256. But see also Raymond A. Esthus, "The Taft-Katsura Agreement—Myth or Reality?" *Journal of Modern History*, XXXI (1959), 46-51.]

[24] [Prince Saionji in his late years lived usually in his small house, designed by himself and called the Zagyosō ("Fisherman's Cottage"), in the town of Okitsu on the warm coast of Suruga Bay southwest of Tokyo. Thus, "to go down to Okitsu" and "to proceed to Okitsu" in the context of this diary means "to call on Prince Saionji." Okitsu had been one of the established "stages" on the Tōkaidō, the famous highway stretching from the old Imperial capital of Kyoto to Edo, the Shogun's capital which became the modern Tokyo.
[The Minaguchiya, an ancient inn in Okitsu, flourished in the 1930s through patronage by Saionji's entourage and by those seeking audience with him. Oliver Statler, in his *Japanese Inn* (New York: Random House, 1961), happily evokes the tradition and the modern situation which account in part for Prince Saionji's somewhat eccentric choice of this spot as his favorite residence.]

also that Count Uchida[25] had expressed himself quite vigorously to Yoshida,[26] the Vice Minister of Foreign Affairs and to Hotta,[27] Chief of the European-American Bureau. "Why," Uchida asked, "why doesn't Japan from the very beginning of the conference take the initiative from Britain and America to bring about a decision at the 60 per cent level? This is an excellent opportunity. Is it not shameful to have the Foreign Ministry trail behind the Navy's General Staff as they do now?"

I mentioned this to the Prince, and he said, "It would be much better for the country to have Saitō devoting himself to the success of the Naval Conference than to have him working for a decade in Korea. My views coincide exactly with what Count Uchida has said; and I've thought so from the beginning."

Since there had been no official communiqué about the London Conference for some time, I went to see the Chief of the Navy General Staff, Admiral Katō Kanji.[28] Angrily he said, "America's attitude is as haggling as that of a street vendor. Utterly outrageous! We ought to be content with the agreement on capital ships and to come home." Even so, Katō expressed admiration for the character of Ambassador Castle. There are a number of sensible men in the Navy, such as Vice Minister Yamanashi, Vice Admirals Nomura and Kobayashi, and Admiral Okada; but they have a tendency to be pulled along by the stronger views of the Navy General Staff.

Katō

---

[25] Uchida Yasuya [(1865-1936)], former Foreign Minister. [He held this post in the Hara cabinet and the two which succeeded it, 1918-23, serving as Prime Minister *ad interim* upon the death in office of two of these cabinet leaders.

[Later he became president of the South Manchurian Railway (1931) and again Foreign Minister in Saitō's cabinet (1932).]

[26] Yoshida Shigeru [(1878-1967) career diplomat, son-in-law of the Lord Keeper of the Privy Seal, Count Makino, and later to become Japan's Prime Minister in the postwar period (1946-47, 1949-55). Vice Minister of Foreign Affairs through this London Treaty period, he was one of Harada's sources of information from this segment of the bureaucracy.]

[27] Hotta Masaaki [(b. 1883), career diplomat, was later to serve as Ambassador to Italy, at the League of Nations, and as delegate to the Geneva Conference of 1937].

[28] Katō Kanji [(1870-1939)], Admiral. [Katō had become Chief of the Naval General Staff in January, 1929, when his predecessor, Admiral Suzuki Kantarō, was raised to the august court office of Grand Chamberlain to the Emperor. Katō's career had included service in the Russo-Japanese War on Tōgō's flagship, as attaché in London, as technical adviser to Admiral Katō Tomosaburō at the Washington Conference. He had also held the Navy's top command post afloat—Commander-in-Chief, Combined Fleet—in 1926. Harada, I, 271, 275; Shidehara, p. 65.

[The principal Army and Navy officials of this period are listed in Appendix I D.]

Or rather, instead of being "pulled along" it would be better to say they are powerless to control it. Even the mild-mannered Vice Minister Yamanashi has told me that he has cautioned the Chief of the Navy General Staff against exceeding his authority, and has advised him to be more circumspect.[29]

In order to provide the Prince with data on the Navy situation with respect to the London Conference, Prime Minister Hamaguchi arranged to have Admiral Okada to go down to Okitsu. I heard many "disclosures" on why this was done. Vice Minister [of Foreign Affairs] Yoshida and others were very anxious to have Admiral Okada go to see the Prince, because if subsequently serious dispute should arise, then in the last resort Admiral Okada might serve as arbitrator. The Admiral did call on the Prince at Okitsu; but I heard afterward that he came with such old-fashioned ceremoniousness that he was not able to say anything. Later, the Prince complained, "I can't understand why Hamaguchi sent him to see me." In the last analysis it seems the situation is so delicate that Okada was deflected from saying even a word on any of the essential points.

> *The American Compromise Plan and the Navy
> General Staff Statement—Admiral Okada's
> Busy Activity—The Observation of the
> Chief of the Navy General Staff—Prince
> Saionji's View on Disarmament Conferences—
> The Anglo-American Messages—Reliances on
> Foreign Minister Shidehara.*

[Dictated March 25, 1930]

The temper of the discussion in the Navy's General Staff circles is very stubborn. And in mid-March the American compromise plan was made public.[30]

---

[29] [These more "sensible" naval officers will reappear many times in the subsequent chapters. Here it is perhaps sufficient to note that they represent the moderate wing of the Navy whom Saionji and Hamaguchi must rely upon to counter the firebrands whom Katō typifies. Wakatsuki was later to describe Yamanashi as a "martyr" to the cause of arms limitation (Wakatsuki, pp. 361-64).

[At this time the first three were all Vice Admirals and held the following posts: Yamanashi, Vice Minister; Nomura, Commander-in-Chief, Training Fleet; Kobayashi, Chief, Navy Technical Department. Okada, a full admiral and a former Navy Minister, was a member of the Supreme War Council.]

[30] [Harada refers, not to an "American" plan, but to the compromise end result of a series of conferences in London, principally between Ambassador Matsudaira and Senator Reed, confirmed by Wakatsuki and Stimson and

Even before this the Navy General Staff had been assiduous with its own propaganda, sending telegrams to the foreign press services.[31] Many of these activities clearly exceeded its proper sphere of authority. Everyone was concerned over this matter. Suddenly in the midst of this situation, a statement was issued from the Navy General Staff. Since it was issued to the Rengō News Agency by Suetsugu, the Vice Chief of the Navy General Staff, it showed that, of its so-called "Three Basic Points," the Navy was still adhering to the two points: demanding a heavy cruiser ratio of 70 per cent, and 78,000 tons of submarines.[32]

The reason why the Navy became so agitated and issued such a statement was that the Chief of the Foreign Ministry's Informa-

---

accepted by the British delegation. It was transmitted to the government in Tokyo for its instruction thereon on March 14. From that date till the Cabinet's decision to accept this so-called "Reed-Matsudaira compromise," taken on April 1, "big-Navy" spokesmen—notably Katō and his aggressive Vice Chief of the Naval General Staff, Vice Admiral Suetsugu Nobumasa—were assiduous in their efforts to have it dubbed an "American" plan to which further counter-proposals might be made and to prevent the Cabinet from making just this decision to accept it. Takeuchi, pp. 290-297, succinctly summarizes contemporary Japanese press reports.

[A chart setting forth the main points of the earlier American and Japanese proposals, and of the compromise plan, is given in Appendix III.]

[31] [The British Ambassador, Sir John Tilley, reported from Tokyo after query from his home government that the propaganda of the Japanese navalists had not merely started overnight (i.e., on government inspiration), but had begun "before the Conference and has been very effective, and . . . fear of the United States . . . was the material on which it had to work." *Documents on British Foreign Policy, 1919-1939*, eds. E. L. Woodward and Rohan Butler (Second Series; London: H. M. Stationery Office, 1946), I, 259-60. (This source is hereinafter cited in the notes as *Br. Docs.*)]

[32] [Suetsugu's statement, issued March 17 without approval or knowledge of the Cabinet, or of the principal Navy Ministry officials, was judged inopportune because it displayed a disharmony within the Navy as between the General Staff and the Ministry, and impolitic because the General Staff was supposedly not involved in government or politics.

[The "Three Basic Points" had demanded (a) 70 per cent ratio with the U.S. in heavy cruisers, (b) the same ratio in categories of auxiliary ships, and (c) maintenance of existing (built and building) submarine tonnage, i.e., some 78,000 tons. See below, Appendix III B. Katō's and Suetsugu's views at this period are given in Aoki Tokuzō, *Taiheiyō sensō zenshi* [*The Historical Background of the Pacific War*] (Tōkyō: Sekai heiwa kenzetsu kyōkai, 1951), I, 10-12.

[Ambassador Castle was quick to report, both to Washington and to Stimson in London, this deliberate misinterpretation of the tentative agreement; and he noted the ire which it aroused in the Foreign Office. Stimson, meanwhile, was told in London that there was "a real controversy between the Japanese civil government and the naval party there" (U.S. Department of State, *Paper Relating to the Foreign Relations of the United States*, 1930 [3 vols.; Washington: Government Printing Office, 1945], I, 66-67). (This source is hereinafter cited as *U.S. For. Rel.*)]

tion Bureau[33] had said to a group of newsmen, "Wouldn't it be best for the conference to settle the issues even if the 70 per cent were reduced somewhat? At a conference you always deal with an opposite number, and you must first make some mutual concessions in order to come to an agreement."

In effect then, the Navy's statement was a riposte to the Foreign Ministry; and in part there was direct allusion to these remarks: "At this time of grave crisis for such a statement to be made, for so plaintive a plea to be heard is bad enough. From the Foreign Ministry, it is utterly inexcusable, impudent and imprudent."

The Government, too, had its viewpoint: "With a request from London for instructions, it is worse to have a Navy that cannot make up its mind." As a result of private talks between Foreign Minister Shidehara and the Prime Minister, Admiral Okada[34] was called to the Foreign Minister's office. Shidehara put it to him point-blank.

"Should negotiations be broken off if there is any change from the 70 per cent ratio, or should they be concluded even if that ratio is reduced somewhat?"

Without hesitation Admiral Okada replied, "By all means come to an agreement even if it's 60 per cent or 55."

"Well then, won't you do your best to bring about agreement within the Navy on this issue?"

Admiral Okada then said, "I'll not be able to check the Chief of the Navy General Staff by myself; but I'll do what I can together with Governor-General Saitō."

Then he met with Saitō and asked him to postpone his return

---

[33] Saitō Hiroshi [(1886-1939)], member of the London Conference delegation staff [later, Ambassador to the United States].

[34] [Admiral Okada Keisuke (1868-1952) was the most adroit of the Navy men in politics in this period. The Introduction examines some of the ramifications of his usefulness to Hamaguchi, Saionji, and the pro-treaty forces in 1930. He had been Navy Minister in the preceding cabinet and was now a Supreme War Councillor *(gunjisangikan)*. Later, he again became Navy Minister and ultimately Prime Minister (1934-36). He survived an assassination attempt in the spectacular February 26, 1936, mutiny and lived into the years beyond the Pacific War giving testimony at the Tokyo trials and publishing his memoirs. While the manuscripts and documents he had been assembling for these memoirs were destroyed in the April 13, 1945 fire raids on Tokyo, his actual diary for part of the year 1930 was by chance stored and rescued with some Buddhist materials and incorporated in his post-war publication. In general it confirms the role Harada ascribes to him. Okada Keisuke, *Okada Keisuke kaikōroku* [*Memoirs of Okada Keisuke*] (Tōkyō: Mainichi shimbunsha, 1950), pp. 42-74.]

to his post in Korea for a few days. But Saitō said he had remained too long in Tokyo and could delay his return no longer. When Admiral Okada sought to elicit from him some statement urging the restoration of unity within Navy circles, the Governor-General said, "You're absolutely right. I endorse your position completely."

Earlier the Chief of the Navy General Staff had said to me, "The present American compromise plan offers us crumbs and tells us to like them. This is extremely high-handed. Yesterday I met with the German Ambassador Ernst A. Voretzsch.

" 'I've just heard something,' he said. 'The French Chargé d'Affaires[35] has learned it from the American Naval Attaché. When Ambassador Wakatsuki was in Washington, the American government then believed Japan's claim for a 70 per cent ratio was not seriously meant, that it was simply bluster; but now, since both our public opinion and the Navy are quite unyielding, it has become more troubled. If this is so, and if you now pushed your demands a little further, you might have surprisingly good results.' "

The Chief of the Navy General Staff was obviously quite pleased with this counsel. A simple-hearted emotional man, he invited the German Ambassador and various Navy leaders, including Admiral Prince Fushimi,[36] to a dinner some four or five days later at the Navy Minister's official residence—largely out of gratitude to the Ambassador for his friendliness.

Since Prince Saionji seemed somewhat disturbed by the tone of much of the material appearing recently in the press, it occurred to me that he might like to receive a visit from the Foreign Minister or from Yoshida, the Vice Minister. At the same time Yoshida, too,

Okada

---

[35] Jean Dobler. [At London the French position seemed to the British and Americans a more significant obstacle to the conclusion of a five-power treaty than the Japanese demands for larger ratio; and they were fearful that France and Japan might secretly make common cause. MacDonald had already suggested to Stimson that the difficulties before Wakatsuki's acceptance of the Reed-Matsudaira plan might have been "instigated by the French" (*U.S. For. Rel.*, p. 58). And the British had sufficient information to ask a member of the French delegation point-blank "whether there was any truth in reports that, on his own initiative . . ., the French Chargé d'Affaires was endeavouring to influence the Japanese against" accepting the Reed-Matsudaira formula (*Br. Docs.*, p. 265, n. 1).]

[36] Imperial Prince Admiral Fushimi Hiroyasu, member of the Supreme War Council. [Born in 1875, Prince Fushimi was the senior member of the Imperial Family in the naval service. He had been educated in Germany, 1889-95; had become an Admiral in 1925, Supreme War Councillor in 1925; and was later (1932) to be made Chief of the Naval General Staff. The House of Fushimi, a cadet branch of the Imperial Family, had been founded in the fifteenth century. The Foreign Affairs Association of Japan, *The Japan Year Book, 1943-44* (Tokyo, 1943), p. 3.]

had become disturbed; and on the eighteenth he journeyed to Okitsu to make a report. I understand that the Prince displayed considerable anxiety. "Each day's delay," he said to Yoshida, "has adverse effects in Japan on attitudes toward Britain and the United States. I want this quickly settled and the reply dispatched immediately so that an agreement may be reached as soon as possible."[37]

On the twenty-first I went down to make a full report on the general situation. There were messages from both the Prime Minister and from the Foreign Minister to this effect: "Ultimately this matter will be settled, but because of our great apprehension over its domestic implications we want to give a little more time for the Chief of the Navy General Staff and his circle to calm down from their present excited state."

To this the Prince responded by saying, "If everyone is agreed, on principle, to settle this matter, what question can there be? Even as early as when Wakatsuki and Takarabe came to see me they expressed a determination to reach a settlement. Even if it should be France or Italy which might directly bring about a rupture in negotiations, it is Japan's shilly-shallying about this reply which may make it possible; and Japan will have to bear responsibility for such a rupture. This could be an extremely important matter. This London Conference is one of the most grave and serious issues before the world today. It's entirely different from such issues in former years as the racial equality question[38] or the Shantung question. I take a most serious view of it.

"Therefore, if it is our principle to conclude the treaty, the reply should be sent as soon as possible to speed the settlement. Why not treat the domestic issues and the Navy reform matter as separate questions? As for breaking off discussions and leaving the conference, this would be quite disastrous. Convey this in general to Prime Minister Hamaguchi. I wish Hamaguchi could display a little more energy and determination.

"Furthermore, at a time like this, it is important to see that the Imperial Household Minister and the Grand Chamberlain as

---

[37] [The British ambassador reported on March 21, 1930: "I saw the *genrō*'s secretary yesterday and was to see his chief today. . . . Although not disposed to talk, he told Sir C. Davidson (Counsellor H. M. Embassy) who was also present that he thought there was too much propaganda going on. Minister for Foreign Affairs suggested to Mr. Castle that one of his staff might have talked with (?secretary) who is personal friend of his" (*Br. Docs.*, p. 265).]

[38] This is a reference to the Japanese amendment to the League Covenant proposed but defeated at the Paris Conference.

well as the Lord Keeper of the Privy Seal have a clear understanding of the problem."[39]

As soon as I returned to Tokyo from Okitsu, I went to see the Prime Minister and told him fully what the Prince had counselled. I also mentioned that the Prince advised that attention be paid to the slackness of discipline in the Naval General Staff.

On Sunday morning, the twenty-third, I called on Admiral Okada. He said, "Somehow this matter will be wound up. But in this present crisis it would be better if I were not summoned by the Prince. I must don the mask of the die-hards and play this role in order to effect a settlement. And settled it shall be. But haste would be damaging. Just today, for example, I must call on Fleet Admiral Tōgō."[40]

The same morning Vice Minister Yoshida visited Count Yamamoto Gombei[41] and had a talk with him. Then, together with

---

[39] [These three officers of the Imperial Court—"advisers close to the throne"—functionally were leaders of the governmental bureaucracy. They were particularly important through controlling access to the person of the Emperor, so that they could prove a troublesome barrier to political opponents who might seek to give advice of which they did not approve. As this record suggests they were one of the fulcrum points in the Japanese governmental structure to which the *genrō* might effectively apply pressure. Though titled "ministers" they were not members of the Cabinet, but held office permanently, or until they desired to retire, and were considered to be above, or outside, "politics." The principal court officials of this period are listed in Appendix I B.

[The Introduction discusses in more detail the men who held these offices at this time and Prince Saionji's relationship with them. The Imperial Household Minister *(kunaidaijin)* was Dr. Ikki (or Ichiki) Kitokurō (1867-1944); the Grand Chamberlain *(jijūchō)* was Admiral Suzuki Kantarō (1867-1948); and in the office of Lord Privy Seal *(naidaijin)*, most important of the three, was Count Makino Nobuaki (or Shinken) (1861-1949).]

[40] Admiral Count Tōgō Heihachirō [(1847-1934). This octogenarian hero of the Russo-Japanese War was a veritable personification of the Japanese Navy, and its only representative on the *Gensuifu*—the Board of Field Marshals and Fleet Admirals. A list of the *gensui* at this period is given in Appendix I. Unlike many of his fellow Satsuma leaders in the earlier Navy (notably Yamamoto), Tōgō had held aloof from politics and this enlarged his prestige among naval and other elements antipathetic to parliamentary politics. His earlier role as tutor to the Emperor in the latter's youth made him a symbol of almost sacrosanct qualities to these same elements. Cf. Edwin A. Falk, *Togo and the Rise of Japanese Sea Power* (New York: Doubleday, Doran and Co., 1936).]

[41] Admiral Count Yamamoto Gombei [(1861-1933)], former Prime Minister. [Of Satsuma origin, Yamamoto had been perhaps the Navy's foremost "political admiral": Prime Minister in 1913-14 and again, after the Great Earthquake, in 1923. Not notably successful in political leadership, his first cabinet collapsed after revelation of the Siemens-Schuckert scandals, his second when confronted by almost unanimous party opposition; yet he remained the leader of a wing of the older Navy. Yoshida, as Makino's son-in-law, rather than as Vice Foreign Minister himself, was a suitable figure to propitiate possible

---

the Chief of the European-American Bureau, I had lunch with him and learned from him what Count Yamamoto had said: "Of course this must be settled. Though some may advocate a 70 per cent ratio, since there are the views of the other parties to consider, there must be some mutual concessions made."

Yoshida went on to recount another incident. The American Ambassador had called on him.

"I've had a message from the President urging Japan's reply," the Ambassador had said. "The message further would have me convey this request directly to Prime Minister Hamaguchi, but I immediately cabled to the President that there is little cause for concern while Baron Shidehara is Foreign Minister. It would be better not to see the Prime Minister directly at this time, but to wait and to rely on the character of the Foreign Minister."[42]

That evening I called on Foreign Minister Shidehara at his private residence. When I spoke of proceeding on to Okitsu that evening, he told me, "The British Ambassador came to see me yesterday. He too has had a message from his Prime Minister to call on Hamaguchi and press for a reply. I told him, 'I have no anxieties in this matter. It will be settled without fail. Let me have a little more time. We will not act in concert with any nations other than Britain and America. Any collaboration must necessarily be together with your own nations. There's absolutely no cause for anxiety.' And the Ambassador's face showed his relief. 'Just pigeon-hole this message,' he said as he handed it over to me."[43]

In a word, both Britain and America are putting their trust in Foreign Minister Shidehara and are awaiting developments. Shidehara cabled a personal message to Wakatsuki so that his reply might reveal whether there were differences of view between him and Takarabe. Further, he noted that counter-proposals were under study.

With what I had thus learned, I reported to the Prince on the morning of the twenty-fourth, and the Prince was quite relieved. "Be sure to convey my greetings to Shidehara," he said. Earlier in

---

opposition from this Navy senior. On Yamamoto's earlier political role, cf. Scalapino, pp. 200-227.]

[42] [See Stimson's instructions to Castle, Telegram No. 155, March 23, 1930, *U.S. For. Rel.*, 1930, p. 75; and Castle's reply, quoted by Stimson in Telegram No. 172, March 28, 1930, *ibid.*, p. 91: ". . .to see Hamaguchi personally . . . would produce a dangerous public reaction."]

[43] [See Henderson's instructions to Sir John Tilley, Telegram No. 142, March 19, 1930, *Br. Docs.*, I, 261-62; and Tilley's reply of March 21, indicating that he was acting in concert with Castle, *ibid.*, pp. 264-65.]

the conversation he had said, "How good it would be if some system were possible permanently to retain a person like Shidehara as Foreign Minister, or at least in the Foreign Office! He certainly should be honored with the Grand Order of the Chrysanthemum."[44]

> *The Navy's Restraints on Takarabe—The Prime Minister's Determination—The Seventy Percenters and the Views of the Grand Chamberlain—The Prince's Illness— The Grand Chamberlain's Visit to Prince Fushimi—The Prime Minister Presents the Instructions.*

[Dictated March 28, 1930]

The leaders of the Navy have been meeting and considering various counter-proposals which the Navy might present; and the Navy General Staff, as stoutly as ever adhering to its "Three Great Principles," is constantly propagandizing for them. Yet a number of men familiar with international affairs, such as Vice Admirals Nomura and Kobayashi, seem to believe that a settlement ought to be reached and that it would be better not to insist upon the 70 per cent ratio. Admiral Okada himself holds the same view; but since it would weaken his role as mediator if he were openly tagged as an exponent of a "soft" policy, he has been working toward agreement as if he were an advocate of the 70 per cent ratio.

Both Wakatsuki's reply to the message from the Foreign Minister and the cables from Takarabe showed these two delegates were in agreement on most matters at the time they had cabled for final instructions. Wakatsuki, however, held that the American proposal was a final one; whereas Takarabe, while expecting the conference ultimately to reach a settlement, yet saw opportunity for further negotiation.[45]

The Navy Ministry, in the meantime, seems engaged in efforts

---

[44] [The highest of nine orders of merit and decoration, created in 1875, "to recognize and reward persons who have rendered distinguished and meritorious services to the State." *The Japan Year Book, 1943-44*, p. 8.]

[45] [Aoki, I, 10-12, and Takeuchi, pp. 292-93, review in more detail how Takarabe's apparently equivocal position seemed to give support and opportunity to the Navy's die-hards. An ill-identified typescript copy of what appears on internal evidence to be Wakatsuki's private report to Shidehara is to be found in the Foreign Ministry achives, *Rondon ikken* (LC Microfilm Collection, S 2.12.0.0.1), pp. 892-901.]

to hold Takarabe in check. The Prime Minister, when I saw him on the afternoon of March 27, said, "The reports from Takarabe are very strange. He asks, 'If the Five Power Conference is not now possible because of the attitude of France and Italy, would it not be preferable to postpone the conference for five or six months so that the Five Power meeting may be possible? Furthermore, if two nations leave the conference and an agreement is to be entered into only by the three countries, Japan, Britain, and the United States, then ought not the instructions from Japan to be changed somewhat from those previously issued?'

"Such a position," continued the Prime Minister, "seems to me quite without logic and very strange indeed."

When I had seen the Prime Minister earlier in the same day, he had expressed his own views in these terms. "I have postponed taking any action until now in order to be as fair and reasonable as possible. I've waited as long as I can wait. I've done what I could. Now my mind is made up, come what may. I intend to act resolutely on my own convictions."[46] Sometime before this, when the Navy members of the Supreme War Council and the Fleet Admiral had met for a discussion, both Admiral Tōgō and Admiral Prince Fushimi had been strong proponents of the 70 per cent ratio. I understood that Admiral Okada, who was present at this meeting, had said, "What we must fear is a break in the negotiations. At all events we must see that a settlement is reached." And he pled earnestly that the agreement be completed for the future progress of the Empire.[47]

Since the Prince had expressed concern that the three officers of the court—the Grand Chamberlain, the Lord Keeper of the Privy

---

[46] [Okada and Katō had together called privately on Hamaguchi the same afternoon—apparently before Harada's visit here recorded—Katō to demand that the "Three Principles" be adhered to, Okada to argue that a head-on clash between Navy and government be avoided. Hamaguchi implied that the Navy was procrastinating in its duty to draft instructions which would prevent the imminent danger of collapse of the conference. When Katō said that he, as Chief of the Naval General Staff, ought to sit in on Cabinet meetings, Hamaguchi testily reminded him that there was no precedent for such action, and that Katō knew the individual cabinet members well enough to talk to them himself. Okada, pp. 50-51.]

[47] [This unofficial meeting had taken place at the Navy Minister's official residence on the morning of March 24. Yamanashi had reported on the government's position, and that it was supported by the *genrō* (Saionji). Okada recorded in his diary his warning that since the government was adamant against action which might give Japan the onus of breaking up the conference, a struggle between government and Navy could be extremely serious. Okada, p. 50; Takeuchi, pp. 295-97.

[A list of the Supreme War Councillors at this period is given in Appendix I F.]

Seal, and the Minister of the Imperial Household—should alike have a clear understanding of this problem, I visited in turn the Imperial Household Minister and the Grand Chamberlain in their respective offices. The Grand Chamberlain, Admiral Suzuki, said:

"Somehow this must be settled. I am very much of the same mind as Prince Saionji on this. If I did not occupy this post of Grand Chamberlain, I should certainly go to explain and clarify matters to Katō and his group, but in my present position I can do nothing. Certainly it behooves the Chief of the Naval General Staff as the Emperor's chief staff-officer to be more discreet and circumspect. It is highly reprehensible to drum up popular support for his own notions and then to try to push them through because of the public opinion thus aroused. Only the mediocre could clamor for 70 per cent or nothing. He who is Chief of the Naval General Staff must be able to utilize whatever strength is allotted to him; whether it be 60 or even 50 per cent that may be decided upon. It's very odd for him to say it must be 70 per cent or nothing, or that the young officers today are different from those of earlier days. It seems to me it is up to the Chief of the Navy General Staff to lead the young officers as he will. I'm sure that as far as spirit and outlook are concerned there is no difference between the past and the present. It may be that Katō is too obstinate and emotional. So it seems to me."

The Grand Chamberlain had spoken on these points because I had asked him to be attentive to these issues. Since he displayed a much more astute understanding than I had expected, I returned from this interview quite relieved.

The Foreign Minister, on whom I called later that evening, seemed quite disturbed. I had planned to go to Okitsu that evening to report to the Prince that a decision had been made to dispatch the reply within the next day of two, but a phone call had come from Nakagawa in Okitsu to report that the Prince had suddenly become ill with a severe cold, high fever, and rapid pulse, and could see no one. Dr. Miura had been called in. I had already had the railroad take a letter for me to Okitsu. Now it seemed better for the Prince not to receive this letter while he is ill. Hence I had Hachirō come to the phone and asked him to hold this letter unopened for me. And to ease the Prince's mind on this disarmament matter, I asked Hachirō to tell him only of the Prime Minister's firm determination. It seemed best that I remain in Tokyo and refrain from going down to Okitsu.[48]

---

[48] [The seriousness of Saionji's illness, diagnosed as pneumonia, is implied by the presence in Okitsu of the three men Harada mentions here:

[Dr. Miura Kinnosuke (1864-1950), a renowned professor of medicine

[Dictated March 31, 1930]

It was not till the twenty-ninth that I left in the evening and arrived in Okitsu on the morning of the thirtieth. When I went to the Zagyosō the Prince's condition did not appear to be at all favorable. Thus I contented myself with talking in the study with Hachirō and others of the family. One of the Prince's attendants came in with the message that if Harada arrived, the Prince had something to discuss with him. Since the Prince's temperature was then 39° [F. 102.2°] and he was in a critical condition, it was thought best that he see no one and hear no reports. Yet in his delirium of high fever two nights before he had muttered over and over again such words as "disarmament," "Italy," or "France." Thus, Hachirō hoped I would speak to him very briefly and simply to put his mind at ease. Hence I went into see him since he was awake. "What a misfortune you've had," I said. "Yes, it's quite a nuisance." Then after he had asked the nurses and other attendants to leave us, he asked me, "How's this disarmament matter progressing?" I spoke of the Prime Minister's resolution, that the Foreign Minister's reply had been drafted, and that the Government's attitude had become strengthened. "Within a day or two," I told him, "Japan will demonstrate quite spendidly her desire to participate in a tri-partite agreement. Rest assured that it will be settled to your satisfaction."

"Ah, that sets my mind at rest," he said with deep satisfaction. Lest it aggravate his illness if I were to remain longer, I bade him adieu; but before departing I assured him that the Grand Chamberlain had an astute awareness of the whole situation.

That same evening I returned to Tokyo and reported the whole circumstance to the Grand Chamberlain. He told me that

at Tokyo Imperial University and long one of the old Prince's personal physicians, had accompanied Saionji to the Paris Conference.

[Nakagawa Kojūrō (1866-1944) was a scion of a family of country squires that had aided the youthful "General" Saionji in the Tamba campaign of 1868 and had come under Saionji's patronage in his youth. He had been secretary to Saionji as Education Minister and later as Prime Minister. Thereafter he had gone on to a notable career in education, founding Ritsumeikan University in Kyōto (its name derived from one of Saionji's earlier literary societies), and becoming himself a Privy Councilor. He still described himself and occasionally functioned as Saionji's personal secretary.

[Saionji Hachirō, born in 1881 the ninth son of Prince Mōri Motonori, the last Lord of Chōshū, had been adopted by Saionji as his son and heir, and was husband of Saionji's (now deceased) elder daughter, Shinko. Long a member of the Imperial Household staff, he had accompanied Crown Prince Hirohito on his European trip; and in 1930 he was *shumei-no-kami*—Chief Equerry or Master of Horse.]

some four or five days before he had called on Admiral Prince Fushimi of whom he had been an intimate friend for many years. He pointed out to the Prince, with respect to his speaking out and arguing as an individual at council meetings, that members of the Imperial family must exercise extreme caution, more especially so since the treaty in question is a matter of grave international importance. The failure to complete it could have serious repercussions in Japan. In fact Japan must give wholehearted support for the successful establishment of an agreement. After this advice, Prince Fushimi seemed genuinely to regret the narrowness of his views and affirmed that he would henceforth be more prudent. No doubt the Grand Chamberlain was able to speak more frankly and earnestly because for so many years they had been close friends during their Navy careers.[49]

The Grand Chamberlain, furthermore, said he would speak with Fleet Admiral Tōgō after the instructions had been dispatched. Since earlier Prince Saionji had been concerned, I had been most apprehensive about the views the Grand Chamberlain held at this time. On the following morning I called on the Lord Keeper of the Privy Seal, Count Makino.

[Dictated April 4, 1930]

I spoke with him about the entire situation and particularly and more fully of the points on which Prince Saionji had been more apprehensive. The Lord Keeper, too, held quite the same views.

On April 1, the Prime Minister presented his disarmament proposals to the Cabinet in mid-morning and they were approved. By three o'clock he had returned from having formally presented them to the Throne.

I understand that before the cabinet meeting the Prime Minister had spoken with the Chief of the Naval General Staff and Admiral Okada: "If we take the most comprehensive view, this agreement must be concluded at any cost for the sake of our overall national policy. On the matter of defense alone it may well seem

---

[49] [Okada, as well as the Grand Chamberlain Admiral Suzuki, called on Fushimi and Tōgō in this period to keep them from being too clearly aligned with Katō and Suetsugu. These latter two were arguing that the final instructions could only be issued after approval by a formal meeting of the Supreme War Council, of which both Fushimi and Tōgō were members. Hence Suzuki's caution to Fushimi about "speaking out." Both Okada and Yamanashi wanted to avoid having the Council meet on this issue, perhaps aware of the constitutional question that might be involved, and preferred to seek an understanding that the government would subsequently support an enlarged supplemental program for the Navy. Okada, pp. 52-54.]

inadequate to one in the position of Chief of the Naval General Staff, but I hope that you may take into account this broader consideration." To this Katō said he was quite unhappy that in strongly urging maintenance of the 70 per cent figure an unexpected impasse had occurred and the matter had been tossed into the maelstrom of political controversy. With this more prudent attitude he seemed to be saying, "If this is the Government's policy, I have to accept it."[50] And with this he calmly took his departure.

Immediately after returning from his audience with the Emperor, the Foreign Minister cabled the instructions to London. Since I had news of this, being at the Prime Minister's official residence at the time, I immediately phoned to Hachirō, "Please give this message to the Prince, for I know it will relieve his anxiety. Just now, after receiving cabinet approval, the instructions have been cabled to London." He immediately went to the Prince's bedside and gave this message. The Prince with considerable pleasure, said, "This is indeed a great success for Hamaguchi."

When his private secretary, Hashimoto,[51] later repeated this to him, the Prime Minister shed tears of happiness. This was on April [1] when the Prince's illness had become increasingly serious, and he seemed to be suffering considerable pain.

---

[50] [Cf. Iwabuchi Tatsuo, *Gendai Nihon seijiron* [*A Discussion of Modern Japanese Politics*] (Tōkyō: Chūō Kōronsha, 1941), as quoted in Shiraki Masayuki, *Nihon seitō shi—Shōwa hen* [*A History of Japanese Political Parties—Shōwa Period*] (Tōkyō: Chūō Kōronsha, 1949), p. 61:

"Katō met three times with Prime Minister Hamaguchi. At the third meeting, Okada as representing the Supreme War Councillors, and the Vice Minister, Yamanashi, were also present. This time, in response to Hamaguchi's explanations, Katō remained silent. Okada remarked that if the government took its decision on the basis of cabinet responsibility, the Navy for its part would build the best possible national defense plans. Hamaguchi took this as the Navy's assent and dispatched the instructions to the plenipotentiaries."]

[51] Count Hashimoto Saneaya, private secretary to Prime Minister Hamaguchi. [Hashimoto (born 1891) was, in a sense, under Prince Saionji's wing for the old prince had been concerned with his education, partly in Switzerland, and his career in minor bureaucratic posts. The Hashimoto were a "branch family" of the Saionji in the old court aristocracy, a relationship originated centuries before. Patterns of patronage and deference involved in such traditional and distant kinship ties were not without some influence in the modern world. This is a reminder of the importance of personal ties in Japanese public life, but it is not clear that Hashimoto's official post at Hamaguchi's elbow was of deliberate political use to either Saionji or Hamaguchi. Hashimoto, because of the distant relationship, was to be in formal charge of the funeral for Prince Saionji a decade hence. After the war he was to write something of Saionji's private life ("Saionji-kō no omoide [Reminiscences of Prince Saionji]," *Kokoro* (September, 1954).]

CHAPTER II

From the Appeal to the Throne
by the Chief of the Naval General Staff
to the Special Session of the Diet

*The Chief of the Naval General Staff Appeals to
the Throne—Suetsugu, Vice Chief of the Navy
General Staff, Exceeds his Prerogatives—The
Statement by the Delegates in London—The
Chief's Dissatisfaction—It Becomes a Politi-
cal Question—Professor Minobe's Views—The
Reports Made to Prince Saionji—The Activities
of Count Yamamoto's Group.*

When the Cabinet's decision had been taken and the instructions dispatched to London, Yoshida, the Vice Minister of Foreign
Affairs, was greatly disturbed by the reported agitation in Navy
circles and very apprehensive about the attitude that Takarabe
might take. He said to me, "I wish there were some way we could
get Admiral Okada to send, as from the Navy here, a cable that
will mollify and reassure Takarabe.[1] Do use your good offices on
this!" Thus, so that I might better approach Admiral Okada and
also learn more of the current situation in Navy circles, it occurred

---

[1] [When Yoshida himself had asked Okada to send a personal message
to Takarabe in support of the instructions, Okada demurred because Yamanashi's official cable had indicated Okada's concurrence (Okada, *Kaikōroku,* p. 54).

[The British ambassador reported on April 5, 1930: "The government
are not, however, free from anxiety, as the Naval Party and their partisans are
still vehemently opposed to compromise and might cause serious trouble in
the Diet which meets April 21. Vice Minister of Foreign Affairs [i.e., Yoshida]
was manifestly anxious as to how the political situation may develop if Anti-
Compromise Party continued their campaign" (*Br. Docs.,* p. 293).]

to me to meet and talk with my old friend, Vice Admiral Ōsumi.[2] I mentioned this to Yoshida and it was decided that he, Ōsumi, Konoe, and I should meet at my house for a discussion in strictest privacy.

Since that evening was not convenient, we met at my home at three o'clock on the afternoon of April 2. The talk turned to Navy topics, and I learned that the Chief of the Naval General Staff had made a formal direct appeal to the Throne yesterday.[3] The original draft of this appeal had contained grave improprieties, even to the extent of attacking the government's policy as spineless diplomacy and asserting its irresponsibility on national defense. Contending that such strong language was far from suitable, Vice Admiral Ōsumi had caused these terms to be deleted. I understand that Katō, the Chief of the Naval General Staff, can understand matters when they are explained to him; so that he assented to the amendment of the text of this document and the direct appeal to the Throne was completed.

[Dictated April 10, 1930]

The officials about the Throne were said to be quite concerned about the contents of this appeal to the Throne. Essentially the appeal asserted that since 70 per cent was the minimum ratio for national defense, and since this could not be obtained, the Naval General Staff would have to change the whole basis of national defense policy. It was, simply, an appeal for the sake of making an appeal, and was quite meaningless. Since it is the duty and function of a Chief of Naval General Staff thus to adjust his strategy to the strength allotted to him when that allotment may be changed,

---

[2] Vice Admiral Ōsumi Mineo [(1876-1941)], Commandant of the Yokosuka Naval Base. [Ōsumi was particularly active at this period as a source of information for Okada; and on more than one occasion he served as Okada's *alter ego* in talking with Katō, e.g. emending the latter's utterances as intimated below. His prior naval service had included residence in Germany and France, and at the League of Nations. Later he was to be Navy Minister in the Inukai cabinet (1931-32) and in the "transcendental" Saitō and Okada cabinets (1933-36). Cf. Okada, pp. 54-56.]

[3] [Neither here nor in his innumerable subsequent references to it does Harada put before his reader the whole story of Katō's audience with the Emperor on the morning of April 2 (*not* April 1, as the text would have it). The "Introduction" suggests an hypothesis about this apparent lacuna in Harada's account. Perhaps it was not clearly understood by Harada at the time; and later he may have felt it his duty to deny, or to seem to deny, the many stories bruited about by treaty opponents that the court officials (prompted by Saionji and himself) had directly and malignly conspired to keep Katō from making this formal "direct appeal to the Throne (*iaku jōsō*)" in time to prevent the new instructions from being sent to London.]

there can be very little importance in an appeal which asserts that he will do those things which he ought to do. Yet because of the present circumstances such a meaningless appeal was made.[4]

It seems to have been Takarabe's attitude and the efforts of the three Vice Admirals, Nomura, Kobayashi, and Ōsumi, and of Admiral Okada that brought the Navy under control. But Suetsugu the Vice Chief of Staff was not yet quieted. He attended a meeting of the Shōwa Club of the House of Peers without permission of the Navy Ministry and there strongly expressed his dissatisfaction with matters which he should not have discussed at all.[5] Furthermore, only the day before he had gone to the Prime Minister in the latter's capacity as Acting Navy Minister, and had said:

"It was highly indiscreet for me to have transmitted that mimeographed material to the Rengō News Agency. It was an action quite unknown to the Chief of the Naval General Staff and the Vice Navy Minister, for I acted wholly on my own. It was quite inexcusable and I can only be penitent and await whatever disposition you, as Minister, wish to make. I might be placed under domiciliary confinement. I am at present assigned to the General Staff to assist the Chief because of the press of business there. I penitently await your decision."

Suetsugu

To this the Prime Minister replied, "What action I shall take will follow due inquiry and deliberation."

It was the very next day that Suetsugu had attended the meeting of the Shōwa Club, had spoken on the results of disarmament,

---

[4] [The fact of Katō's appeal, however, was not meaningless; for this became the basis of the principal attack on the government action as an unwarranted if not unconstitutional affront to the agencies through which the Emperor exercised the "supreme command." Doubtless this minimizing of Katō's appeal is Harada's mimicry of the views of his luncheon guests. He later records an early anxious awareness of the political implications of this "meaningless" appeal (below, p. 117 f.).]

[5] [The House of Peers was considerably more important in the legislative process and in politics than, say, the British House of Lords since 1910. Its members usually belonged to groups, styled "clubs" or "societies," that did not parallel or reflect the parties in the lower House but rather the several "orders" among the Peers themselves. The dominant such group was the Kenkyūkai (Research or Investigation Society), centered upon the count and viscount members and especially subject to the influence of the Lord Privy Seal, Count Makino. The Shōwa Club, here involved in inviting Admiral Suetsugu's criticism of the government, was a recently formed informal bloc of some Peers in opposition to the Kenkyūkai (Charles B. Fahs, "Political Groups in the Japanese House of Peers," *Am. Pol. Sci. Rev.*, XXXIV [1940], 896-919). See Okada, *Kaikōroku*, pp. 56-59, for this particular episode; also Aoki, I, 54; and for a detailed analysis of the structure and composition of the House of Peers in 1930, see Tiedemann, "The Hamaguchi Cabinet," chaps. viii-ix, and Appendix C.]

and had laid bare his grievances, touching on matters which should have been kept strictly confidential. This, of course, highly incensed the Prime Minister. In anger he said to me,

"This is quite unwarrantable from the standpoint of maintaining discipline. Personally I find it presumptuous and brazen. The man must be punished."

Then I met Vice Minister Yamanashi at the Navy Ministry and learned from him, as also later from Okada himself, that Admiral Okada had just been there and had severely admonished Suetsugu.[6]

[Dictated April 28, 1930]

At the meeting of the Chief Delegates to the London Conference on April 4, our delegates announced Japan's acceptance of the pact on the basis of the instructions.[7] Britain and the United States rejoiced at our participation; and grateful and friendly messages were cabled to Foreign Minister Shidehara by MacDonald and Stimson.

I was anxious to report these developments to the Prince, but his illness remained serious so that I was not yet able to do so. It was reported that the signing of the pact would take place on the twenty-second. Hence, of course, Takarabe would remain in London until that date to participate in the signing.

At home, however, dissatisfaction still rankled among many in the Naval General Staff who continued their hypercritical talk. On April 7, or perhaps the eighth, I chanced by the Navy Ministry and talked with Vice Admirals Kobayashi and Nomura. They told me that the Chief of the Naval General Staff had recently failed to appear in the staff ward room, and they asked me to find out what the situation might be. Somewhat later I went to Katō's

---

[6] [Okada's diary for April 7 records an evening call from Baron Yabuki, the Navy's Parliamentary Vice Minister, to relate the great umbrage which Hamaguchi had taken at Suetsugu's behavior and virtually to appeal to Okada to take some appropriate measures. Yabuki reported that when he and Suetsugu had been called before Hamaguchi on April 2 to be urged to act with prudence since the instruction had finally been issued, Suetsugu had thereupon spoken his *mea culpa* with great punctilio. Even so, he had no compunction about again airing his personal views to the Shōwa Club on April 5. Okada held a number of conferences the next day, including admonitory sessions with Katō and Suetsugu, but he came to the conclusion that no punitive measures be taken till after Takarabe's return from London. Okada, pp. 57-59.]

[7] [The Japanese government's acceptance of the Reed-Matsudaira compromise was actually made known by statements issued on April 2 (Greenwich Time) by the delegation in London. *Documents of the London Naval Conference, 1930*, p. 535; *Br. Docs.*, I, 282-89.]

office. He inquired about the Prince's health, and when we had
exchanged the usual greetings, I remarked, "You may, of course,
be dissatisfied with the results; but still the Conference has wound
up its task and that is a fine thing."

To this he rejoined, "It's as if we had been roped up and cast
into prison by Britain and America. When I and my kind have
gone, it will be you and your kind who must bear the brunt of it.
Since there's no fixed national policy, it follows that the program
for national defense will also vacillate. This is indeed disturbing.
In the days ahead officials and people should be rallied and a
national defense conference should be held. There should be discussion of the obstacles to Japan's expansion in the Far East, especially in China, and of the ways to avoid or minimize these obstacles
as much as possible. It is essential that we build sufficient strength
so that it may constitute a threat to any opponents. What has
caused me the gravest concern recently has been the activity of
those about the Throne. When I note such activities as those of the
Lord Keeper of the Privy Seal pushing forward his own personal
views, it makes me sick at heart."

From this it occurred to me that it may have had harmful
consequences for the Grand Chamberlain to have talked with Admiral Prince Fushimi and with the Chief of the Naval General Staff
himself. But I changed the subject, "Be that as it may, according
to the newspapers, you do not want to make this question a matter
of political antagonisms and have said you must always be careful
lest you become involved in the maelstrom of political disputes;
and you have solemnly foresworn all temptations to do so. These
remarks you gave the press are eminently praiseworthy."

"Well, all sorts of political party groups have come to ask me
to meet with them, but I've refused them all and have seen no one
at all."

In the next several days, though commenting on a variety
of subjects, the newspapers seemed to contain nothing of particular
consequence. I heard, however, that some were spreading the
rumor that the Chief of the Naval General Staff had sought to
present a direct appeal to the Throne before the Prime Minister
had reported to the Throne on the instructions, but that the Lord
Keeper of the Privy Seal had prevented him from doing so.

Further rumors which are rife now include the following:
that as the Diet session draws nearer, the whole matter will tend
to become a political question; that when the treaty is referred to
the Privy Council, the Council will prefer not to recommend ratifi-

cation because it feels that the national defense is gravely insecure with a treaty not approved by the Chief of the Naval General Staff; or that the Council will assert the Treaty violates the Emperor's prerogative of supreme command;[8] or that ratification should only be considered when the full Supreme War Council has met to determine whether or not, under such a treaty, national defense can be assured. All these rumors aim at sabotaging the completion and ratification of the treaty.

About this time, when I met with Admiral Okada, he said:

"If there are plans to convoke the Supreme War Council or to seek the opinion of the Board of Field Marshals and Fleet Admirals prior to Imperial ratification of the treaty, I'll do my best to have such undertakings take place after instead of before the formal ratification. Thus, I ought not to leave Tokyo until the Navy Minister has returned from the conference."

In the Diet circles, of course, there are various views of the prerogative of the supreme command and of cabinet responsibility, especially as related to interpretations of Articles XI and XII of the Constitution;[9] and to develop ammunition to attack the present

---

[8] [Here Harada first uses the phrase *tōsuiken kampan,* "violation of the supreme command prerogative," which soon became central as a charge against Hamaguchi and pro-treaty elements (court officials and the *genrō*). The word *kampan,* a literary rather than a legal term, might also be translated as "transgression, infringement, encroachment, or contempt." It almost immediately came to carry pejorative implications of an illegality and an unconstitutionality akin to *lèse majesté.* It contrasted with similar but less harsh words translatable as "disregard, slight, or by-pass." It became customary to say the Navy (and especially Katō) had questioned the constitutionality of the government's action. Recent Japanese studies (cf. Kobayashi Tatsuo in Tsunoda Jun, *Taiheiyō sensō e no nichi,* I) emphasize that it was Hamaguchi's civilian opponents in the Diet and Privy Council, rather than Navy men, who initiated and developed this critical charge against him. Harada's usage here and later bears out this interpretation.]

[9] [See Appendix II A. In the first chapter of the Meiji Constitution defining the position and attributes of the Emperor, two articles directly bore on the Emperor's prerogatives with respect to the military and naval establishments. Article XI, in the Itō translation, declares that "the Emperor has the supreme command *(tōsui)* of the Army and Navy;" and Article XII: "The Emperor determines the organization *(hensei)* and peace standing of the Army and Navy." Thus, "*tōsui*" and "*hensei*" are parallel attributes or prerogatives of the Emperor's sovereignty, and conceivably quite separate. Institutionally, the Emperor exercised the supreme command *(tōsui)* through the agency of the Army and Navy General Staffs and the Supreme War Council; and the power to organize *(hensei)* the military and naval establishments and to determine their standing through the agency of the respective Ministers in the Cabinet. Here then, in the interpretation of the constitutional basis of its action in concluding the London Naval Treaty, was the possibility of forcing the Hamaguchi cabinet to a position which might cause its collapse. If it claimed to be

government heated arguments are being developed on exactly where, under the Constitution, does the responsibility for national defense lie. Hearing all this talk, I thought it might be well to go to the University and elicit the views of such a scholar as Professor Minobe.[10] Luckily he had two hours free at the noon hour that

---

acting under Article XII or could be shown to have acted in defiance of the views of the Naval General Staff it could be condemned as disregarding if not usurping *tōsui*, the prerogative of the supreme command.

[In the face of a clear majority which Hamaguchi's Minseitō enjoyed in the House of Representatives, such an argument was addressed less to the possibility of anything like a "no-confidence" vote there, than to the influence of this argument in the two sectors of government outside the Diet which might effect the downfall of the cabinet. If either or both of the service ministers, Admiral Takarabe or General Ugaki, could be induced to resign on these grounds, the cabinet would fall. Further, since the treaty had yet to be submitted to the Privy Council, it might be an effective argument in this quarter, the more so because of the role taken by the Privy Council in defeating the Wakatsuki cabinet in 1927.]

[10] Dr. Minobe Tatsukichi [(1873-1948)], of the Law Faculty of Tokyo Imperial University [from 1900 to 1932. Minobe was the leading exponent of an orthodox but so-called "liberal" interpretation of the Meiji Constitution and of the Japanese state.

[His disposition normally to give interpretations which magnified the authority of the cabinet and asserted the primacy of parliamentary vis-à-vis other agencies of government was consonant with Saionji's own views of the elasticity of the constitution and the direction in which its interpretation should evolve in practice. From an earlier day before World War I Minobe had advanced his "organic theory *(kikansetsu)*," the thesis that the Emperor was one of the organs of the state, having no authority over and above it. Now, as Hamaguchi's opponents were advancing to constitutional arguments, he was soon to publish a series of articles justifying the cabinet's action with respect to the London Treaty. These appeared in the leading newspaper, *Tōkyō Asahi*, in the first week in May while the Diet was still in session, under the title, "Kaigun jōyaku no seiritsu to tōsuiken no genkai [The Conclusion of the Naval Treaty and the Limits of the Power of Supreme Command]," and in the journal *Kaizō* [*Reconstruction*] XII,, No. 6 (June, 1930), 19-26. Together with other discussion pertinent to London Treaty issues, these were later republished in a separate volume of essays, *Gikai seiji no kentō* [*A Study of Parliamentary Politics*] (Tōkyō: Hyōronsha, 1934), pp. 97-143.

[Minobe's position on this issue may be summarized as follows: the power to decide military and naval strength and to determine Army and Navy organization appertains ultimately to the throne's prerogative over state affairs on which the cabinet alone gives responsible advice, with the views of military and naval authorities being purely advisory to and without binding force on the cabinet. And more specifically in the context of this issue over this London Treaty, Minobe asserted that it appertained exclusively to the political organs (i.e. the cabinet) to assume full responsibility for exercising the imperial prerogative to conclude treaties. Thus, as Professor Takeuchi epitomizes this view: "the cabinet was clearly within its exclusive competence to advise the throne concerning the subject matter of the treaty, and even granting that the naval general Staff had the constitutional power to advise the Emperor as to the subject matter, the London Treaty, being a treaty, it was within the exclusive competence of the cabinet to give responsible advice to the throne." (Takeuchi, *op. cit.*, pp. 310-13).]

day, so I arranged a luncheon at the Sumitomo villa and also invited Okabe, Hotta, Chief of the European-American Bureau, and Arita, Chief of the Asian office, to hear Professor Minobe.[11] Before we adjourned we gained some clarification of the constitutional points that have been under discussion.

In general the government is inclined to adopt Dr. Minobe's views. Prime Minister Hamaguchi himself speaks approvingly of them.[12] Even so there was some discussion that the professor may be putting it too glibly when he says, "The Naval General Staff, as one of the headquarters agencies, participates in planning under the sovereign authority of the Emperor. The Staff's views, as a matter of reference, should be given every serious consideration by the government; yet it does not at all have the right of decision."[13]

---

[11] [These three men, near his own age, were friends as well as information sources and "pressure points" with whom he met more frequently than the Memoirs indicate. Viscount Okabe Nagakage (b. 1884), descendant of a *daimyō* family, was chief secretary to the Lord Privy Seal. The other two were Foreign Office career men—Hotta Masaaki (b. 1883) and Arita Hachirō (b. 1884). Hotta was the Foreign Ministry officer responsible for drafting much of that Ministry's documents on the treaty and for representing that Ministry in negotiations with similar senior staff men in other ministries and later vis-à-vis the Privy Council secretariat. This luncheon preceded not only the Diet session but also the publication of most of Minobe's articles on the treaty issue. Perhaps the meeting was more profitable to the professor than to the others.]

[12] [Minobe's constitutional views were widely accepted by the higher bureaucracy, the civil service largely recruited from Tokyo Law Faculty graduates. Dr. Ikki, the Imperial Household Minister and later President of the Privy Council, had been Minobe's teacher and was identified with similar views. Harada later records the Emperor's own acceptance of them and admiration of Minobe (Harada, IV, 237-39).

[Examples of this pre-war "liberalism" are included in Ryusaku Tsunoda and others (eds.), *Sources of the Japanese Tradition* (New York: Columbia University Press, 1958), pp. 718-58. A succinct statement of the range of orthodox philosophies about the state that is not lost in the niceties of a particular issue (as is here involved) nor in the imprecision of the terms "liberal" and "moderate" is presented in John K. Fairbank, Edwin O. Reischauer, and Albert M. Craig, *A History of East Asian Civilization*, Vol. II: *East Asia—The Modern Transformation* (Boston: Houghton Mifflin Co., 1965), pp. 531-38.

[Frank O. Miller, in his *Minobe Tatsukichi, Interpreter of Constitutionalism in Japan* (Berkeley: University of California Press, 1965), cites (in chap. iv, *passim*) this episode from Harada as "the only firsthand report we have," apart from the professor's published writings, of Minobe's part in the treaty affair. Yet Miller misdates, misplaces, and mistranslates Harada's account and omits (without indicating any elision) the politically critical part of Minobe's advice. Though perhaps minor flaws in his otherwise remarkable study as a whole, such error together with some ten other egregious misstatements of fact unfortunately make Miller's portmanteau account of the treaty issue quite unreliable.]

[13] [This remark attributed to Minobe may illustrate the acuity of Harada's reportorial ear and memory, for he has the professor use precisely the

There was talk that it ought not to be put as bluntly as this; for it might have unfortunate emotional repercussions and the Army too might become involved. Better simply let it be known that military views are given fullest consideration, lest the atmosphere become more and more tense.

There are many rumors current that, with the Diet session drawing near, groups tending to oppose the government both in the House of Peers and in the Privy Council are preparing to make this issue a means of attacking the government.

I consulted with Dr. Katsunuma[14] and with Hachirō on the condition of the Prince's illness, and it seemed reasonably sure that he would have recovered sufficiently for me to see him about the beginning of May to make my report. Meanwhile I would be attentive to all aspects of the situation. On the morning of the twenty-third, however, I had a call from Okitsu that I should come as early as might be convenient, though there was no urgent business.

Thus I left on the evening of the twenty-fourth and reached Okitsu the next morning. After consulting with Dr. Miura and Hachirō and first deciding that we should not speak for more than fifteen minutes at a time, I went to the Prince's room. "Well," he said, "this is not at all urgent. It's just that I've been confined to bed for so long I'm out of touch with things. It's like a youngster in primary school who for illness' sake has been so long absent that he cannot coordinate what was taught with what is being taught and is thought to be stupid. Not wanting to be in such a plight I've called you to learn what's happened since I've been bedridden. And I may have a few words to add."

Thus I gave him a general report. He then asked, "What have been the British and American reactions to Japan's stand at the London Conference? It would be splendid if these have been favorable." He seemed happy with my reply that the results were eminently satisfactory.

Minobe

---

terms of Article III of the Naval General Staff ordinance (see Appendix II H) that define its function, though Harada may not have recognized this was so. This is not mere pedantry. The principal term (*sankaku*, here translated as "participates in planning") might be understood as analogous for military affairs to the "assistance *(hohitsu)*" given by ministers of state on state affairs; and both might be translated as "advice." But Minobe, both in his general theory and in this specific instance, drew a sharp distinction between these two kinds of "advice." Minobe could not, of course, speak of the Staff as being in any direct sense "advisory" (i.e. subordinate) to the cabinet.]

[14] Dr. Katsunuma Seizō [b. 1886], Professor in the Aichi Medical School, Prince Saionji's personal physician.

"Be particularly watchful of this issue in the House of Peers and the Privy Council," he cautioned.

I returned to Tokyo the same day and found a message from the Prince upon my return. "When you see Prime Minister Hamaguchi, tell him, 'Once again your conceptions have become realities. If it can be said that Japan's full participation has made possible the splendid conclusion of the naval conference's agreement, it is due to your efforts. My heartiest congratulations!' And to the Lord Keeper of the Privy Seal, to the Imperial Household Minister and the Grand Chamberlain for their concern over my illness, please convey my grateful thanks."

The Prince had also asked me if the men in Count Yamamoto's entourage had been involved in any political maneuvering during his illness.

[Dictated May 1, 1930]

In general I reviewed for him the developments that had taken place since he became ill. I reported that the Privy Council might seek to overthrow the Cabinet on this issue, or that the opposition group in the House of Peers might try to use the disarmament issue for the same result. I mentioned also that Kabayama[15] and others of the Satsuma clique were said to be involved in a movement to organize a group advisory to the Lord Keeper of the Privy Seal so that after Prince Saionji's death Count Yamamoto, Hiranuma Kiichirō,[16] and Prince Ichijō,[17] might function as a three-man

---

[15] Kabayama Sukehide, member of the House of Peers [was associated politically with Yamamoto Gombei, for whom he served as Chief Cabinet Secretary in Yamamoto's last cabinet].

[16] Baron Hiranuma Kiichirō [(1867-1952)], Vice President of the Privy Council, a former Home Minister [in the second Yamamoto cabinet, and the most prominent civilian promoter of ultra-conservative nationalism. The *Kokuhonsha* (National Foundation Society) which he founded in 1924, drawing its original membership from bureaucratic protégés in the Justice Ministry of which he had been a long-time official, was now burgeoning as the leading right-wing patriotic society. It was to be a sort of brood-mother for a flock of more explicitly reactionary groups in the years ahead. Prince Saionji had a strong antipathy to him personally as well as politically and on more than one occasion used his influence to check Hiranuma's patent ambition. Later, predominantly Army pressure elevated Hiranuma to the Prime Ministership for some eight months in 1939. Later still he was indicted as one of Japan's major "war criminals," found guilty on six counts, and sentenced to life imprisonment by the International Military Tribunal of the Far East, and died in prison. Cf. Togasaka Masanari (ed.), *Dantai sōran* [*A Compendium of Associations*] (2d ed.; Tōkyō: Dai Nihon Teikoku Sangyō Sōrenmei Dantai Kenkyūjo, 1934), especially Part IV; the useful brief *Kokka shugi dantai keitō ichiranhyō* [*A Table Showing the Lineage of Nationalist Organizations*] August, 1935 (LC Microfilm Collection, SP 251); *Shuyō kokka shugi dantai benran* [*A Handbook on the*

group within the Lord Keeper's office to advise that official in such matters as changes of administration and the like. To this the Prince said, "I won't stand for such talk."[18]

> *Katō's Statement and the Movement to Bring*
> *About the Fall of the Cabinet—The*
> *Question of Navy Minister Takarabe's Resig-*
> *nation—Koga and Others go to Meet the*
> *Returning Navy Minister—The Views of*
> *the Chief of the Naval General Staff—*
> *The Strategy of the Privy Council and the*
> *Seiyūkai Party—The Question of the Lord*
> *Keeper's Alleged Blocking of Katō's Attempted*
> *Direct Appeal—Attacks on the Government*
> *in the Diet.*

On the subject of the House of Peers and the Privy Council, it was just after his direct appeal to the Throne that the Chief of the Naval General Staff created a terrific stir by issuing a public statement: "Under the terms of the American proposal I cannot bear the responsibility for national defense. I disapprove of it completely."[19] What the Naval General Staff thus condemns as an

---

Principal Nationalist Organizations], May 1935 (*ibid.*, SP 250); and *Documents Relating to the Organization, History and Personnel of the Black Dragon Society* [*Kokuryūkai*], *Kokuhonsha, Jimmukai* . . . , *1927-1942* (*ibid.*, IMT 344). Storry, Maxon, Butow and Maruyama, in their several studies that concentrate on the next fifteen years, necessarily have much to say on this man who is already, in 1930, a symbol of arch-conservatism.]

[17] Prince Ichijō Sanetaka, member of the House of Peers. [Like Saionji and Konoe a scion of the pre-restoration court nobility, Ichijō was a retired naval captain.]

[18] [Saionji, as is discussed in the Introduction, hoped that the role of *genrō* as extra-legal, extra-constitutional but ultimate arbiter under the Emperor might come to an end with himself, and that practices should evolve whereby regular governmental agencies would function with more unity and responsibility under the Prime Minister. In the parlance of the "liberal 'twenties" this was called *kensei no jōdō*, constitutional government's normal course. But in the context of modern Japanese politics, the prospect that the aged Saionji's present illness might be his last not unnaturally led to speculation and to maneuvers to continue the *genrō* system or some near alternative for purposes of mediating in the recurrent crises that seemed bound to erupt because of the pluralism of the Japanese state; or at least to formalize the *genrō's* responsibility in nominating a new Prime Minister. With all such schemes brought to his attention, as here, Saionji expressed impatient irritation. (See also below, chap. iv, p. 173 and n. 19; and pp. 234-35.)]

[19] [The episode of Katō's direct appeal to the throne *(iaku jōsō)* on April 2, after the government's decision to accept the Reed-Matsudaira formula had been sent to London, is reviewed in more precise detail in Aoki, I, 15-20.]

"American proposal" is no American proposal at all, but represents a compromise of both the Japanese and American claims. Yet if they do not say it is an "American" proposal crammed down our throats, they would be at a loss for the means to attack the Government. Hence the Staff is so insistently proclaiming to the world that it is "American."

In the last analysis I believe this disarmament question will end eventually with Imperial ratification. Yet those who oppose the Government will use Katō's statement in an effort to overthrow the Cabinet, and the disharmony between Staff and Government will be stressed. The Government may say that it gives full consideration to the views of the General Staff; but if this is so, it could be asked, what of the fact of Katō's statement? The Prime Minister has said that since it has not gone beyond the inner circles there is no need for a reply.[20] Nevertheless, the fact is that nothing is so troublesome as this statement.

Ultimately it may be that both the Chief and the Vice Chief of the Naval General Staff must resign, but this would bring about the resignation of Navy Minister Takarabe at the same time. Since the Cabinet would thus be incomplete, it would necessarily fall. This is precisely what the opposition parties and schemers are planning.[21]

For this reason Takarabe's course of action will have utmost significance, and it is this which gives grave concern to such right-thinking men in the Navy as Admiral Okada, Vice Minister Yamanashi, and others. Thus, Captain Koga,[22] the senior secretary

---

[20] [To use American political parlance, Hamaguchi is thus prepared to claim "executive privilege" rather than to disclose internal processes of his administrative arrangements to other governmental agencies, whether the Diet, supreme command agencies, or the Privy Council.]

[21] [If this "estimate of the situation," presumably at the end of April, is not a later interpolation in the record, it may suggest the quality of political calculation and, perhaps, prescience which made Harada so useful to Saionji. The issues as forecast in these two paragraphs do indeed dog the Hamaguchi government in the ensuing five months.]

[22] Captain Koga Mineichi. [According to Aoki, he carried distinct messages from at least six persons: Okada, Hamaguchi, Yamanashi, Harada (as from Saionji), Shidehara, and Katō. All but the last sought by various methods of argument to apprise him of the political danger in comments of any kind prior to his return and to dissuade him from them. Okada, who saw Koga on April 27, urged the necessity of maintaining outwardly the appearance of unity in the Navy, argued against action which might involve the Army in the matter, and for Takarabe to entertain no thought of resignation at this juncture. On May 1, Hamaguchi's message also counselled against Takarabe's return till after the Diet session was concluded, thus denying the opposition in the Diet an opportunity to question the Navy Minister directly (Aoki, I, 27-32; cf. Okada, pp.

to the Navy Minister, is to be sent to Harbin to meet Takarabe before he has returned to report on the political situation and to convey these views of Admiral Okada:

"The Navy Minister should refrain from any comments whatever until the whole delegation has returned. It seems likely that some reservist groups, among others, will question the Minister's responsibility and will press for his resignation. I trust that, since there was considerable conviction shown by him in signing the treaty, the Navy Minister will remain firm and will do nothing that might be interpreted as a sign that he may repudiate his action. After the Chief of the Naval General Staff resigns and before the consideration of the treaty by the Privy Council, it should be relatively easy to reach a decision that national defense is being maintained, whether by Imperial inquiry to the Board of Field Marshals and Fleet Admirals or by assembling the Supreme War Council."[23]

I reported to the Prince that Captain Koga had been sent to acquaint the Navy Minister fully with the situation and to apprise him of the great importance of taking no action which might overthrow the Cabinet. The Prince not only agreed, but urged the wisdom of having someone from outside Navy circles say the same thing to Takarabe.

This very point had given some concern to Vice Minister Yoshida, who seemed to have some difficulty in finding a suitable man to send to meet Takarabe. I discussed it with him; and he

---

59-61). Captain Koga subsequently rose to highest rank, and was Commander-in-Chief, Combined Fleet, at the time of his death in a plane crash in March, 1944.]

[23] [Additional points in a fuller account of this message, presumably Captain Koga's, will help us to understand better some of the intricate maneuverings that lie ahead. Perhaps Okada did not tell Harada the whole of his counsel to the returning Takarabe, in keeping with his general line that these issues be solved within professional navy circles without involving outsiders. First, Okada pointed out that, though Katō wanted a formal meeting of the Supreme War Council and the *Gensui*, Okada himself was against such action until it could be pre-arranged that any "request for advice" to the Council would elicit the reply that "under the treaty terms national defense can be made secure"; and that this must precede any reference to the Privy Council. In brief, the Staff must be led to give assurance that, through the development of naval aviation and other internal measures and adjustments, it will be able to make an adequate defense possible. Secondly, despite the precedent of "consulting" both the Army and the Navy after the Washington Conference, Okada thought it would be "extremely harmful" to involve the Army in the present situation. Thirdly, if Takarabe immediately upon his return will be attentive to obtaining the understanding of Tōgō and Fushimi, "there will be no serious difficulty with the Supreme War Council." And finally, "I shall do whatever is possible to support your position and your efforts." (Aoki, I, 27-28)]

also consulted with Count Kabayama Sukehide, and with the Lord Keeper of the Privy Seal, and Count Yamamoto Gombei as well. As a result, it was decided that Matsukata Otohiko might be personally effective with Takarabe; but for some reason Matsukata was hesitant and seemed likely to decline the mission.

Finally it was decided that Count Kabayama Aisuke,[24] privately and as a personal friend, should go to meet Takarabe, and also that Baron Yabuki,[25] the Navy Parliamentary Vice Minister, should go part of the way.

Since Kabayama Aisuke had previously been on quite intimate terms with Hiranuma there was some fear lest the matter become known to Hiranuma's faction and this would be to the grave disadvantage of the Government. Yet since the recovery of the Prince was assured and this completely altered the situation, it was said that Kabayama would think only of Takarabe and would not go so far as to lend his friendship to the schemes of Hiranuma. Thus, the decision to approach Kabayama was made. I told the Prince of this entire matter, and then returned from Okitsu to Tokyo.

The Diet vigorously attacked the Foreign Minister and the Prime Minister, concentrating on the differences of opinion between the Naval General Staff and the Government.[26]

[Dictated May 5, 1930]

When after some time I called on the Chief of the Naval General Staff at the Navy Ministry on May 3, he still expressed deep dissatisfaction with the disarmament conference.

"Shidehara's speech on foreign affairs in the Diet the other day is highly provocative and defiant.[27] It was aimed directly at

---

[24] [Count Kabayama (1865-1953), eldest son of the late Admiral Kabayama Sukenori, was not only of Satsuma provenience and thus apt as emissary to Takarabe; he was also associated with "internationalist" (that is, "cosmopolitan") viewpoints and, like Saionji, felt Japan's best future course lay in alignment with Britain and America. He was lately returned from London where he had been an adviser to the Japanese delegation.]

[25] Baron Yabuki Shōzō, member of the House of Peers [and a former Parliamentary Vice Minister of Foreign Affairs, a post he resumed in the second Wakatsuki cabinet in April, 1931, and which he also held under the Okada cabinet from 1934].

[26] [During the special session of the Fifty-eighth Diet, convoked April 23 and prorogued May 14, vigorous attacks by the Seiyūkai on the Foreign Minister and the Prime Minister sought to develop the constitutional arguments previously alluded to. Harada's summary of this session is given below, pp. 129-31. For a summary of the official record, see Takeuchi, pp. 305-9.]

[27] [Shidehara's principal speech on the subject, on April 25, had in fact

---

the Naval General Staff. Before the Government dispatched the instructions to the delegation in London, they ought to have listened to our views on this matter; and yet when I had wanted to present explanations at meetings of the Cabinet, I was prevented from attending. They constantly talked behind my back, and told me only two hours before dispatching the instructions that they were going to do so. They are altogether defiant of the General Staff. It would have been acceptable if they had allowed me to have my say and then had given me to understand before the instructions were issued that there was no alternative after considering the matter from various angles. But they didn't even do that. The very issuance of the instructions shows a disregard for the Navy General Staff and is equivalent to ignoring the prerogative of supreme command. Can I stand by and allow decisions on the national defense to be made in this way?"[28]

He was critical, too, of what he regards as a tendency to consider the power of supreme command and the power of administration—that is, the power to determine national defense—as being in opposition. "No cabinet of political parties," he said, "can resolve this situation. The cabinet should be limited to officials. Absolute monarchism is the only solution."

"Such an argument," I said, "shows you completely misunderstand the state of affairs. Such a cabinet nowadays, even if it could be formed, would have absolutely no followers and supporters. There is no other method under a constitutional regime than to work for the improvement of the character of the political parties. There is no other way than to wait for the awakening of the people. The announcement which you gave to the press, when you had just come from making a direct appeal to the Throne, was highly unfortunate. It is altogether regrettable that no one cautioned you against urging your strong views with such belligerence."

---

been reviewed in advance and presumably accepted by Yamanashi; but it nonetheless stirred up much ire among high Naval circles because of its blunt assertion that national defense was yet secure and that opposition was "absurd" and "utterly wide of the truth." Okada, p. 62-63. Shidehara's speech is included in the 400-hundred page printed classified collection, *1930-nen Rondon kaigun kaigi kankei bunshoshū* [*A Collection of Documents Concerning the 1930 London Naval Conference*], May, 1931, in *Rondon ikken* (LC Microfilm Collection, S 2.12.0.0.1), pp. 983-88.]

[28] [As early as April 2 Katō had petulantly talked with Okada about resigning. While obstensibly agreeing with him, Okada insisted that timing was all-important and that he owed it to Takarabe to await the latter's return from London (Okada, p. 56).]

When I returned from talking to Katō, I met both Vice Admirals Nomura and Kobayashi and told them of the incident. I had also invited Yoshida to supper, so the four of us repaired to the Kinsui restaurant and talked of many things. I'm told the Seiyūkai is giving currency to the story that the Grand Chamberlain, with the knowledge of the Cabinet, had prevented the Chief of the Naval General Staff from making a direct appeal to the Throne before the Prime Minister presented the instructions. The story has it that after due investigation the Seiyūkai will publicly disclose these indiscretions of the advisers about the Throne. The Privy Council, even more than Seiyūkai, seems to be keeping an eye on those who have any connection with the Palace.

All this, of course, is the work of scheming intriguers. Two or three days ago I met with the Grand Chamberlain and told him of these stories.

"I've been warned about that story," he said, "by the Kempeitai.[29] The fact is, of course, that I did absolutely nothing to block an appeal to the throne by Katō before the instructions were presented. In the first place, my office has nothing to do with direct appeals [*iaku jōsō*] to the Throne. These are in the purview of the Chief Aide-de-Camp. Even so His Majesty's calendar of official duties was so full that there was not time; and it was inevitably delayed till after the instructions had been presented."

From the Prime Minister I heard another curious story. It seems that an old and intimate friend came to the Prime Minister from Count Kiyoura.[30] His message was that the Count had heard the following: "The Lord Keeper of the Privy Seal was in attendance upon His Majesty when the instructions were presented. His Majesty asked, 'Does the Chief of the Naval General Staff agree with these instructions?' And the Prime Minister had replied affirmatively. All this was told to me privately, but I rejoined that it was not so and I quashed it then and there. But with this in mind you should not tell many people of this episode."

Count Kiyoura's advice is undoubtedly well-intentioned, but the episode as he tells it is a complete fabrication. Not only was the Lord Keeper not present when the Prime Minister reported

---

[29] [The Kempeitai—the Military Police or Gendarmerie—were reputedly as efficient in their intelligence activities as they were brutal in their more usual police duties.]

[30] Count Kiyoura Keigo [(1850-1942), octogenarian former bureaucrat, head of the last purely bureaucratic cabinet for six months in 1924 after the collapse of Yamamoto's second cabinet and before Katō Kōmei's first cabinet].

on the instructions; His Majesty also asked no question about the Chief of Staff's acceptance of the instructions. While the Prime Minister remarked that it was strange counsel indeed, it seemed to me to be further evidence of the lengths to which the schemers will go.

According to Vice Admiral Nomura, "Some extremists among the reservists are saying that to produce Takarabe's resignation, they will go Harbin to threaten him and if worse comes to worst, they will assassinate him. If only Governor-General Saitō could return to Tokyo to take these reservists in hand, particularly those of flag-rank. . . ." Yesterday's papers were saying quite openly that the Governor-General of Korea expressed considerable satisfaction with the current disarmament conference and was quite displeased with the actions of the Naval General Staff.

Caught up with this matter in the Diet discussions are such questions as whether or not an Acting Minister of War should be designated, and whether or not a civilian official would be acceptable. As devices which might bring about the collapse of the Cabinet in some way or other, all sorts of questions on the disarmament conference and the supreme command are being raised: that it is urgently necessary for the hospitalized War Minister Ugaki[31] to attend; that a close inquiry be made into the relation between the right of supreme command and the right of state administration; has there been any encroachment *(kampan)* on the prerogative of supreme command?[32] If on the one hand, Navy Minister Takarabe's behavior in connection with disarmament has indicated his anxiety, and if on the other, the War Minister's views on whether it is under Article XI or Article XII of the constitution

[31] [No official cognizance had been taken of the fact that General Ugaki Kazushige, the War Minister, was ill and in the hospital. Like Takarabe, he was part of the ministerial team with which Hamaguchi had long been familiar. To countenance his resignation, or even temporary official withdrawal, at this time, would play into the hands of the Cabinet's enemies.]

[32] [More clearly than in his first use of this phrase, *tōsuiken kampan* (p. 112 and n. 8), Harada here puts it in the context of the opposition's real use of it, less as a genuine constitutional argument between "strict" and "broad" constructionists than as a general cover-slogan for stratagems to alienate the Navy and, if possible, the Army too, and thus bring about the collapse of the Hamaguchi cabinet. That such stratagems were commended to them stemmed partly from their patent present inability to find any parliamentary means to this end (faced with Hamaguchi's clear majority in the lower house and his understandings in the upper house), and partly from the old habit of many Japanese politicians of making unprincipled deals with oligarchs, bureaucrats or military men for momentary political advantage.]

that the treaty has been concluded differ from those of their cabinet colleagues, then are not both the Navy and War Ministers—that is, the military representatives in the Cabinet—together in their disagreement with the Cabinet? This being so, if they can be both brought to resign, the Cabinet can no longer continue.

General Ugaki, thus, is not simply the War Minister. Among the Ministers of State he is clearly the most important, and his action can have the gravest political consequences for the Cabinet. Various elements in the Diet and elsewhere, lumping together Articles XI and XII of the Constitution, charge the Prime Minister with ignoring the prerogative of the supreme command and with depending on ministerial advice in the matter of the disarmament conference. At the same time, albeit reluctantly, the Prime Minister is maneuvering to avoid these questions as far as possible. He is quite insistent that "if from a constitutional viewpoint you set up clearly the distinction between the administrative power and the command power, then I accept responsibility for the disarmament conference since it is without question within my competence to offer advice as a Minister of State. But I shall refrain from any discussion of the constitutional issue that may be involved." In other words, considering the unusual circumstances affecting both service members of the Cabinet—War Minister Ugaki and Navy Minister Takarabe—during this session of the Diet, the Prime Minister is in the awkward position of wanting to proceed safely through this session of the Diet without touching on these questions lest the Cabinet be brought vainly to an end and its main purposes be nullified.

Taking advantage of the fact that naval men are relatively ignorant of constitutional matters, some of the Privy Councillors are arguing that since the Privy Council is the highest authority on the interpretation of the Imperial Constitution, thus whenever a constitutional inquiry is made to the Council, the Emperor must accept as correct whatever interpretation is decided by the Council. Therefore, they say, when the Cabinet's views differ from those of the Council, His Majesty necessarily follows the interpretation decided by the Council. This being so, the Cabinet should resign. This argument is being talked up among some of the Navy leaders in hope of bringing about the downfall of the Hamaguchi government. Some of the schemers think they can tempt War Minister Ugaki into resignation, and various maneuvers are under way about the disarmament conference. Thus the disarmament conference question has in fact become the football of politics.

Prince Saionji's Concern—An Interview with Governor-General Saitō—The Conspiracy in Privy Council Circles—Captain Nakamura's Activity—Takarabe's Attitude.

Saitō

I left for Okitsu on the evening of the third and reached there the next morning when I saw the Prince and tried to give him a full report, especially on the political scene. He expressed surprise at the number of stubborn men.

"If the advisers about the throne, such as the Lord Keeper of the Privy Seal and the Grand Chamberlain, remain steadfast, the matter of the Privy Council will be all right. But this ought to be settled once and for all while I am yet alive. As in the present instance, it can be deeply disquieting."[33]

Governor-General Saitō, interviewed by newsmen in Korea, has said, "Our participation in the disarmament conference and acceptance of an agreement that is deemed essential in international affairs in no way jeopardizes *(kampan)* the prerogative of supreme command. It seems to me extremely unfortunate, moreover, to have this question used as a plaything of politics. Doesn't it seem to be a serious mistake for the military groups to broach the subject of the alleged "disregarding" of an important agency of the state and to call into question a treaty which the government has quite properly negotiated and signed? If you examine the terms of the agreement I believe you will find nothing in them which can cause a flaw in national defense up to 1936. National defense is of course endless, but in view of the figures in the agreement I believe it should be quite evident, even to a novice, that there will be no deficiencies with respect to national defense. It is henceforth up to the military men to secure the national defense within the terms that have been agreed upon."

These views came very fittingly from Governor-General Saitō, and I believe they have had considerable influence in the Navy.

It is reported that Yabuki, the Parliamentary Vice Minister, by arrangement with the Diet, will go part way to meet and welcome Takarabe, the returning Navy Minister. The story may not

---

[33] [Saionji's impatience with Privy Council pretensions, with its "flaws," frequently led him to such explosive criticism; yet it is unlikely he had any broad general reform in mind as a "settlement." Later in the summer he will commend two specific measures to the Prime Minister and to court officials in case the Council should prove to be intransigent on the treaty; but they were not needed, and thus not tried. (Chap. vi, especially pp. 211 f., 224; 248 f.)]

be entirely correct, but I understand that four or five days ago when Railways Minister Egi[34] called on Count Itō Miyoji,[35] the Count said, "It is most fortunate for Japan that an agreement has come out of the disarmament conference; but I'm very troubled that the Chief of the Naval General Staff has opposed it." It occurred to me that what he found so "very troublesome" in short, is the prospect of the days ahead when the matter will come before the Privy Council; and the Count is gloomy wondering if it can be forestalled.

It seems to be a fact that the Vice Chief of Staff is running about amongst the Privy Councillors, and it has become known that Chief of Staff himself has actually said: "The actions of a Government which disregards the power of supreme command violate the very spirit of the Constitution. On the right or wrong of this I am anxious for His Majesty to obtain the advice of the Privy Council." Thus, although on the surface the Navy General Staff circles seem more calm than before, the facts are still disagreeable and intolerable to them.

[Dictated May 16, 1930]

Navy Minister Takarabe finally left Harbin on May 15, and he will go by way of Changchun to Korea where he is expected to meet with the Governor-General about the nineteenth.[36] Captain Nakamura, who had accompanied the delegation to London, had already returned to Tokyo two or three days before and issued statements apparently favorable to the Naval General Staff's side. Even as he was en route to Japan, he had hinted to newsmen at various dissatisfactions; and articles had appeared attributing rather cynical remarks to him. From what I have heard, matters revealed by America in strictest confidence to Japan during the private talks between Matsudaira and Reed were leaked to the

---

[34] Dr. Egi Yoku (Tasuku) [(1873-1932)], member of the House of Peers, counsellor of the Minseitō. [Egi was commonly understood to be the chief of Hamaguchi's political brain-trust. He had been Chief Cabinet Secretary in the third Katsura cabinet, 1913, and in the following Ōkuma cabinet. He had entered the House of Peers in 1916. He had been Justice Minister in the Katō cabinet, 1925.]

[35] [Count Itō Miyoji (1857-1934) enjoyed, in some circles, a special prestige in the Privy Council because, with the aged Viscount Kaneko, he was a relic of the constitution-drafting days of 1888-90 when he had been a chief secretary to Prince Itō Hirobumi. He had been vitriolic in opposition to the first Wakatsuki cabinet and to Japan's signature of the Kellogg-Briand Pact.]

[36] [Shidehara recalled receiving private assurances from Saitō, at this time, that he supported the Foreign Minister and Cabinet rather than the Navy high command (Shidehara, pp. 123f).]

Tokyo newspaper, the *Jiji Shimpō*.[37] I understand from various sources that it was Captain Nakamura who purposely allowed these secrets to be disclosed so that the Matsudaira-Reed talks might end in failure. It was apparently the deliberate strategy of Navy General Staff circles to have him return before the Navy Minister just so that he might give a report favorable to the Staff's position.

From the beginning the Prince had said persistently, "The attitude of the present staff is fanatic and inexcusable." When I saw him on the fifteenth, after the Diet session was concluded, the subject recurred. "If only from the standpoint of maintaining discipline, shouldn't something be done, lest there be trouble?"

On this issue Prime Minister Hamaguchi proposed, "As soon as possible I'd like to have Foreign Minister Shidehara review at some length for the Prince the full situation on disarmament. Rather than meeting with him myself, it would be better for him first to meet with Takarabe." When I told the Prince of this request, he mused, "Since my health is again quite good, it's not impossible to meet with him, and I'd prefer to go to see him. Yet if I meet with the Foreign Minister, then I'll also have to see Takarabe when he returns a few days hence. But from another standpoint, for me to see the Foreign Minister first could invite public speculation and conjecture with unhappy results. Might it not be better for me to see neither the Prime Minister, nor the Foreign Minister, nor the Envoy until I'm completely recovered? See if you can't handle this smoothly."

Thus when I returned from Okitsu I decided to tell both the Foreign Minister and the Prime Minister that the Prince was seeing no one for the time being.

Someone of those who went to meet Takarabe as he was en route home must have properly briefed him on the situation, for since then no comments which might cause concern have been attributed to him by the press.

In retrospect one might note that many questions had arisen in the recent Diet session, but the two issues of disarmament and unemployment had provided the principal issues for attacks on the government. Just as had been feared from the start, Katō's

---

[37] [A manuscript report of such disclosures to the *Jiji* at London, apparently early in February, is to be found in the Foreign Ministry archives (LC Microfilm Collection, S 2.12.0.0.1, pp. 226-31). From the files of the London embassy there survives a further group of documents on the leaking of top-secret telegrams *(kimitsu dempō rōei)* in that portion designated "after the London Conference *(Rondon kaigi igo)*" of the whole file headed "Military Disarmament *(Gumbi shukusho)*" (LC Microfilm collection, UD 55-3).]

public statement and the words and actions of the Naval General Staff had contributed mightily to political controversy.

Since Konoe was due to leave for China on the evening of May 13, I invited him and Admiral Okada to dinner at my house on the evening of the 8th. During dinner I had Admiral Okada give Konoe a first-hand account of the situation between the Naval Ministry and the Naval General Staff as concerns the disarmament conference so that he might have a full understanding of the circumstances to date.[38]

The Question of the Prerogative of the Supreme Command—The Cabinet's Moves against Diet Opposition—The "War of Interpellations" —Prime Minister Hamaguchi's Reply.

The question of the prerogative of supreme command ran through the entire special session of the Diet, and was the focus of sharp debate. Moreover, no solution had been reached at the time of adjournment so that the matter remains an open question following the Diet session. The government had anticipated that argument about the responsibility for the conclusion of the London Treaty would serve as the crux of attack by the opposition party and in the House of Peers. The appropriate officials had been set to study means of coping with the Diet and had concentrated on a reply to this very question. In general their position was as follows:

"There was no point, in its handling of the negotiations of this treaty, in which the Government contravened the Constitution. The conclusion of a treaty is simply one of the 'duties of state.' The present matter is a treaty concerned with determining the strength and manpower of the Navy. That is, although there may have been some difference of opinion with the Naval General Staff when the instructions were issued, the power to decide rests, now as before,

---

[38] [Konoe had inherited from his father a role as patron of certain traditionalist activities stressing Japan's ties with China, such, for example, as expressed in the private cultural exchange activities the Tōa Dōbunkai (East Asia Common Culture Society) which maintained institutes and schools in China. As an officer of this society he was about to spend a week in China attending ceremonies for that society's thirtieth anniversary (Yabe, *Konoe,* I, 180-182). This Konoe patronage gave rise to various kinds of covert or oblique relations between Konoe and the adventurer types called "China *rōnin*" as Harada will have occasion to note below (in Chapter ix). See Marius B. Jansen, *The Japanese and Sun Yat-sen* (Cambridge: Harvard University Press, 1954).]

with the government. Thus on this point it is quite clear that there can be no question of any violation of or encroachment on the prerogative of supreme command." They took the following points as basic for their replies to be offered on this matter: (1) The views of the Naval General Staff have been given the greatest respect and consideration; (2) the responsibility for national defense before the Diet is assumed by the government; (3) there is no necessity to reply to questions on internal procedures employed at the time of issuing the instructions, or to enter upon discussions of constitutionality.[39]

From the first interpellations to the very end of the session, there was a constant bitter verbal struggle whether on the floor, in budget committee, or in other committees. Ranged against the government in the House of Representatives were Inukai Ki, Hatoyama Ichirō, Uchida Shinya, Maeda Yonezō, Uehara Etsujirō, and Yamazaki Tatsunosuke; and in the House of Peers the opposition included Shimizu Koichirō, Ikeda Nagayasu, Inouye Seijun, Hanai Takuzo, Uzawa Fusaaki, Ishiwata Toshikazu, Sakamoto Shuntoku, and Ichijō Sanetake.[40] If one were to study in detail the course of these discussions the main points of the critics would be the following:[41]

    1. When the government decided on the instructions to be dispatched to Wakatsuki, it disregarded the views of the Naval General Staff and accepted the American proposals.

[39] [Compare this "position" devised by these "appropriate officials" with what Harada has earlier recorded as Professor Minobe's advice on the matter (see pp. 113-15).]

[40] [These six members of the lower House were all prominent leaders in the opposition party, the Seiyūkai: Inukai, its new president; Hatoyama, chief cabinet secretary under the Tanaka government (and in post-World War II Japan the leading contender with and eventual successor of Yoshida Shigeru for conservative leadership); Maeda, a party counsellor (*komon*), head of Tanaka's Legislative Affairs Bureau, was later to be a minister in the Inukai cabinet; Uchida, a quondam secretary to Katō Kōmei but now a Seiyūkai partisan (below, chap. iv, n. 7); Uehara, a member of the party's Standing Committee, had been a parliamentary councillor on foreign affairs under Tanaka; Yamazaki, a member of the party's Executive Committee, like Maeda and Uchida, was later to become a cabinet minister.

[Of the Peers, Prince Ichijō, Baron Inoue and Baron Sakamoto were retired naval officers; some, like Uzawa (former president of Meiji University), were directly affiliated with the Seiyūkai despite the fact that party groupings in the House of Peers were unique to that body and did not mirror those of the lower House (above, n. 5). On Uzawa, see below, chap. ix, n. 13.]

[41] [Harada is not, of course, attempting to give a full summary of the Diet session; but to list the individuals and questions most sharply critical of the government. Takeuchi, pp. 305-9, gives a more succinct précis from the official record, *Kampō gōgai*.]

According to the Naval General Staff, which is wholly responsible for the disposition of forces for national defense, the security of national defense cannot be devised by any means in terms allowed by this proposal. Yet Prime Minister Hamaguchi and Foreign Minister Shidehara are aligned in asserting that the national defense can be secured. Is this so? (Inukai's interpellation from the floor in the House of Representatives, April 25.)

2. If the minimum established by the Naval General Staff is set aside and another standard is said to provide a secure national defense, there would seem to be two "minimum standards." But in the forty-fifth session of the Diet, did not Railways Minister Egi assert there could not be two minimum standards? (Uchida's interpellation of April 27 from the floor of the House of Representatives.)

3. Are the items on the power of supreme command and on the power of administration, under Articles XI and XII of the Constitution, within the spheres on which Ministers of State are responsibly to give advice? (Maeda's interpellation at the House of Representatives Budget Committee meeting of April 30.)

4. Since the rupture which has occurred between the Cabinet and the Naval General Staff cannot be resolved by legal argument, a political solution is essential for the future political fate of the nation. How does the Prime Minister propose to deal with this situation? (Shimizu's interpellation from the floor of the House of Peers, May 6.)

5. Because scholars may differ in interpreting the Constitution is no reason why a clear response cannot be made; and it is inexplicable in a constitutional politician. (Baron Ikeda from the floor of the House of Peers, May 7.)

6. Does the Prime Minister possess the qualifications of a Navy Minister, so as to serve as Navy Minister pro tempore? (Hanai at the Peers Budget Committee Meeting, May 9.)

7. Do you hold the interpretation that the responsibility for proffering advice with respect to the power of supreme command is found elsewhere than in Article LV of the Constitution? Report has it that you will give no reply respecting the supreme command. Then let me phrase it another way: Do the Ministers of State assert that they do possess responsibility for advising on national defense? (Hanai, Peers Budget Committee, May 9.)

8. If the power of supreme command is jointly exercised through the Navy Ministry and the Naval General Staff conferring together, may the Ministry on its own authority proceed to change what has been set by the General Staff as the minimum standards for national defense? (Prince Ichijō's interpellation in the House of Peers' Budget Committee, May 11.)

In the face of all these questions, Prime Minister Hamaguchi proceeded in line with his original resolution to avoid, as far as possible, making any replies; for since he considered that the course of the Diet debate might have important repercussions later, especially in the Privy Council, he kept sedulously aloof from verbal riposte. Once one enters upon a constitutional argument, one is always pressed, in practice, to discuss a particular constitutional interpretation, and one must not only limit responses but also dodge arguments.

On the thirteenth, the very last day of the session before the full House of Peers, the Prime Minister answered both Shimizu and Hanai and took pains to change his earlier statement from: "The views of the Naval General Staff were taken into consideration" to "The views of military men, including the Naval General Staff were heard; and the Government, which includes both the War and Navy Ministers made its decision." Thus, at long last, the Government took a stand on the matter of the correlation between Article XI and Article XII involving a constitutional interpretation which it had approached with the utmost caution. That is, the Prime Minister's statement had clearly implied official responsibility for the deployment of forces as well as for military organization and administration; but the reason for not making this absolutely apparent was, as Dr. Hanai had clearly explained in the Diet on the thirteenth, the Government had done no more than be attentive to the delicacy of relations with certain elements. These certain elements, of course, are the military services, and this question will be argued again and again, when Navy Minister Takarabe returns and on numerous other occasions as well, so that it is like a canker plaguing the Government.

CHAPTER III

From Takarabe's Return
to Katō's Resignation

*Takarabe's Return to Japan—His Deter-
mination—The Question of the Vice
Minister of Navy—Admiral Okada's Views.*

[Dictated May 22, 1930]

When Takarabe finally returned to Tokyo on the morning of May 19, I went to the Tokyo station to greet him. It was quite a warm welcome that he received. Among those thronging to meet him, many, of course, had come on instruction from the political parties; and yet, it was a much more rousing homecoming than I had expected to witness.[1] I hope that Wakatsuki's homecoming may be as auspicious.

---

[1] [Not all who "greeted" Takarabe were applauding his achievements. The day before, at the Shimonoseki railway station as Takarabe had just returned to Japan from Korea, a young man stepped forward to present him with a dagger and a memorial commending suicide as the most suitable apology he could make for having placed the national defense in jeopardy. And despite precautionary arrests to prevent a similar or more violent demonstration in Tokyo, at the Tokyo station members of the Aikoku Kinrōtō (Patriotic Workers Party), a recently organized extremely chauvinist group distributed handbills denouncing the Navy Minister as a traitor. Perhaps Harada failed to note such episodes because the contemporary press reported them. Cf. Takeuchi, *War and Diplomacy in the Japanese Empire*, p. 313, n. 86; Yanaga, *Japan Since Perry*, p. 496; Young, *Imperial Japan, 1926-1938* [New York: William Morrow and Co., 1938], p. 54.

[The Aikoku Kinrōtō was not actually a political party in the parliamentary sense but one of the proliferating "murder and hokum" groups through which professional patrioteers—in this case one Amano Tatsuo, a Tokyo lawyer and quondam student of the ultra-conservative legalist Uesugi Shinkichi—recruited simpletons and gangsters for deeds of political terrorism and blackmail. Amano was later to confess to a leading role in the extraordinary

My heart was full, for I recalled from my student days the lonely impression of meeting Komura[2] when he returned to Shinagawa from the splendid achievement of concluding the Portsmouth Treaty—the Treaty responsible for the international position which Japan has reached today. Then there was widespread dissatisfaction with Komura; but as historians have more recently discussed that Treaty's significance, it is generally accepted as marking a crucial turn into the diplomatic destiny of Japan. Had this been realized by the people at the time, their reaction might have been different and the great diplomat's return would not have gone unmarked.

Takarabe

Immediately upon his return, Takarabe went to the Prime Minister's residence. About three o'clock, before he was to meet with the Chief of the Naval General Staff, I called on him at the Navy Minister's official residence. He asked about the illness which had befallen the Prince while he had been away and spoke of the gratitude with which all of our countrymen have received the news of the Prince's recovery. Then he had many things to ask about Prince Saionji's attitude in connection with the Naval Conference. I said:

"The Prince sends this message, 'I want to express my deep appreciation and gratitude for the untiring efforts Your Excellency has made to bring about this naval agreement. Especially so, because in distinction from the other chief delegate, Your Excellency was in a sense the representative of the military services. Though this placed you in a most difficult position, the ultimate result is certainly one to bring utmost satisfaction to our people.'

"From the depths of his heart," I added, "he is most pleased that you carried the agreement through to signature of the treaty."

"It would take too long," he said, "if I were to review the whole situation now. Of course, when there were differences of opinion, we argued. But it was argument among gentlemen. No one in our delegation behaved disgracefully and nothing was done to mar our prestige. I cannot but greatly admire the skill which our senior delegate, Wakatsuki, displayed. My own first efforts, now that I've returned, must be directed at bringing about the Imperial ratification of the entire agreement we formulated. And secondly,

plot known as the "*Shimpeitai* (God Sent Troops) Affair" which the police nipped in the bud in July, 1933. Cf. Storry, *The Double Patriots*; Yanaga, *Japan Since Perry*, pp. 505-6; Byas, *Government by Assassination*, pp. 213-25.]

[2] Marquis Komura Toshitarō (1855-1911), former Foreign Minister, Japanese plenipotentiary at the Portsmouth Conference [concluding the Russo-Japanese War in 1905].

I want to try to patch up the differences within the Navy. At the same time, since there seems to be something of a misunderstanding among the Prime Minister, the Foreign Minister, and the Naval Staff, it is perhaps my most important duty to try to dispel their mistrust.

"Please convey my best wishes to the Prince."

Since I was planning to go down to Okitsu that evening, I wanted first to have chats with both the Prime Minister and Admiral Okada. When I saw Hamaguchi he told me:

"I've just had lunch and a leisurely talk with Takarabe on a number of things. What splendid resolution he has! Speaking of his relations with the Chief of the Naval General Staff, he said, 'Since Katō and I are old friends of long standing, I'd like to try to explain the situation to him. I'm quite confident I can. Please leave it to me.' "

When I inquired what is likely to be done on the matter of the Vice Minister of Navy, he said, further: "Yamanashi has been most energetic and industrious and of great assistance to me. For this I'm very grateful. His recent proposal to resign may have been made to force a re-examination of the Vice Chief of the Naval General Staff and ultimately to bring about the Chief of Staff's resignation. He seems quite worn out; perhaps he should take a leave of absence."[3]

I then reached Admiral Okada by telephone. "Please wait two or three days," he suggested, "Instead of coming to see me now, it would be better if you waited a few days." Thus I phoned to Okitsu and postponed my next visit. Since there seemed to be no urgency on the Prince's part, I decided to wait till the evening of the twenty-second before leaving for Okitsu.

On the twenty-first I called on the Navy Minister at his official residence to inquire into recent developments. Takarabe said,

"I've tried several approaches in talking with the Chief of the Naval General Staff. He seems clearly to understand that regarding numerical military strength—as far as concerns disarmament—or the whole course taken up to the completion of the treaty, I could only do my best. He takes no exception on this point. But he is quite determined in his views on the prerogative of the supreme command; especially on what he regards as the very serious dis-

---

[3] [In his message sent by Captain Koga to Takarabe while the latter was en route back to Japan, Yamanashi had indicated his intention to request relief from his duties as Vice Minister on grounds of ill health. Aoki, *Taiheiyō sensō zenshi*, I, 30.]

regard of the Naval General Staff and the interference *(kampan)* with the prerogative of the supreme command. This, he believes, is a matter of grave concern. I think it is quite probable that he is incited to this view by Hiranuma and his clique in the Privy Council. To have this made the issue of political controversy is indeed troublesome. Because this is not a good development, just now I am being very cautious. But if it eventually comes to a quarrel, I intend to act with determination. Since it would have been necessary to pound the nails in the right places beforehand, I am cognizant of this now and am doing something about it."

That same evening I called on Admiral Okada to inquire about developments. "On other topics Katō may be all right," he said, "but he is impervious to argument on this matter of the prerogative of the supreme command. It seems quite likely that he may have to resign. First of all, if one considers what is actually meant by his assertion that the prerogative of the supreme command has been contemned and that his views as Chief of the Naval General Staff have been disregarded, it would seem to mean in short that unless his views are accepted, there can be no agreement on national defense. It follows from this, then, that no one else can exercise plenipotentiary powers. But the Navy as a whole is represented by the Navy Minister as a Minister of State [member of the Cabinet] and the Naval General Staff is included within the entity which he thus represents and a controversy between the Staff and the Navy Minister cannot become a direct controversy between the Staff and the Government. It would be a sad thing, indeed, if we could enter no international treaties which the Chief of the Naval General Staff opposes. With this argument about a "violation of the supreme command prerogative" he is simply being used by those intriguers who want to prevent ratification of the treaty. This disturbs me so much that I think it may be best for Katō to resign as Chief of the Naval General Staff.[4] Yet I think I should try once again to dissuade him. There are those who would urge me to ask that a meeting of the Supreme War Council be convened to make it known that the national defense is not secure, in fact, is in great jeopardy. But it is quite impossible for me to say any such thing. Of course the Navy has in no sense discarded the Three Great Principles it sought to maintain at the London Conference. The present agreement may be unsatisfactory; but since

---

[4] [Okada's diary records that as early as April 2 Katō, in indignation over the government's instructions, had raised with him the question of resigning as Chief of the Naval General Staff (Okada, *Kaikōroku*, pp. 56f).]

it has been concluded there is nothing to do under the circumstances but make the best of it. At any rate, Vice-Minister Yamanashi has been working so assiduously and with such fatiguing effect that this is perhaps the time for him to retire. Vice Admiral Kobayashi, for example, might take over in his stead as Vice Minister of Navy.

"I'd like to have another day to go over this matter both with Katō and with Takarabe."

I returned home that evening to receive various reports. It seems that Katō, who has been strangely quiet while Suetsugu has been on leave, is intractable again now that Suetsugu is back. In the last analysis, as Katō is controlled by Suetsugu, so, too, behind Suetsugu one can discern Hiranuma and his group in the Privy Council. The matter seems to have endless ramifications, but I think Katō's resignation may bring it to an end.

> *A Talk with Mori—All Sorts of Rumors—*
> *The Attitudes of Admiral Prince Fushimi*
> *and of Fleet Admiral Tōgō—Opposition of*
> *the Kuroshio-Kai to Takarabe—Prince*
> *Saionji's Policy vis-à-vis the Privy*
> *Council.*

A call came for me from Mori,[5] the Chief Secretary of the Seiyūkai. He said, "I have something to discuss with you; where can I see you later this evening?" So preferring not to make it too late, I stopped by at the Seiyūkai headquarters where he had this to say:

---

[5] Mori Kaku (or Tsutomu) [(1883-1932)], member of the House of Representatives, Chief Secretary of the Seiyūkai. [Mori was closely connected with rightist and military leaders. As Parliamentary Vice Minister of Foreign Affairs under the preceding cabinet he was deeply involved in expansionist schemes in China. Later, as Chief Cabinet Secretary to the Seiyūkai cabinet of Inukai, he is reported to have frustrated Inukai's attempts, following the Army's invasion of Manchuria, to reach a viable agreement with the Chinese government. Cf. Takehiko Yoshihashi, *Conspiracy at Mukden* (New Haven: Yale University Press, 1963), *passim;* Iwasaki Sakae, "Inukai misshi: Kayano Chōchi no nisshi (The Diary of Kayano Chōchi, Inukai's secret emissary)," *Chūō Kōron,* No. 690 (August, 1946), 82-88.

[Seventeen years earlier, at the time of the Kuomintang "July Revolution" against Yuan Shih-k'ai, Mori, then a Mitsui executive and an official of the recently formed China Industrial Company, had attempted to provide Sun Yat-sen with financial and military support in return for the cession of Manchuria. Sun agreed, but the plan was blocked by Makino, the present Lord Keeper of the Privy Seal who was then the Foreign Minister. Cf. Jansen, *The Japanese and Sun Yat-sen,* p. 165f.]

"There's an extraordinary story going around. Perhaps you've heard it. I'd like to know the straight of it. It's said that when the Chief of the Naval General Staff planned to make a direct appeal to the throne before the Prime Minister reported on his instructions, the Emperor's military Aide-de-Camp, General Nara Takeji, conferred with the Grand Chamberlain, who talked with the Lord Keeper of the Privy Seal. The Lord Keeper, in turn, called on Harada to have him seek the *genrō*'s views; but while this was being undertaken he was persuaded by the Prime Minister to delay this consultative procedure until after the Prime Minister's instruction proposal had been submitted to the throne. In other words, the direct appeal, which should have preceded the Prime Minister's proposals, was deliberately shunted aside. That is, the Grand Chamberlain and the Lord Keeper quite improperly blocked the direct appeal. What do you know about this?"

"I know nothing whatsoever," I said. "In the first place, a direct appeal is made directly through the Imperial military Aide-de-Camp. Neither the Grand Chamberlain nor the Lord Keeper has anything to do with it. Furthermore I had no such request from the Lord Keeper. To say so is pure fabrication. While I've heard it was because of His Majesty's own preference that a direct appeal not be made, still it is not for me to speak of this for I know nothing of the matter."[6]

So Mori continued: "It is, in fact, being said that His Majesty did convey a message to the Chief of the Naval General Staff. It seemed to me very strange if it had happened in this way. At any rate, I wanted to see you today to inquire into this point."

When I saw Admiral Okada, I gave him the gist of this con-

Mori

---

[6] [It has already been suggested that Harada's various references to Katō's audience on April 2 are either ill-informed or somewhat less than candid (p. 108, n. 3). Note that here, confronted with Mori's story, he says that *as a matter of normal procedure* it is the Aide-de-camp who attends upon the Emperor when he receives his chiefs of staff. He avoids saying this was so on April 2. He denies that the Lord Keeper made the specific request that Mori mentions. But a careful reader of this diary will note that Harada has already recorded as fact that on Friday, March 28, he had talked with the Foreign Minister and with the Prime Minister twice, and had gone to the Palace there talking with the Imperial Household Minister and the Grand Chamberlain; that on Saturday he had made a quick trip to Okitsu; that on Sunday he was back in the capital again and again talked with the Grand Chamberlain; and that on Monday, March 31 (the very day when Katō was deflected from scheduling the audience when he first asked for one), Harada was again at the Palace for a talk with the Lord Privy Seal himself. Had the Seiyūkai made up the story from having kept a watch on Harada's comings and goings? Or had Mori's story more nearly hit the mark than Harada could politically admit?]

versation with Mori; and I told him that while there seemed to be some maneuvering in Privy Council circles, largely on the matter of the alleged violation of the power of the supreme command, I could not envisage in what concrete form it might be expressed.

[Dictated May 26, 1930]

Admiral Okada said, "What a strange mind Katō has! He seems to believe whatever he is told—that the present government is bad because it is leftist, and the like.[7] Since he seems to be so completely ruled by impulse and emotions, I think it would be best for Katō to resign. Still because there are many among the young officers who nearly idolize Katō,[8] and because anti-Takarabe sentiment is so strong among some reserve groups,[9] I'm concerned lest they may be driven to some foolish action in connection with Katō's resignation which could be very harmful to him. If I want to avoid harm to the Navy, I also want no harm for Katō, the Chief of Staff. What can we think of that will have the smallest possible repercussion? That is our real problem!"

Furthermore, because Admiral Prince Fushimi and Fleet Admiral Tōgō seem to be in sympathy with Katō's views, it would be difficult to let matters take their own course. Since he emphasized once again the need to face these facts, it seemed probable that Admiral Okada and Vice Admiral Sakonshi[10] should call on these dignitaries again and redouble their efforts at persuasion.

Later when I met Admiral Takarabe again, he said:

"Katō, in discussing the suicide of Lieutenant Commander Kusakari, remarked 'What a truly fine man he was—a martyr to

---

[7] [Okada's diary for May 7 includes a report of Katō's making this charge against the Cabinet in an effort to persuade Okada that the Supreme War Council should be called forthwith. Okada rejected the notion of taking any action that would thus undermine the yet absent Takarabe. "Whatever one may think of the Cabinet as such, there's no real cause for concern if the Navy Minister is sound. Furthermore a man in your position cannot go around calling the present cabinet leftist! Think of the repercussions it would have in the public mind!" See Okada, p. 61.]

[8] [Okada was aware of his own current unpopularity among certain of the Navy's younger officers, some of whom at Yokosuka had recently contemptuously tossed a plaque bearing his autograph into the pond of a Navy-patronized restaurant. See Okada, p. 52.]

[9] [Aoki publishes an epitome of such views expressed at a meeting of admirals at the Suikōsha on the evening of May 20 (Aoki, I, 37f).]

[10] Vice Admiral Sakonshi Masazō [(b. 1879)], member of the Naval General Staff, a technical adviser to the London conference delegation. [He was subsequently to become Vice Minister of Navy and Chief of the Naval General Staff. Upon his retirement in 1934, he became president of the North Sakhalin Oil Company.]

disarmament!' And to this I rejoined, 'It may be all right for you to speak to me like this. But to talk in the same vein to others, especially outsiders, can only call your own integrity into question. You must be more careful.' He was quite angry at this advice." Actually Kusakari had been a man of pronounced instability and subject to periodic breakdowns.[11]

When I called on Admiral Okada again, he remarked:

"There are too many of these journalists and newsmen about. They're saying the government has put plainclothesmen to watch Katō, Suetsugu, and Tōgō, to keep tabs on the comings and goings of their visitors and pry into their movements and activities. This sort of rumor and report can only serve to heighten the opposition of these three men and their antipathy to the government."

This report so disturbed me that I discreetly phoned the Chief of the Metropolitan Police[12] to learn the truth of the matter. When he assured me that such a story had absolutely no basis in fact, I immediately conveyed this assurance to Admiral Okada. Here is another example of the underhand methods by which certain groups are stimulating these men's antagonism to the government. In fact the newsmen currently frequenting the Navy—members of the Kuroshio-kai—are entirely sympathetic to the Chief of the Naval General Staff.[13] In my own calls at the Navy Minister's office they try to corner me with various questions. I shrug off their questions with "I know nothing of that." But from their line of questioning it is apparent that anti-Takarabe sentiment has mounted considerably.

Some of them wanted at least a meeting of the Supreme War Councillors and were trying to pressure Admiral Okada into asserting that the national defense has become insecure.

---

[11] Lieutenant Commander Kusakari Eiji [(1881-1930)], assigned to duty with the Naval General Staff. [Kusakari had attended the London Conference as a member of the technical staff. He was found to have committed suicide in a railway car at the Numazu station, May 20, 1930. Right-wing groups claimed he had died in protest over the treaty. Okada explained the suicide as Harada does (Okada, p. 70.]

[12] Maruyama Tsurukichi [(b. 1883), police expert who had served in various posts in the Home Ministry and the Chōsen (Korea) administration, had been a member of the Japanese delegation at the Geneva Conference, 1927, and served as Chief of the Metropolitan Police Board under the Hamaguchi cabinet].

[13] [The Kuroshio-kai (Japan [*lit.* Black] Current Society), a club of journalists assigned to the Navy Ministry, is mentioned in Okada's diary at an earlier point, under date of April 2:

["Late in the morning Suetsugu sought to have the Kuroshio-kai publish some quite improper documents, but those in the Navy Ministry who knew of this in advance toned them down, as I later learned" (pp. 56-57).]

"I can't indulge in such a foolish move," Okada said. "As far as the Navy is concerned, there has been no discarding of the Three Great Principles. But since the Treaty has been decided upon, the national defense must be made secure within its framework. What could not be obtained in one way must be accomplished in some other fashion. In no sense is it possible for the Naval General Staff to be independent of the government. In the first place it must deal with the government through the Navy Minister; and in fact it may have no direct dealings or negotiations with outsiders. But since the Navy Minister seems to be conducting himself with prudence and resolution, there should be no need for worry."

I put it to both the Navy Minister and to Admiral Okada: "If the Chief of the Naval General Staff has decided to resign, wouldn't it be best in view of the repercussions to bring it about as soon as possible rather than to let it drag out for some time? If it is prolonged there may be altogether too much slanderous and foolish questioning. To bring it about simply will be the best all around."[14]

They seemed to feel, however, that too much haste would also be harmful.

On May 23 I went again to Okitsu to report on the general situation, placing before the Prince what I had learned from both the Prime Minister and Admiral Okada. I pointed out: "The right man has been found to succeed Katō. Furthermore, the Vice Minister of Navy, now in poor health, is to be replaced because he must bear responsibility for the confusion during the absence of the Navy Minister. Yet this must be most carefully thought out, for the Vice Minister's wish to resign is also designed to confront and confound the Vice Chief of the Naval General Staff who is really responsible for this confusion."

The Prince remarked, "Isn't it likely that the Navy men, if they lend their efforts to it, can settle this matter and that they should take a new stance vis-à-vis the Privy Council? And yet, as far as concerns the Privy Council, both the Prime Minister and the Foreign Minister ought to be thoroughly informed; and they need certainly to elicit the counsel of constitutional scholars. It wouldn't

---

[14] [Though Harada nowhere mentions the matter directly, this comment appears to show he knew that Katō had given to Takarabe on May 19, the very day the Navy Minister returned to Tokyo, a formal petition to the Throne resigning from his post as chief of staff. Correctly, such a resignation like all other personnel changes were presented to the Emperor by the Navy Minister. Takarabe cannily refused to have his own position forced by Katō and he pigeonholed the petition. The text of the document is given in Aoki, I, 33-35.]

surprise me if there were some in the Privy Council who are trying to nose out some constitutional question. The government ought to be mindful on this point."

I told him I would remind both the Prime Minister and the Foreign Minister to be cautious about this when I returned to Tokyo.[15]

> *Position of the Imperial House—Rumors from Many Quarters—The Facts about the Chief of the Naval General Staff's Tacit Consent—The Luncheon Meeting of the Supreme War Councillors—The Grand Chamberlain's Visit to Prince Saionji— The Report of the Chief of the Information Office.*

[Dictated June 2, 1930]

Since the Emperor was to be at Shizuoka after May 28 and because I would have to stay in Okitsu for three or four days, I wanted to see the Navy Minister, the Prime Minister, and also Admiral Okada by the twenty-seventh. Admiral Okada, however, was ill abed with a cold so that I was unable to see him. I did see the Navy Minister just after he had gone to the Palace on the twenty-fifth and had been received privately by the Emperor to make his first report on his mission since returning to Japan.

"I've just come from a private audience with His Majesty," he said, "and I was quite overcome with awe that he should take the trouble to thank me, in a most deliberate way, for the work that I had undertaken. Some Navy men, even Fleet Admiral Tōgō and Admiral Prince Fushimi, are still indulging in all sorts of strident comments. This is because Katō has been seeing them almost daily and insistently implanting his own ideas. This I find quite annoying. While it may all work out well in the end, I am disturbed that Prince Saionji and his circle do not seem to be giving this consideration. It can be extremely troublesome for a member of the Imperial family, after achieving a high position of responsibility, to engage

---

[15] [At this point Harada incorporated the full text of an editorial from the newspaper, the *Tokyo Asahi*, of May 25, 1930, which argued at length that if this treaty question had come to involve any violations of the Constitution, it was the naval clique which sought to usurp the proper function of the Cabinet by intervening and seeking to override the proper treaty-making authority of the Emperor acting on the advice of the Ministers of State. In general, in this period, the *Asahi* was stalwart in support of the Hamaguchi cabinet.]

in such arguments and disputes. Hence it seems to me it would be much better for members of the Imperial family to hold only honorary positions so as not to be involved directly in matters of controversy. I am deeply anxious lest some grave difficulties may result in the future if the Imperial family becomes involved in controversy."

He went on to say, "I think the Supreme War Councillors might be brought together unofficially, say for a luncheon meeting at which I might deal with this matter of the Chief and Vice Chief of the Naval General Staff. It can probably be handled quite smoothly and expeditiously."

Just after this, on the evening of the twenty-seventh, the Foreign Minister entertained the members of the House of Peers who had been of help to him at the Yamaguchi; and I was invited too. Afterward, as we had pre-arranged it, I called on the Prime Minister about nine o'clock and talked with him until after ten.

"As Navy Minister Takarabe, who was here just before you, has suggested, I think an informal session of the Supreme War Council should be held soon. I'd rather not have the matter of the supreme command prerogative touched on more deeply than it was in the Diet; and I'd like to have it stipulated that overall military strength be proposed by joint undertaking of the Chief of the Naval General Staff and the Navy Minister. It is being strongly urged, in domestic circles, as a fact which persons such as I must accept, that both Admiral Okada and the Vice Minister and the present Chief of Staff are in essential agreement. The Chief of Staff's assent seems to have run along such lines as these: 'Considering the general situation I agree. On the matter of operations I think there's cause for concern. But though I can't agree on manpower and operations, yet in the general situation inevitably I must assent within the determined sphere.'"

When I took leave of the Prime Minister he asked that his greetings be conveyed to the Prince.

On the preceding day several newspapers had boldly played up a story of the questioning of War Minister Ugaki by Baron Ikeda of the House of Peers on the matter of the supreme command prerogative. Ikeda is reported to have said, "Because of his illness War Minister Ugaki is quite uninformed, but he told me he cannot assent to this treaty if, as a matter of fact, the Chief of the Naval General Staff has not approved of it." The Cabinet ascertained that there was nothing to this story but propaganda, yet it clearly had the endorsement of the Vice Minister of War.

Egi, the Railways Minister, had a chat with me. "This is a secret matter," he said, "but just the other day I had a call from Tomii.[16] 'The recent arrogance of the military cliques,' he said to me, 'is quite disturbing. Even though the government is very careful, there are those in the Privy Council given to violent talk. Thus, if constitutional government is to be maintained, you must exercise utmost vigilance. The government must at all costs strengthen the bulwarks of its position.' He was considerably relieved when I told him before his departure that that was just what the government is intending to do.

"Please mention this only to Prince Saionji for I am anxious that it not leak out to others."

Some four or five days previously, venerable Okazaki Kunisuke[17] called at my house. "This disarmament question is getting to be another case like that of Chang Tso-lin," he said. "Don't let it topple the cabinet." And he went on to comment on the sad state of the financial world and to criticize the present cabinet's policies before he took his departure. It was after this that Ichinomiya[18] dropped by late one evening. "According to what I hear," he said, "the Naval General Staff seems to have gone on a general strike. Is this really the case?" Since there would probably be no limit if I were to try to answer all such variously originated and ill-founded stories, I listened but made no reply. Shortly afterward, when I raised this latter question with Vice Admiral Nomura he said, "It doesn't seem so; but it might happen."

Afterward I met with Vice Admiral Kobayashi. "There's something I've wanted to discuss with you for some time," he said. "At the time when the Chief of the Naval General Staff met with all of us at the Navy Minister's official residence to discuss the instructions, both the first proposal and that which had come from London were considered. The General Staff urged, 'Let's discard the first proposal. Let us then accept, since it is inevitable under the circumstances, the second proposal with three conditions appended.' This was accepted. When this was done neither the Chief of the Naval General Staff nor anyone else spoke to interpose

---

[16] Dr. Tomii Masaaki, Member of the Privy Council. [See below, p. 211.]

[17] Okazaki Kunisuke [(1854-1936)], a member of the House of Representatives, counsellor to the Seiyūkai, former Agriculture Minister [in the first Katō cabinet, 1924-25].

[18] Ichinomiya Fusajirō, member of the House of Representatives, parliamentary councillor of the Home Ministry (Minseitō). [Ichinomiya, just returned from a brief trip to China in the suite of Prince Konoe (above, chap. ii, n. 38), sought from Harada a briefing on political developments during his absence.]

any objection. Had there been any opposition, why didn't it come out then? Having remained silent then, how can they raise objection later? As soon as he returned Navy Minister Takarabe ought to have talked with the Chief of Staff. Since they didn't speak of it, the whole matter has become obscured. How would it be if we had Matsuda[19] raise this question with Katō since they are close friends?"

When I raised this question with the Prime Minister, he said, "Let's not meddle with this when the Navy Minister has just returned. Moreover, Katō is saying, 'That's the only time I passed this over in silence. I never assented or agreed to it.' " Thus despite Kobayashi's suggestion, after this chat with the Prime Minister, I let the matter pass without speaking to Matsuda.

I went to Okitsu and saw the Prince early on the morning of the twenty-eighth. After I had made a full report, the Prince said, "It's best that this whole business be concluded as soon as possible."

When I had occasion to telephone from Okitsu to the Foreign Office, Hotta, Chief of the European-American Bureau, told me, "A meeting of the Fleet Admiral and the Supreme War Councillors,[20] called by the Navy Minister, seems to have ended just thirty or forty minutes ago, but I don't yet know what is the upshot of it. . . ." Yes, indeed, I said to myself, this must be the luncheon meeting suggested the other day. When I checked on this by later phoning Admiral Okada, he told me, "The talk at this meeting ended quite without incident. Everything seems to be going according to plan."

Since Wakatsuki had earlier suggested that Saitō[21] the In-

---

[19] Matsuda Genji, Minister of Overseas Affairs; Minseitō, Member of the House of Representatives.

[20] [An unofficial meeting of the naval members of the Supreme War Council, called by Takarabe May 29, met at the Navy Minister's residence, to establish a formula for agreement between the government (i.e. the Navy Ministry) and the staff in determining the naval strength of the state. There was agreement on the necessity for "complete understanding" between the Navy Minister and the Chief of Staff, and on the desirability of embodying the understanding in a written memorandum. But when it came to drafting an explicit statement, Katō refused to sign that drafted by the Navy Ministry and Takarabe withheld his signature for that drafted by Katō. Both Okada and Takarabe now came to the decision that Katō should be replaced (Aoki, I, 42-48; Takeuchi, pp. 314-15).]

[21] [Saitō Hiroshi (1886-1939) had been assigned by Shidehara from the Foreign Office staff to be Wakatsuki's chief aide at London. Later he became ambassador at The Hague, and in Washington where, having had earlier experience as Consul-General in New York, he had unusual popularity for a Japanese. Following his death at his post in the United States, his body was returned to Japan with due honors aboard a U.S. naval vessel. See above, ch. i, n. 33; and Shidehara, p. 65.]

formation Bureau Chief, should see Prince Saionji upon his return to Japan to report on the London situation, it was decided to have him meet the Prince; and I made it a point to phone him to come to Okitsu immediately.

About seven-thirty on the evening of the twenty-eighth, Grand Chamberlain Suzuki, who had come to Shizuoka in attendance upon the Emperor, came to Okitsu to call on the Prince at the Emperor's request and to present a gift of fruit and cakes from His Majesty. They spent more than an hour together discussing thoroughly all the recent talk in court circles on disarmament. The Prince was highly pleased, and commented, "Suzuki, himself, has worked well on this and seems to have an excellent comprehension of the matter."

Then he went on to say, "I tell you this for yourself alone, for I'd be concerned if you spoke of it to others—even to Konoe. Before Takarabe departed for London, I had a message from him that he wanted an Imperial Conference to be called to determine Japan's position and to unite public opinion behind it.[22] At that time he said he came with this suggestion in fact also approved by the Grand Chamberlain. But I told him, 'Do nothing of the kind. In diplomacy one does not burn his bridges or show his hand. And that's what you would inevitably be doing, is it not? Please also tell the Lord Keeper of the Privy Seal, Makino, as strongly as possible that Saionji is absolutely opposed.' Thus they finally dropped the idea because of my opposition. I was very much disturbed then that Suzuki had agreed to any such thing. Now he has come to me gratefully to say: 'It was because of your objection that no Imperial Conference was held then. And when I think back on it today I realize it might have invited the most unfortunate results. It was thanks to you that I did the right thing then.' And he indeed now seems to comprehend the situation much better. But that I should have been

---

[22] [An Imperial Conference *(gozen kaigi)*, or more properly a Conference in the Imperial Presence, was a device occasionally used to cut through the hydra-headed pluralism of the Japanese state in order to reach and record (and in this sense to impose) unanimity among the Emperor's advisers. A document prepared for the Tokyo Trials describes it thus broadly:

["Although no authority can be found in the Constitution, laws or ordinances for the Gozen Kaigi, or Conference before the Throne, it has existed as an instrument in the Japanese government for hundreds of years. It has continued to function as the organ for reconciling the conflicts arising from the division of authority into various spheres. As a body, it meets only under the gravest of conditions to determine matters of gravest policy. The membership [of the *gozen kaigi*] has varied both in size and in the nature of the membership" (IMTFE, I.P.S. Doc. No. 0004, "Decisions of Imperial Conferences, Liaison Conferences, Privy Council Meetings, etc. . . .," p. 1).]

concerned to the point of questioning Suzuki's judgment is not the sort of thing to be mentioned to others."

Then Saitō of the Information Bureau, arrived on the evening of the thirtieth. He spent more than an hour with the Prince the next morning reporting on the proceedings of the Naval Conference—much to the satisfaction of the Prince. Shortly after noon Saitō and I returned by train to Tokyo.

> *The Demand for an Imperial Conference—*
> *The Navy Minister's Illness—A Report*
> *on the Luncheon Meeting—The War*
> *Minister's Wish to Resign—Navy Person-*
> *nel Changes—The Prince's Message to*
> *the War Minister.*

When I talked with Admiral Okada on the morning of June 1, he said,

"I told you everything would go as planned, but actually the Naval General Staff and the Navy Ministry have come to be poles apart. Even though the Navy Minister may now be minded to replace the Chief of Staff, it may take some time to accomplish, and the outlook is that it will inevitably have wider repercussions in the Navy than had been expected."

Using a previously arranged telephone code, I called the Prince to inform him that the expected decision had been taken but that, according to Admiral Okada, it may take some days to accomplish and a certain amount of commotion cannot be avoided.

[Dictated June 9, 1930]

A number of people, subsequently, expressed the hope that an Imperial Conference be held on the naval treaty question,[23] and Admiral Yamamoto[24] appeared to be one of them. But Admiral

---

[23] [This "hope for an Imperial Conference" is a reminder that the use of a *gozen kaigi* in the Meiji and Taishō periods arose "chiefly out of the necessities of pre-war or wartime international diplomacy, and concerned matters lying within the overlapping spheres of competence of the supreme command and the civil government (Yale Candee Maxon, *Control of Japanese Foreign Policy* [Berkeley: University of California Press, 1957], p. 63). Butow epitomizes the early use of this device more critically and gives fuller account of its use later during the Pacific War (Butow, *Tojo*, pp. 169-77).]

[24] [This refers to Admiral Yamamoto Eisuke, Commander-in-Chief, First Fleet, and concurrently Commander-in-Chief, Combined Fleet, rather than to the older Satsuma leader, Yamamoto Gombei. Before Takarabe's return, Yamamoto had talked with Okada about the desirability of the Minister's resigna-

Okada opposed these suggestions, saying, "The only time for an Imperial Conference is when the Minister and the Chief of Staff agree; for if their views differ, how can His Majesty make a decision? Thus irresponsibly to seek the Emperor's judgment, vexing his mind in this way, is a matter about which we must be extremely careful."

Soon after this the Navy Minister became ill with an abdominal ailment and finally took to his bed. Since this kept him away from the activity of the Navy Ministry, it gave rise to a number of rumors, and newsmen indulged in speculation. It was even rumored that he had resigned. When I took occasion to pay him a sick call, he said:

"As far as I'm concerned my own attitude has come to be increasingly strengthened. At any event when I had an informal meeting of the Supreme War Councillors with twelve or thirteen admirals on the retired list present for informal discussion at my official residence, they all grasped the situation readily and were good enough to express a high regard for my labors in connection with the Naval conference.[25]

"For example, the atmosphere at this meeting was such that Admiral Tochinai was led to remark with some pleasure: 'A happy picture of harmony like this is never seen in the Army.' And Admiral Yamaya put it this way, 'There may be some concern that some Navy men, whether belonging to the Yōyōkai or to the Kai kōkai,[26] may proclaim strong views, but I think no great harm will result even if they are allowed to do so. Since it could become extremely troublesome if we tried to stop them, perhaps it's best to let them alone. As long as I understand the situation it's quite all right. Don't be bothered by their outbursts of opinion; for I give you my word....' "

In fact in the newspapers and elsewhere it was reported that

---

tion. The treaty issue, in all its aspects, contributed significantly toward bringing about that division in the naval officer corps between the so-called "fleet group" *(kantai-ha)* and the older bureaucratic group usually termed the "administrative group" *(gunsei-ha).*

[An Imperial Conference *(gozen-kaigi,* conference in the Imperial Presence) at this juncture would presumably maximize the position of Katō and his partisans, and would imply reaching a final irrevocable decision.]

[25] [This was a luncheon meeting at the Navy Ministry on June 1. Both Admiral Tochinai Sōjirō (1866-1932) and Admiral Yamaya Tanin (1866-1940) were former Commanders-in-Chief, Combined Fleet. Cf. Aoki, I, 46f.]

[26] The Yōyōkai and the Kaikōkai were both influential unofficial organizations of officers on the reserve lists. The Yōyōkai, a naval group; the Kaikōkai had both army and navy members.

very strong resolutions had been passed at a meeting of Naval Reservists. My own estimate was that though the gesture was strong, there was nothing really serious in it.[27] According to the Navy Minister's later word, he had met the Chief of the Naval General Staff, argued with him vehemently, and had worsted him—in fact so admonishing him for the flaws in his behavior up to this time that Katō even seemed to show some remorse.[28]

According to the newspapers it was just about this time that the Naval General Staff transmitted a colossal budget proposal to the Navy Minister. Thus it now became a public question whether the Navy Minister, in his dilemma, might not have to resign along with the Chief of the Naval General Staff. As luck would have it, since he was still bedridden, the Navy Minister did not attend the Cabinet meeting on the sixth. That afternoon, however, despite his illness, he did attend a meeting at his official residence to discuss urgent personnel matters. To my own thinking it seemed that however important the morning Cabinet meeting may have been, the Navy Minister gave it very little weight. But when it came to the important afternoon personnel meeting at the Ministry, he had to attend even though ill. Viewed from the outside, of course, for the Navy Minister to appear at his office while absenting himself from the Cabinet meeting might give rise to speculations that he had encountered such difficulties that he would resign.

Afterwards when I went to the Cabinet, I learned that Prime Minister Hamaguchi had sent Chief Secretary Suzuki[29] to call on the Navy Minister at his private residence, and when he reported finding the Navy Minister already out, even the Prime Minister was a little incredulous. He asked me to find out the truth of the matter. Since I thought it would be rather strange if I were to dash after the Navy Minister, I went to Admiral Okada's residence to ask about the situation. He told me, "Everything's going just as planned, in fact even better. There's no cause for worry." Certainly if there were something wrong Admiral Okada would have reason

---

[27] [At a meeting on June 2 the Yōyōkai adopted a resolution "strongly condemning the government's action at the time of issuing the final instructions, insisting that the consent of the naval general staff was absolutely essential and expressing grave apprehension as to the security of the national defense under the treaty. Although the resolution was given publicity in the press, it was not presented to any officials" (Takeuchi, p. 315, n. 91).]

[28] [Aoki publishes what purports to be the substance of an hour-long conference, presumably the one Harada here refers to, between these two officers on June 6 (Aoki, I, 49-53).]

[29] Suzuki Fujiya, Minseitō member of the House of Representatives, Chief Secretary of the Hamaguchi cabinet.

to know about it. If the Admiral's words are to be taken literally there is no need to worry. What makes the public restive is that they do not have the inside facts. Since it seemed foolish to be taken in by this public clamor, I hastened back to the Prime Minister's residence, saw Hamaguchi, and gave him this report. It seemed to relieve his mind.

That evening I was invited to the home of the Vice Minister of the Imperial Household, where Konoe, Okabe, and Kido were also present.[30] As we left later in the evening, Konoe walked along with me. He said;

"A little while ago Mizoguchi came to see me. 'Since War Minister Ugaki's illness is prolonged, he will sooner or later resign. I have orders from the Minister to go to Korea for preliminary talks with General Minami who will be his successor.' "[31]

Kido

---

[30] [These three men, close friends of Harada and near his own age, met more often and informally than this diary reflects. Viscount Okabe had been in the diplomatic service, in both the London and Washington embassies and in bureau posts in the Gaimusho before he entered the Imperial Household and became Count Makino's official secretary (see above, p. 114). He relinquished this post to Kido in October of the year (1930), and entered the House of Peers where Konoe was becoming one of the politically most active members despite his relative youth (see above, p. 90, n. 20).

[Marquis Kido Koichi (b. 1889), a grandson of the able Chōshū samurai, Kido Koin (Toshimichi), who with Ōkubo of Satsuma had been a key leader of the Meiji Restoration, thus became official aide to Makino, who was Ōkubo's son. Kido remained in this post of Chief Secretary to the Lord Privy Seal till 1937, a friend and confidant of Harada. From 1937 to 1939 Kido was successively Education Minister and Welfare Minister in the first Konoe and the Hiranuma cabinets; and his relations with Harada became less cordial. From 1940 till 1945 Kido was himself the Lord Privy Seal.

[Charged before the International Military Tribunal for the Far East as a major war criminal, Kido found his own diary used with telling effect by the prosecution. The Tokyo court sentenced Kido to life imprisonment, but he was released on parole in 1956. A translation of his diary between July 11, 1931, and December 9, 1945, is to be found in the LC Microfilm Collection as IMT 2.]

[31] [Hamaguchi had been careful, as the Introduction mentions, to include a number of influential peers within his administration. Count Mizoguchi Naoyoshi (b. 1878), who held the political office of Parliamentary Vice Minister of War, was descended from a *daimyō* family, elder brother of Count Maeda, nephew of Viscount Sawa, married to a daughter of Count Tokugawa. A member of the House of Peers since 1924, he was a leader of its Kenkyūkai. Note, however, that it is a series of "private" disclosures—from Mizoguchi to Konoe to Harada to Hamaguchi—that makes it possible for the Prime Minister to begin the complicated moves adumbrated here and in the next chapter to keep Ugaki from resigning. Note also that Harada is confident enough of his own role and of Saionji's undoubted interest to take the initiative (to see first Hamaguchi, then Ugaki) before relaying this news to the old Prince.

[Mizoguchi was himself a retired major general who had served as parliamentary councillor to the War Ministry under Ugaki in an earlier administration.

At that time it seemed to me that even if it was a resignation because of illness, it would not be an easy matter either for General Ugaki himself or in terms of the present political situation. I thought to verify as soon as possible whether the Prime Minister knew of this or not. I went to the Prime Minister's official residence the following day and found him completely ignorant of the matter. He was much concerned and said: "I'm very much disturbed lest General Ugaki should resign now. Think of some way to stave it off." Since, in the present case there was no way to be sure without seeing and questioning the War Minister, I called on him at the Army Hospital. He did not tell me definitely that he would resign, but he gave his comments this meaning: "The preparation of the budget is a most difficult task. In the present state of the financial world there are few accommodations that the Finance Minister can make. This disturbs me very much. When the opportune moment comes, I want to transfer my office to another. Since my illness may last three or four more months, I would like to resign." Even before this, some such talk had once before come to my ears, and I had been taken aback and become disturbed. At any event, the Prince himself has considered Ugaki's role as War Minister of great importance, and so this time I commented:

"There may be various occasions for resignation, but it will be very troublesome if you do not remain to see through at least the ratification of the naval treaty, whatever is done about other present problems."

I was on the point of leaving when an adjutant announced that the Navy Minister had come to pay him a sick call. I left the room but waited at the hospital till after the two ministers had met. Then I greeted the Navy Minister in the vestibule as he was leaving and went together with him by car to his official residence. Our conversation, begun in the car, continued for about an hour at his residence. He had this to say,

"Actually this meeting with Ugaki was quite by chance. I

[General Minami Jirō (1874-1955), then commanding general of the army in Korea. Minami did in fact later succeed Ugaki, becoming War Minister in the second Wakatsuki cabinet the following April, and he held this post when active aggression against Manchuria began in September, 1931. He was a Supreme War Councillor from 1931 to 1934; for the next two years he was concurrently Commander-in-Chief, Kwantung Army, Ambassador to Manchukuo, and Kwangtung Governor-General. Thereafter he was for six years Governor-General of Korea. From 1942 to 1945 he was a member of the Privy Council. Like Kido he was sentenced to life imprisonment by the Tokyo War Crimes court, but was subsequently released owing to ill health.]

had no special reason for seeing him. I was merely going to drop by to pay my respects in a courtesy call and to inquire about his health after my return home. But word had come that the War Minister wanted to see me. When I entered his hospital room he grasped my hands and said, 'What a lot of trouble you've gone to.'

"Now according to information from certain quarters people are trying to arrange a joint meeting of both Army and Navy Supreme War Councillors with the *gensui*.[32] I had felt this would be very impractical and had thought of speaking to the War Minister but it was he who opened the subject and remarked, 'This disarmament is a Navy matter and the Army has no share in or knowledge of it. A joint Army-Navy meeting would be quite superfluous. The Navy alone must handle it. I would myself flatly oppose a joint conference.'" Thus Takarabe gave me the gist of their conversation. Inasmuch as such a meeting is impossible unless the two ministers should be of like mind, the Navy Minister was encouraged by his colleague's views and put much feeling into his words when he said, "That reassures me considerably."

The Navy Minister went on to say, "On the tenth I intend to replace the Vice Minister and the Vice Chief of the Naval General Staff, and I shall make various transfers in personnel which ought to have been accomplished while I was away. Since, of course, I need the assent of the Chief of the Naval General Staff to remove Suetsugu as Vice Chief I have already talked with him. First he was much opposed to the idea, but I told him, 'The Navy to maintain its own independence cannot put personal matters first. If we put it off till there is a clamor among the political parties, it will appear that we were forced to it by the parties, and this would all the more reflect on the prestige of the Navy. Naturally what is best for the Navy must be done so that this cannot be said.' And so, seeming to accept it as inevitable he said, 'Well, all right.' Thus Suetsugu is to be removed. Everything is going very satisfactorily. I've just come from the Palace where this morning I reported to His Majesty on the personnel changes to be made on the tenth. It's bad enough to have all sorts of falsehoods bruited about, and if this is botched I'll be the prey of every vulgar ambitious politician. So—I've decided to make these changes first, and then—perhaps ultimately there should

---

[32] [The *gensui*, the generic term for the highest ranking Army and Navy officers—Field Marshals and Fleet Admirals—here refers to Fleet Admiral Tōgō.

[Captain Koga, Takarabe's chief secretary (above, p. 118 f.), in his record of the June 6 conference of Takarabe and Katō reports Katō as then asking for such a joint conference (Aoki, I, 51). Thus, Takarabe has assurance from this conversation of War Minister Ugaki's support against Katō and his partisans.]

be a change in the Chief of the Naval General Staff, too. But for the time being, let's see what develops."

We talked on various other matters and I left the Navy Minister's official residence about five o'clock, and looked in at a rugby game that I'd agreed to see with friends. But I couldn't help being quite apprehensive about General Ugaki's possible resignation;[33] and because of the Prince's earlier comments, I decided to leave for Okitsu the same evening, reaching there past midnight. I went to the Prince's room about eight o'clock the next morning and spent about an hour giving him the details.

"The truth seems to be," I said, "that General Ugaki has some intention of resigning since his prolonged absence could seriously inconvenience both the War Ministry and the Cabinet as well. Mizoguchi said as much, according to Konoe. I can't help wondering if such action by the War Minister were taken today, would it not give rise to wide repercussions? The Prime Minister, too, is greatly disturbed today lest Ugaki resign. He wants to stave it off somehow. Yet the War Minister himself seems to have thought of resigning suddenly without speaking with anyone."

The Prince therefore instructed me,

"I want you to go back to Tokyo immediately and give this message to the War Minister: 'While I sympathize with you deeply in your illness, I want you to give up any thought of resigning at this juncture. The resignation of a Minister of State is a matter of vital importance. Especially today is Your Excellency's responsibility to the nation of such particular significance that I strongly urge you to give up any notion of resignation. I myself would come to ask this; but since my illness prevents it, I have asked Harada to do so. I make this request of Your Excellency for the sake of our country.' But before you give this message to Ugaki," Saionji went

---

[33] [Note that after this chance meeting with the Navy Minister at the Hospital, Harada does not record that he in any way discussed a possibly imminent Ugaki resignation with Takarabe, but that he obtained precisely that information from Takarabe (that Ugaki was opposed to involving Army agencies in the London treaty imbroglio) which gave especial reason for averting the War Minister's resignation at this juncture.

[Another general succeeding Ugaki now might not similarly want to keep clear of the "supreme command" arguments against the government. But Ugaki himself had already gone on record in April, in reply to written interpellation from the Diet, as opposing the temporary appointment of any deputy or interim minister during his illness. Furthermore, there was no other minister of state (i.e., cabinet member) who was technically qualified to be temporarily assigned to act for Ugaki during a formal leave of absence. See Asahi shimbun seijikeizaibu, ed., *Kaigun shukushō no hanashi* [*On Naval Disarmament*] (Tōkyō: Asahi shimbunsha, 1930), pp. 195-96.]

on to say, "see the Prime Minister, give him the gist of it, and ask if there is anything to be added to it."[34]

I took the nine-thirty train back to Tokyo, reaching there at two o'clock that afternoon. I immediately got in touch with Prime Minister Hamaguchi at Kamakura by phone. After mentioning that it would be best if no one else knew of the communication from the Prince to War Minister, the Prime Minister assured me there was nothing to add to the message. I called on the War Minister in the hospital later in the evening and delivered the message. Looking somewhat perplexed, he said:

"Well, I had made up my mind to resign without making it a subject of discussion. As far as the War Ministry is concerned, for all I can participate in its affairs I might as well be in the deaf-man's gallery; and as far as the Cabinet is concerned I must be an embarrassment. But I do want to resign at the right time. Once this disarmament matter is cleared up would seem to be the time for it." To which I replied,

"It seems to me that Your Excellency's action is extremely important just now. It would be especially unfortunate for your own sake if this matter were to be bungled. Recently there's been that talk of Ikeda Nagayasu and others." General Ugaki then remarked,

"Please give my greetings to Prince Saionji. And tell him Ugaki is saying nothing and keeping his thoughts to himself. But especially because of the Prince's kind advice, I shall certainly reconsider the matter carefully. Yet with circumstances as they are, there are bound to be difficulties with respect to my official duties. Perhaps it can be arranged that an Acting Minister may be designated who can attend cabinet conferences. Of course, for formal legal and other reasons, this should be someone of ministerial rank. Please keep this a confidential matter, secret even from Prime Minister Hamaguchi."

When he had spoken thus, I took my departure. But since, of course, I was bound to talk with the Prime Minister, I immediately phoned to him in Kamakura and spoke with him briefly. I called

---

[34] [This message to Ugaki appears in a different form in Harada's pocket notebooks, his jottings on the spot that were raw material for his later dictation of the diary. No doubt the words in the notebook are the ones Saionji actually used, as if dictating to Harada. They are the abrupt forms of common masculine speech as between equals. But as Harada records the message in the above text, and as he must have spoken it to Ugaki, the same message has been transmogrified into the correctly formal language appropriate to his own station vis-à-vis the War Minister. Both Japanese versions are given in the "Introduction" where some implications of the variation are discussed.]

his attention to the fact that I had received this information in strictest confidence, to be kept secret from Ugaki's cabinet colleagues including even himself.

Then I wrote a detailed letter of report to Okitsu and dispatched it by registered mail.

> *The Chief of the Naval General Staff*
> *Presents His Resignation to*
> *the Emperor—The Change of the Chief*
> *of the Naval General Staff—Prince*
> *Saionji's Opinion—Prince Saionji's*
> *View on Disarmament.*

[Dictated June 13, 1930]

On the morning of June 10 I met with Vice Minister Yoshida of the Foreign Office. He said,

"This is confidential, but this morning I had a telephone call from Mori, the Chief Secretary of the Seiyūkai. He asked, 'Do you know that it's said that the Chief of the Naval General Staff Katō has made a direct appeal to the Throne?' I told him I knew nothing about it. Have you any knowledge of this?" I had had no inkling of it and told him so.

The tenth was the very day when the transfers of the Vice Minister of Navy, the Vice Chief of the Naval General Staff, and others were to be announced. The Vice Minister's post went to Kobayashi, Chief of the Naval Technical Department; and that of Vice Chief of the Naval General Staff went to Vice Admiral Nagano. Yamanashi and Suetsugu were both posted to duty at the Navy Ministry. The new Chief of the Naval Technical Department was Vice Admiral Fujita; and as Training Bureau Chief, Rear Admiral Terashima.[35] Then and there from the Foreign Office I

---

[35] [Vice Admiral Nagano Osami (1880-1947), a native of Kochi (old Tosa), was thus advanced from the superintendency of the Naval Academy. He later became a Supreme War Councillor (1933), Chief Delegate to the London Naval Conference of 1935—from which Japan withdrew, Navy Minister in the Hirota cabinet (1936-37), Commander-in-Chief, Combined Fleet in 1937, Supreme War Councillor for the second time in 1940, Chief of The Naval General Staff (1941-44), and finally the unusual post of Supreme Naval Adviser to the Emperor (1944). Charged as major war criminal before the International Tribunal, he died before that trial was concluded.

[Vice Admiral Fujita Hisanori, until this change, had been commandant of the Yokosuka Navy Yard. He was later to become a full admiral and a Supreme War Councillor. Harada has occasion to note him as a "stalwart" later this year (below, p. 257).

phoned Vice Admiral Kobayashi to ask if he knew about Chief of Naval General Staff Katō making a direct appeal to the throne this morning. His reply was, "I know nothing whatever about it. Just now I'm in the process of clearing out my office." Then I recalled that the Chief Secretary of the Privy Council had given a hint of this to newsmen the other day: "In a few days Chief of the Naval General Staff Katō may independently memorialize the throne." Thereupon I thought to telephone to the office of the Imperial Household Minister to ask there. But it occurred to me to go to ask the Prime Minister about the situation. He said, "Well, it seems the Chief of the Naval General Staff did make some sort of report to the Throne at eleven this morning and I'm told that when his audience was ended he went to seek a conference with the Navy Minister." About two o'clock that afternoon I had planned to make a call on the Grand Chamberlain, but I was told, "Come two or three hours from now." And about four o'clock I called on the Grand Chamberlain. "Yes," he said, "Katō did submit a report to the Throne this morning. It's indeed a troublesome matter. For the details about it, I prefer for you to ask the Navy Minister rather than me." Afterward, I had been talking with Chamberlain Honda at the Board of Chamberlains.[36] The telephone was ringing insistently. Though I thought of leaving, I had no idea who might be calling, so I answered it while Honda was out of the room. It was the Emperor's voice I heard clearly. "When the Navy Minister comes to the Palace at four-thirty I want to see him." Less than fifteen minutes later the same phone rang again. This time, too, it was His Majesty's voice saying, "There's something I must give the Navy Minister, please don't forget." I wondered what it was all about. At four-thirty the Navy Minister was entering the Palace and I passed him just as I was leaving. I went to his official residence to await his return.

When he came back about five-thirty, he had this to say, "The distressing thing is that Katō has had the audacity to approach the Emperor directly to beg to be relieved of his post, and his reasons for this were virtually an impeachment of the government. His Majesty listened quietly to Katō but made no reply. Apparently

[Rear Admiral Terashima Takeshi (Ken) (b. 1882) had been on duty in the General Staff office. He became Vice Admiral in 1932 and retired two years later to become president of the Uraga Shipbuilding Company. Still later he was communications and railways minister in the Tōjō cabinet (below, p. 243).]

[36] [Viscount Honda Naoichirō, after graduation from Tokyo Imperial University, had entered the Home Ministry and subsequently the Imperial Household Ministry.]

this considerably flustered the Chief of the Navy General Staff, for no sooner had he submitted his memorial at eleven o'clock then he came to seek a conference with me. 'I've just made a report to the Throne,' he said, 'but His Majesty had nothing whatsoever to say! What should I do now?' "

To this Takarabe apparently had said he would have to give it some study and had questioned Katō on his reasons for submitting his memorial. All this had taken place before noon.[37]

When the Emperor saw the Navy Minister, he said "Katō brought this to me and spoke to me about it; but what he said seems quite improper. As far as his resignation is concerned I leave it to your discretion and I turn this document over to you."

The Navy Minister immediately assented, and taking the document quickly examined it. He then proposed, "I believe that Katō should be relieved as Chief of the Naval General Staff. Admiral Taniguchi, now Commandant of the Kure Naval District, might be appointed as his successor."[38] And with this he withdrew

---

[37] [Captain Koga's record of what the Imperial Naval Aide-de-Camp, Vice Admiral Imamura, reported to him of this episode and its immediate forerunner may elucidate these various reactions. Some days earlier, after the Emperor had sat through a lecture by Suetsugu on the naval reduction and supreme command issues, Imamura had ventured to suggest that Suetsugu's comments were "academic" and not spoken in his official capacity as Vice Chief of the Naval General Staff. To this the Emperor tartly observed, "Constitutional matters are for the Privy Council, after all."

[Arriving at the Palace for his audience on June 10, Katō brusquely announced, "His Majesty knows [of this matter] from what Suetsugu said to him the other day" (Aoki, I, 56).]

[38] [Admiral Taniguchi Naozane, previously unknown to Harada, had had a sturdy though unspectacular naval career since 1894, in command and administrative roles. The latter had included service as secretary *(fukkan)* to the Navy Minister, chief of the Bureau of Personnel, commandant of the Naval Academy, and of the Kure Naval Base before he became Commander-in-Chief, First Fleet and Combined Fleet in 1928; and thereafter for a second tour as Kure commandant.

[He thus belonged to the post-Satsuma generation of Navy leaders topped by and typified in Okada and Takarabe, and was not likely to be involved with Katō and his young "stalwarts." His availability at this time was increased because he was a native of Hiroshima, as was Kobayashi, the new Vice Minister of Navy, and Abo, Takarabe's chief technical aide at London and a Supreme War Councillor.

[Takarabe's preparation to act swiftly following Katō's "improper" personal presentation of his resignation is made clearer in his own fuller account of this audience. The Emperor also asked Takarabe how Taniguchi stood on the "strength of forces" issue. The Navy Minister replied, "The successor-designate holds sound moderate views. As I was returning to Japan he unexpectedly came to meet with me in Seoul. He held it essential to cooperate in unifying views on the strength of forces. When I said I hoped we might work together effectively, Taniguchi said he would make every effort to do so." (See Aoki, I, 59-60.)]

from the Imperial presence. Afterward Takarabe told me he would carry this out immediately.

I called on Admiral Okada at his home that evening. "This is a bad business," he said, "the worst that could be expected. Katō has been inveigled into this by others, for it's not his own way. It's a bad business indeed." I could not help thinking that bad though it might be, it would probably mark the end of the whole episode. All the while, of course, Admiral Okada had been working quietly to effect a solution satisfactory alike for Admiral Katō and for the Navy as a whole; so that it was natural for him to deplore that Katō's attitude had gone to such extremes.

Taniguchi

I had planned to go down to Okitsu the same evening, but when Admiral Okada suggested it might be well to wait another day, I did stay over and planned to go to Okitsu the following day.

The next day I called on Vice Admiral Nomura and heard a good deal of Navy talk. And when I saw Lord Keeper of the Privy Seal Makino at eleven-thirty, he said, "This has been a very troublesome matter; but it should keep the Navy men calmed down for a while.[39] Those of us who are, so to speak, actors behind the scenes are not supposed to mix in outside affairs. It is best for me not to say anything to the public about questions which His Majesty may put to me." After talking of various things, I returned home about noon.

In the afternoon I called on the Navy Minister at the Ministry. He related his final moves dealing with Katō.

"Just a short time ago I called Katō here and gave him my decision. I told him of the formal steps that had been taken: that when His Majesty had ordered me yesterday to act on Katō's resignation at my own discretion, I had immediately replied that Katō could be transferred to the Supreme War Council with Admiral Taniguchi posted as his successor as Chief of the Naval General Staff, if these moves met with Imperial approval; that a message had come late last night from the Chief Aide-de-Camp conveying the Imperial sanction to these proposals.

"Katō then said to me, 'I am truly and deeply appreciative of this kindness you have done, despite the fact that I took steps beyond your control as Minister. Henceforth whatever my billet

[39] [The Emperor and the court had apparently understood that Katō's *jōsō* audience was to be for the fairly routine purpose of reporting on preparations for the forthcoming fall "grand maneuvers" of the fleet, and were thus taken aback by the resignation which he also presented. His unexpected action was thus irregular, "troubling," and "not sensible." Cf. Aoki, I, 59.]

I shall act neither to contravene Navy regulations nor to be of embarrassment to you as Minister.' "

Thus it was that with Admiral Taniguchi from Kure succeeding as Chief of the Naval General Staff, Vice Admiral Nomura replacing him at Kure, the various transfers were all accomplished. The Navy Minister went on to say, "Well, one more stage has been reached. Please report on this to the Prince so that he may feel reassured."

Then I saw the Prime Minister for a second time and left late that evening for Okitsu. I gave the Prince the particulars the next morning. His comment was: "This has been quite unavoidable. Still, it's just as well that the Navy has settled it alone. You say it was the Seiyūkai that was first to know beforehand about Katō's memorial and that the Chief Secretary of the Privy Council also spoke of it. It seems to me there is a natural connection here." Though I had previously written to the Prince of my talk with General Ugaki, I now reported on it in some detail. I pointed out that the previous evening's papers had carried detailed stories that Ugaki would resign for reason of illness, stories apparently emanating from reporters who frequent the War Ministry. The Prince found such indiscriminate stories in the press both disgraceful and an indication of laxity of administration in the Army.

Afterward I again spoke of having been invited, along with Konoe, Okabe, and Kido, to dine with the Vice Minister of the Imperial Household on the evening of the sixth. When the talk turned to the subject of disarmament, our host had said, "Certainly disarmament, if thus brought about, means whittling away our national defense by treaty. . . ." At that time I thought this was a strange thing to say; but I told the Prince, "Many people seem to think this way."

"Oh, but that's quite wrong," said the Prince. "Today when new impetus has been given to peace through the new agencies devised after the Paris Peace Conference, agencies based on a spirit of peace for the promotion of human welfare, no nation should have offensive armaments. In a word, then, may we talk of weapons for defense, but nowhere can anyone today talk of weapons for aggression. These may seem to be wholly new schemes and principles, but if we go back a little further, we find they have a long and splendid history. This is what Jean Jacques Rousseau advocated so long ago. Men are not beasts; hence they should cease chewing each other up. For the welfare of mankind, let us preserve peace: this is the spirit that has come forth as the new principle today since the Peace Conference. Both the disarmament treaties and the Anti-War Pact stem from a fine long-developing tradition. There's no intention of using treaties to threaten or reduce a particular nation's armaments. On the contrary, these treaties should be considered as undertaken for the sake of human happiness which can come from a spirit of the love for peace. Please pay my respects to the Navy Minister and to the Prime Minister, too, for their stalwart efforts. It's spendid that this Navy matter has been brought to an end." As for the publicity about Ugaki, the Prince wondered if it weren't a case of schemes by Hiranuma and his group. As soon as I returned to Tokyo, I saw the Prime Minister and transmitted the Prince's message.

CHAPTER IV

*The Question of the War Minister's Resignation
and the Activities of the Navy General Staff
and the Privy Council*

*Background of War Minister Ugaki's
Decision to Resign—Egi Earnestly
Entreats Him to Reconsider—He
Talks with the War Minister—The
War Minister Reconsiders—The
Prince's Reassurance.*

[Dictated June 16, 1930]

About eleven-thirty on the morning of June 14 when I was calling on Konoe, a message came by telephone from the War Ministry that Parliamentary Vice Minister Mizoguchi wanted to see me. When I called back I was asked if I could call at the hospital to see the War Minister about five that afternoon. I made a point of seeing the Prime Minister at his official residence about 3:30 P.M. He told me, "At one o'clock today the Chief Secretary was called to see the War Minister. Ugaki told him, 'In the first place, I've been remiss in my duties toward the Emperor, and because of illness have accomplished nothing with respect to urgent administrative duties. In the second place, I've been remiss in my responsibilities to the Army, unable even to attend cabinet meetings, but sitting on the side lines[1] have made no progress at all. In the third place, I have no excuse to make to the cabinet. Now at the present

---

[1] [Here Ugaki is again said to have used the same colloquial phrase, *tsumbo-sajiki* (literally, "deafman's gallery"), that Harada had heard from him a week before to indicate how much he felt himself to be "out of things" because of his present affliction, a severe case of tympanitis. If he indeed thought the Navy "disarmament question" was now concluded, he was in fact somewhat "out of things." See Ugaki, *Nikki*, p. 138.]

moment, since the disarmament question, on which the Navy raised such a fuss, has reached a conclusion, and since—thinking also of myself—I've been told I must have three or four months of absolute rest, I want to resign and recommend some suitable successor as minister.' "

The Prime Minister continued, "Now Ugaki's resignation at this time would be extremely embarrassing. Perhaps he might somehow relinquish the routine tasks of administration, but I certainly want him to give up the idea of resignation. I even instructed the Chief Secretary that when he saw the War Minister he must under no circumstances accept any letter of resignation for delivery to me. For these reasons, then, the Chief Secretary simply said, 'I shall report what you have said,' and then left. Somehow I want to prevent Ugaki from taking this step. Since he and Railways Minister Egi have been close friends from the time they entered the Cabinet, I've decided to have Egi see if he can dissuade him. When he left here a short time ago, Egi said, 'It would be well if you asked Harada not to go to Ugaki's until after I have returned.' "

Ugaki

Necessarily, then, I had to wait for about an hour and a half at the Prime Minister's. Somehow a crowd of newspapermen followed the Railways Minister. I sent the General a message that I might be delayed for about an hour; and arranging to be notified by the Prime Minister when the Railways Minister should have returned, I returned home for a while. Just before five o'clock word came from the Prime Minister and I went out again. The Railways Minister said, "When you go to Ugaki's I wish you'd do your utmost to get him somehow to change his mind. When I was with him just now I told him, 'I'm the one who has kept Harada from coming to see you. It would be awkward if your determination were made known to the *genrō*. Three or four months of rest will put you back on your feet. Why not give up this talk of resignation.' Ugaki replied, 'Well, perhaps I may.' So it's up to you to get him to put aside this notion of resignation."

I went immediately to the Army hospital and saw the War Minister. He said, "This Navy muddle has been cleared up, and since all's quiet for a while, I want to take this chance to recuperate. I think I've already told you that's why I want to resign. But Egi has been to see me, and on behalf of the Prime Minister has strongly urged me to give up this idea. So I called in Abe[2] and asked if

---

[2] Major General Abe Nobuyuki [(1875-1953, having held a number of posts in the Army's administrative hierarchy, was at this time Ugaki's Vice Minister. A decade hence he was to become Prime Minister—a post his mentor never reached—for a short five months at the end of 1939].

he could serve as my deputy in administering the department. Abe said, 'Of course I can undertake it, but if you go I shall need to consult you on so many matters it will be impossible for you to relax. I cannot vouch for everything.' I've had him go just now to see the Prime Minister, so that whatever he may say, it will probably end by my putting him in charge. How will that be?"

I replied, "There's no reason at all for you to resign. Your stubbornness is giving opportunity for all sorts of wild rumors to crop up. It's doing you a pound of harm for every ounce of advantage. If it should turn out actually that you will not be up to it physically, you can always resign later. Why not try to handle your duties either through a deputy or by an *ad interim* appointment, and at the same time see if you can't get sufficient rest to recuperate? This way should work out smoothly for all purposes and the danger should be small."

Then the War Minister himself said, "I can see that I shouldn't have stirred up people with my foolish talk, nor brought embarrassment to you all." And finally, he said, "Well, wait a while to see what Abe says upon his return." So I waited at the hospital until after ten o'clock. But since there was no sign of Vice Minister Abe's return, the War Minister said, "Why not come back at eight in the morning. If you do, this can be straightened out; and I'd like you then to take word of it to Okitsu."

No sooner had I returned home than a call came from the Railways Minister to ask how I made out. "Well, he seems about seven-tenths persuaded. He seems to understand what we've all been telling him," I replied. Later that evening I phoned the Prime Minister to inquire about the situation.

"In the course of my talks with the Vice Minister of War," he said, "the Vice Minister offered to convey my views to the Minister of War since Parliamentary Vice Minister Mizoguchi is in the hospital. And when he had done so the War Minister's rejoinder was, 'It's inevitable, then; I leave it entirely up to the Prime Minister.' This being so, I've decided to proceed with the appointment of a deputy."

Thus the matter, now decided, allowed of no more maneuvering.

I visited the War Minister at the Hospital at eight the next morning and he gave me the following message for Prince Saionji.

"I deeply appreciate the advice you recently sent me. Being ill in the face of many duties, and accomplishing nothing, I have no excuse to offer His Majesty. I had considered quite earnestly this matter of resignation. Since both the naval disarmament question and the complications with Navy circles have been generally allayed, I thought I might be allowed at this juncture to retire so that I might recuperate; and I frequently so entreated the Prime Minister. But he repeatedly came back with, 'Since there are other ways of taking a holiday, please don't resign.' So that rather than persist in this to the point of quarrelling or bringing about complete difference of opinion, I've made it a point of leaving the matter entirely up to the Prime Minister. I'm certainly sorry if, in this short time, I've done anything to stir things up. I'll go over further details when next I see the Prince." Thus it was finally decided that by some means Vice Minister Abe be persuaded to take over for the time being while the War Minister himself is recuperating.

I took an express to Shizuoka and went immediately to Okitsu for a talk with the Prince, who was very pleased at my report.

"Well, that puts my mind at rest. At any rate, for the War Minister to resign today would not be good. It's fine that it has come out this way. Please take this message from me to War Minister Ugaki: 'It makes Prince Saionji very happy that you have been persuaded to remain in office. Never before have I asked such a favor of anyone. Whichever one of us recovers first should call on the other for a leisurely chat about my reasons for this advice. At all events I'm especially pleased you've relinquished the idea of resigning now, and wish to express my deep appreciation. Meanwhile it is my earnest hope that, with ample rest, you will make a speedy and complete recovery.' "

Returning to Tokyo by the special express that same day, I called on the Minister at the Army Hospital about 8:30 P.M. and conveyed the Prince's message.[3]

While it seemed likely that the newspapers of the day would publish various fanciful slanders, few in fact contravened the regulations. Rather than stir up trouble, many seemed concerned that this be not so; and all was relatively calm. My own analysis of

---

[3] [Ugaki's diary says it was "in the dead of night" on June 14 that he changed his mind and decided not to resign, and that he called in Harada early the next morning to give him this information (apparently unaware that Harada already knew it from Hamaguchi). The episode as a whole is more briefly treated than by Harada and is captioned, "Prince Saionji stops me from resigning," though it will be noted it took a full week for Saionji's advice of June 8 to take effect. Ugaki reproduces two messages delivered by Harada from Saionji: in substance the same as Harada's versions, but in language rather different (chap. iii, n. 34). See Ugaki, *Nikki*, pp. 134-36.]

the situation would be that the motive behind the War Minister's proposal to resign was seven parts ill-health and three parts the officious meddling of others.

> *The Question of an* ad interim *War Minister—The Return of Ambassador Wakatsuki to Japan—General Ugaki's Future—A Talk with Prince Kaya— A Visit with the New Chief of the Navy General Staff—Opposition from the Fleet to Takarabe.*

[Dictated June 19, 1930]

On the morning of the sixteenth I visited the Prime Minister and summarized briefly the message of greeting from Prince Saionji the previous day to the War Minister. We discussed the matter of setting up a War Minister *ad interim.* He pointed out that there is nothing in statutes or regulations against such a course, yet it is sufficiently unusual to consult the Lord Privy Seal. There seems to be no precedent for one of *chokunin* rank to function as a Minister of State; and this may be cause for concern.[4] I mentioned that I had learned from Chief Secretary Okabe that the Lord Keeper of the Privy Seal was expected to return from Kamakura to Tokyo on the following day.

"That's too bad," he said, "for I am to have an audience with His Majesty at two o'clock this afternoon. And it is essential that I have an understanding with the Lord Keeper of the Privy Seal before then. I realize it may be trying for you, but could you go down to Kamakura to have a chat with him about it?"

When I phoned Makino's official residence at Takanawa, in an effort to comply with this request, I learned happily that he had already set forth for the capital and was in fact at the Palace. I went to the Palace immediately, saw the Lord Keeper of the Privy Seal, and told him the circumstances which had changed the War

---

[4] [Ministers of State were officials of *shinnin* rank, the highest in the Japanese bureaucracy. Such rank implied direct personal appointment by the Emperor, and was held by such high officials, in addition to cabinet members, as privy councillors, ambassadors, and a few others. The second rank, *chokunin*, signified indirect Imperial appointment, and was held by vice-ministers, bureau chiefs, prefectural governors, etc. Cf. Quigley, pp. 142-59; also Leonard D. White, *The Civil Service in the Modern State* (Chicago: The University of Chicago Press, 1930), pp. 513-55; below, Appendix II B, n. 1.

[Hamaguchi, of course, could not afford to jeopardize his handling of the Ugaki case by provoking a purely procedural dispute with the court officials.]

Minister's resolve to resign; and I tried to speak only of those aspects I'd been asked by the Prime Minister to include on this point. But on the matter of the legality of these measures there seemed to be a certain hesitancy. The Lord Keeper of the Privy Seal professing ignorance of the legal aspect, this was natural.

Immediately afterward I stopped at Okabe's office in the Board of Ceremonies and found him idle. "You know," I said, "the Lord Keeper of the Privy Seal, the Grand Chamberlain, and the Imperial Household Minister are all meeting in the Lord Keeper's office at this very minute with their heads together discussing some Army matter. You've got a good understanding of legal affairs; why don't you go and explain it so they'll understand the points of law that are involved." And with a look of surprise on his face, Okabe dashed off to the Lord Keeper's office.

Okabe

Later I gave the Imperial Household Minister a detailed account of the discussions between Prince Saionji and War Minister Ugaki, and remarked, "At this time, if there is no actual infringement of law, to hesitate on some legal quibble—as to whether there are precedents or not, or whether this would be a unique exception—such hesitation can only have unfortunate results in view of the total situation." And I went on to recall Prince Saionji's oft-repeated earlier counsel:

"You may say what you will about precedents, but if it is essential for the conduct of government (as long as no law is contravened), all sorts of exceptions and even new precedents are unavoidable, are they not? To be so bound up in observing precedents that the conduct of government is delayed is extremely bad."

Since the Imperial Household Minister seemed to listen to this advice, giving it his full assent, I took my departure and returned home.

In the afternoon I went to the Prime Minister's official residence and reported on these conversations. Then, since Okabe seemed to have some further business to discuss with me, I went back to his office at the Imperial Household Ministry about three o'clock. He said, "I thought you'd like to hear that this whole matter has now been safely concluded."

Afterwards, as I was on the way to attend the funeral of Sir Colin J. Davidson,[5] I chanced to meet Kobayashi, the new Vice Minister of the Navy. He told me, "There's something I'd like to talk over with you. Won't you come to see me?" So, on my return,

---

[5] The Counsellor of the British Embassy who had died June 14, 1930. [See above, chap. 1, n. 37.]

I stopped by the Navy Ministry to talk with him. He said, "Katō, the Chief of Naval Operations in the Naval General Staff,[6] should probably be persuaded to resign. It ought to be done quickly before the preparation of the new national defense plans are drawn up and before the advice of the Privy Council on the Naval Treaty is sought." The talk then turned to various topics about the present situation in the Army, but I myself had nothing to say on this, so I left and returned home.

When I reported to the Prince that I had conveyed his orders about the War Minister, I also put before him the tales being bruited about in Privy Council circles and their maliciously intended arguments. Some in these quarters are saying, "The War Minister is most outrageous. For him to hold on to his post when he is bedridden and cannot perform his duties must be most embarrassing to His Majesty."

Then, since I had already so promised Admiral Okada, I had lunch with him and Uchida[7] of the Seiyūkai on the seventeenth and we had a leisurely discussion until past three o'clock.

When Ambassador Wakatsuki returned to Tokyo on the morning of the eighteenth, I was present as Prince Saionji's representative. There was a huge turnout to welcome him and the crowd was in much better spirits than expected. Twice while he was in London, and again to reach him in Singapore on his return trip, I had written him in some detail on the political situation at home. As soon as I spied his face and greeted him, the Ambassador with a broad smile remarked, "Thank you very much for those good letters. I want to see you soon to discuss them more leisurely."[8] I conveyed the Prince's welcoming message and was on the

---

[6] [Rear Admiral Viscount Katō Takayoshi reappears later in this narrative as one of those seeking personally to range Imperial personages, such as Prince Fushimi, on the side of the "stalwarts," i.e., the anti-Treaty forces (below, pp. 182, 193).]

[7] [Uchida Shinya (Nobuya) (b. 1880), prominent as a businessman in politics, was a leading (though sometimes dissident) member and financial supporter of the Seiyūkai. He had connections with the Mitsui interests, was head of the Uchida Ship Company, had served as parliamentary Vice Minister of Navy, and was later to become Railways Minister in Okada's cabinet, a post to which he turned in a post-war Yoshida cabinet.]

[8] [A manuscript record survives of an undated (but presumably mid-April) message sent by Harada through the Foreign Office to Wakatsuki in London informing him of Saionji's recovery from his serious spring illness (LC Microfilm Collection, S 2.12.0.0.1, p. 490).

[Wakatsuki, in his memoirs, has written: "I understand that Saionji was extremely concerned about the London Conference. Though he was seriously ill at that time, he was attentive to the Conference developments and expressed the hope that it might be speedily concluded. The government regularly made

point of departure when the Chief of the Army General Staff[9] happened by. Since he said there was something he wanted to discuss with me, I accompanied him to the General Staff offices and we talked for about an hour. Principally he was concerned with Ugaki's future, for the War Minister seems to have informed him in detail on the discussions with the Prince. Briefly put, it was General Kanaya's hope that General Ugaki would not be made subject of political involvements, but that he might eventually become Governor-General of Korea. And because I myself had often thought this might be a suitable development, I suggested, as I took my departure, that he might so advise Ugaki.

While I was at the Chief of the General Staff's Office, a message came from His Imperial Highness Prince Kaya[10] that he wished to see me when our business was over. In fact, I had thrice before had messages to see the Prince, but I had been both busy and cautious and had not become involved. Now, however, it was unavoidable, so as I was returning I met him.

He asked me, "In terms of future development, I've been wondering about Naruse,[11] who was made Chief Secretary to the House of Peers on my advice. What do you think of him?"

"In character and good sense he is, I think, an altogether suitable person. I've known him well since we were schoolmates together." This reply of mine seemed to please him.

But he had a further request, "I'd like very much to see Prince Saionji, for I want to ask him about his views on the future for

---

known to him the principal reports coming from London. He seems to have seen the views expressed in my lengthy private message at the time of requesting final instructions. I understood later from Shidehara, 'When he read your dispatch he said, "This is worthy of the *Tō-Sō hakka*." ' But though I was eschewing officialese in this paper in order the better to express my own opinions, it did not merit comparison with Han T'ui-chih!" (Wakatsuki, *Kōfuan kaikōroku*, p. 365).

[The phrase *Tō-Sō hakka* refers to eight masters of classic Chinese prose in the great T'ang and Sung periods (7th to 13th centuries, A.D.): Han T'ui-chih (Han Yü), Liu Tsung-yüan, Ou-yang Hsiu, Wang An-shih, Su Hsün, Su Shih, Su Ch-ich, and Ts'eng Kung. Wakatsuki's proud reminiscence of this little colloquy will remind the reader of another dimension of Japan's ancient heritage, the Confucian one, different from the oft-noted *samurai* tradition but yet with traces in the twentieth century.]

[9] General Kanaya Hanzō, [(1873-1933), an Ugaki man in the higher army echelons, had become Chief of Staff in Feburary, 1930.]

[10] [Imperial Prince Kaya Tsunenori, thirty-year-old head of the cadet house of Kaya which had been founded by his father in 1892, was assigned as a cavalry captain to duty with the Army General Staff.]

[11] [Naruse Tatsu was later to become president of the Nihon Seimei Hoken Kaisha (Japan Life Insurance Company).]

members of the Imperial family." Since I'd been thus cornered, I could only say, "The Prince himself would like to be able to meet each member of the Imperial family and to present his views on various matters, but because of his advanced age it is regrettably not at all possible for him to do so. I shall, however, look for an opportunity to request an audience with Your Highness." And then I took my leave.

Nowadays in connection with the matter of disarmament there is much serious discussion, especially in the case of Admiral Prince Fushimi, of the propriety of placing members of the Imperial family in positions of responsibility, considering it both from the standpoint of administration and in view of possible antagonism between elements of the Imperial House and the government.[12] Perhaps this has prompted the thought, as the Navy Minister expressed it, that such persons might well be limited to purely honorary posts and offices in the future. It occurred to me that it would be well, before Prince Saionji should see His Highness, to have someone implant this idea in His Highness' mind by frequent theoretic discussions. And so I took my leave.

I then called on the new Chief of the Naval General Staff. When I told him that I was calling both to extend my greetings and to apologize for being unable till now, because of other duties, to offer congratulations on his induction into office, Admiral Taniguchi replied with most dignified mien, "Although I have not previously had the opportunity or the honor of knowing you, I have already heard about you from others. I trust that henceforth I may ask to see you from time to time, to exchange views with you and to beg for your friendship."

After this most formal and respectful greeting, I responded, "I am, of course, necessarily involved in political affairs. Mindful that such activity may be embarrassing and quite out of the question for you, even so I trust our acquaintance may grow closer in the days ahead. If there is any way in which I may be of service to you along the lines of your new public duty, and if you have any request to make of me, please do not hesitate to call upon me."

While meeting and talking with Admiral Taniguchi, I couldn't help feeling that the new Navy disposition, as contrasted with the former regime, would exhibit greater strength.

---

[12] [Saionji's circle was to to be further worried by this problem in the next two years. After war began in Manchuria in 1931, the Army drew more immunity to itself by making an Imperial prince, Field Marshal Prince Kan'in Kotohito, its Chief of Staff in December of that year; and the Navy followed suit by making Prince Fushimi *its* Chief of Staff in February 1932 (Harada, II, 199 *et passim*) pp. 134 f.]

In returning from this meeting, I called at the Navy Ministry, saw the Minister, and found him much more composed. I told him, "Some days ago, when the First Fleet put in at Osaka and the Commander-in-Chief and his staff were entertained by Sumitomo, they talked about how annoyed they were that some people have been so noisy in expressing their dissatisfaction with Your Excellency, and in putting forth propaganda quite at variance with the truth." The Navy Minister seemed very pleased to hear me speak thus.

The Disclosure of the Memorandum on the Naval Replenishment Program—The Prince's Admonitions on Military Discipline—Schemes in Privy Council Circles and the new Chief of the Navy General Staff—The Rescript to the Plenipotentiaries—The General Reaction within the Navy.

[Dictated June 23, 1930]

Leaving Tokyo on the evening of the nineteenth, I saw the Prince on the morning of the twentieth. I reported on the general situation of Ambassador Wakatsuki's return, and conveyed Wakatsuki's message that he would like to see the Prince as soon as it might be convenient for him to call. The Prince's reaction seemed to be that there was no need for rush, but he'd be pleased to see Wakatsuki.

It was just some two days before this that what purported to be the joint memorandum of the Navy Minister and the Chief of the Naval General Staff on the replenishment program was published in the press. The story was so written that it appeared to be a report made by the Navy Minister as a member of and at a session of the Supreme War Council, whereas in fact the Navy Minister had brought about a meeting of the *gensui* and the Supreme War Councillors on the matter of a Special Inspector. The memorandum on replenishment was not touched on in the slightest degree.

This memorandum, between the Navy Minister and the Chief of the Naval General Staff had been drafted some time before. Actually, such matters relating to the implementing of the terms of the treaty are quite within the competence of the Navy Minister and the Chief of the Naval General Staff acting together. Ordinarily, up to this time it had been customarily handled between Ministry and Staff without being especially elaborated in writing. But it was inevitable, under present circumstances, that this agreement be put in memorandum form. For the full details of such a memorandum to be published in the press with scarcely a single word changed must certainly mean that it was "leaked" by someone within the secret planning group.

The Prince commented: "If this has been made known by Navy personnel, it is a serious breach of discipline. Most improper conduct! Certainly Fleet Admiral Tōgō and the other elders of the Navy ought to be concerned for and to pay attention to such deterioration of naval discipline, instead of carping about strength of forces and the treaty and such matters, oughtn't they? No matter how satisfactory this strength of forces, for the Navy to have no discipline, is to be harmed a hundred times for one paltry advantage. This is just the matter which Tōgō should concern himself with, and the General Staff should be taken severely to task."

When I asked, "Well, then, when I next see Fleet Admiral Tōgō, should I try to put it to him tactfully?" The Prince said, "No, let the matter ride." He went on to reminisce, "In earlier days when Miura Gorō was a member of the Privy Council, there were several amongst the Councillors who were actively involved in politics. In protest he proffered his resignation with this comment, 'In circumstances like this, I cannot properly fulfill my duties as Councillor. It will lead to a corruption of correct discipline.' It may have been unexpected for a man like Miura to be so concerned, but his thought on this problem of discipline was quite proper.[13]

"So now I think it best for the Privy Council's deliberation on the Naval Limitation Conference to be begun as soon as possible. Also, please convey my greetings to Wakatsuki."

Upon my return to Tokyo that afternoon, I found some newsmen waiting to quiz me. "Some of the Privy Councillors are anxious to know definitely whether or not the new Chief of the Naval Gen-

---

[13] [Is Saionji speaking ironically here? Major General Viscount Miura Gorō (1846-1926) is known in the West almost only for his involvement in the brutal murder of the Korean Queen Min shortly after his arrival as Minister to Korea in the fall of 1895. Saionji, then Acting Foreign Minister, had quickly disavowed Miura and recalled him, and was disappointed that he received no suitable punishment. (See Hilary Conroy, *The Japanese Seizure of Korea, 1868-1910: A Study of Realism and Idealism in International Relations* [Philadeliphia: University of Pennsylvania Press, 1960], pp. 283-321.) Here Saionji is not just giving the devil his due; for, later purged of this Korean odium, Miura rose to be a Privy Councillor and somewhat surprisingly for a bureaucrat he on occasion acted to support party politicians—his last such deed being to foster the three-party "Defend the Constitution" coalition, headed by Katō Kōmei, that unseated Kiyoura's cabinet in 1924.]

eral Staff considers national defense to be adequately safeguarded under terms of the treaty. Tell us what the real situation is on this."

Clearly these Councillors wish to embroil Taniguchi either with the Government if he answers it is not adequately safeguarded, or with the former Chief of Staff if he holds the opposite view. That Taniguchi is listening to everything but saying nothing himself must be extremely annoying to these Councillors and other critics.

Later in the day I called on Taniguchi at the Naval General Staff offices. "In view of these reports, I think Your Excellency's policy of making no comment on today's questioning was a very wise and prudent one. This is just what the schemers on the Privy Council would do." The Chief of the Naval General Staff easily understood this. "Of course I voiced no comment," he said. Then I told him of the Prince's concern over matters of discipline. And when I reviewed to him, for information's sake, what the Prince had had to say about Fleet Admiral Tōgō, his comment was, "That's entirely right. I will devote myself to the maintenance of proper discipline." On my return from this call on Taniguchi I also talked for a time with the Vice Minister of the Navy.

This was the day on which Ambassador Wakatsuki and the others were entertained at a court dinner, and were graciously given an Imperial Rescript which read:

"To all of you, envoys plenipotentiary, who have attended the London Naval Conference and have reported to me, for your patience over the months of negotiations, for your diligence, and for the conclusion of your arduous tasks, I am deeply grateful."[14]

In the next few days there was some talk on the matter of this Imperial Rescript. "It's outrageous! The court officials have used this device to shield the government with apparent imperial approval. It puts the Privy Council in a most awkward position." From newsmen I heard that Futagami, the Privy Council's Chief Secretary, has been saying, "Since his last illness, Prince Saionji is clearly in his dotage. It's a shame, but I have it from a close friend who has just recently seen him." This is strange talk, indeed![15]

---

[14] [Cf. *Rondon kaigun kaigi teikoku zenken fukumeisho oyobi hōkokusho* [*Report of the Japanese Plenipotentiaries to the London Naval Conference*], June, 1930 (LC Microfilm Collection, SP 227).]

[15] [Futagami Hyōji (1878-1944), Doctor of Laws, Member of the House of Peers and Chief Secretary of the Privy Council, seems to have been a particular *bête-noire* to Harada, typifying the pettifogging bureaucrat and ready cohort of such major schemers as Hiranuma (see below, chap. vi.).

[Later Futagami was to become president of the Court of Administrative

On the evening of the twenty-second, I gave a dinner at the Hōryu restaurant in the Tsukiji district for the four Vice Admirals, Ōsumi, Nomura, Kobayashi and Sakonshi, with Rear Admiral Terashima, Konoe, and Okabe also invited, and our talk turned to many topics.[16] Quite a number of young officers in the fleet units and at the naval bases seem to be wholly sympathetic to Katō, the former Chief of the Naval General Staff.[17] They are moved to propaganda without knowing the real facts. And these senior officers seem definitely concerned about the matter. As the party was breaking up, Vice Navy Minister Kobayashi turned to me, saying.

"Men like Railways Minister Egi seem to be rushing this matter of the Privy Council hearings on the treaty. But until the Naval General Staff plans are quite set, I wonder if it might not be better to consider the matter as fully as possible, perhaps delaying it a little rather than rushing it too much and thus putting the new Chief of the Naval General Staff on the spot. Might you not put in a word or two, indirectly, with the Prime Minister suggesting the possible difficulties of too much haste?"

It was about this time I understood that Vice Admiral Ōsumi had been receiving threatening letters of various sorts. Many who felt his position was too moderate also showed great antipathy to the Navy Minister, saying that Takarabe is responsible for all this confusion and ought to resign.

> *Talk That the Emperor's Chief Aide-de-Camp*
> *Tenders his Resignation—The* Jiji Shimpō's
> *Article, "Idle Chatter in Political Circles"*
> *—The Spreading Rumors—The Schemes of*
> *the Chief Secretary of the Privy Council*
> *—The Prince's Views on Financial Policy.*

[Dictated June 26, 1930]

On the following twenty-fourth or twenty-fifth, some newsmen unexpectedly came to see me to report what they had heard from Futagami, whom they quoted as follows:[18]

"His Majesty's Chief Aide-de-Camp at the time of the recent

Litigation (*Gyōsei saibansho*) in 1934; and subsequently (1939) a member of the Privy Council. Cf. Fukai Eigo, *Sūmitsuin jūyō giji oboegaki* [*Private Notes of Important Privy Council Proceedings*] (Tōkyō: Iwanami Shoten, 1953), p. 481.]

[16] [These are the "moderates" to whom Harada has made reference in earlier chapters.]

[17] [For Okada on this topic, see above, chap. iii, n. 7.]

[18] [Harada has already recorded (above, p. 137, n. 6) another version of this story of court officials' interference with Katō's "just" prerogative of *iaku jōsō* (direct appeal to the Throne).]

attempted appeal to the Throne—prior to the issuance of instructions to the London Naval Conference delegates—when it was blocked by the Grand Chamberlain and the Lord Privy Seal, felt himself so disregarded that he offered his resignation. On this score Katō, the former Chief of the Naval General Staff, felt these actions of the court advisers so improper that he could not remain silent, and thus it was so much the responsibility of the Grand Chamberlain, the Lord Keeper of the Privy Seal, and the Imperial Household Minister that they may resign. Now, perhaps, some one from Count Kiyoura's circle might serve as mediator between the two groups."[19]

Kiyoura

This seemed very strange to me, but for precaution's sake, I phoned Chamberlain Honda to ask about the matter; and it seems there was nothing whatever to it.

When I went early the next morning to see General Ugaki at the hospital, he said, "If it were a question of resigning because he has reached the age limit, he would have to resign, of course, but there's no reason why he should now. Since I'm not conversant with the details, why don't you ask Abe?" And so, when I went to see Abe, the War Minister pro tem, at his office, he told me, "Well, the fact of the matter is that, evening before last, newsmen were quizzing me until a late hour on this point, and when I told them there was absolutely nothing to it, the papers suddenly stopped trying to make something of it for their columns."

The very same morning in an article entitled "Idle Chatter in Political Circles," the *Jiji Shimpō* ran a story with a mixture of authenticity and fable, purporting to give a secret discussion among the Prime Minister, the former Chief of the Naval General Staff, the Lord Keeper of the Privy Seal and the Grand Chamberlain. It

---

[The Chief Aide-de-Camp was elderly General Baron Nara Takeji who had been personal military aide to Saionji at the Paris Conference and who was later to serve as chairman of the Military Valor Society (Butokukai) and of the Patriotic Soldiers' Relief Society (Aikoku juppeikai), and to become a member of the Privy Council. Cf. Fukai, p. 481.]

[19] [See above, chap. ii, n. 30. Count Kiyoura, the oldest living former prime minister, except, of course, for Saionji himself, was a relic of the "clan politics" of the Meiji and Taishō periods when he had functioned as an adopted member of the Chōshū clique. In these latter days he was anxious to play and to be recognized in the role of an elder statesman. Faced with Saionji's known reluctance to contemplate the continuance of a *genrō* system as such, Kiyoura's ambition was long frustrated. Conservative bureaucrats, like Futagami, were beginning to argue that some formal recognition should be given to like-minded venerable dignitaries, such as ex-prime ministers and prominent spokesmen for Japanese traditionalism like Hiranuma, to serve as counterweight to party politicians and to the "too cosmopolitan" Saionji and his authority with the court advisers. (See below, pp. 234-35 and n. 1.)]

was written from a viewpoint highly favorable to the former Chief of the Naval General Staff. And in spite of the fact that on the matter of the appeal to the Throne, the Grand Chamberlain was not present, it was written as if he were and as if the Chief Aide-de-Camp were not concerned. To involve the Lord Keeper of the Privy Seal and the others was purely tendentious propaganda. The article gave a strong impression of originating with Suetsugu, the former Vice Chief of the Naval General Staff and his group.[20]

The Navy Vice Minister is greatly worried and said, "If it is possible to check on the source of this, something certainly must be done about it." The Lord Keeper of the Privy Seal was also highly indignant. In all likelihood the Imperial Household Ministry and the Lord Keeper of the Privy Seal's office will require a complete retraction. I went to see Admiral Okada, who is concerned at the mounting antagonism to Takarabe within the Navy. He said, "While everything else seems to be going well, this is still a troublesome matter."

The Navy Minister had thought it would be best if neither Katō, the former Chief of the Naval General Staff, nor the former Vice Chief of the Naval General Staff were in Tokyo at the time of the Privy Council's deliberations. Repeatedly he had proposed that, by way of holiday, they make a tour of the South Seas area; but they stubbornly would not listen. I ventured to suggest to the Navy Vice Minister, "Instead of Okada, why not send Admiral Katō as Special Inspector?" At this time, Admiral Okada, at any rate, seems to think that national defense is adequate in terms of the treaty and that the Privy Council will not take serious exception.

Early the next morning I had a phone call from Mr. Wakatsuki. "Since His Majesty has graciously received our report, I'd be pleased if you would report it to the Prince at your next meeting with him." To which I replied, "I shall see him within the next two or three days and will convey your message promptly."

Since it was recently being bruited about that the Prince was doddering in senility, whereas his health in fact is quite good, the Prince himself thought it a good idea to see various people from time to time.

Then I called on the Prime Minister, who said, "The Board of Fleet Admirals and Field Marshals is about to meet.[21] We'll prob-

---

[20] [Lengthy extracts of this article which appeared on June 23, are reproduced in Aoki, I, 65-74.]

[21] [The Japanese editors of Harada's text question this reference by Hamaguchi to "the Board of Field Marshals and Fleet Admirals" (*gensui kaigi*), assuming it to be a mistake or slip-of-the-tongue by Hamaguchi or Harada for

ably have some trouble with them because His Highness' group is entrenched there; so we must work at it." Further, "On this Navy Ministry matter, when we know the whole of it after investigation, I'll show no mercy," he commented very angrily.

There's a good deal of wild talk, for example that since the Navy has not set up a defense policy, Governor-General Saitō is being brought back from Korea to devise one; that a new defense plan is impossible under the treaty; and that the Navy Minister will resign because of his responsibility for this situation.

There are, in fact, a great many more wild rumors being circulated than I have known in the past. And those apparently stemming from Chief Secretary Futagami are the worst I've encountered. It seemed to me that something drastic should be done about official discipline; but there was no shred of evidence. Yet, in the words of the Foreign Minister,

"Futagami has been calling on each of the Privy Councillors and inciting them to take a stand against the government on such issues as the prerogative of the supreme command. If a Councillor has the least thing to say in approbation of the government, he says no more; but if a Councillor shows a disposition to be critical, he works on it to incite opposition to the maximum. It is utterly improper behavior on his part."

"the Supreme War Council" (*gunji sangikan kaigi*); perhaps because it was the Council and not the Board that was in fact called upon a month later to give formally the supreme command's advice to the Throne on the new naval program.

[More probably it is no mistake. In Harada's pocket diary, in the jottings made during or just after his conferences—the raw material for his subsequent dictation, the reference is to a "*gensui* conference" (Harada, IX, 94). Kobayashi, the new Vice Minister of Navy, also refers to "a *gensui* conference" a day or two later (see below, p. 178). If we recall that for this whole London treaty matter Hamaguchi was deliberately following the practices at the time of the Washington Conference treaties as his procedural model and that at the parallel stage with those treaties it had been the *gensui* whose advice was obtained, it appears that at this time (late June) the *gensui* reference is correct.

[But Navy leaders, particularly the intransigent Katō, were now insisting that it should be the Council and not the Board that should give this advice; for Tōgō was the only naval member of the Board, whereas Katō himself would be a direct participant in a Council deliberation. Hamaguchi, in accepting this change from his procedural model, would not be merely "giving in" but really strengthening his chances. The larger Supreme War Council conference would also include his Navy Minister, and Admiral Okada, and the new staff chief, Admiral Taniguchi, all more receptive to his program's needs than old Tōgō alone might be, or at least anxious to avoid public humiliation for Takarabe.

[That Harada does not refer directly to the short sharp issue of just which supreme command agency to approach for advice on the new naval program under the treaty illustrates the curious, but explicable, lacunae found in Harada's text. Such "gaps" are discussed in the Introduction.]

I went to Okitsu on the morning of the twenty-fifth and saw the Prince, reviewing for him the current situation. He then expressed himself as follows:

"The prospects are good, are they not, for this disarmament matter to proceed through the Privy Council. To plan too far ahead is rather meaningless. Let's push this matter through this stage first; then we can take consideration for the future."

The Prince seemed quite concerned over the financial depression which is apparently worsening. "The basic government policy should not be changed. It is best to try to cope with the situation with the present policies. I'm convinced that interim measures to produce a short-lived prosperity could be of no avail. Because the situation is a response to general trends, we must adhere to the fundamental policy of limiting the national budget even if it causes momentary hardship. Many have come to speak of the present situation. However diverse these spokesmen, they bear the same tale. It seems to me that we can only borrow to ease the present slump if we are prepared to face a worse subsequent crisis, and thus I'm opposed to borrowing by the government now.

"Long ago in Kyoto, during the last years of the Shogunate, I saw many collapsing in the streets from starvation and crying loudly, 'I'm hungry. I'm hungry.' Some then claimed the depression and shortage of goods resulted from trading with the outside world, and were loud in condemning the Shogunate for opening the country. That was a far worse depression than the present one.

"Be that as it may, the disarmament matter must be concluded as soon as possible."

Having decided with the Prince that Wakatsuki should call on him at nine-thirty on the morning of the thirtieth, I left Okitsu and returned to Tokyo.

> *Wakatsuki Calls on the Prince—Admiral*
> *Prince Fushimi Makes a Request of the*
> *Emperor—The anti-Takarabe Clique and*
> *Fleet Admiral Tōgō—Recent Attacks from*
> *the Privy Council—Mori, Chief Secretary*
> *of the Seiyūkai, Seeks an Interview with*
> *Prince Saionji.*

[Dictated July 3, 1930]

On the thirtieth Ambassador Wakatsuki, chief delegate to the London Naval Conference, came to Okitsu to report to the

Prince. They talked together for nearly an hour and a half. The Prince seemed to listen and talk in good spirits and without tiring. When I met Wakatsuki, after his return to Tokyo, he told me how pleased he was to find the Prince in such unexpectedly good health. "I recounted fully my activities and ideas from the time of the London Conference up to the present, which no one has understood so clearly as Prince Saionji. And it has made me happy that he has recovered his health and was good enough to see me today. I'm indeed grateful."

Afterward, since I had some business with him, I called on the Grand Chamberlain. He told me, "This is a highly secret matter, which I trust you'll convey to the Prince. Some ten days ago Admiral Prince Fushimi paid his respects to the Emperor, and he made a direct request to the Emperor, 'I should like to speak to Your Majesty on the matter of disarmament, if Your Majesty will be graciously pleased to listen.' But His Majesty remained silent and made no response. Thereupon Fushimi withdrew from the Emperor's presence. His Majesty immediately summoned the Lord Keeper of the Privy Seal and said to him, 'Admiral Prince Fushimi has just told me such and such. But I have not now inquired into these matters. I think it best not to hear him at this time. I wish to make this known to Prince Fushimi through the Chief Aide-de-Camp. Do you agree with this?' The Lord Keeper of the Privy Seal thought His Majesty's proposal most suitable and said it would be splendid if handled in this way. His Majesty's prudence in managing it in this manner was indeed awe-inspiring and reassuring. His Majesty's adamantine firmness in this manner will also greatly reassure Prince Saionji, I am sure."[22]

It was about this time that a large Court dinner was given on behalf of those concerned with disarmament questions. And not long afterward Chief Delegate Wakatsuki, Navy Minister Taka-

Fushimi

---

[22] [Harada has already recorded the general concern of his mentor's circle lest members of the Imperial Family be used in partisan political maneuverings (p. 121). Here the Grand Chamberlain sends report to Saionji that he and Makino, and the Emperor himself, have been alert to the impropriety of Fushimi's approach and to block its intent. Not till two years later does Harada's diary hint at Fushimi's purpose on this occasion. Ōsumi, the then Navy Minister, told him that Fushimi planned to submit representations from Katō but that His Majesty cut him short, saying, "Now is not the time to listen to you *(Ima kiku jiki de nai)*." The phrase can equally mean, "I am not asking about this now." This is almost the same formula the Emperor used on June 27, 1929, in rejecting Tanaka's effort to present the Army's version of the Chang Tso-lin murder. Tanaka's resignation followed in less than a week. (See Harada I, 11; Harada II, 199.)]

rabe, and Foreign Minister Shidehara were summoned to an informal dinner at the Palace.

And again, after this incident, there was a good deal of talk and both the opposition and those aiming at a more middle-of-the-road cabinet gave voice to critical propaganda as they had on the matter of the rescript earlier.[23] When I saw Navy Vice Minister Kobayashi at this time, he said, "I understand that there may shortly be a meeting of the *gensui*, but I am greatly concerned about it for the anti-Takarabe faction has quite strongly influenced Fleet Admiral Tōgō and I'm very much afraid their hold on him is tightening."[24] According to the Navy Minister, Vice Admiral Viscount Ogasawara Naganori is the man who stands in closest rapport with Fleet Admiral Tōgō; and thus the Navy Minister had called on the Viscount himself to have him speak with the Fleet Admiral. But then Vice Admiral Ogasawara unexpectedly showed himself to belong to the jingoist group by saying, "Frankly it would be better for Japan if these treaty proposals broke down completely." Viscount Ogasawara, Fleet Admiral Tōgō and men like Inoue Seijun of the House of Peers were talking in almost precisely the same words as those used by Vice Admiral Suetsugu, the former Vice Chief of the Naval General Staff.[25]

I was greatly surprised at the pervasiveness of these ideas, and that our position had been so thoroughly distorted in the minds of this group of elder statesmen. Fleet Admiral Tōgō with the intransigence of an old man, said, "This treaty should never have been negotiated." Taniguchi, the new Chief of the Naval General Staff, has already talked with him two or three times without pro-

---

[23] [The term *chūkan naikaku* may mean, depending on context and user's intent, either "temporary, interim, or stop-gap" cabinet, or "middle-of-the-road, neutral, or independent" cabinet, or "nonparty, national, or transcendant" cabinet.]

[24] [Opposition to Takarabe was combined of many elements in addition to those transparent in Harada's reports: from such personal complaints as Tōgō's grumbling to Okada about "petticoat rule"—Takarabe's wife, a daughter of Admiral Yamamoto Gombei, had accompanied him to London; to the deliberate castigation by anti-bourgeois chauvinist ideologues like Kita Ikki asserting that Takarabe was a tool of capitalist politicians (Okada p. 46; Tanaka Sōgorō, *Nihon fuasshizumu no genryū* [*Origins of Japanese Fascism*] [Tōkyō: Hakuyōsha, 1949], p. 310).]

[25] [Viscount Ogasawara Naganori was one of the few elder naval officers with close personal affiliations with the civilian right-wing groups such as those of Kita Ikki and Ōkawa Shumei. Harada has further report of him below, pp. 193-94.

[Baron Inoue Seijun (Kiyozumi), a retired captain in the Imperial Navy and a member of the House of Peers, was active in opposition to the Hamaguchi government (above, p. 129), as a member of the Kōseikai.

[Aoki devotes a short chapter to this "anti-Takarabe" movement (I, 81ff).]

ducing the least understanding on Tōgō's part. Even though the Chief of the Naval General Staff had formerly belonged to Tōgō's group and understood his manner, he is reported to have said, "There's no other way than to preach at him, slowly, tenaciously, patiently until he understands." But on the other hand, there is the danger of delaying the Privy Council considerations of the treaty on this account, so that on the evening of July 2, the Navy Minister went secretly by car to Kamakura to talk with the Lord Keeper of the Privy Seal. Some members of the Privy Council have been intensely critical, especially of the high court officials. In fact they are scheming to oust them and replace them with persons whose views are favorable to their own position.

Sometime before this I had gone to see Mori of the Seiyūkai at his office. He said to me,

"Perhaps Prince Saionji is not conversant with the present state of things in the Seiyūkai. Of course I have every confidence in you; but certain elements in the party suggest that, since you are so friendly with Uchida Shinya, it is Uchida's views that you put in the Prince's ear, or that, having been Katō Kōmei's private secretary, and consequently close to the Minseitō, you may speak ill of the Seiyūkai. When I answered them that you are not that sort of person, they have yet expressed deep concern."

To this I replied, "I'm not concerned with what others may say, for I can only do that which I think right. And I certainly have no intention of acting with any partiality. You mustn't make much of talk like that. Still, I appreciate your speaking to me about it."

Thereupon Mori said, "It may be somewhat presumptuous to ask it, but I have been thinking that I might like to call upon Prince Saionji—entirely at his convenience, of course—in case he should want to inquire into these matters." To which I replied, "I'm sure that he would welcome a call from you. Because he is once again in good health, see him whenever you can in the near future and that will be the best."

When I told the Prince in Okitsu of this talk with Mori, he said, "Certainly, why not arrange it soon?"

Then, because both the Foreign Minister and the Lord Keeper of the Privy Seal had asked to have interviews with the Prince as early as possible, I relayed these requests and suggested that the Prince might be up to seeing both men in one week—and now a third man had asked to come to see him. And on the fifth, Prime Minister Hamaguchi was scheduled to see the Prince after a long interim.

CHAPTER V

The Meeting of
the Supreme War Council

Fleet Admiral Tōgō's Obstinacy in Discussion—
The Question of Voting in the Supreme War Council
—The Movement to Involve the Imperial Family
—The Prince's Views.

[Dictation date unclear]

Several newspapers are publishing stories that Fleet Admiral Tōgō's views are quite uncompromising; and it is rumored that some on the Privy Council are saying that this matter will never proceed to a reference to the Privy Council; that there is bound to be a complete deadlock.[1] The Navy itself is having great difficulties. The Navy Vice Minister has frequently suggested, "Perhaps Fleet

---

[1] [A deadlock, that is, within the supreme command agencies. Harada nowhere deals directly with the decision on the agency to be consulted on the treaty and the modified defense program it required. There were other factors (than the ones mentioned above, chap. iv, n. 21) for now preferring the Supreme War Council to the Board of Field Marshals and Fleet Admirals. The latter, though the more august body, was now little more than a ceremonial vestige. Further, both its Army and Navy members joined in its deliberations. In contrast, the Council, by Article VIII of its governing ordinance (see Appendix II F), could act in separate sections: Navy members alone to take up purely Navy matters; or Army members only, to deal with wholly Army matters. War Minister Ugaki, whether because the London treaty dealt solely with naval disarmament or because the Navy had not yet reached a consensus, had already agreed that the Army not be involved (p. 151). The decision lay with the command agencies and the court functionaries and not with the Prime Minister. Perhaps Takarabe's "private" visit to Count Makino (p. 179) was related to this decision.

[Takeuchi's study gives a careful review of the contemporary press reports (pp. 313-22).]

Admiral Tōgō might be persuaded by someone from Count Yamamoto's group of the Satsuma clique, that is, by someone of the same lineage of old clan politics."

But when Count Yamamoto was asked to talk with Fleet Admiral Tōgō, he refused, saying, "Since this is not my own position, and since what you would have me say is not what I think, it is quite out of the question." Chief of the Naval General Staff Taniguchi, Admiral Okada, and Navy Minister Takarabe have gone by turns to see Fleet Admiral Tōgō; but he seemed to express only the views of the group around him and to be quite unyielding. Since, then, there is no other course than to make progress slowly, Taniguchi, Takarabe and Okada have called on him together to discuss and refute Katō's views, and to present their own views with as much congruity as possible. Okada asserted: "I cannot understand what on earth Admiral Katō really means."

To put it briefly, the first argument is the alleged infringement of the prerogative of the supreme command. If this question is disposed of, then there is raised the question of the replenishment program and the right to decide on military strength, and finally it comes to the opposition to ratification of the treaty.

Tōgō

Tōgō also raises these objections. As far as the Navy is concerned, the Fleet Admiral is its unique Grand Old Man and there is no desire to give umbrage to the man who is regarded, historically, as the very incarnation of the Navy. Yet it would be a very grave matter, indeed, if the ratification of an international treaty, signed by plenipotentiaries representing the Emperor's sovereignty with respect to foreign affairs in accordance with Imperial policy, could be set aside by one man, even though he be the Fleet Admiral. And it could be a grave crisis for this nation if he were to express contrary views to a replenishment program which has been declared acceptable by both the Minister of State who is responsible for offering such advice and the new Chief of the Naval General Staff who is the agency for offering advice with respect to the supreme command, and if he were to oppose ratification of the treaty. Certainly those who are urging such a course on the Fleet Admiral could thus cause him to make a tremendous mistake. With such arguments these three men, Taniguchi, Takarabe, and Okada, tried earnestly to gain the understanding of the Fleet Admiral; but whenever they called upon him, his house was always thronged with those who, for the sake of preventing the ratification of the treaty, were daily urging upon Fleet Admiral Tōgō their own reckless schemes.

Then Admiral Okada had to leave, on July 8, to go to Ōminato[2] as Special Imperial Inspector. It had been planned, if arrangements could be completed, formally to ask for the Privy Council's advice on or about the tenth; but by the evening of the eighth, no such progress had been made. I saw Admiral Okada on the evening of the seventh and we discussed the general situation.

"The matter does not go as smoothly as one would want. The outcome, on the whole, is clear; but we've spent much precious time, and I've delayed my departure till today, in hope of keeping Tōgō from making a serious mistake that would hurt his reputation. It's a difficult situation, but it will be managed somehow."

On the afternoon of the eighth I called on the Navy Minister. He said, "Since I had called on Fleet Admiral Tōgō a few days ago and talked with him for more than two hours, I supposed that he now understood the situation fully. Yet today, when Admiral Okada, just off on his tour as Special Inspector, stopped at Fleet Admiral Tōgō's house for a brief chat, he found that he had not changed his views in the least. This is most disturbing.

"Until Admiral Okada returns on the fourteenth, there's nothing to be done but wait. What troubles me most, though I'm not mentioning it to others, is that when the Supreme War Council is called into session, decisions are made by a majority vote. Now Fleet Admiral Tōgō, because he is senior, will probably be in the chair; and with His Highness Prince Fushimi, Admiral Okada, Admiral Katō, Chief of the Naval General Staff Taniguchi, and myself, there will be six of us in all. If we consider His Highness, the group is evenly divided—three against three. Now for a member of the Imperial family to participate in decisions on affairs when the times are good may be quite all right; but in bad times it might arouse popular resentment. It's not simply a question of one member of the Imperial family, it may well stir popular resentment against the whole Imperial family. Somehow it should be arranged that an Imperial personage is not involved in the impending decision. Heretofore it has been quite usual for Prince Fushimi to express no views at all at such meetings. It is most highly regrettable that he has now been so misled by members of his entourage. According to reports that come to me, it is Rear Admiral Katō Takayoshi who has most direct access to him. There seems to be a movement of sorts to involve others of the Imperial House as parti-

---

[2] Naval station in Aomori-Ken, at the northern end of Honshu Island.

sans in political matters, for example, to have Prince Chichibu[3] and Prince Higashi-Kuni[4] and others participate in sessions of the Privy Council.[5] In this direction Fushimi seems to be urged on by Vice Admiral Suetsugu, the former Vice Chief of the Naval General Staff, who is a frequent visitor. It is matters like this which are giving me concern. Though I cannot speak of this to others, I believe that this is a matter on which Prince Saionji and his circle should become concerned."

I took the night train down to Okitsu and saw the Prince on the morning of the ninth, telling him along with other current reports, that Fleet Admiral Tōgō is still holding stubbornly to his views. I also spoke about this matter involving the Imperial House. The Prince said,

"It's a great shame that Fleet Admiral Tōgō takes this position. Those who have been urging the Navy Minister to resign will now have added cause. But Takarabe definitely must not do so now. He must be rebuffed in any attempt to resign by pointing out that official service is at the pleasure of His Majesty, and that one may not for a moment consider that resignation is purely a personal matter. Again, if it is a question of holding everything in abeyance until Admiral Okada's return, then in the meanwhile perhaps something can be done on the matter of these Imperial personages. Please see that the Lord Privy Seal and his group give some thought to this." To this I suggested,

"Since Prince Konoe is coming to call on you this afternoon, perhaps you might like to talk with him about it and get his opinion." I thought I would leave it wholly up to Konoe.

I returned on the eleven o'clock train. But since our trains would be passing each other on the way and because I had not spoken to him on this matter of the Imperial House, I hurriedly wrote a message about it, saying, "Please take careful note of everything the Prince tells you on this," and left it with the Numazu

---

[3] Imperial Prince Chichibu Yasuhito [1902-53], a younger brother of the Emperor, was at this time a captain of Infantry assigned to the Army War College.

[4] Prince Higashi-Kuni Naruhiko [(b. 1887)], first head of the cadet house of Higashi-Kuni, was also an Army officer. At this time he held the rank of Brigadier General and was attached to the General Staff. [Subsequently, during World War II, he seems to have been aligned with Army factions antagonistic to Tōjō; and at war's end he was for fifty days Prime Minister of Japan's first post-war government.]

[5] [For the Imperial Message which empowered Princes of the Blood to attend in Privy Council sessions, issued within a month of the establishment of the Council in 1888, see Appendix II, E.]

station agent. Then I went on into Tokyo. On the way the station master at Kōzu brought me word that the Numazu agent had given my letter to Prince Konoe.

As soon as I reached Tokyo I went to the Foreign Ministry and had a talk with Vice Minister Yoshida. I found him to be extremely anxious about the safety of Lord Keeper of the Privy Seal Makino, his father-in-law, because of a recent scurrilous document. It is quite outrageous and he believes the ultimate source is Katō, the former Navy Chief of Staff. The document attributes it to Makino's "machinations" that Okabe, his chief secretary, had on two occasions privately called on Katō at his home. The fact is that when Okabe was in the foreign service and stationed in London some time ago, Katō had also been there and they had come to know each other well. Okabe had said nothing of these visits even to the Lord Privy Seal; but rather he remarked on taking leave of Katō, with whom he was on particularly good terms, "This talk is just between the two of us." And Katō had replied, "Of course, I shall speak of it to no one."

Yet in this scurrilous document it was plainly written, "The Lord Privy Seal secretly sent his private secretary to the home of Navy Chief of Staff Katō to say that, because of the Emperor's grave concern, he hoped it might be possible to ease His Majesty's mind." Yoshida is certain not only that this statement is false but also that it can have come from none other than Katō.

If so, this is truly scandalous; and I, too, was greatly shocked that Admiral Katō should be guilty of such a breach of trust.

At the same time Vice Minister Yoshida was deeply anxious about the personal safety of Lord Keeper of the Privy Seal Makino, and he said, "The Metropolitan Police must inquire immediately and fully into the source of this scandalous writing." Since I felt the same way about it, I went immediately to call on the Police Commissioner. He said, "The case is presently under investigation. We may find out something since this is our third inquiry. We shall certainly exert every effort to solve it." After asking to be supplied with the full details, I took my leave of him. I also asked about providing a guard for the Lord Privy Seal.[6]

---

[6] [Yoshida's worried complaint rings the changes once again on the charge that court officials had acted improperly if not illegally to "block" Katō some four months before. It does not seem to be the truth or falsity of the story that troubles Harada, but rather that the Emperor's closest official adviser is criticized with malign intent—a reminder, perhaps, of his awareness that the arrant violence of the outlaw *rōnin* tradition was close kin to the vituperation of nationalist tirades.]

*The Question of the Supreme War Council
Chairman's Voting Rights—The Question
of Participation by Imperial Family
Members—A Policy for Handling the
Meeting of the Supreme War Council—The
Chief of the Naval General Staff's Hasty
Action—The Army's Attitude.*

Since the time for the Privy Council's deliberations had not yet been set, it was arranged that the Emperor would go down to Hayama on the eleventh, to return when the matter was to be placed before the Privy Council. Some in the Privy Council surmised that the Emperor's departure for Hayama meant the usual opportunity to leave town for the summer, and that probably no request for advice would be made.

I was taking a bath on the evening of the eleventh when a telephone call from the Navy Minister unexpectedly came, asking me to see him as soon as possible. So I hastened to his official residence.

"This matter of Prince Fushimi has me very much upset. Isn't there any way we can keep him from participating in the voting? Of course, as a member of the Supreme War Council he *may* vote, but to the world at large his role is that of a member of the Imperial House. And the fact that this very serious matter may be decided by his vote should be of utmost moment to the Prince himself. I can't help thinking that it is most urgent, from the standpoint of the Imperial House, that His Highness not participate in the voting. I was wondering if some such advice might not be conveyed to him by some of His Majesty's advisers as from the Emperor; but this troubled me for the other questions which it might raise. What do you think might be done on this?"

Then he turned to the matter of whether the chairman of the Supreme War Council had two votes; i.e., the right to vote as well as the right to cast a deciding vote. Generally speaking a Chairman does not vote except in case of a tie. For the sake of following the precedents set, up to now, by the Diet and the Privy Council, the Chief of the Naval General Staff Taniguchi in preparation for this, his first session of the Supreme War Council, called on Fleet Admiral Tōgō to say, "Since Your Excellency is Chairman of this Council, there would seem to be no occasion for Your Excellency to express your views."

At this, the Fleet Admiral, with a dubious look on his face

said, "This is strange, isn't it? According to recent discussions, since a Chairman, who is at the same time a member, possesses as a Council member the right to vote, he also possesses as Chairman the right to cast a deciding ballot. Thus, there being five other members of the Council, three may be supporters of a proposal and two may be opposed. If I, too, am opposed to it, and if I cast my vote with the two—the matter would be tied. Then if, by use of my power as Chairman to cast a deciding vote, I were to vote against the measure, our side would win completely, wouldn't it?" Chief of the Naval General Staff Taniguchi remarked only, "Well, I must study this more carefully." Then, after leaving some documents and chatting a while, he took his departure.

For his part, the Navy Minister had called on Railways Minister Egi for his expert views on the matter of the Chairman's right to vote as a Council member, and the Railways Minister undertook a careful study of it. When I had stopped by at the Foreign Office and was chatting with Vice Minister Yoshida, a phone call came from the Prime Minister's residence saying the Prime Minister wished to see me immediately. When I arrived at his official residence, the Foreign Minister was also in the office with him. And the Prime Minister said to me, "The Foreign Minister will leave tomorrow to go to Okitsu. Is there anything you would like to ask on his talk with the Prince?" To this I ventured to reply, "There is nothing that I would especially suggest, but since the Prime Minister cannot frequently go down to Okitsu himself, it might be well, if he has not already spoken to the Prince about the government's stand toward the Privy Council, for the Foreign Minister to touch on this subject." To this he agreed.

Both the Prime Minister and the Foreign Minister, too, were apprehensive lest the effect of voting by members of the Imperial House cause widespread uneasiness. "Might there not be some way to prevent the Imperial Prince from casting a vote? Direct intervention in the Emperor's name would probably be wrong, wouldn't it?" I contented myself with saying, "Well, it might be considered; indeed, it might." Since I had promised to see the Lord Keeper of the Privy Seal at seven o'clock, I went to his official residence in Takanawa. Since he, too, had heard of this problem and was concerned about it, we discussed the subject of whether Fleet Admiral Tōgō, as Chairman, had a dual vote. The Lord Keeper of the Privy Seal said, "From the standpoint of precedents, as a rule the Chairman does not vote. He only casts a deciding vote in the case of a tie. On the matter of the propriety of employing the Emperor's authority to determine the question of whether Prince Fushimi casts a ballot or not, of course it would be best for Fushimi not to vote. But since the Supreme War Council is one of His Majesty's highest advisory bodies, would it not be a contradiction to use the Emperor's powers to determine the actual voting? A very difficult matter indeed." I also conveyed the message from Prince Saionji to the Lord Keeper, "Wouldn't it be well not to rush this beyond the point already reached?" And we spoke of the desirability of awaiting Admiral Okada's return on the fourteenth.

Returning from this call on the Lord Keeper, I stopped in for a short time at Kuwana because Konoe, whom I had not met since his last Okitsu visit, had sent a message for me to join him there. Later, after 9:30, I called on the Imperial Household Minister and the Grand Chamberlain who were in attendance upon his Majesty at the Chōjaen in Hayama. We talked of many things. Dr. Ikki shows an especially apt understanding and concern about what may develop. Both he and the Grand Chamberlain thought they should avoid taking a direct message from the Emperor to Fushimi.[7] On the matter of the Chairman's voting rights Dr. Ikki had previously maintained, as an expert on constitutional law, that the Chairman had the right both to vote and to cast a deciding vote. Hence he said, "For me this is difficult. The Grand Chamberlain suggests, 'According to the Supreme War Council's own rules, interpretation of the regulations appertains to the Navy Minister. Thus, if he were to rule that the Council Chairman may not vote, the matter would stand there, would it not?' "

Ikki

Say, for instance, that a conference of the Supreme War Councillors were held, and that there were three votes supporting the national defense proposal of the government. There are two opposing it. Fleet Admiral Tōgō, though chairman, could vote also in opposition. The vote would then be three to three; and Tōgō, as chairman, could then cast the deciding vote with the opposition. However, both Fleet Admiral Tōgō and Admiral Katō would have to submit their resignations if this matter were brought

---

[7] [Ikki was consulted on this matter not because he was an expert on the Constitution but because of his official position. It was not the Constitution or any of its agencies or instruments but the quite separate and parallel *Kōshitsu tempan* (officially translated as "Imperial House Law" but not a "law" in the ordinary sense) that provided for the governance of the Imperial Family whose members were thus marked off from all ordinary subjects whether peers or commoners. Technically subject to no external controls, members of the Imperial Family might be given advice and direction only through the Imperial Household Minister.]

before the Emperor and His Majesty were to decide instead to take the proposal of the Chief of the Naval General Staff and the Navy Minister, who also act in an advisory capacity. Thus it will greatly confuse matters if one faction in the Privy Council is busy conniving and consequently produces so serious a political problem. It is the province of the Privy Council to meet to receive and respond to a particular request from the Throne; and of the Supreme War Council to assemble to offer technical advice. The present authorities might say to the Privy Council that they take full responsibility for the assertion that "the new national defense plans are adequate within the terms of the new treaty." If, even so, the Privy Council took the position that it could tender no advice on ratification of the treaty without the prior assent of the highest military advisers, then the responsibility for the delay of the Privy Council meeting must inevitably be held by the Privy Council itself. In the last analysis it might be resolved by requesting an Imperial decision. But, if it is at all possible, His Majesty should not be troubled. Hence, the procedure of asserting that, on the basis of precedent, the Council Chairman does not have the right to vote would be much the best procedure whether Prince Fushimi participates or not.

I reached Ōfuna at 11:55 P.M. and took the express to Kōzu, but the train was so stifling that I stayed overnight at Kōzu and took the 5:40 A.M. train for Okitsu. When I had given my full report on these details, Prince Saionji said, "It would be best not to have to bother the Emperor directly, but it may be preferable to submitting to the notion of the Chairman's right to vote." We then talked of various matters, and I reminded him that Foreign Minister Shidehara was to call on him the next day. I returned to Tokyo in the evening.

When I reached the Shinagawa station there was a message from the Prime Minister's private secretary, "The Prime Minister will go this evening to Kamakura and would like you to see him there when it is convenient. The Railways Minister and the Navy Minister, however, will remain at their offices until about five o'clock." So I left the train at Shimbashi station and went immediately to the Navy Minister's official residence. I told him, "Since precedent has it that the Chairman does not vote in cases like this, might not Your Excellency, who has the power to interpret the regulations, proceed to make the decision?"

"What troubles me now," he said, "on this matter of the Chairman's right to vote, is that Chief of the Naval General Staff

Taniguchi who has been studying it for the last several days has taken the results of the inquiries by Army and Navy secretaries and by members of the Legislative Bureau to Fleet Admiral Tōgō and has represented this as the common agreement of Army and Navy, saying, 'Your Excellency does indeed have two votes: both the right to vote and the right to cast a deciding vote.' This would seem to be a new theory."

I was greatly surprised to hear this rash story, but with word that the Railways Minister had even now sent for Vice Minister Kobayashi to inquire into this matter, I presumed it might be so. Since the Navy Minister suggested that I wait until Kobayashi returned, I did so for some time. But since time was dragging on, I myself went to the Railways Minister's office. He informed me, "I've made various inquiries. In neither the Privy Council nor in the Imperial Diet does the Chairman have the right to vote. In fact, if one went according to custom, it could not be done. I had thought of telling this to Kobayashi now; but since he had already given the contrary view to Fleet Admiral Tōgō, why should I proffer my views? Still I'm extremely disturbed about it."

Since I understood the Imperial Household Minister had returned to his official residence in Banchō I called on him, related the ins and outs of the matter, and then reached the Prime Minister's house in Kamakura about eight-thirty. In the course of our conversation, he said, "On this question of the Chairman's right to vote there seems to be no alternative to forcing a showdown with the Navy." To the comment that it would be well for an effort to be made through the Army to produce agreement with the Navy, the Prime Minister rejoined, "I wish War Minister Ugaki would try to do this. A word of advice to him as from Prince Saionji would be desirable. Would you be good enough to go to see him at Hakone?" Since I thought a rash handling of such a suggestion could have serious consequences for the Prince, I left Ōfuna on the 9:28 P.M. express, went again to Shizuoka, and reached Okitsu at daybreak. I went to the Prince's study about seven o'clock and we discussed the situation. The Prince said,

"It would be extremely embarrassing to have it said that I interfered directly in this matter either by dissuading the Army members of the *Gensuifu* [Board of Field Marshals and Fleet Admirals] from attending its meetings or the Generals and Army members from sessions of the Supreme War Council. Besides I should dislike doing so. But I see no harm in your summarizing this situation to General Ugaki and in your conveying a message from me that since the Government is greatly concerned, I trust he will somehow exert himself at this present critical juncture."

Whereupon I left by the eight o'clock express for Numazu, and went by car from Numazu to call on General Ugaki, at Gōra in Hakone.

Ugaki said, "Well, up to the present it has not been customary for the Council Chairman to vote. Whatever the theory of the matter, why not stick to usage? If we can thus effect a solution which will slight no one, it should be perfectly all right. At least I'll call Sugiyama[8] this evening and tell him so."

Then, after a brief stop at Odawara, I returned to Tokyo. I immediately called the Chief of the Army General Staff [Kanaya Hanzō] thinking to go to speak with him about my talk with Ugaki; but since it was just at this time that Chief of the Naval General Staff Taniguchi was calling on him, I hung up and went first to the Navy Minister Takarabe's office, gave him the details of this conversation and on the way back I called on the Chief of the General Staff. The latter said,

"Well, we'll do what we can. I can take the responsibility of having the Field Marshals refrain from voting, but on the chairman's voting rights I have my doubts. Since it is such a serious matter we will think of some solution."

And then I went home.

That evening there was to be a dinner for Ambassador Wakatsuki at the Shinkiraku restaurant, and just as I was leaving to attend a phone call came from Honda.[9]

"General Ugaki had intended to call in Vice Minister Sugiyama this evening. This could not be arranged; so he had me make inquiries on the matter of the Chairman's right to vote insofar as concerned the practices of various other agencies. I have just reported by phone to General Ugaki that the Army and Navy have already come to an agreement on this matter. War Minister Ugaki asked me to inform you."

I thought this very strange, but thanked him and hung up, and then immediately phoned the Chief of the General Staff. "What kind of talk is this! We're back where we started from. It is because I had thought this might be the upshot that I went directly to Ugaki. This is indeed a most irregular situation. In view of your assent to what I had to say earlier, I trust there'll be some reconsideration." To this General Kanaya replied that he understood.

---

[8] Lieutenant General Sugiyama Hajime (Gen), Vice Minister of War.

[9] Lieutenant Colonel Honda Seizai was Private Secretary to the War Minister.

On the following morning I telephoned to him again. He said, "I'm going to General Ugaki's to ask about this whole matter up to the present. Meanwhile something must be said to Abe, who is serving as War Minister pro tem." Since I knew that Lieutenant General Abe was expected to call on the Chief of the General Staff at the General Staff Headquarters at eight-thirty in the morning, I made it a point to call on him before then for a brief chat. Lieutenant General Abe himself generally agreed, but he said, "Since an agreement has already been made on the matter of the right to vote, to set it aside now might do appreciable harm."

At nine-thirty that morning, the Chief of the Naval General Staff was to call on the Chief of the General Staff with the new national defense plans. Thus the three officers—the War Minister pro tem, the Chief of the General Staff, and the Chief of the Naval General Staff—met together and conferred on various subjects.

The same morning I received an urgent call from the Lord Keeper of the Privy Seal. I saw him immediately and acquainted him with the latest details. He greatly regretted Chief of the Naval General Staff Taniguchi's precipitate action in reporting to Fleet Admiral Tōgō on the status of the Chairman's powers.

Later the same morning I went again to see the Chief of the General Staff, learned of the morning's discussion, and was shown a copy of the agreement. In brief it said, "On this question there are diametrically opposed theories. Since they cannot be reconciled, both the Army and Navy will agree to accept, in this instance, the discretionary judgment of the Chairman of the Supreme War Council." The present chairman holds that he has two votes. Yet it may be that he will limit himself to a single deciding vote in case of a tie. The Chief of the General Staff went on, "Please mention this only to the Prince. On the matter of the new naval defense program, since the Chief of the Naval General Staff confidently assumes the responsibility, I place fullest trust in it." In a most friendly way he concluded, "The General Staff will do its utmost to work out a national defense plan consonant with that of the Chief of the Naval General Staff."

Since Admiral Okada returned to Tokyo that same morning, the afternoon was spent in various discussions with naval leaders who were continually calling, through the afternoon, at the Navy Minister's official residence. The Vice Minister, Kobayashi, was very pleased to report, "Well, Katō, the former Chief of the Naval General Staff has finally said he will himself go to speak with Fleet Admiral Tōgō; and today (July 15) Chief of the Naval General Staff Taniguchi will go to Karuizawa to see His Imperial

Highness Prince Fushimi. So isn't this to some extent a good thing? It's not bad, at least. Or rather, it is a turn for the better."

Yet I couldn't help thinking that all is not yet entirely satisfactory.

Without recalling this precisely, I believe it was on July 16 that I heard this from the Chief of the General Staff. The Chief of the General Staff that morning returned the formal call of the Chief of the Naval General Staff at the Admiralty where he announced, "Because it has full confidence in the responsibility of the Chief of the Naval General Staff, the Army will seek to develop its national defense plans in concert with those of the Navy."

> *The Position of Prince Higashi-Kuni—*
> *Prince Fushimi's Attitude Moderates—*
> *Fleet Admiral Tōgō and Vice Admiral*
> *Ogasawara—The Draft Reply to the In-*
> *quiry from the Throne—Prince Saionji's*
> *Views on Hastening the Reply to the*
> *Throne—Opinions about Navy Minister Takarabe's*
> *Resignation.*

About this time, since I understood that His Highness Prince Higashi-Kuni was to become commander at Nagoya, I called on him at his palace to pay my respects. And I took the occasion to raise certain questions with him. "There are many stories current that concern you and the former Vice Chief of the Naval General Staff Suetsugu: that he called on you to discuss the details of the disarmament conference from the standpoint of the Naval General Staff, and that he found Your Highness most sympathetic to his viewpoint; that Your Highness thereafter called on His Imperial Highness Prince Chichibu and spoke to him in this vein, 'When this disarmament treaty is submitted to the Privy Council, Your Highness as an Imperial Prince is entitled to be present.[10] Hence in so grave a matter as this you ought by all means to attend and exert your responsibility to the utmost.' Since this is the nature of the talk that is going around I would greatly appreciate your telling me the real facts of the matter."

The Prince's [i.e., Higashi-Kuni's] reply was that some time ago Saitō Hiroshi[11] of the Foreign Office did call on him to discuss

---

[10] [See above, pp. 182-183, and n. 5, for Takarabe's account which is a prelude to the call by Harada on Higashi-Kuni.]

[11] [See note on Saitō, above, chap. iii, n. 21.]

various aspects of the London Conference, and that Vice Admiral Suetsugu did indeed indicate a desire to talk with him about it. "I heard him in order to obtain the opposition party's views," the Prince said. "However, it is quite false to say either that I was sympathetic to his views or that I went to His Imperial Highness Prince Chichibu on this matter. To have done so would have been most embarrassing for the Prince. This distresses me deeply. That this distortion of the true facts has been the subject of propaganda makes me most anxious."

I had heard indirectly from Kobayashi, the Vice Minister of the Navy, that the source of this story is Katō Takayoshi, Chief of Naval Operations—Naval General Staff. Thus I asked Higashi-Kuni if he knew a certain Rear Admiral named Katō Takayoshi. His reply was, "He's quite unkown to me." Then, leaving the Prince's palace I relayed this conversation to Admiral Okada, the Navy Vice Minister, and the Navy Minister. These stories about the Prince's [i.e., Higashi-Kuni's] ideas and actions seem to be rumors devoid of truth.[12]

Higashi-Kuni

Both the Chief of the Naval General Staff and Admiral Okada are frequently calling on Fleet Admiral Tōgō, and seem to be trying to mollify Admiral Katō Kanji. Prince Fushimi, for his part, has recently come to have a changed attitude; and he is reported to have said:

"It will be quite bad for the nation to act as if the disarmament treaty cannot be ratified. As far as deficiencies in military strength are concerned, the government on its own responsibility can accomplish some remedy. Hence I myself have no opposition to the treaty on this ground." This would seem to be the result of Admiral Taniguchi's visit to Karuizawa.

Meanwhile as far as Tōgō is concerned, a Vice Admiral named Ogasawara Naganori has been constantly in attendance acting as if he were the spokesman for the old Fleet Admiral. Newsmen gathered about him, and he would make such comments as "Takarabe, being responsible for this mess, must resign"; or, "It's

---

[12] [Harada's conclusion about "these stories" should not be read to imply that Higashi-Kuni was in fact inhospitable to right-wing ideas and actions, as Harada is to report in the later volumes of his diary. Cf. the hearty endorsement of him given by one of the very active pre-war chauvinists, Kodama Yoshio, who was sought to re-interpret nationalist dogma for postwar Japan in his *I Was Defeated* (Tōkyō: Robert Booth and Taro Fukuda, Publishers, 1951), translated from a somewhat fuller Japanese original, *Ware Yaburetari* (Tōkyō: Tōzai Shuppansha, 1949); Storry, *The Double Patriots, passim*; and Morris, *Post-War Nationalism*, pp. 443-44, and *passim*.]

America's doing that our submarines must be less than 50,000 tons"; or, "It is because, with 70,000 tons of submarines or more, Japan could bring pressure on America that Japan is allowed only a maximum strength of 50,000 tons." It is reported that so many are constantly coming and going at Vice Admiral Ogasawara's house that in a single day he has some forty or fifty callers. Newspaperman often partly in fun come away with quite one-sided material and in fact write it up to make what Vice Admiral Ogasawara had said seem foolish. One of them said, "As we were leaving, after having gotten our stories for the present, the Vice Admiral seemed extremely pleased and self-satisfied, gesticulating with a large folding fan as if he fancied himself some great statesman." Some among the newsmen remarked that the Vice Admiral is a very annoying person. I, too, was concerned for there seemed to be no one among his associates with whom I could talk seriously.

At eight-thirty on the morning of July 20, the Big Four of the Navy—Okada, Taniguchi, Takarabe, and Katō, met for two hours; but Admiral Katō's position was quite unclear. Although it seemed likely that at the unofficial meeting of the Supreme War Council on the following day, the twenty-first, Admiral Katō would insist upon his position, even so the other three—the Navy Minister, the Chief of the Naval General Staff, and Admiral Okada—had made up their minds and were determined to accomplish as much as possible whatever might occur there.

Till now the prime purpose of these meetings had been to agree on a draft response to be given to an Imperial request for advice. The argument turned on the choice of words for the formula of the reply to the Throne. Either, "The military strength allowed by the London Conference Treaty is deficient"; or, ". . . is inadequate"; or, "will cause difficulty"; or, as Katō's circle insists, "has grave flaws." If stated bluntly Katō's position seemed to be: "I question the responsibility of Takarabe as Ambassador for he has recognized that the contents of the treaty are such as to produce grave defects. Yet it is not Ambassador Takarabe's responsibility alone, but that of the whole government. Thus the government as a whole should resign." At all events he seemed determined to have the words "grave defect" used. The government itself wanted to avoid such words, yet even Prime Minister Hamaguchi himself in his reply to interrogation in the Diet had spoken of "grave defects." But by this he had not meant the Treaty itself was at fault. Rather it referred to a change from the Navy's plans for strength adopted secretly in 1923.[13] The responsible authorities, however, contend that the discrepancies are remediable, and thus men like Okada are content with the assertion that there is no "defect" in the treaty as such.

I had gone to Okitsu on the evening of the eighteenth, and on the morning of the nineteenth accompanied the Prince as he was moving to Gotemba.[14] On the way we encountered a violent thunderstorm, but reached Gotemba safely. The Prince had had this to say,

Saionji and Harada

"The other day I was saying that the government ought not to rush these matters, and that it were better to await Admiral Okada's return from his inspection tour and once again discuss them with him in a leisurely fashion. There's no point in trying to rush matters in two or three days' time. This does not mean, however, that it might be best to postpone things till September. You must not be taken in by the opposition stratagem of postponing action until the political season in September. It must be settled soon—by the middle or the end of August. The other day the Lord Keeper of the Privy Seal came to say it might be best to proceed slowly, deferring action till September. But on this I can't agree with him. He even insists, 'If Takarabe were to resign it would be amicably settled. Egi has consented to his resignation.' But this can't be, I believe."

My reply was, "If Takarabe does resign now, there'll be a lot of turmoil. And Railways Minister Egi is quite aware of your view that Takarabe be deflected from any notion of resigning. He told me himself that I should try to keep up Takarabe's spirit so that he will not resign. I'm so sure of this that I'm convinced someone must be deliberately fooling the Lord Keeper of the Privy Seal."

The Prince had said, "Well, I then asked Makino who it was had recommended Takarabe's appointment as Navy Minister in the first place. I implied that as long as it is the Prime Minister's responsibility to appoint his cabinet and he had recommended Takarabe, it ill becomes third parties to volunteer advice. And with this, of course, Makino agreed."

---

[13] [This refers to the detailed National Defense Plan *(Kobubō hōshin)* prepared and Imperially approved after the agreements of the Washington Conference, and by extension, to the operational plans derived from it (below, n. 20).]

[14] It was Prince Saionji's custom to spend the summer season at the resort community of Gotemba, on the slopes of Mt. Fuji, where he maintained a house.

I returned that night to Tokyo and met with Prime Minister Hamaguchi, Admiral Okada, and Railways Minister Egi. For their consideration I passed on to them the Prince's counsel: "Now that the relationships within the Navy have been settled it is essential to proceed speedily to the formalities of the Imperial request for the Supreme War Council's advice on the treaty. To postpone this to September would be quite undesirable." All three of these men were strongly of the same opinion.[15]

> *The Informal Meeting of the Supreme War*
> *Council—The Navy Minister's Defense*
> *of his Position—The Formal Session*
> *of the Council and its Reply to the*
> *Throne—The Emperor's Question to the*
> *Prime Minister.*

The informal meeting of the Navy members of the Supreme War Council opened at the Navy Minister's official residence at eight-thirty on the morning of the twenty-first.[16] After a detailed explanation of the contents of the new national defense plan by the Chief of the Naval General Staff, taking some four hours, Admiral Prince Fushimi turned to the Navy Minister to ask if the government possessed sufficient resolution to remedy the defects, from a strategic and tactical viewpoint, stemming from the strength of forces stipulated at the London Conference. He asked for details with respect to what numbers would be readied during what years ahead. The Navy Minister became quite tense. "I am not in a position," he replied, "to go into such matters at this time. Continuing studies are being made. . . ." And to this Admiral Katō interposed, "Such vagueness is most alarming. In this case I must put

---

[15] [Here again Harada writes obliquely. He has previously noted that at the "Big Four" conference on the morning of the twentieth, the other three leaders had "made up their minds" and were "determined" to proceed despite Katō's continued intransigence. He then implies that a factor in their "determination" was the certain knowledge, which he had relayed the previous evening, that Saionji thought it was time to do so. Another factor, as also doubtlessly in Saionji's advice, was the understanding that Fushimi's views had become moderated. That is, the earlier apparent even division among the Councillors, over which Harada and others had been so anguished, has disappeared. Indeed, he makes no further reference to it. A consensus seems near at hand. It is time to involve the Court directly, to decide on the specific wording of the "Imperial request for advice" to set the precise terms that will elicit the desired "reply to the Throne."]

[16] [Aoki, I, 86-89. Harada's account of these days' activities accords in general with that of Aoki which is based on official papers.]

Gotemba

*Saionji's summer house,
a modified seventeenth century
farmhouse on the
slopes of Mount Fuji*

197

my query directly and immediately to the Prime Minister." And to this the Navy Minister replied, "In the present circumstance, with no formal inquiry from His Majesty, it is quite impossible to ask that the Prime Minister offer an explanation directly on this matter. I, myself, on my own responsibility, might try to guess what is in the Prime Minister's mind. . . ." Since it was patently impossible to conclude discussion in one sitting, he then adjourned the meeting till the morrow.

After the adjournment I went to the Navy Minister's official residence. Vice Admiral Kobayashi met me and said, "I'm quite disappointed in my boss. Even when material is given to him in carefully written form he cannot handle it well. To the Prince's question he should have said, 'Together with the Chief of the Naval General Staff I take full responsibility and I am confident the government can remedy any flaws with respect to strength of forces.' Instead, he became quite tense, mumbled, 'I'll have to think this over. . .' and so the matter continues to drag on."

When I met the Navy Minister, he was with the Military Affairs Bureau chief and others. I asked why he had not assumed, jointly with the Chief of the Naval General Staff, the responsibility of remedying any inadequacies. To this he replied that for a bystander like me it was easy to say anything; but in his position it was extremely difficult. The Military Affairs Bureau chief, however, also felt that this impasse was highly regrettable.

Then I met with the Prime Minister and chatted briefly by phone with the Lord Keeper of the Privy Seal. The Navy Minister was scheduled to meet with the Prime Minister at seven that evening. Vice Admiral Kobayashi asked me to call on Egi, before this meeting, to have him give as much encouragement as possible to the Navy Minister.

That evening, Egi, Adachi, and Shidehara met at the Prime Minister's residence.[17] Takarabe, of course, was there as the Prime Minister had asked, to confer with him on the reply to be given

---

[17] [To this important strategy conference Hamaguchi has summoned, in addition to Takarabe and Shidehara as the ministers directly concerned, his two most powerful party chieftains: Egi, his principal "brains-truster" whom Harada has already depicted as more involved than might be expected of a Railways Minister; and Adachi Kenzō, the Minseitō "god of elections," who is here mentioned for the first time. Adachi (1864-1948), who won his sobriquet because as Home Minister he bossed the majority-producing election machinery, led an important wing of the party. A rival of Egi, upon whom Hamaguchi placed such reliance, Adachi was prone to dissidence, partly because in character and background he differed from the more gentlemanly bureaucratic origins of his cabinet colleagues. A native of Kumamoto, as a young man he had been involved

the Supreme War Councillors on the morrow. I saw Hamaguchi the next morning. "When we met last night," he said, "we decided that the Navy Minister should say that necessary replenishments would be made as needed, within the limits of the government's financial condition and the general situation. The Navy Minister, on his own responsibility, is to tell them he has full confidence in my ability to realize this purpose."

That morning the Supreme War Councillors' conference opened at eight-thirty. Beforehand there had been a discussion among Admiral Okada, the Chief of the Naval General Staff, and the Navy Minister in which they agreed that such a phrase as "within the limits of financial and other circumstances" would be bound to become an issue with the Supreme War Councillors. Hence Takarabe took the initiative of changing it to: "The greatest efforts will be made to realize these objectives by utilizing finances and other circumstances as may be necessary."

At the conference itself Admiral Katō had much to say, such as stressing the need to adhere firmly to the "Three Basic Principles," but in the last analysis the Navy Minister's reply was acceptable. Following it, the Chief of the Naval General Staff made the formal request to the Throne for the calling of an official session of the Supreme War Council. The Emperor immediately dispatched the Chief Aide-de-Camp to the home of Fleet Admiral Tōgō, Chairman of the Supreme War Council; and it was decided to open the official session at ten o'clock on the twenty-third.[18]

I met with the Lord Keeper of the Privy Seal and the Minister of the Imperial Household to report these developments; and after a further meeting with the Prime Minister I went to Gotemba to relate these developments to the Prince. When I returned to Tokyo a little after three o'clock, the meeting of the Supreme War Council had already been successfully concluded, with unanimous approval of the reply to the Throne. It was decided that Fleet Admiral Tōgō and the Chief of the Naval General Staff would proceed together to Hayama to report formally on the completion of the conference.

Though I do not know the exact contents of this reply to

---

in Genyōsha-affiliated "continental *rōnin*" activities and intrigues, including the murder of Queen Min of Korea.

[On the strategy devised at this meeting Harada also quotes a later explanation by the Prime Minister (p. 214).]

[18] [This was a meeting of the naval members of the Supreme War Council, not of the whole council. Those present were Tōgō, Fushimi, Okada, Katō, Takarabe, Taniguchi assisted by appropriate staff subordinates.]

the Throne, it appears that the word "insufficient" was used rather than the more critical word "fault."[19]

The day before, the Navy Minister had said to me with some anxiety: "It is my incompetence that has delayed this conference. I have no excuse to offer for the incompleteness of everything." He obviously felt his responsibility keenly. Feeling sorry for him, I said, "The real blame lies with those who are deliberately creating this confusion. It is not at all necessary to feel this responsibility so keenly. The blame really belongs to those puppets of the politicians who are opposed to the treaty."

By telegram I reported to the Prince at Gotemba that the conference had been successfully concluded.

The Prime Minister held an extraordinary cabinet meeting [the same day] at which it was decided formally to petition the Throne to request the advice of the Privy Council [on the treaty]. This the Prime Minister did in formal audience at Hayama the following day [the twenty-fourth].

Meanwhile Fleet Admiral Tōgō and the Chief of the Naval General Staff had also been received in audience to present the Supreme War Council's reply to the Throne and had petitioned that the Prime Minister be questioned by His Majesty on its contents. Thus, by the Emperor's command, the Chief Aide-de-Camp called on the Prime Minister to inform him of this Supreme War Council document and of the Emperor's wish to grant him an audience forthwith to question him on its contents. Prime Minister Hamaguchi received this imperial message reverentially and the Chief Aide-de-Camp took his departure.

The Government, for its part, held no extraordinary cabinet meeting on this matter; but it was fully reported at the regular meeting on the twenty-fifth. The Government's address to the Throne [on this matter] had been drafted with the assent of various cabinet members. Now, with their formal approval, it was presented in a second formal audience with the Emperor at Hayama.[20]

---

[19] [Harada's impression on this point was incorrect: the word *kekkan* (fault) had not been softened to *fujūbun* (insufficiency) (Aoki, I, 87; below, n. 20).]

[20] [The Supreme War Council's reply asserted that the terms of the London treaty created "defects" (*kekkan*) in the maintenance of the Navy operations plans under the overall Defense Plan, that if the treaty were to be ratified because of its short duration certain specific measures must be undertaken to minimize the effects of these defects: among them, to improve existing vessels and to build to the maximum in unlimited categories; to maximize naval aviation; to increase and improve experimental research, training schedules, etc.

I returned from Gotemba and saw the Prime Minister and the Foreign Minister. It had been a quite formal audience, lasting only forty minutes for the presentation of the national defense plan. There had been no discussion and both Ministers were pleased and relieved that it was over.[21]

[Hamaguchi's address to the Throne, in response to this reply, said to be modeled after that which Admiral Katō Tomosaburō, as Prime Minister, had presented at a parallel stage in the ratification of the Washington Naval Treaty, bespoke his responsibility and readiness to execute the program "taking into account financial and other circumstances" (Aoki, I, 68-88; cf. Takeuchi, *War and Diplomacy in the Japanese Empire*, pp. 321-22, n. 110).]

[21] [Harada's careful use of the special formal Japanese terms for address and report to the Throne is difficult to render into mundane English. More importantly, it obscures the political significance of what Harada is recording. Put simply, Hamaguchi has had two audiences with the Emperor at Hayama: at the first he formally asked that the treaty be referred to the Privy Council; at the second he gave the government's comment on the Supreme War Council report. Is this perfunctory performance of protocol?

[The first audience *preceded* his official knowledge of the contents of the Supreme War Council document; the second *followed* the formal initiation of the Privy Council's review. Note that it was only after the formal Supreme War Council's meeting on the twenty-third that the first of these audiences took place. If he had asked for Privy Council review earlier, he would seemingly have given clear evidence of that violation of the supreme command prerogative (*tōsuiken kamban*) that his opponents were already charging against him. But by submitting the treaty to the Privy Council before he took official cognizance of the Supreme War Council document, on the other hand, he in effect excluded that document and his government's answer to it from the matters into which the Privy Council might inquire. (See the prefatory note to the next chapter.)

[Thus once again, by timely and entirely proper action, Hamaguchi was moving to deny to his opposition the data on which to make their case against him and the treaty. This would seem to be just that "drastic" and "resolute" action that Saionji has been urging upon him.

[This may also appear to be another instance of a gap in Harada's whole account. Yet though literally obscure, this segment would be transparently clear to Saionji (for whom, after all, Harada was writing); for Saionji was entirely conversant with its contextual meaning.]

CHAPTER VI

*From the Privy Council Meeting
to the Advice for
Unconditional Ratification*

Translator's Note: The Constitution did not require that treaties as such be referred to the Privy Council (see below, Appendix IIA, Art. LVI); but in practice, as a result of the inclusion of "treaties" in the enumerated matters on which the Emperor might request Privy Council opinion (see below, Appendix IID, Art. VI), virtually all treaties were submitted to the Council before ratification and the Council's advice had been invariably followed.

The monarchic character of the Japanese state, with its formal attribution of all action and decision to the absolutist ruler as aspects of his sovereignty, imposed a special terminology as well as a peculiar behavior pattern upon the Japanese governing elite and its instruments. Privy Councillors were technically lifetime officials of the Emperor's court and constitutionally defined as his "highest advisers" on certain matters. Hence they could easily regard themselves by virtue of this proximity to the Throne as clearly superior to and not merely coordinate with the Cabinet, an attitude not dissimilar to that on the supreme command agencies in their own sphere. In common parlance the Privy Council (Sūmitsuin) was known as the acronym sūfu, a term suggesting that it was at least parallel with the seifu (Government). This chapter breathes with the attitude that the sūfu must chide or chastise the seifu. In this confrontation the term seifu can stand narrowly for the Cabinet, i.e., the government of the day and specifically the Hamaguchi cabinet; or more broadly it may mean the cabinet-plus-parliamentary majority—the whole trend toward kensei no jōdō of which Saionji was sponsor.

Yet the Privy Council suffered a serious handicap if it were to try to exercise its vaunted "general surveillance over the whole government of the state," to use Councillor Kubota's phrase (see below, p. 218). It could only give advice when specifically asked to do so. Other officials (ministers of state, especially the Prime Minister) enjoyed a right of direct access or direct appeal (jōsō); and the possession of a similar right (iaku jōsō) by certain high military officials is familiar as the point of leverage from which the military finally extended their control over the whole state. But the Privy Council, like the Supreme War Council, could give advice only when a formally documented "Imperial inquiry" or "request from the Throne for advice" (goshijun) had been duly issued. The advice thus elicited was a "reply to the Throne" (hōtō) and its formal text (hōtōbun) could not properly go beyond the terms of reference of the originating "request from the Throne."

Clearly, then, the precise wording of an "Imperial request" as well as its timing might well have direct bearing on the political outcome of the matter at hand no less than the wording and timing of the "reply." Theoretically a prime minister had no direct relationship to this consultative process and his power to control it was compounded of many strengths and weaknesses vis-à-vis these other agencies. He could initiate it by "petitioning the Throne to request the advice" (goshijun sōsei) of those advisory agencies, and could bring some influence to bear on its course.

If Katō had bungled in his efforts to use the iaku jōsō to block the treaty in April, and later to give the Supreme War Council's hōtōbun an explicit condemnation of the Cabinet, Hamaguchi could try to exclude both matters from the terms of reference of the "inquiry" to the Privy Council.

Hamaguchi was well aware that the Council could be the final hurdle on which he might stumble before obtaining ratification of the treaty; and much of his apparent caution up to this time is perhaps explained thereby. The Council was prospectively a threat for two principal reasons: It regarded itself as the palladium of the Constitution and in the Diet and, reportedly, in the military establishment there had been grave charges against the constitutionality of the government's action. Furthermore, the Councillors were not only generally critical of parliamentary parties and their present hegemony but had a particular animus against the Minseitō. It was the Council which had brought an end to Wakatsuki's first cabinet on a domestic issue in 1927; and in riposte the Minseitō had put through the lower house a dangaian (resolution of im-

*peachment) against the Council. A wing of younger Minseitō mem-
bers was quite vociferous against the Council, which they regarded
as a doddering anachronism.*

> *The Throne's Formal Request to the Privy
> Council—The Prime Minister and the
> President of the Privy Council—The Text
> of the Government's Report to the Throne—
> The Privy Council's Advisory Committee—
> Rumors about the Audience of the President
> of the Privy Council with the Emperor at
> Hayama—The Request by the President of
> the Privy Council for the Submission of the
> Reply—The Question of Errors in the Trans-
> lation of the Treaty Text.*

Some time before, the Prime Minister had told the Emperor,
"I think it would be well to obtain the advice of the Privy Council
on the London Naval Treaty as soon as possible."[1] Now, on the
morning of July 24 he went to Hayama and requested a special personal audience with the Emperor. Recalling his earlier conversation, he said, "As I have mentioned before, I had been anxious that
Your Majesty request the Privy Council's advice before the summer
vacation period. It has been necessary to postpone action in order to
draw together the views of the military establishment. Fortunately
these views have now been fully elicited, and for this reason then,
even though the summer holidays are upon us, I would especially
ask for the Privy Council's advice at this time." With these prelim-
inaries the Prime Minister then formally petitioned the Throne to
obtain the Privy Council's advice. He told me of this at his official
residence when he returned from Hayama that afternoon. He proceeded to call on the President of the Privy Council[2] at his private

---

[1] Cf. Colegrove, "The Treaty-Making Power in Japan," *Am. J. Int. Law*,
XXV (1931), 270-97; "The Japanese Privy Council," *Am. Pol. Sci. Rev.* XXV
(1931), 589-604, 881-905.

[2] Baron Kuratomi Yūsaburō [had been Vice President of the Council
under Baron Hozumi, the former dean of the Tokyo Imperial University law
faculty whose appointment the Katō (Kōmei) ministry had obtained in an effort
to reduce the political activity of the Council. Upon Hozumi's death in 1926,
the first Wakatsuki government sought the appointment of Dr. Ikki, the *kunai
daijin* (above, chap. i. n. 39), a constitutional liberal, to the Council presidency.
But Ikki had only the preceding year become Imperial Household Minister, and
Saionji preferred that his services be retained in the immediate court circle.

residence, and requested that hearing be held at once. Thus by the fact of asking the Privy Council President to initiate hearings, the whole matter passed into the hands of the Privy Council.

The following morning, when I went to Gotemba to report that the matter was now formally in the hands of the Privy Council, the Prince seemed to be quite satisfied and asked me to relay this message to Hamaguchi on my return: "The country has reason to be grateful. My congratulations to the Prime Minister; indeed to the whole Cabinet."

On the twenty-fifth the Cabinet held a regular meeting at 10:30 A.M. The Prime Minister presented the text of a reply to the questions raised in the response of the Supreme War Council which had been presented to the Throne on the twenty-third. And then he left for his villa in Kamakura.

Since the treaty text, submitted to the Privy Council for advice on the twenty-fourth, is a most serious matter, and because the Government wished it to be considered during the summer's heat, the preliminary inquiries under the direction of Futagami,[3] the Chief Secretary of the Privy Council, were begun at 9:00 A.M. on the twenty-sixth. Hotta, Chief of the European-American Bureau [of the Foreign Office], informed me of this, "As might be expected, Chief Secretary Futagami is going into this with a fine-toothed comb to investigate in minute detail this submitted treaty text. Since it's the nature of the man, there's no help for it. But if there is some urgency, his niggling at detail can be a nuisance."

On the morning of the twenty-eighth, the Privy Council President went to Hayama, reported on the treaty investigation procedure, had lunch with His Majesty, and returned after a lengthy audience.[4] Thus the papers all at once began to write this up as if the audience implied that the situation is extremely serious. The following day, both the Grand Chamberlain and the Imperial House-

Futagami

Thus Kuratomi, clearly not Wakatsuki's first choice, was advanced to the presidency and Baron Hiranuma became Vice President.

[When the presidency again became vacant in 1934, however, Hiranuma was not advanced to this post; and Dr. Ikki was transferred to it from the *kunaishō*.]

[3] [Futagami Hyōji has already been marked as improperly privy to Katō's maneuvers (above, p. 155) which he made known to the opposition; and as a tale-bearer meriting only contempt (above, p. 171). This first meeting under Futagami was attended by three Privy Council secretaries, three bureau chiefs from the Foreign Office (including Hotta), and two naval captains.]

[4] [Cf. below, Appendix II D, for the pertinent Privy Council regulations on organization and procedure.]

hold Minister accompanied His Majesty on his return from Hayama to Tokyo for the ceremonies of Meiji festival.[5] Thus I went to
the Palace to find out from them privately how the situation was
developing. They told me it is quite customary for high officials
who come to pay their respects to the Throne during the summer at
Hayama to be entertained at a luncheon if it is convenient for His
Majesty. Some days before, in fact, the Prime Minister and other
Cabinet members had been so entertained. This case of the Privy
Council President was quite the same—simply a matter of "paying
respects." On this particular day His Majesty had been making
some collections at the seashore,[6] and, since he was more than an
hour late in returning, the President of the Privy Council had had
to wait for some time. The lunch itself was thus delayed and the
whole affair of Kuratomi's visit was long drawn out. From first to
last, however, it was simply a call to pay respects and there was
nothing more to it. It became clear that it was from this quite formal audience that Chief Secretary Futagami, the newsmen, and
others in Tokyo had devised and circulated their rumors. Some of
these reports would have it that "the Privy Council President's audience at Hayama today is a closely guarded secret; but it has already leaked out to the press that he went secretly to make most
urgent representations to the Throne." Etc., etc.

The President of the Privy Council called on the Prime Minister on August 4, to ask, "I shall appreciate your sending me the report of the Supreme War Council for use in the Privy Council deliberations." The Prime Minister replied, "I believe this report is
in the hands of the Emperor. I do not know whether the Naval
General Staff or the Supreme War Council have retained copies;
but the Government as such does not have one. Thus I cannot provide you with a copy."

To this Baron Kuratomi rejoined, "But could you not require
the Navy Minister, in accordance with Article VII of the Cabinet
Regulations,[7] to procure this report? Would it not then have come

---

[5] ["The Meiji-Tennōsai is observed . . . on July 30 to mark the anniversary of the demise in 1912 of the Emperor Meiji, grandfather of H.I.M. the Emperor. Offerings are made and a ritual performed at his mausoleum on the same
day." *The Japan Year Book*, 1943-44, p. 10].

[6] [This refers to the Emperor's well-known personal interest in marine
biology. The Hayama Imperial Villa is situated on the coast of the Miura
peninsula south of Tokyo.]

[7] [Kuratomi's appeal to this article, of which a translation is given in Appendix II B, suggests it had larger meaning than that assumed by Colegrove,
who saw it simply as a device for assuring the exclusion of the cabinet as a whole

into the hands of the Government? I again ask that you provide a copy for the Privy Council."

But the Prime Minister said, "Then, is Your Excellency venturing into political matters? Whether or not to ask for a report from the Navy Minister is up to me. It is not a matter in which the Privy Council may intervene." To this Kuratomi replied, somewhat flustered, "It is not at all that I propose to intervene. It is simply a case of obtaining a copy of the report for reference purposes." Hamaguchi continued, "This is not at all a kind of report to be had simply for the asking; nor is it at all necessary to your deliberation. In the last analysis it is only His Majesty of his own volition who can grant permission to see it. Hence, it is quite impossible for me to transmit it to you. Regardless of this I trust that your hearings may be conducted as soon as possible. On the matters of national defense I see no reason why you should not have testimony from the Navy Minister. But if you yourself wish to be given this report, I must remind you that it is a matter for the Imperial Court alone."

The Privy Council President said, "For me alone to see this report would not satisfy the general need for it as reference material for our hearings; and to place me under the compulsion of not discussing it with others, if I were to read it, is quite impossible. I imagine this may make our inquiry the more difficult." And with this he left the Prime Minister.

The press increasingly writes fictitious tales of what happens and what does not happen. The Prime Minister has called the Railways Minister and the Navy Minister to discuss the problem together. The Chief of the Naval General Staff has also said, "Since the text of the Supreme War Council report to the Throne was shown to the Prime Minister alone, and since no copy of it was circulated amongst members of the Cabinet, then—quite apart from

---

from rendering advice on military affairs (Kenneth Colegrove, "The Japanese Cabinet," *Am Pol. Sci. Rev.*, XXX [1936], 916-70).

[It is clear in this reference by Kuratomi that the article in question could also be employed by a Prime Minister to claim access to information transmitted to the Throne by the military under their right of *iaku jōsō*. Hamaguchi, who of course knew of the War Council's reply in detail but wanted to deny it to the Privy Council, refers by implication, in his answer to Kuratomi, to the Privy Council's ordinance which stipulated that the Council "shall not interfere with the executive" (below, Appendix II D, Art. VIII).

[Miller's study of Minobe (p. 99) makes the same assumption about this Article VII as Colegrove had done. He does so, however, as with his use of Harada's quotation of Minobe (chap. ii, n. 12), by giving only a partial translation with no indication that his ellipsis changes the meaning of the basic text.]

the matter of its being shown to the Privy Council President—I feel it is quite impossible to have copies circulated among the members of the Privy Council committee." Both the Naval General Staff and the Navy Ministry, thus, have presented a solid front. Both the Navy Minister and the new Chief of the Naval General Staff seem to be cooperating suitably with the Government and are firmly resolved to oppose the Privy Council in this.

The Privy Council President again visited the Prime Minister on August 8, and said, "I've already seen you twice and have brought this matter up formally. Today I want to talk to you quite informally. Without making an argument, I wonder why this report of the Supreme War Council cannot be transmitted to the Privy Council? Should not the Government thus demonstrate its good intentions and make it available without question?"

To this the Prime Minister replied: "Since what I said before was the result of very careful thought on this matter, there's nothing more for me to say than I have already said; but I would again urge that the Privy Council hearings open as speedily as possible." The Privy Council President said, "It has come to my ears that the Navy Minister and the Staff do not see eye to eye. If this be so, it is a further reason why I want to see the text."

The Prime Minister replied, "There's no such lack of agreement. In the first place, the text was unanimously accepted by the full meeting, and if you have been apprised of this fact, I think you'll find this point quite clear."

"Isn't it rather that to show me the text might seriously inconvenience the Government?"

But the Prime Minister replied, "I wouldn't venture to say what the outcome might be for me personally. Since I have already told you the reasons for my position, there is nothing further for me to say." And then he excused himself and they parted. According to the Prime Minister, the Privy Council President said something which sounded like a direct command, "Turn over to us, for reference purposes, both the text of the request to the Supreme War Council and the reply made by it." On this conversation I reported in like manner to the Lord Keeper of the Privy Seal, to the Imperial Household Minister, and also to the Grand Chamberlain, as well as to the Prince. The Prince had, in fact, earlier advised me to be careful on this score.

All kinds of propaganda continue to appear. In many instances, that aimed at harming the Government seemed to stem from the loose tongue of Chief Secretary Futagami. For example, he

said that the Government, that is, the Foreign Ministry, has transmitted a treaty filled with mistaken translations, and thus hearings
have been delayed—it has to be rewritten; or that the text of the
Supreme War Council's reply to the Throne has been withheld because it reveals the Government's weaknesses, and if it were shown,
then the Government must inevitably fall. Such rumors of errors in
the treaty text were designed particularly to embarrass the Foreign
Minister. The papers have published ridiculous stories: that the inquiry has pointed to such errors as the use of the word "inches"
when the metric system is more appropriate, and the use of [a literary word of the Edo period], rather than [the proper contemporary
legal term]. Some papers played up such items with a droll humor
that seems to have been highly resented by some of the Privy Council group.

Councillor Okada's Questions—The Personnel
of the Advisory Committee—The Prince's
Views on How to Deal with the Privy Council—
Dr. Minobe's Views—Liaison with the War
Minister.

At the end of its last previous session, when the Privy Council
had been discussing the matter of the World Court, Privy Councillor Okada[8] had arisen and asked to speak, but the Chairman had
said, "Since this session is already closed, this is not the place for
further official discussions. Would you postpone your point until
our next informal discussion?" Okada had accepted this as suitable.
Hence, he had no sooner taken his seat at the next conference than
he raised his question thus.

"It seems very strange to me, but more than a fortnight has
elapsed since the Imperial request for advice on the Disarmament
Treaty was handed down to the Privy Council on July 24. And
today, though I am a member of the Privy Council, I have not the
slightest knowledge of the contents of this request, nor does it seem
to be forthcoming. I shall welcome a report on this most serious
matter to the full Privy Council at the earliest moment. Why has
nothing been done about it thus far? The press has printed quite
varied reports: that the Privy Council has hardened its attitude,

---

[8] [Okada Ryōhei, an older bureaucrat and former Minister of Education,
was elder brother of Dr. Ikki—the Imperial Household Minister. Colegrove
characterized him as "one of the younger and more liberal councillors" (*Am. Pol.
Sci. Rev.*, XXV, 901). Okada was sixty-six; the average age of the Councillors as
a group at this time was seventy-two. See below, p. 254.]

that the Privy Council is softening; or that the Government is preparing to put up a fight. Whatever the situation is, I cannot make it out. In the first place, it appears in the newspapers as if only two or three Councillors other than the President have dealings with the Government; and yet with neither committee chairman not committee membership appointed thus far, everyone's conjectures are being played up in the press while not the slightest outline of the matter is available to us. Why has this been so long delayed?"

The Privy Council President, somewhat flustered, replied, "Well, according to Privy Council custom there are various preliminary inquiries to be made. Since the proposal from the Government has a number of mistakes and because these are being corrected, it has taken some time."

Then Okada continued his questioning: "Can it be that the text of the treaty, even though it has been submitted to the Emperor, has not yet finally been decided?" To this, of course, the reply was, "It's quite settled." Okada continued: "For Foreign Office officials to make serious mistakes and flaws in translations must be due to their lack of seriousness. Such lax morale is highly regrettable. This slackness must be tightened up."

To this kind of admonition Foreign Minister Shidehara struck back by saying, "As far as I am aware, there have been no mistranslations in this treaty text, no matter if the press may say that the Foreign Ministry's mistranslations are causing the delay. It is quite natural for such stories to be highly irritating to the officials concerned. Just where are there mistakes and mistranslations? The copies you have are photostatic copies of the original. At most, then, there may be misplaced commas or periods, or such trivial omissions due to the photographic reproduction. Beyond this there can be no errors 'in translation.' Who has in fact made any such assertions?" And the vigor of the Foreign Minister's statement seemed to have dumbfounded the Chief Secretary, and left him speechless.

As if in retaliation to Shidehara the evening papers published stories implying that the Foreign Minister had been quite helpless before Privy Councillor Okada's questioning, with headlines such as "Privy Councillor Okada admonishes the Foreign Minister," or "Privy Councillor Okada strongly criticizes the Government in the presence of the Foreign Minister," or again "The Privy Council takes a very firm stand." Certainly this was Chief Secretary Futagami's effort at retaliation.

On August 11 the Chairman and other members of the subcommittee were designated. When the list is examined, it is found that the members of the committee, of which Count Itō is chairman, are neither experienced diplomats nor yet jurists, but are drawn wholly from those interested in finance.[9] There were those who said, "Because of the relation between the treaty and the need to lighten the burdens of the people so as to effect the supplemental program skillfully in the present financial crisis—with this very aim they are seeking to embarrass the Government financially in this matter of the supplemental program.'" For example, it was said that by omitting from the subcommittee those who might naturally be favorable to the Government—such as Dr. Tomii[10] or Councillor Ishii[11] and including those ill-disposed toward the Government, the Privy Council leadership has particularly resolved to bring about a head-on collision.

I took a full report on this situation to the Prince at Gotemba. He said,

"I want the Government to persist consistently in following the path of logic and reason. If it shows no logic now, there'll be great trouble later. I may not be expressing this clearly now, but if it should turn out that the Privy Council opposition is irrational, wouldn't it be better for the Prime Minister, by the power of his office and at the Government's convenience, to dismiss both the President and the Vice President of the Privy Council and thus cause the reply to be given by new officers subsequently designated? At all events, the Government must move toward greater rationality."

It was as if the Prince was thinking that this might be an excellent opportunity, if only the Government were determined to take a strong stand, for reforming some of the deep-rooted evils

Tomii

---

[9] [This belatedly appointed subcommittee of ten Councillors included the two surviving members of a group who had drafted the constitution—Count Itō Miyoji and Viscount Kaneko Kentarō, with Count Itō as chairman. Its personnel (Appendix IC) was generally judged to be antipathetic to the government of Minseitō: Count Itō, for example, had taken a leading part in bringing on the fall of Wakatsuki's first cabinet three years before (see above, p. 82; Royama, p. 454). Count Itō had been a councillor since 1899; Viscount Kaneko since 1906, though with earlier service on the council, 1888-1894. Both had held ministerial posts in cabinets of Itō Hirobumi.]

[10] [Baron Tomii, distinguished emeritus professor of administrative law at Tokyo Imperial University, had been appointed to the Privy Council during the first Wakatsuki cabinet. Harada has already mentioned an episode indicating Dr. Tomii's pro-Minseitō disposition (above, p. 143).]

[11] [Viscount Ishii Kikujirō (1866-1950), a former Foreign Minister (in the wartime Ōkuma cabinet of 1915), was the Council's one notable expert from the diplomatic field. He fathered the Lansing-Ishii Agreement, and had been a delegate to the abortive Geneva naval conference of 1927.]

within the Privy Council, saying, "It's these irrationalities that trouble me. For the sake of prudence, the Government ought also to inform itself—at far as possible—of the views of qualified scholars and legal experts." After my departure I took this advice both to the Prime Minister and to Railways Minister Egi.

The general feeling at least among the subcommittee was that the text of the Supreme War Council's reply must be submitted to them before their decision is to be made. Since the Prince had asked me earlier to get the views of constitutional scholars, I visited Dr. Minobe[12] at Chigasaki. I posed to him the question whether it was proper for the Privy Council to ask to see the test of the reply. The Professor said,

"If it is essential to their deliberations it cannot be avoided. But it is a mistake for the Privy Council to cite Article VII of the Cabinet Regulations. On the question of the aforementioned text of the reply, it is reported to have a bearing on the Imperial sanction of national defense plans; but as the reply of the Supreme War Council it is quite otherwise. If it comes to the point of the Privy Council saying 'Since the Government does not cooperate in making this reply available to us, our deliberations cannot be accomplished,' the Government will be perfectly justified in charging the Privy Council with procrastination, or even with refusal to fulfil its official duties. Since the Privy Council's advice is not even essential to the ratification of treaties, the Government might be justified in proceeding to ratification without such advice. For example, at the conclusion of the Anglo-Japanese Alliance, Prime Minister Katsura, because he thought secrecy absolutely essential, formally petitioned for ratification without having obtained the prior advice of the Privy Council. This is at least one example of a precedent.[13]

"It might be better to propose that the Government make a request to the Emperor that the document be made available to the Privy Council. And in such a case, the Chief of the Naval General Staff might reply, 'This reply to the Imperial inquiry ought not to be shown,' and this would be perfectly acceptable. In the present circumstances for the Government to seem to be keeping it dark for secrecy's sake can do the Government great harm."

Earlier the Prince had asked me to say to the Prime Minister, "In the present serious circumstances it can do the Government

---

[12] [See above, pp. 113-15.]

[13] [Katsura's example in 1902 was not entirely unique. Takeuchi, examining the constitutional niceties of a variety of instances, concludes that the submission of treaties to the Council was indeed general practice but "merely a matter of form" (*War and Diplomacy in the Japanese Empire*, pp. 37, 429-34).]

great harm if it appears to lack an effective continuing rapport with War Minister Ugaki. It would be best if the Prime Minister sent one of his Cabinet colleagues or the Chief Secretary of the Cabinet to talk with General Ugaki. If this should not be possible, you yourself ought to volunteer to go in the Prime Minister's stead to call on the War Minister, General Ugaki, to report on the latest political developments and to serve as liaison between them. What do you say to seeing the War Minister as soon as possible?"

When I had spoken of this to the Prime Minister, he speedily assented, "Of course I want you to do this." Hence when I left Chigasaki after talking with Minobe I went to call on the War Minister at Gōra in Hakone but found that he was out walking and would not return till four or five o'clock. To utilize this time, then, I went over to Gotemba by crossing the Nagao Pass and called on the Prince, reported on my talk with Dr. Minobe and with the Prime Minister. Then I once again crossed back over the pass and talked with the War Minister for about an hour, from seven-thirty on, after I'd made it plain that I'd come on behalf of the Prime Minister. The War Minister said,

"The reply perhaps need not be shown; but since the replenishment program relates to state affairs, perhaps it ought to be shown. But if you say it should not be made available to the Privy Council, it needn't be. What I'd heard before was that the reply which the Chief of the Naval General Staff gave to General Kanaya was comparatively simple and brief, whereas what the Prime Minister reported to the Cabinet seemed quite complicated. If the request for advice to the Supreme War Council had been simply, 'From the standpoint of national defense, are there defects in the treaty or not?' then either a simple affirmative or negative answer would have sufficed; and then the so-called replenishment program would have been left to measures to be designed by the Navy Minister and the Chief of the Naval General Staff. But for the Supreme War Council to involve itself in this matter by its reply is altogether unprecedented. To inquire into the replenishment program is, I feel, very much like invading the proper jurisdiction of the government. I have a feeling it goes somewhat beyond the proper scope of either the request for advice or the reply thereto."

The War Minister expressed himself as grateful to the Prime Minister for having sent me, and expressed his appreciation also of the Prince's good wishes.

The following morning I met the Prime Minister, told him that the Lord Keeper of the Privy Seal had seen the Prince on the thirteenth and speaking of other aspects of the situation, I also touched on the matter of my visit with General Ugaki. The Prime Minister said,

"Well, I was concerned lest, if the Imperial request to the Supreme War Council had been simply 'Are there defects?' it would provoke an affirmative reply. It was thus arranged that by making the request somewhat more political, the reply might be 'There are defects, but counter measures are available.' Quite probably General Ugaki is not yet fully conversant with this matter. It was intended that he be informed by the War Minister pro tem; but it seems this has not yet been done."

Then I told the Prime Minister that the Prince had felt somewhat irritated and impatient with the Government's attitude, saying, "It's like scratching itching toes with one's shoes still on."

The Prime Minister said, "According to reports up to last evening, the fourteenth, Chairman Itō seems to be in a conciliatory mood and to have no intention of raising the question of the Supreme War Council's reply. His questions to the Government will generally center on the relations between the state of defense, the replenishment plans, and financial policies; and yet, on the Supreme War Council's reply, the situation is not clear."

The Lord Keeper of the Privy Seal had gone to Gotemba on the thirteenth. When I saw him that evening, he said with much pleasure, "This is the first time I've seen the Prince since his illness and he seems in much better health than before." And he went on, "Tomorrow I'm going to Ikaho. If you're not otherwise occupied, why not come along too?" But I replied and asked,

"I'm much too busy. Besides I'd like to have Okabe's help. Would you be good enough to tell him to remain in Tokyo?"

> *The Change in the Office of Parliamentary Vice Minister of War—The War Minister and the Problem of Control of Armaments—Count Itō's Policy—The Prime Minister's Call on the War Minister—The Meetings of the Privy Council Subcommittee—The Decision to Limit Attendance—A Talk with Privy Councillor Mizumachi.*

I visited the Prime Minister at his official residence on the morning of August 15, told him of Dr. Minobe's views, and of meeting the Prince and War Minister Ugaki, and I conveyed General Ugaki's appreciation of his courtesies. The Prime Minister said,

"If I can get a little free time, I'm going to go down to Hakone on the seventeenth to see the War Minister." And he went on to speak of having Mizoguchi, the Parliamentary Vice Minister of War, resign and he wondered whether to appoint Viscount Itō Jirōmaru in his stead.[14]

The Prime Minister left from Fujisawa a little after seven o'clock on the morning of the seventeenth. And since he had spoken of seeing General Ugaki at Hakone, I went along in the same car as far as Ōiso. As we were travelling I said,

"The other day as you'll remember the call I made on General Ugaki was made on your behalf. In the talk we had then, General Ugaki gave the impression of placing perhaps too much confidence in Mizoguchi. Perhaps you should bear this in mind." I mentioned also that General Ugaki had said he would call on the Prince in the near future. The Prime Minister then responded,

"There's something I'd like you to do for me while there's yet time. When General Ugaki goes to see the Prince, since the whole matter of armament controls cannot be settled without Ugaki's help, I would very much like to have the Prince comment on this to Ugaki."

I left the train at Ōiso[15] and went on to Gotemba in the afternoon. I mentioned to the Prince that the visit of Tawara,[16] the Minister of Commerce and Industry, to Count Itō was purely personal and was made quite without the knowledge of the Government; that the situation with respect to the Privy Council is unchanged; and finally, "The Prime Minister asks that you urge on General Ugaki the need for military reorganization." The Prince replied,

"Of course I will take this up with War Minister Ugaki. On the other matter, Privy Councillor Itō may say he will not touch on the matter of the Supreme War Council's reply to the Throne, but this is no assurance that the subject will not be brought up. It is almost a habit with Itō to insist he will not bring up such-and-such a subject, but when the matter subsequently is broached, he will assert it was beyond his power to stop it. In other words, we must yet be careful."

---

[14] [On Mizoguchi, see above, chap. iii, n. 31, and p. 160. Viscount Itō, a member of the House of Peers, a former Parliamentary councillor for Navy, did in fact become Parliamentary Vice Minister of War this year.]

[15] [Harada maintained a country villa at Kōreisan in Oiso, Kanagawa Prefecture, southwest of Tokyo.]

[16] [Tawara Magoichi was a bureaucrat who had served in administrative posts under the Home Ministry before "entering politics" with the Kenseikai-Minseitō groups in the early twenties. Harada, as ever, is sensitive to what may have seemed a defection.]

The first meeting of the Privy Council subcommittee was held at one o'clock on the eighteenth at the Privy Council office. Privy Council members alone were present and the general procedure for the hearings seems to have been established. On the afternoon of the nineteenth I called on the Prime Minister after his return from Kamakura. He said,

"When I saw War Minister Ugaki in Hakone he expressed his pleasure at my coming. He spoke also of the London Treaty, and he again said, on the matter of the reply, that there was no reason at all why it should be shown to the Privy Council. I had intended not to refer, except with circumspection, to the matter of armament control, but it seemed his intention to press the matter strongly."

After passing on two or three bits of advice from the Prince, I left and returned home. According to the talk of the day, there will be a session of the Privy Council subcommittee on the twenty-third at which only three cabinet members—the Prime Minister, the Foreign Minister, and the Navy Minister—may be asked to attend to represent the Government; and this strikes me as being a somewhat ill-tempered and possibly mischievous action. About eight o'clock on the morning of the nineteenth I called on Privy Councilor Mizumachi[17] at his home to ask about the situation. He told me,

"Of course on my own responsibility I cannot discuss these confidential matters; but we can speak of probabilities. First speaking of conclusions, I think it is absolutely certain, on the matter of advice on the treaty, that the ultimate recommendation will be for Imperial sanction of the treaty. However, I also think it is inevitable for unhappy developments to take place before them. In the first place, the Privy Council intends to inquire into the matter of Prime Minister Hamaguchi's disregard of the Naval General Staff at the time of issuing the instructions. The questioning on this topic may very well also give rise to the matter of the supreme command prerogative. In the second place, there's the question of whether or not dissension exists within the military establishment. In the third place, the matter of the prerogative of the supreme command. Fourthly, the contents of the Supreme War Council's reply, especially the necessity for an explanation of its relationship to state affairs. Fifth, there's the matter of replenishing the gaps in strength of forces; that is, the financial question. All of these points will probably be touched on.

"As far as possible the Government should avoid talking in

---

17 [Mizumachi Kesaroku (1864-1934), a member of the Privy Council, recently appointed (under Hamaguchi's ministry), was Harada's inside source for information on the subcommittee.]

generalities, and should not stick to petty logicalities. It would be better to look at the total situation; and if there are flaws in the matter as it actually stands, to admit openly and sincerely that there may have been flaws in procedure. After all, the Privy Councillors as a group are, in their own intentions, the true leaders of the nation. And because they are decent men, I hope that the Government, too, will treat them with utmost respect. A man like Privy Councillor Kaneko[18] has a large number of friends in America. When he read the text of the Foreign Minister's address, he said,

" 'Foreign Minister Shidehara has asked that the London Treaty be ratified as speedily as possible because of its importance for international good faith, and to show our sincere desire to further the cause of peace. But the reason that America hopes it will be ratified before November has nothing to do with international good faith; but rather, since a third of the United States Senate may be changed by the election in November, they want to accomplish the ratification before that change. That is, Britain and America are not talking about international good faith. That Japan alone is thinking in terms of honesty and good faith, is utterly absurd. Let's finish with the Foreign Minister once and for all.' "

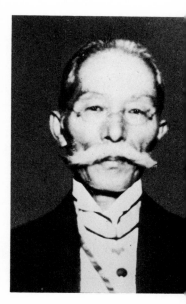

Mizumachi

Upon leaving Privy Councillor Mizumachi's house, I went to the Foreign Office, saw the Minister there; and, as we spoke of the foregoing matter, he said, "I never said anything about speeding the ratification for the sake of international good faith. They're quite mistaken about this."

Furthermore, the limitation that only the three ministers might attend, according to Mizumachi, had been proposed by Mizumachi himself. It had been most unfortunate to have previous Privy Council discussions leak out; and since this was because there had been altogether too many "ears," he had asked that all vice-ministers, bureau chiefs, secretaries and the like, and even other members of the Cabinet not directly involved, be excluded, and that admission be allowed only to most important ministers—with the ultimate objective of stopping all leaks of confidential data. Thus, I was told, whether it was the remarks of the Chairman Itō or

---

[18] See above, n. 9. Viscount Kaneko had attended Harvard Law School in 1872 and rather preened himself as an expert on America. His conversatism was not merely the result of his age, which was seventy-seven. Nearly a half-century before, in 1881, his *Seiji ronryaku (Essays on Politics)* had essentially translated selections from Edmund Burke, had been circulated by the government to counteract democratic doctrines and the influence of Rousseau's ideas (Osatake, *Nihon kenseishi taikō,* II, 621). His correspondence a decade later with Herbert Spencer elicited strong support for the conservative and absolutist elements of the new constitution (Michio Nagai, "Herbert Spencer in Early Meiji Japan," *Far Eastern Quarterly,* XIV (November, 1954), 55-64.]

of Mr. Mizumachi which might be given out, it was to be left to Chief Secretary Futagami to decide.[19]

When I heard this I couldn't help thinking that the very cause of the leaks of such confidential matter might be, in fact, the Privy Council's Chief Secretary himself, and so I called it to the attention of Privy Councillor Mizumachi. The limitation of members of the Government to three might somehow give a wrong impression; though I understood it was done from the very best intentions.[20] Naturally Privy Councillor Mizumachi himself admitted that from time to time, as it was necessary, Vice Ministers, Bureau Chiefs, and such assistants, might need to come to the next room.

Privy Councillor Kubota's[21] views on this matter were put this way, "Basically it's the function of the Privy Council to exercise a general surveillance over the whole governance of the state. Perhaps then, there's been enough quibbling on matters of form and ceremony: and we should call a halt to further hair-splitting."

> *Prince Saionji and the Limits on Attendance*
> *at the Subcommittee Meetings—Questions*
> *Raised by Privy Councillors Kaneko and*
> *Kawai—Rumors of American Purchase of*
> *the C.E.R.—Detailed Explanation on the*
> *Issuance of the Instructions to the London*
> *Delegation—Propaganda of the Chief*
> *Secretary of the Privy Council—Questions*
> *on the Prerogatives of the Supreme Command.*

[Dictated September 1, 1930]

When I went to Gotemba on August 19 to report to the

---

[19] [Despite an injunction of secrecy placed on Council debates and votes, they "have become almost public property. Despite the oft-repeated warnings of the President that members must not divulge the proceedings, in some occult way the newspapers are able to publish, not only full accounts of the speeches, but also a record of the votes cast. A general similarity of information throughout the press seems to indicate common sources of communication; and the accuracy of these press reports is generally assumed, even in references to the Council from the rostrum of the House of Representatives" (Colegrove, "The Japanese Privy Council," *Am. Pol. Sci. Rev.*, XXV, 608).]

[20] [Does the "wrong impression" of which Harada is apprehensive relate to another point of friction between the Council and Hamaguchi less than a year earlier? "When the Hamaguchi ministry in 1929 refused to accede to the demand of the Council for an increase of two seats, the Councillors in turn brought forward a proposal to amend their regulations so as to deprive the ministers of their votes" (Colegrove, "The Japanese Privy Council," *Am. Pol. Sci. Rev.*, XXV, 605).]

[21] [Baron Kubota Yuzuru, at 83 the second oldest member of the Council, had been Education Minister in the first Katsura government, 1903-06.]

Prince on the meeting of the Privy Council subcommittee the preceding day, the Prince said,

"I doubt very much that the subcommittee has any power to limit the attendance of ministers of state at its sessions. Speaking broadly, when Ministers of State (who have the responsibility to proffer advice) may seek audience with the Emperor, even His Majesty cannot refuse them a hearing. Still more in the case of the Privy Council must the Ministers of State be able to be present and to speak, whatever the subject under consideration. This disturbs me very much; for it's only the latest in a long series of flaws in the Council through the years."

On my way home I stopped in at Dr. Minobe's villa at Chigasaki and again sought his scholarly advice on a number of questions. Then, on my return to Tokyo I saw the Prime Minister and related to him the Prince's views.

The subcommittee's meeting on the twenty-third was limited to the statements of the three ministers. The third session was held on the twenty-sixth, and was largely limited to Viscount Kaneko's questions on the negotiations. The principal topics he asked about were: why was the Chief Delegate so guided to press for the 70 per cent ratio as soon as he had landed in the United States en route to London; what was the nature of the "free conversation" between Matsudaira and Reed; what of the Saitō[22] talks with Craigie;[23] also why should there have been a telegraphed request for instruction, and what were the reasons for Ambassador Takarabe's associating himself with this request for instructions?[24]

Following Kaneko, Privy Councillor Kawai,[25] as if delivering a monologue, wondered whether Admiral Takarabe ought to have

[22] [Saitō Hiroshi, chief of the Foreign Ministry's Information Bureau and member of the London delegation staff. See above, chap. iii, n. 21.]

[23] [Sir Leslie R. Craigie, member of the British delegation staff at the London Conference.]

[24] [Harada is less interested in the substance of these questions than in the demonstration they give of the argument, palatable to his chief, that the Councillors are improperly concerning themselves with political activity—the supervisory intervention presumably forbidden under Article VIII of the Imperial Ordinance on the Privy Council (below, Appendix II D). Hamaguchi's handling of such questions was essentially that laid down as doctrine before the Fifty-Eighth Diet session (above, pp. 128 ff.), except for the exercise of more patience and precision with the Council. In the Diet there was a clear Minseitō majority. Privy Council opposition must be as firmly confronted as that in the Diet, but not to the point of provoking a negative response if such could be avoided. The Prime Minister's tactics become clearer in Harada's account of the later sessions of this subcommittee.]

[25] [General Kawai Misao (1864-1941) was a former Chief of the (Army) General Staff.]

gone to London as a plenipotentiary; or rather as Navy Minister to have remained in Japan. If he had it to do over again now, which would he prefer? The Navy Minister gave what seemed a very clever reply to this when he said, "To try to answer such a question would be very hard indeed. Whatever I might say would sound so like self-justification that I really cannot answer." Then Viscount Kaneko again arose and questioned the Foreign Minister:

"The Emperor has graciously announced that the summer recess has begun. And yet the Government has now transmitted a formal request for advice in this proposal for ratification of the treaty. Just what is the reason for this haste?" Somewhere Foreign Minister Shidehara had said that Imperial sanction was being hurried along because it was hoped that Japan might thus show a desire to promote international goodwill and a love of peace. With senatorial elections approaching, the United States might have a good domestic reason for hastening its ratification. Thus Viscount Kaneko implied that it was foolish for Japan alone to promote international goodwill.

The Foreign Minister, who well understood this scheme, replied succinctly, "There may be no reason from the standpoint of law for haste; but from the standpoint of convenience, the Cabinet hopes that ratification may be accomplished quickly."

The Prime Minister, very much irritated that this matter had become so protracted, suddenly arose to say, "I am wholly in agreement with the Foreign Minister's views. From the standpoint of domestic affairs it is time to formulate the budget. Hence, without suggesting there should be any time limit imposed, I believe that we should proceed as speedily as may be to recommendation for ratification."

To this Viscount Kaneko insisted on saying, "The remarks of the Foreign Minister and of the Prime Minister contradict each other." But Count Itō, the committee chairman, interrupted, saying, "The Government's explanations are never contradictory. I think this is enough for this time." Thus he brought the matter to an end. It is understood that he added, "But I want to reserve to a later occasion my own views on the budget which the Prime Minister speaks about."

The fourth session of the subcommittee was held on the twenty-eighth. It was spent in relatively inconsequential questioning of the Foreign Minister and the Navy Minister. Just what turn the general attitude of the Privy Council might take, it seems at this juncture impossible to guess. One question which did arise at this session was the matter rumored in the press of a pending American purchase of the Chinese Eastern Railway. The Privy Council is maneuvering to get the facts on this matter as well as to inquire into the treaty. Within the Privy Council it is a case of promptings from Chief Secretary Futagami, who probably represents it as another case of America's trying to infringe on Japan's preeminent rights in Manchuria. I am sure that Chief Secretary Futagami's visit to the head of the America and European Bureau, as soon as this story appeared in the press, was not without special significance.

[Dictation date unclear.]

On the twenty-seventh[26] I went to Gotemba, reported on the Privy Council situation on the twenty-eighth, and then I returned home.

At the Privy Council session on September 1, Privy Councillor Kawai asked for details on the Navy Minister's concurrence in the request for instructions. Privy Councillor Arai[27] raised many questions on consultations with the Naval General Staff that had taken place at the time before decision upon the final instructions. To this the Prime Minister replied, "I'm firmly of the belief that the Chief of the Naval General Staff had no objections," and politely and in some detail he explained the circumstances of that period. And finally Chairman Itō said, "What the Prime Minister has just told us is quite at variance with what has generally been reported. I believe there will be a number of further questions to be raised about this matter."

On the morning of the second, I went to Gotemba, saw the Prince, and discussed this situation with him generally. The Prince seemed rather tired because of a slight cold.

"I'll see no one for the time being. But when the Imperial Household Minister comes on the fifth, I want to be sure to see him because I have some business with him. You may cancel everything but this." On my return trip I stopped at Kōzu and called on War Minister Ugaki. The newspapers are busy spreading propaganda, making the worst of the situation between the Government and the Privy Council.

This was all the deliberate intention of Chief Secretary

---

[26] [This appears to be an error in the manuscript, and the date presumably was September 29.]

[27] [Arai Kentarō, a former Agriculture Minister in the Admiral Katō cabinet 1923-24.]

Futagami and his group. Privy Councillor Itō actually said, in the Privy Council, "It is extremely pleasant to note that nothing whatever has leaked out from the Privy Council meetings this time. It's spendid. All that's appearing in the press is complete fabrication. What fools the newsmen are! If one were to say to them that it is most troublesome for Privy Council activities to be leaked out, they'd accept it with pride. They are really quite stupid." But if one were to inquire where these reports came from and who was responsible, the principal source would turn out to be the Privy Council's own Chief Secretary.

At the September 3 meeting Privy Councillors Arai, Kawai, and Kaneko arose, one after the other, and in centering their remarks on the question of the prerogative of the supreme command, said, "Though the Prime Minister may say, as he did the other day, that we should accept that the Chief of the Naval General Staff had no objection to the final instructions, yet this is extremely doubtful." And they produced various sorts of evidence to prove the contrary to the Prime Minister's assertion. Much of this had been put together by reservists, members of the Yōyōkai or the Kaikōkai, based on drafts made by Katō, the former Chief of the Naval General Staff, or Suetsugu, the former Vice Chief of the Naval General Staff, and hence altogether partial to their position and wholly at variance with the real facts. "Why," they queried, "has the Government leaned so heavily on Admiral Okada? And why were the final instructions not handed directly to the Chief of the Naval General Staff, but rather were transmitted to the Vice Minister of Navy by Hamaguchi through the chief clerk of the Navy Ministry? Let us bring forth the former Chief of the Naval General Staff to confront the Prime Minister."

These are all topics on which strict secrecy should be maintained and which on no account should be discussed publicly. The Government has clearly made up its mind to deal with such activity on the part of the Privy Council with the utmost firmness. When I met with the Prime Minister on the afternoon of the third, I told him I would leave for Gotemba early the next morning, the fourth, and he asked me to postpone my departure till the afternoon. I had the impression that he was about to come to a decision of some sort. Later in the day I called on the Minister of the Imperial Household, at his private residence, to give him a general report on the Privy Council proceedings of the day, and to converse on various matters.

*The Government's Determination—The
Foreign Minister's Illness—The Prime
Minister's Message to Prince Saionji—
Saionji's Message of Support—Questions
on the Contents of the Treaty—The
Railways Minister's Visit to Prince Saionji.*

Early on the morning of the fourth I called on Railways Minister Egi at his private residence and we discussed various aspects of the Privy Council situation. Judging from his attitude, it seemed to me that the Government is quite firm in its determination. He showed me the Privy Council Regulations, established by Imperial Rescript, and asserted, "We absolutely cannot permit expressions and activities which clearly violate Articles I and III of these regulations."[28] And he went on, "I believe the Prime Minister would like to see you about ten-thirty. Why not ask if that is convenient instead of awaiting his call?" When I phoned the Prime Minister about ten o'clock, he asked me to call at ten-thirty. So I dropped by at the Foreign Ministry first and went from there to the Prime Minister's office. At the Foreign Ministry I was told that sudden severe stomach pains had kept Shidehara from coming to the office, and I was anxious lest he again be suffering from appendicitis.

When I saw the Prime Minister at half-past ten, he gave me the following summary of the situation:

"I explained to the Privy Council, 'As a result of the liaison activities of the Navy Ministry's Chief Secretary with the Chief of the Naval General Staff, I was firmly convinced that the Naval General Staff was resolved to do its utmost to establish effective alternatives to secure the national defense if the Government had made its determination on this matter from the point of view of overall national affairs, even though from a strictly professional operational viewpoint the treaty provided inadequate strength. Hence I issued the new instructions.'

---

[28] [Articles I and III of the *Sumitsuin jimukitei* (Regulations for the Conduct of Business of the Privy Council), to which Egi referred, read as follows:
     I. The Privy Council shall formulate its opinions on matters submitted to its deliberation by order of the Emperor.
     III. The Privy Council shall have official connection with the Cabinet and with the Ministers of State only, and officially shall not communicate or have any connection whatever with any other governmental offices, with the Diet, or with any of His Majesty's private subjects.
Cf. Appendix II D, below; Harada, I, 281-82.]

"Each member of the subcommittee, however, has received a good deal of material from outside sources and they may not be prepared to accept my statement. About four o'clock Itō, the Chairman, arose to enumerate several of the points from the materials he held and remarked, 'The Prime Minister's comments differ markedly from the information which we have. In order to sweep away the doubts which this causes, I would like to ask, through the Navy Minister, that the former Chief of the Naval General Staff come before us so that we may hear his explanation. The Government is asked to grant this request of the Privy Council.'

"The items which the Chairman had offered up were various items, scattered in time, and bearing very little relation one with another, and obviously favorable only to the side of the former Chief of the Naval General Staff. If they are rounded out with the insertion of all that actually happened during the period in question the ultimate picture will be as I have already explained. But thinking it unwise to refute these comments at that moment, I contented myself with saying, 'We will take this request into consideration.' But I am quite determined to reject this suggestion without further ado.

"After I returned, I conferred with members of the Cabinet and we decided, of course, to reject this request. This morning I simply wrote on a piece of paper, without giving any reason for this decision, 'Your suggestion is much appreciated, but it is impossible to grant your request that Admiral Katō appear.'

"I shall appreciate your reporting all this to Prince Saionji. Perhaps because it has been turned down in this matter, the Privy Council may take some action against us. If so, the Government is determined to take strong measures; and thus I would like to have the Prince's support. Please so convey this message to the Prince."

I immediately took the 11:04 A.M. train to Atami, changed to a car at Odawara and drove to Gotemba by way of Hakone. I gave the Prime Minister's message in full detail and outlined the general situation in detail. The Prince responded quietly.

"Thank the Prime Minister for his message. I understand and agree with him completely. If it is necessary and reasonable to do so, I would have him take drastic measures today. Provided the action is clearly within the Constitution, I see no reason to be bound by precedent. I want him to act with firmest determination. Please convey this message to the Prime Minister. If there is anything beyond this which you would want to add I leave it to you to do so. Since you know what my wishes are, please act accordingly."

Upon leaving him I went by car to Odawara, reached Shim-bashi at five-thirty and went immediately with the Prince's message to the Prime Minister. The Prime Minister seemed much relieved and said to me, "I'm really grateful to you. This relieves me very much indeed."

Prince Saionji had asked me, just as I was leaving Gotemba, to inform the Lord Keeper of the Privy Seal, the Minister of the Imperial Household, and the Grand Chamberlain, and he felt some-what remiss that the Lord Keeper of the Privy Seal had not been informed earlier. Thus I planned to relay this information early the next morning through Okabe, since both the Lord Keeper of the Privy Seal and the Minister of the Imperial Household were at the Imperial Villa at Nasu. The Grand Chamberlain, I discovered, was fortunately returning to Tokyo that evening so that I could report to him in person and in detail early the next morning.

I wondered how the Privy Council meeting on September 5 might develop. At the outset Chairman Itō read the Government's reply to the committee's inquiry at the last meeting and then remarked,

"Members of the Privy Council are requested not to question the reasons why the Government has rejected their request, nor to ask the Prime Minister to explain such reasons. To avoid complications, I ask you all to refrain, whether in your questions or in comment, from reference to the reasons for this action by the Government."

Thus, when Privy Councillor Kawai seemed about to raise some question, Chairman Itō interrupted him and would not let him continue. Of the questions that were put, Privy Councillor Kaneko raised a point about Article XXIII of the Treaty; Privy Councillor Yamakawa asked about the source of funds for the supplemental program and whether or not taxes might be reduced; and Privy Councillor Kawai asked why, by 1936, Japan's ratio should be so much lower than America's. These were all questions relating directly to the treaty. The meeting ended after about two hours without special incident or difficulty.

The Prime Minister commented, "Although we should be careful not to cast off our guard, the situation seems quite different from that of two days ago."

I left Tokyo on the morning of the sixth, arrived at Gotemba in the afternoon and reported to Prince Saionji. His comment was, "Isn't it outside the terms of the inquiry to the Privy Council to raise questions on tax reduction and the like? Why didn't the presiding officer forbid questions of this nature? Are they confusing the Privy Council with the House of Peers?" And he went on to say, "At any rate I want you to tell War Minister Ugaki about it."

Thus I spent the night at Ōiso and the following morning—Sunday morning—I visited the War Minister at Kōzu, and returned home after reporting in general on the situation.

On that same Sunday morning the Railways Minister called on Prince Saionji at Gotemba to pay his respects and to report on the general situation. It just so happened that I took the same train as the Railways Minister after his call on the Prince, and heard his comments on how young the Prince seemed and in what good health. And from his evident pleasure in these remarks, I surmised that the Prince had said much to encourage the Government.

> *Questions on the Supplemental Program—*
> *Should the Subcommittee Hearings be Post-*
> *poned or Not—Newspaper Propaganda—*
> *Count Itō's Attitude Softens.*

Although the papers were seeking to magnify the bad elements in the situation, the Privy Council hearings on the eighth in fact went quite smoothly. Since there was no special reason for going to Gotemba, I contented myself with reporting by telephone.

At the next meeting of the committee on the tenth, Privy Councillor Arai arose with this question:

"It is said that the national defense is defective. How on earth can the supplemental program be accomplished? How is the budget shaping up? Can a reduction on the tax burden be effected? Will the surplus be spent entirely? I would like to know the total sums involved in the supplemental program. It would be quite unreasonable if these matters have not been decided upon up to this time. Without these data how can we proceed with our deliberations?"

To this the Prime Minister replied, "As far as 'total sums' are concerned, it is unreasonable to stipulate them until the annual estimate of the budget is made."

Then Privy Councillor Arai put in with, "All right then, let us postpone our deliberations until the annual estimate is made." But the Prime Minister objected, saying, "This we cannot permit. We cannot wait. Generally speaking, of course, there is no limitation in law on the time for your deliberations here, but there should be a certain *reasonable limit*. And I would like to have this matter concluded within such *reasonable* limits."[29]

Once again Privy Councillor Arai insisted, "I'd like to ask if the Navy General Staff and the Navy Ministry are of the same mind on this matter?"

To this the Navy Minister replied, "These matters are presently under discussion, and as you may know, they involve and concern the Finance Ministry and other agencies as well, so that I cannot yet comply with your wishes."

The Prime Minister began to speak, saying, "Mr. Arai ought indeed to know of this situation from his former experience. . . ." But Privy Councillor Arai stuck to his point, "No, I want to know if the Staff and Ministry are in agreement."[30]

And to this the Navy Minister replied, "Again I cannot meet this request. But on my own responsibility I would like to reassure you and assert that the supplemental program will be accomplished well within the limits of the surplus fund."

Having waited for the close of this session I met with the Prime Minister immediately afterward and he showed his firm resolve. "The atmosphere continues to be in general as before, but I felt that they are about to launch an attack. Whatever happens, the Government can never concede what is impossible. While I can't predict what the outcome may be, as far as the Government is concerned, we shall take whatever firm measures are needed by the Privy Council's actions."

Subsequently I related all this to the Minister of the Imperial Household and to the Grand Chamberlain; and I called Okabe and told him to report the matter to the Lord Keeper of the Privy Seal upon his return. I had planned to go to Gotemba later that same evening, but the Railways Minister had said he wanted to see me about eleven o'clock. Thus I called at his private residence, and he had this to say:—

"The general tactics of the Privy Council seem to be something like this: Since the Government indicates no definite method for achieving the supplemental program and shows no source of funds to finance it, the Government's own plans cannot yet be

---

[29] [The italicized words signify that Harada quotes Hamaguchi as using these English words. Perhaps he recalls them because they express one of Saionji's favorite notions.]

[30] [Cf. Arai's questions at the committee's fifth session (above, p. 221). Hamaguchi, in asking Arai to recall the complexities of budget drafting from his service in the Katō Tomosaburō cabinet, is perhaps obliquely critical of the majority of the committee members who were men without such ministerial background.]

established. Therefore the Privy Council has insufficient data to judge if the treaty can be acceptable or not. Thus they may suggest a postponement of further hearings until the Government's program is complete. If such a postponement is not allowed, they may reject the treaty. Such would seem to be their tactics. I think they may want to suspend their hearings to wait until the plans are made available to them. The Government, for its part, on its own responsibility, will make the supplemental program and reduce taxes as well. If the Privy Council has no confidence in the Government, there will be no way but to await the opening of the Diet session. If they say they want a postponement, our reply will be for them to continue. If they say they cannot continue, we will ask that their deliberations be concluded within a certain limit of time. Then they will counter with the assertion that the Government is forcing their exhaustion in deliberation. In a word there'll be a lot of questions at the next session."[31]

---

[31] [The Government had already agreed, vis-à-vis the Supreme War Council, to implement such supplemental program as the Navy Minister and Chief of Naval General Staff jointly propose "within limits of financial conditions and the general situation" (see above, p. 199). It was part of Hamaguchi's strategy, apart from the logic of the argument that the budget would depend on whether the treaty was accepted, to deny that the Privy Council in examining the treaty had any right to request budgetary data. His bluntness (or candor) on this point was softened somewhat by his statement that, were the details of the supplemental program complete, he would have voluntarily presented them.

[Egi, it will be recalled, was the chief political tactician for Hamaguchi. Note that he has called on Saionji on the preceding Sunday morning (above, p. 203), and will do so again the following Tuesday (below, p. 232). Note also that in Harada's account these are dismissed as calls "to pay respects" and to make "general report." Harada's record, of course, is of his own activities and his gathering of evidence (hearsay or direct) *for* Saionji. In this sense it did not need to include that data to which the old Prince was himself privy; but as a record for posterity, there might well be significant lacunae, except as Saionji made additions. The reader will have noticed that Harada generally pays little heed to the press, which of course is available to Saionji in Okitsu, except as it presents "problems." Egi's visits were in fact reported in the contemporary press; and the story was that his September 7 visit was to convey the Cabinet's determination to ride out the Privy Council storm and to petition the Emperor directly for ratification if the Council rejected it or attached reservations implied Saionji's support; the more so when Egi was received a second time on the sixteenth, on the eve of the committee's final decision. (Cf. Takeuchi, p. 330, n. 143. Takeuchi's account of this issue is derived almost exclusively from the contemporary daily press, and does not seem to require substantial revision from these and other subsequent disclosures.)

[The final completion of the supplemental program, which is the subject of Harada's Chapter viii (below, pp. 251-71), was of course contingent on several developments yet to appear: notably, the treaty ratification itself; the continued life of the Cabinet; its ability to permit Takarabe to resign and find a successor without upsetting the neat balance which kept the "moderate" admirals on top.]

On the morning of the eleventh I went to Gotemba to make a general report. The Prince's comment was that this time the Government, as long as the action was reasonable, would have to take drastic measures. Being in a hurry that day I returned by way of Odawara, crossing over at Hakone.

The newspapers are making propaganda at a great rate: "The session of the twelfth will result in a complete rupture between the Privy Council and the Government," and the like. Chief Secretary Futagami himself made some of this by announcing to a group of reporters playing up the Privy Council's "hardheadedness"—which made for lively reading—that the Privy Council's attitude was unshakable. The press is doing a bustling business.

At the meeting on the twelfth, Privy Councillor Kaneko arose to state:

"The relations between Japan and America are wholly peaceful. Although it is said that America is a land filled with a peace-loving spirit, still it is a cunning land that must be watched. And thus we Japanese must be sure to take suitable precautions against her."

Privy Councillor Kubota expressed himself thus: "It is very reassuring to learn that the military agencies are in agreement in their attitude on the prerogative of the supreme command. From the beginning, the historical development of the Japanese Empire has depended on the Army and Navy. Adequate armament has been the primary national policy since the founding of the country. It is for this reason that the increase in our national defense has meant the firm and steady development of our country. We cannot make light of this."

Then Privy Councillor Kawai arose to speak:

"I would like to know whether the Supreme War Councillors, at their meeting on this matter, placed much or little weight on the deficiencies in military manpower?" And his attitude showed this was no idle question, but Chairman Itō interrupted him saying, "Privy Councillor Kawai, don't you think there's been enough questioning already on this topic?"

Thus the meeting of the twelfth, at which an open rupture between the Privy Council and the Government had been predicted, was concluded more quietly than had been expected. This was no doubt because the Privy Council came to realize that the Government position was quite firm and thus they were led to soften their own attitude. The papers the next morning seemed to suffer quite a let-down.

Chairman Itō's Suggestion for Informally Presenting the Supplemental Program and the Supreme War Council's Reply—The Prime Minister's Definite Rejection of this Suggestion—Reasons for Hastening the Ratification—The Railways Minister's Visit to Prince Saionji—The Sudden Change of the Privy Council's Attitude—The Recommendation for Unconditional Ratification.

At the subcommittee's meeting on the fifteenth, Chairman Itō turned politely to each of the Councillors to ask, "Have you any further questions to put to the Government?" But there were none of any importance. When he was certain there were none further, the Chairman arose and quietly said,

"I now speak addressing the Government on behalf of the whole committee. First of all, there is the prime question of the prerogative of the supreme command. I note that the Government has made a *volte face* from its attitude expressed in the Diet and has now admitted to this committee that it must have the consent of the Chief of the Naval General Staff. There is thus no further discussion of this point. Secondly, there remains an uncertainty about the contents of the telegram sent by the former Chief of the Naval General Staff Katō to Ambassador Takarabe in London on April 2. I shall likewise let this matter rest. In the third place, this committee has asked the Government to provide it with data on the supplemental program. Since the Government has rejected this request, the Councillors have been unable to fulfil their duties adequately. Fourthly, we must see the text of the Supreme War Council's Reply to the Throne; without it we cannot adequately judge of the supplemental program. Accordingly the committee urgently again requests the Government to present the text of the reply. We do not press for an immediate answer to this request. It will be perfectly agreeable if the Government answers in writing some time in the days ahead."

At this Prime Minister Hamaguchi immediately arose and stated, "I can answer immediately the questions which Count Itō raised on behalf of the committee. With regard to the prerogative of the supreme command, which he has raised as the first point saying that the Government's answer to this committee differs entirely from that made to the Diet. When he speaks of a '*volte face*,' he is quite mistaken. In the Diet it is necessary to weigh each word carefully; but here in the friendly environment of the Privy Council discussions, I thought it better to go into more detail. While the words I have used may have differed according to the place, yet I cannot at all admit they indicate any change in meaning. As to the third point, the request for the presentation of materials which have not been submitted, both the Navy Minister and I have already replied in minute detail. Although we have not presented the material in question, I am convinced you have the fullest evidence necessary for your deliberations. I feel that it is not incumbent upon the Government to reveal the figures on the supplemental program. Yet if they had been fully prepared by this time, the Government of its own volition would have presented them for your information, even though it is under no obligation to do so. Now as to the fourth point, the question of the Supreme War Council's reply, let me offer you this assurance, the Navy Minister has already given you an explanation in great detail, so much so that I was fearful lest he touch upon the text of the reply itself. As for your request that the text itself be presented, there is nothing further I can say; for the document is not at the disposition of the Government; it did not originate with the Government and further it is not the kind of document which should be in the hands of the Government."

Itō

Then Chairman Itō, turning to each member of the committee, answered for them quite clearly.

"You have all heard the answer which has just been given by the Prime Minister. That is, is it clear that what the Prime Minister has just said is in reply to my formal request?"

Among those who put questions on this day, Privy Councillor Arai asked, "Why is the Government in such a rush to obtain ratification of the Treaty?"

The Prime Minister arose slowly, to give this reply:—

"As you may know from each day's newspapers, a sense of insecurity reaches today to all levels of society. Because of the urgency of domestic affairs it is most necessary to dispose of this problem without a day's delay. In the present parlous situation rumors are rife that a political crisis will result from whatever advice—pro or con—may be proffered by the Privy Council; that because of this crisis, should the Government be changed, there may again be an embargo on gold shipments. For myself I have not the slightest concern for the life of the Cabinet, but I cannot forego deep concern for the economic future of the nation."

Then Chairman Itō arose to announce that the next meeting

would be on the seventeenth, for members of the subcommittee alone. Prime Minister Hamaguchi glanced back at Chairman Itō and queried, with a trace of irony, "Are the Cabinet members not required to be present?" To which the reply was, "No, sir, they are not." All this I heard from the Prime Minister when I met with him just after the meeting. He went on to comment,

"Since it may be risky to depend for victory on the majority in the next regular session of the Diet, it seemed necessary to be quite careful. It may have been too early for me to do so, but I thought it better for me to reply directly at that point. I do not know what will come from the Privy Council, but I intend to deal with them as firmly as possible. Please report on this to Prince Saionji."

I immediately reported on this in some detail to the Lord Keeper of the Privy Seal and then to the Minister of the Imperial Household and the Grand Chamberlain. I returned home about eight o'clock to find Okabe and Konoe waiting to see me. While I was talking with them I was told a message had come from the Railways Minister Egi that he wishes to report to Prince Saionji on behalf of the Prime Minister on the most recent developments and thus asked me to phone him from Gotemba if this met the Prince's convenience.

Konoe was quite concerned lest the Railways Minister's visit be too conspicuous and thus harmful to the whole situation, but I could see no harm since he merely wished to report on developments.

After a dinner held for the International Statistics Conference at the Prime Minister's official residence that evening, the Railways Minister stopped in at my house about ten-thirty to talk with Konoe and me on various matters.

The following morning, the sixteenth, I went to Gotemba to report in detail on the Government's firm attitude toward the Privy Council and relayed the Railways Minister's request to call on the Prince. The Prince said, "If he must come, have him do so openly." So I immediately phoned Tokyo that the Prince was waiting to receive the Railways Minister. It was arranged that he would come by the four o'clock train. In the evening, then, the Railways Minister reported in detail and returned to Tokyo the same day.

On the seventeenth of September there was some anxiety as to the decision which might be made at the meeting exclusively of the Privy Council members of the committee. All the papers were

writing that the Privy Council could not avoid a head-on collision with the Government. Yet when I phoned from the Foreign Ministry about three-thirty to Privy Councillor Mizumachi at his home, I learned that the meeting had been concluded amicably and without incident, that the Privy Council committee had unexpectedly changed its attitude and had reached the resolution to recommend unconditional ratification of the treaty.[32] On this action after a two-hour session the meeting adjourned. Everyone seemed quite surprised at this apparently unexpected and sudden change of attitude. To me it seemed a very splendid result.

---

[32] [Harada gives his report on this crucial meeting, from data received from Mizumachi and Tomii at the beginning of the next chapter (below, pp. 235-37); and on data from Privy Councillor Egi together with his own assessment (below, pp. 242 ff.).] For the official record of these Privy Council subcommittee meetings, see the "Minutes of Committee Meetings for the year 1930: Secretariat of the Privy Council," Document No. 1124, Exhibit No. 910, in the manuscript document collections of the International Military Tribunal for the Far East, "Proceedings" and "Exhibits." The Japanese text, of which the foregoing is a partial translation, is found in the documents on Privy Council proceedings, *Shōwa gonen iinkai roku* [*Minutes of Committee Meetings for 1930*] (LC Microfilm Collection, IMT 200).

[The detailed epitome given in Aoki (I, chap. xxv; "Sumitsu-in no shingi [Privy Council Inquiry]," pp. 89-100) confirms in general the accuracy of Harada's summary reports for Saionji.]

CHAPTER VII

*From the Privy Council's
Sudden Change of Attitude
to the Ratification of the Treaty*

*Propaganda for Remedial Measures—The
Motives of Count Itō's Sudden Change of
Attitude—Councillor Yamakawa's Per-
plexity—Unconditional Approval—The
Asahi's Editorial: "The Privy Council's
Sudden Change and the Seiyūkai."*

After the subcommittee's action on September 17 for approval of the treaty became known, newsmen came with a variety of
stories. Here is an example:

"According to current reports, Chief Secretary of the Privy
Council Futagami and others are saying that the two chief agencies
under the Constitution—the Privy Council which is the Emperor's
highest consultative body and the Government which is the administrative body—should not be allowed to develop such opposition to
each other. In cases of this kind it is the appropriate responsibility
of the elder statesmen to mediate between the two agencies. In the
present circumstance perhaps Count Yamamoto or Count Kiyoura
may be called upon to intervene both to save the face of the Privy
Council and to put the Government in its proper place. Some such
mediators will probably step forward now to settle these issues."

Such propaganda was addressed partly to relieve the embarrassment of the Privy Council, but partly also to project Yamamoto
and Kiyoura as elder statesmen in succession to the *genrō*—whether

they be termed "successor *genrō*" or "senior statesmen."[1] It seemed to me that the followers of these men considered this a favorable opportunity and were thus responsible for the rumors.

There were also other reports, such as this: "The reason for the unexpected *volte face* was that the Emperor while at Nasuno had become increasingly concerned and had dispatched the Grand Chamberlain to Tokyo for each session of the committee to inquire personally of the Chairman about the situation. The matter has taken this course because of His Majesty's deep anxiety."

This, too, seemed a kind of excuse, not at all in accord with the facts. The Emperor was at Hayama when the Grand Chamberlain, on his own volition, called only once on the Committee Chairman to inquire into the situation. Beyond this the Grand Chamberlain came from Nasu to Tokyo on four or five consecutive days because of the illness of and possible operation on his brother, General Suzuki,[2] but not once did he see the Chairman again. I had met with him two or three times to report in some detail. Such were the propaganda stories but none of them revealed the true facts.

By telephone I reported to Gotemba simply that the matter had been passed unconditionally. On the morning of the nineteenth I visited both Privy Councillor Tomii and Privy Councillor Mizumachi. Privy Councillor Tomii's comments were as follows.

"To tell the truth, I had been almost overcome with worry in this case. I had even thought to go to Gotemba myself to speak

---

[1] [The term *jūshin*, here translated as "senior statesman," is an old feudal term signifying "chief retainer." It was being increasingly used by those arguing for some continuance of *genrō*-like high advisers or overseers. Such discussion (called *jūshin-ron*) cropped up again and again (see above, Chap. ii, n. 18; and Chap. iv, n. 19); and Harada adverts to it recurrently in subsequent volumes of his diary.

[Yamamoto and Kiyoura were both former prime ministers. Such *jūshin-ron* was partly ambition, partly antipathy to Saionji and his circle (as Harada quickly senses), but also partly genuine if archaistic concern to forefend the sharpening antagonisms rending Japanese public life—the familiar bureaucratic (and "oriental") preference for consensus. Ultimately Saionji gave it some recognition four years later when he informally called all former prime ministers to meet with him and court officials at the palace prior to his own decision to recommend Admiral Okada to be the new prime minister. At this *jūshin kaigi* (senior statesmen's conference) of July 4, 1934, Kiyoura at last reached his goal of becoming a kind of super-adviser; but old Count Yamamoto had died the year before. See Harada, III, 341-50; and Iwabuchi Tatsuo, *Jūshin-ron* (Tōkyō: Takayama Shoin, 1941).]

[2] Suzuki Takao, a Supreme War Councillor, was a younger brother of the Grand Chamberlain.

to the Prince about it. But when I realized that a powerless person like myself could not be of much help, I refrained from going to see him. The situation, however, was so complicated that I ventured to call on Count Itō at his home an hour before the subcommittee meeting was to open on the seventeenth. I spoke my mind as clearly and resolutely as possible; and found him to be equally firm in his determination. He said, 'In the situation as it is at present, I'm prepared to wager even my official position in the effort to have the treaty ratified and in short to resolve this issue.' And with this assurance from Count Itō I returned home."

Tomii went on to deplore, "It is the trickery of two or three members of the Privy Council which is harming the basic reputation of the Privy Council and is destroying the confidence of the public."

I next went to see Privy Councillor Mizumachi about the situation. He gave me the following story:

"Privy Councillor Kaneko has had this suggestion to make, 'The Government's position on the relationship between the prerogative of supreme command and Articles XI and XII of the Constitution is ambiguous. As one of those who drafted the Constitution I want to call on the Government to clarify its position and offer assurance. As far as the treaty is concerned, our approval with conditions should be the solution.' But the Chairman rejoined, 'We may not recommend ratification with reservations.' And then he went on, explaining with great emphasis to the members, 'If this subcommittee proposes postponement of its consideration of this treaty, the government will demand that we conclude our deliberations within a certain time limit. If further deliberations are impossible, we must return the Imperial request for advice. If we reject the treaty, the Government may report a counter-proposal to the Throne. Whichever we choose the result will be to beg His Majesty's decision, a result which can only trouble His Majesty. This would indeed fill me with awe and trepidation. Furthermore, in considering the situation in the Privy Council, there is no prospect that such a proposal from this subcommittee would be accepted by a plenary session. If the subcommittee's proposal is rejected by the plenary session, we must resign. In any case, it is a serious matter. In such circumstance, then, we must change our direction completely, and can only vote for unconditional ratification. I appeal to you to take account of my sincere devotion and to agree with me.'[3]

-----

[3] [The reader may surmise that the iterated shibboleth about "troubling

"At this point Privy Councillor Yamakawa,[4] an expression of deep doubt on his face, stood up to say, 'By nature and profession, I am only a humble scientist. In jurisprudence and diplomacy I am a complete amateur and thus till now I have trusted the guidance of the Committee Chairman, Count Itō, who has the skill and proficiency of long experience. I am now very much perplexed to be told to go in a direction completely different from the one he has been urging us to follow heretofore. Perhaps because I am a dullard I cannot simply sit here and say I agree. Please let me think it over for a while.'

"Then both Privy Councillor Den[5] and Privy Councillor Kuroda[6] tried to mollify him, saying 'We, too, are quite dissatisfied with this treaty, but there's nothing else we can do.' And the Chairman, bowing humbly, again sincerely appealed to Privy Councillor Yamakawa who finally gave in and shouted reluctantly, 'I'll agree!' It was an embarrassing situation and I felt a certain sympathy with him."

The final text of the resolution is not completed as yet, but its main purport is the following:

"Provided that the objectives of this treaty can be accomplished through the fulfillment of an adequate supplemental program devised in cooperation with the military departments, we believe the ratification of this treaty is acceptable."

His Majesty" is only part of Itō's reason for now standing for a report to approve ratification. As Itō notes, it was not certain that a negative report of the committee would be sustained by the whole Council. While treaty advice from the Privy Council had always hitherto been followed by the Emperor, Hamaguchi had demonstrated fairly clearly that he was not only capable of appealing for ratification in face of an adverse Council report, but also entirely likely to succeed in such an appeal. Were not the Navy moderates still on top? Had not the Army refrained from taking up the "supreme command issue" as it might have done in the Supreme War Council or through Ugaki's resignation? Was it not clear that Hamaguchi's position was supported by the court officials "about the Throne" and by the *genrō*? Both Itō's personal prestige and the whole position of the Council in the Japanese governmental scheme would be seriously discredited if Hamaguchi were given the opportunity to prove himself more powerful than the Council. His Majesty, in effect, would be "troubled" to hand the Council a stinging rebuke.]

[4] [Baron Dr. Yamakawa Kentarō (1854-1931), a physicist, had been president of Tokyo Imperial University at the beginning of the Taishō era.]

[5] [Baron Den Kenjirō (1855-1930) had been an active political figure in the Meiji and Taishō periods. Hiranuma had succeeded him as Justice Minister in the second Yamamoto cabinet (1923). He had been the first civilian governor-general of Formosa, in one of the reforms undertaken by Hara, the first commoner Prime Minister.

[6] [Marquis Kuroda Nagashige (1867-1939) was, of course, a member of the House of Peers as well as of the Privy Council.]

A further meeting is planned for the twenty-fourth or twenty-fifth to complete the draft, and on October 1 it will be submitted to the plenary session of the Council. Because the text of this resolution might appear to be conditional, the Cabinet is holding several further meetings to study the matter attentively, especially because it could not thoughtlessly be assumed to be entirely settled.

Thus, on the evening of the nineteenth, after I had reported to the Lord Keeper of the Privy Seal, the Grand Chamberlain, and to Dr. Ikki in some detail, I went to make my report to the Prince at Gotemba. The Prince was especially pleased that the situation had turned out like this.

The Seiyūkai had planned a general party rally on the sixteenth to work up party spirit in anticipation of the fall of the Cabinet on the seventeenth in connection with this Privy Council matter.

Public opinion at this time was strongly inclined to favor completion of the treaty as speedily as possible. To illustrate this I might refer to an editorial in the *Tōkyō Asahi* on the eighteenth.[7]

> *President of Seiyūkai Inukai's Speech—*
> *The Suzuki Group and Vice President of*
> *Privy Council Hiranuma—Chief Secretary*
> *of Seiyūkai Mori's Judgment—Talk with*
> *Kodama, President of the Yokohama Specie*
> *Bank.*

Since Prince Saionji was to return to Okitsu from Gotemba on the twentieth, I went to Gotemba early that morning to accompany him to Okitsu on the eleven o'clock train. He talked further

---

[7] [Harada here incorporates into his account an extensive quotation from the *Asahi*, which throughout this period gave staunch support to the Hamaguchi government, especially on the Treaty issue. The editorial in question berated the opposition Seiyūkai party for cottoning to the enemies of constitutional parliamentarism on the treaty issue; and its opening paragraph might well be quoted:
> Congratulations are certainly in order, for a step taken toward world peace as well as the upholding of our Constitution. Just when a head-on collision between the Privy Council and the Government seemed inevitable, the Council's subcommittee unexpectedly and without warning has recommended that the Treaty be returned for Imperial sanction. There is no reason and there is no influence at work to deflect the full session of the Council from accepting and approving its subcommittee report. It is now up to the Government to implement the true spirit of the Treaty and the purport of the London disarmament conference by decreasing the burdens on the people and relieving the nation's finances of excessive military expenditures.]

about what Inukai had said in the latter part of his speech at the Seiyūkai general rally, that "the London Treaty should be set aside."

"Why on earth should President Inukai have delivered such a speech?" queried the Prince.

From the reports that had come to me, I understood the original plan was for this speech to inveigh against the depression and to attack the Minseitō government's financial administration. This attack on fiscal policies was written by Horikiri.[8] In his own mind at first Inukai does not appear to have thought of making such criticisms as were in the latter part of his address. And the matter of setting aside the treaty was added later because of the urgent insistence of the Suzuki faction[9] in the party.

Basically the Suzuki faction is tied in with Hiranuma, the Vice President of the Privy Council. Hiranuma, from the very first, has insisted on discarding the treaty, and has been active in the movement to prevent Imperial ratification, arguing that the Emperor should not ratify the treaty. At the same time he suggested the prospect that the Seiyūkai, by pushing this line of attack, could bring about the downfall of the Minseitō government. Thus it was natural for Suzuki's group, following Hiranuma's lead, to insist on the insertion of this matter in the President's address in an effort to accomplish this purpose—the fall of the present Cabinet.

Hiranuma

Thinking back on it now, I recalled that Mori, the Secretary-General of the Seiyūkai, had phoned me from time to time and would present the same argument whenever we chanced to meet.

"The Cabinet will fall on this issue. To argue that the Emperor should ratify a treaty which would not guarantee the national defense under its terms is to deceive the young Emperor and is unworthy of a faithful subject. The fact that Katō, the former Chief of the Naval General Staff, did not agree with this view is apparent, is it not, because of his direct appeal to the

---

[8] [Horikiri Zembei (b. 1882), a prominent Seiyūkai member of the Diet, had served as secretary to Takahashi Korekiyo as Prime Minister.]

[9] [Dr. Suzuki Kisaburō (1867-1940), member of the House of Peers, adviser to the Seiyūkai, had been Justice Minister in the Kiyoura cabinet (1924) and Home Minister in the Tanaka cabinet (1927), a post he was forced to resign because of his flagrant interference with the Diet election. Subsequently (1932) he resigned from the House of Peers to be elected to the lower house and become president of the Seiyūkai after the assassination of Inukai. His political faction was on the extreme right, affiliated with such nationalist groups as the *Kokusuikai* and the *Kokuhonsha*, and implicated in many of the violent incidents of the politics of the thirties. Cf. Scalapino, *Democracy and the Party Movement in Pre-war Japan, passim.* See below, p. 277f.]

Throne the following day? In the Privy Council the Government has at last struck a hidden rock. Surely the Cabinet will founder within the next four or five days."

I had replied, "Well, I don't know; but I doubt that this treaty matter will result in a political upset." Mori seemed quite skeptical and remarked, "Somehow all the reports that come into my office are quite contrary to what I hear from people in the Foreign Ministry and from you."

"Perhaps it's wishful thinking on your part that accounts for it," I replied.

After my return from Okitsu on the twentieth, I called on Mori at the Seiyūkai headquarters the next day. He said, "As the situation has turned out, the Seiyūkai, beginning tomorrow, is going to push as vigorously as possible to oust the present Cabinet."

Generally speaking the Seiyūkai had made a completely mistaken estimate of the situation because it was misled by the propaganda of Hiranuma's faction. At this juncture the Privy Council seemed busily engaged in clarifying that the contents of its text did not attach any conditions to ratification of the treaty; yet, though I could not but think of the anxiety it had forced upon the Government, it had seemed clear that matters would work out satisfactorily.

On the morning of the twenty-third Mr. Kodama Kenji[10] came to visit me.

"Since the London Treaty has been before the Privy Council," he said, "there has been all sorts of talk: that the treaty could not be found acceptable and that a change of government would be provoked over this issue. It has also been rumored that, in the event of a change of government, the next cabinet, composed of Seiyūkai members, would again embargo gold shipments and devalue the currency. This would be done on the grounds that the Minseitō government's resumption of gold export was a real cause of the depression and a great mistake. To save the situation, then, gold shipments must be again prohibited and the currency depreciated. Because of the fearful expectation of such a development, over ten million yen in gold has been flowing out of the country each day since the Specie Bank began to sell exchange. And this run, of course, was of grave concern to the Bank. When finally the London Treaty was approved on the seventeenth and the political situation became more stable, the demand for yen

---

[10] President of the Yokohama Specie Bank.

suddenly dropped to less than a million per day. The anxiety is dissipated and no one now talks of it. Recently it has been decided that from September 26 on, each regularly scheduled sailing of the Nippon Yūsen Line ships will carry five million yen in gold in order to maintain our credit in the outside world and to meet our foreign payments. At the same time a statement will be issued clarifying the reasons for this action."

Looking back on it now I recall that it was when daily gold shipments had mounted above ten million that Mori had said to me: "Just check with Kodama of the Yokohama Specie Bank. Gold is flowing out of the country at a great rate. The Seiyūkai cannot condone such a situation without a word. We'll make a big thing of it."

Considering that the situation was largely brought on by Seiyūkai propaganda I couldn't help thinking what an inconsistent and illogical way for him to speak!

> *The Subcommittee's Report—Vice President Hiranuma is Forestalled— Privy Councillor Egi and Count Itō —The Committee's Affirmative Vote —The Visit of Vice Admiral Ōsumi and Rear Admiral Terashima— Prince Saionji's Views on the Report —A Successor for the Navy Minister.*

On the twenty-fourth I called on Privy Councillor Mizumachi and asked to be allowed to copy the report distributed to the Committee members; on the understanding, of course, that it was for the Prince alone.[11] The entire contents, from first to last, seemed based on the implicit premise, "With confidence in the Government's declaration of its responsibility." Yet every phrase of the text breathed distaste for the Government. It was filled with remarks such as "Britain will probably not ratify the London Treaty till after November because the Irish Problem is not decided. Therefore there is no need for Japan's haste." Or there were needless expatiations on the prerogative of the supreme command. Altogether it seemed to me to be much too long and filled with unnec-

---

[11] [Harada's full verbatim copy of this report into his pocket notebook (Number 14, with notes beginning in September, 1930), made during this call on Mizumachi, is found in the auxiliary volume to the Iwanami edition (Harada, IX, 102-04).]

essary clauses. Privy Councillor Mizumachi said, "It's quite well done. As usual, Count Itō has labored long over this." And he went on to tell me:

"As early as the fifteenth [of September] it seemed to me that Committee Chairman Itō had made up his mind to change his direction. I don't believe he conveyed this determination in any way to Vice President Hiranuma. From the first Hiranuma had believed that the Cabinet could be forced out if the treaty were destroyed: that is, by a recommendation against ratification. But if he had known of the Chairman's determination, I am sure he would not have allowed anything to be said at the Seiyūkai rally on the sixteenth about abrogating the treaty. Count Itō certainly put one over on him. I don't think even Chief Secretary Futagami knew anything of it till that very day. Needless to say, Hiranuma holds a grudge against Count Itō on this matter."

When I had called on Privy Councillor Egi[12] on the sixteenth, he told me that Count Itō had called him on that very day and had asked him to persuade Privy Councillors Okada and Ishii to be well-behaved at the full meeting of the Privy Council; that is, that they raise no question of confidence in the Chairman and voice no criticism of the Committee. He went on to tell me that Count Itō had showed his determination in these words.

"Even if it costs me my position, I'll settle this question. I have changed my previous views; the treaty must be ratified."

In other words, it was to get Egi to prevent men like Privy Councillors Okada and Ishii, men with grudges against the subcommittee and its chairman, from speaking up in the full Privy Council session that Itō had invited Egi to see him.

When I met Privy Councillor Tomii on the seventeenth [of September], just an hour before the Committee was to convene, he had told me, "I have severely criticized the Chairman for the impropriety of his attitude." But actually, at the time when he met with Tomii, the Committee Chairman had already made up his mind. Of course Privy Councillor Tomii's opinion had been indirectly considered, but it is not true that Itō suddenly changed his mind as a result of talking with Tomii. The truth of the matter seemed to me to be that he had decided on or about the evening of the fifteenth that it would be better to change his position and that of his committee than to face a situation in which it would

---

[12] Egi Chiyuki, whose Privy Council post capped a long civil service career, had been Education Minister in the Kiyoura cabinet. [The Railways Minister was his adopted son.]

be patently impossible to lead the full Privy Council to reject the treaty by unanimous action; a situation in which if the Privy Council were to vote down the subcommittee's recommendation, it would discredit the committee and shatter the prestige of its Chairman.

Then I visited Privy Councillor Sakurai.[13] He seemed very dissatisfied. "The Privy Council's knowledge of international affairs is extremely meager," he said. "The so-called right wing tries to deal with such affairs with extremely narrow ideas. Their deficiency in knowledge of international problems makes me very apprehensive both for the present and for the future as well." And this was an opinion I fully shared with him.

Be that as it may, as I was awaiting developments in the sub-committee meeting on the twenty-sixth, I had a phone call from Privy Councillor Mizumachi. He informed me, "After two or three corrections in the wording of the report the committee unanimously decided to recommend ratification. It's all safely settled."

I reported this to the Minister of the Imperial Household and also spoke of it to Konoe and Okabe.

On the previous evening both Vice Admiral Ōsumi and Rear Admiral Terashima had come to call on me. I might summarize their various comments in this way.

"When the Privy Council Committee was asking the Government to bring the former Chief of the Naval General Staff Katō before its hearings, the fleet was assembled for tactical maneuvers at Funakawa near Aomori. Both Katō, the former Chief of the Naval General Staff, and Suetsugu, the former Vice Chief of the Naval General Staff, happened to be there. They had planned to remain there until September 1 to observe the maneuvers. But about August 22 a telegram came to the Navy Ministry from Katō reporting that he was returning to Tokyo, changing his plans because of the serious illness of his niece; but that he would not, in these circumstances, present himself at the Naval Ministry. Yet when Rear Admiral Terashima went to Funakawa on the twenty-fourth, Katō was still there one or two days after sending his telegram. Then on the evening of the twenty-fourth, accompanied by Vice Admiral Suetsugu, who has no family relationship with him, Katō returned to Tokyo ostensibly because of his niece's serious illness. As we mentioned, it was just at this time that the Privy Council Com-

---

[13] [Dr. Sakurai Jōji (1858-1939), who had travelled widely abroad on many occasions, was President of the Imperial Academy and a member of the House of Peers.]

mittee was asking for the presence of former Chief of the Naval General Staff Katō. If the Government had acceded to this request, then Admiral Katō could have been present on the twenty-sixth [of August]. Since Admiral Katō was ostensibly back in Tokyo only because of his niece's illness, it was obvious that he and Vice Admiral Suetsugu were involved in this scheme in concert with certain outside quarters."

Considered from various angles this is a most deplorable situation for the Navy. I felt that it was especially regrettable for the future of the Imperial Navy that even such men as Vice Admiral Nomura are subject to censure as "the moderate party's admirals."

Ōsumi and Terashima stayed talking with me till about midnight.

The Privy Council Committee's meeting on the twenty-sixth [of September] was concluded without incident. Having left Tokyo late in the evening I saw Prince Saionji on the morning of the twenty-seventh. No sooner had I entered his room than he remarked,

"The only report I've seen is that in the newspapers. It's very strange, isn't it? Do Hamaguchi and others regard this as a good result? The Privy Council would put the whole responsibility on the Government when they say 'with confidence in the Government's declaration of its responsibility.' In such a case what reason can there be for continued existence of the Privy Council. What do you think about it?"

I said, "Well, I think it's a highly irresponsible report. Instead of replying on their own responsibility to His Majesty's request for advice, they've put the responsibility wholly on the shoulders of the Government."

When I read to him the text of the report that I had brought with me, the Prince commented. "It's filled with such superfluous verbiage. I'm sure it was written by Itō; it's so dull, isn't it? I remember years ago, when the Yamamoto cabinet—that is, the earthquake cabinet—was set up, an Imperial rescript was issued. The author of this, too, was Itō, and what a long thing it was. How on earth could the people, reduced to misery by the earthquake, have time to read such a verbose rescript! What was needed then was a sympathetic statement of few words through which the people might easily and immediately understand His Majesty's 'great sympathy and understanding.'"

I went on to tell him that there was something of a movement to have Navy Minister Takarabe resign and to have Admiral Abo[14] succeed him. The present Chief of the Naval General Staff, the Navy Vice Minister Kobayashi and Kawasaki, Chief of the Legislative Bureau, are all from Hiroshima and thus want to elevate one of their own group to this post. And I also told him that the Lord Keeper of the Privy Seal had earlier said, when he had called on me, that Ōsumi would be the best man for the post. Admiral Okada had also urged that Ōsumi is the man for the post. The Prince said, "I'm inclined to agree. Though I don't know Ōsumi, people do say he's a good man."[15]

Since the Prince had nothing further to say about the present attacks on the Government I went on to tell him that the Government would like to seize some chance, while the Prince is yet alive, to change both the President, the Vice President, and the Chief Secretary of the Privy Council as well.

I returned to Tokyo on the evening of the twenty-seventh, visited the Prime Minister on the twenty-ninth to report on the situation.

The Cabinet, when it read the Privy Council Committee report, was somewhat dissatisfied; but it seemed prepared to let the matter pass without action or comment.

Ōsumi

*The Plenary Session of the Privy Council—
The Circumstances Surrounding Admiral Abo's
Elevation—The Problem of the Privy Coun-
cil President's Report to the Throne—
The Change in the Naval Ministry—Ratifica-
tion of the Treaty—Dispatch of the Formal
Imperial Ratification.*

In advance of the session of the whole Privy Council on October 1, the President, Vice President, and Chief Secretary of the Council were apprehensive lest Privy Councillor Egi proclaim his lack of confidence in the President of the Privy Council or that

---

[14] [Admiral Baron Abo Kiyokazu (b. 1870), a member of the Supreme War Council, had been chief technical advisor to the Japanese delegation at the London Conference. Subsequently, upon his retirement from the Navy in 1934, he was elected to the House of Peers.]

[15] [Vice Admiral Ōsumi, currently commandant of the Yokosuka base, has already been encountered as Okada's agent in earlier tussles with Katō (above, p. 108). And Harada, after one of his dinners for his naval friends, has recorded criticism of Osumi as being "too moderate" (above, p. 172).]

Privy Councillor Ishii should speak in like vein in the Emperor's presence. When the plenary session was opened at ten o'clock on the morning of October 1, Count Itō, the Chairman of the sub-committee, reported on its proceedings and findings.[16]

Next Viscount Ishii arose to ask of the Privy Council President sharply why, in the light of the 60,000 ton "parity" in sub-marines which had been projected at the Geneva disarmament conference, it should now be necessary to demand 78,000 tons; and why more than a month had been wasted since this problem had been referred to the Privy Council.[17] Addressing the Naval Minister he remarked, "When other nations refrain from realizing the full rights to which they are entitled under the treaty, may it not bring calamity in the future for Japan to be the first to seek to implement its full rights to build up to the maximum allowed under the treaty?"

Then Viscount Ishiguro[18] raised the question, "What does the Prime Minister mean when he speaks of the danger of social disorders?" The Prime Minister explained in some detail that every day's delay in the matter of this advice to the Throne was producing rumors touching on economic, political and social fields and might have very serious consequences in the resultant political instability.

Finally this session of the whole Privy Council was concluded, without much trouble, in less than two hours. It had thus unanimously approved of ratification. About three o'clock that afternoon I met with the Prime Minister and learned the above from him.

---

[16] [Cf. "Record of the Privy Council regarding the Imperial Ratification of the London Naval Treaty of 1930," IMTFE, Doc. No. 891-A, Exhibit No. 911A. This document is also found in LC Microfilm Collection, IMT 120.]

[17] [The inconclusive Geneva three-power naval conference of 1927 had failed because of the inability of Britain and the United States to agree on what constituted "equality" or "parity" in the matter of cruisers. The Japanese delegation, headed by Admiral Viscount Saitō (then as now Governor-General of Korea) and Viscount Ishii, appears to have stood largely on the sidelines observing the apparent irreconcilable arguments of the other two. Ishii argued then that for Japan submarines were essentially a defensive implement and urged their exemption from limitation. U.S. Congress, Senate, *Records of the Conference for the Limitation of Naval Armaments, Held at Geneva, Switzerland, from June 20 to August 4, 1927*, U.S. Senate, 70th Cong., 1st Sess., Doc. No. 55 (Washington: Government Printing Office, 1928), pp. 46-47, cf. Philip J. Noel-Baker, *Disarmament and the Coolidge Conference* (London: L. and V. Woolf, 1927).]

[18] [Viscount Ishiguro Tadanori, the oldest member of the Council (born in 1845), had taken up the study of "Dutch medicine" before the Restoration, and had become Surgeon-General of the new Imperial Army. He retired in 1890.]

"We plan," he said, "to have a special Cabinet meeting tomorrow, the second, to formulate the request to the Throne for ratification. When the Emperor has approved it, the instrument of ratification will be sent to Britain."

Returning from my talk with the Prime Minister I called at the Foreign Ministry and at the Naval Ministry. And I thought also to see Admiral Okada to inquire further about the matter of the Navy Minister's possible resignation; but when I phoned his residence he was not at home. Happily, though quite by chance, I encountered him; and when we could find no suitable place to chat, he said, "Let's go to your house." He accompanied me there, and we talked of a number of things.

I asked, "Why are the members of the Supreme War Council calling so frequently on the Chief of the Naval General Staff?"

"I imagine," Okada replied, "it has to do with the supplemental program or some such matter. I think, too, that Navy Minister Takarabe will resign as soon as possible. Until a few days ago, I thought Ōsumi would be the best successor to Takarabe; but he is wise, I think, not to accept it before the budget estimates have been settled. If we consider Admiral Abo, he too will probably refuse it. It goes without saying, that the confusion of having no successor now for the Minister is most unfortunate for the nation and of course very bad for the Navy. As far as I am concerned, I think it would be best to persuade Admiral Abo to accept the post as successor to Takarabe. Thus it would be best to have the formal ratification of the treaty by the Emperor without delay. Admiral Abo is by no means a person of mere stubbornness and obstinacy. He is skillful at coordination and able to control his men; and I think he is eminently suitable. If Admiral Abo is acceptable to the Government, I will do my best to make this come to pass. Both from the Naval Ministry's situation and for the benefit of the Government Admiral Abo is the most suitable successor and there's no one else."[19]

When I afterwards called on Vice Minister Kobayashi at the Naval Ministry to inquire into the situation, he too insisted there

[19] [Note that Okada, after earlier sponsoring Ōsumi for this post, now supports Abo. It is difficult to assess all the factors in these personnel choices. Ōsumi had been tagged as a "moderate"; but perhaps more important was the fact that Abo, a full admiral, was not only the senior, but also was involved in the London decision. That he was expected to work well in harness with three other Hiroshima men already in high naval posts is a reminder that bureaucratic clique patterns often predominate over matters of policy (above, p. 245).]
[Harada records Ōsumi's own version of this transfer (below, p. 252).]

was no one but Admiral Abo for the post. The Vice Minister went on to say:

"If you were to ask why it should be necessary that there be a change in the Ministry, it is that when it comes to the new budgetary estimates there may be a complete change of atmosphere. Even if the same sum is involved, if it were under the present Naval Minister it would be concluded that there was not a larger budget because of Takarabe; but if it is put through under Abo the same sum would be acceptable because of Abo's approval of it. This seems to be how the matter stands. Quite apart from this, I hear that Minister Takarabe is extremely tired, and in the circumstance this is a very appropriate time for him to resign. If it is objected that as Vice Minister and as owing my post to the recommendation of the Minister, I should not speak this way, I am sorry that I must do so; but these are the facts of the matter.[20] Of course Abo is on good terms with the Chief of the Naval General Staff, and for that reason I think things will go 'smoothly.' "

In order to report this conversation to the Prince I took the night train on October first to Shizuoka; and saw the Prince with my report the following morning, the second. I related the circumstances of my meetings with Admiral Okada and with Vice Admiral Kobayashi. When I mentioned that a change in the Naval Ministry was imminent he had this to say:

"It would be the best thing to see this matter through with Takarabe, but if the situation doesn't permit this, it cannot be helped. Will you convey to Admiral Okada that Saionji has listened in silence to your report from beginning to end, and that finally he said that of course Admiral Okada would take a most careful attitude on matters of national defense. This goes without saying. And yet even so, it is from a broader view that I am expecting him to exert himself for the country, both directly and indirectly, to stabilize the political situation as soon as possible.

"Then I want you to tell Railways Minister Egi in detail about this circumstance in the Naval Ministry as soon as possible after your return to Tokyo. Furthermore on the matter of the Privy Council, we must end that strange custom maintained up to the present, which allows the Privy Council President to appeal directly

---

[20] [Kobayashi had earlier undertaken to criticize his superior, Takarabe, to Harada at the time of the Supreme War Council meetings (above, p. 198). Cf. the statement by an astute journalist in Japan in this period: "The young officer, or official, in Japan not only expects to do part of his chief's work, but thinks he has a right to do it" (Byas, *Government by Assassination*, p. 76).]

to the Throne.[21] He must not be allowed to infringe upon the office and prerogatives of the Prime Minister. This is a problem to be tackled later at more leisure, but that concerning the Naval Minister is urgent, so take it up with the Railways Minister as soon as possible."

He also asked with some anxiety, "The papers report that the so-called 'big wheels' in the Navy are thronging the Naval General Staff. What is their actual purpose? Are they not instigating something?" I promised him to inquire further into this situation when I saw people in the Navy; and I returned to Tokyo immediately that evening. I tried to find both the Prime Minister and the Railways Minister but could not meet either of them that evening.

The next morning I called on the Railways Minister at his home and spoke of the situation in the Naval Ministry.

Egi

The Railways Minister spoke quite calmly, "Yes, this problem emerged quite suddenly. In fact neither the Prime Minister nor I had any sleep last night because of it. The matter arose when it became known that on his return from London Navy Minister Takarabe intended to resign. I dissuaded him from this step then by pointing out that since he had affixed his signature to the treaty he ought not to resign until it was ratified; and I urged him to remain in the post for the good of the country. Now yesterday evening Minister Takarabe told the Prime Minister that he wished to resign now that ratification was accomplished. At first our thoughts turned to Ōsumi as a suitable successor, but after making various inquiries, it was evident there was no one but Abo. I immediately talked with Takarabe continuing till one o'clock in the morning. At two o'clock Takarabe went to see the Prime Minister, then Abo was also summoned. About three in the morning Abo and the Chief of the Naval General Staff Taniguchi met at the Navy Minister's official residence. Taniguchi, Abo, and Takarabe shook hands and Abo agreed to become Navy Minister without conditions. The formal investiture ceremony, then, will take place about one o'clock this afternoon."

Later, about nine-thirty in the morning I saw the Prime Minister and heard the same story from him. At his request I phoned to Prince Saionji at Okitsu, and to the Lord Keeper of the Privy Seal. The latter was surprised that the matter was disposed of so speedily.

The Prime Minister, acting on the decision taken in the Cab-

---

[21] [Saionji would seem to be hearkening back to Kuratomi's audience on July 28 and the consequent press speculation on the "serious situation" (above, p. 205). On the matter of Privy Council reform: see below, pp. 254 ff.]

inet meeting which had been advanced to the second, formally appealed to the Throne for immediate ratification of the London Treaty. On the afternoon of the same day, official notice came from the office of the Lord Keeper of the Privy Seal to the Cabinet that the treaty had been sanctioned by the Emperor at 2:35 P.M. On the third the Emperor will have returned the London Naval Treaty together with its ratification, and with this action only India and Ireland remain to ratify it. Since India requires only final government approval, its ratification is expected in the near future. Ireland's action will be delayed because its parliament will not be in session until November 19. By late November, thus, each signatory nation will have ratified the treaty. There is some indication that Ireland may consider some method of expediting its ratification. Thus all ratifications may be deposited on or about Armistice Day, November 11.

Thus the Japanese document of ratification was placed on board the Hikawa Maru of the Nippon Yūsen Line on its departure at 3:00 P.M. on the fourteenth for Seattle. The document will cross Canada and be forwarded to the Japanese Embassy in London. It is due to arrive there on October 28 or 29 and will be deposited with due ceremony by the Japanese Ambassador.

CHAPTER VIII

From the Appointment of a New Navy Minister to the Solution of the Supplemental Program

*The Appointment of the New Navy Minister
—Ex-Navy Minister Takarabe's Intentions
—Admiral Katō's Apology—Criticism
of the Privy Council President's Action—
Plans to Reform the Privy Council—
Takarabe is Granted the Privileges of his
Former Post.*

The formal investiture of the new Navy Minister took place at the Palace at 1:30 P.M. on October 3. On the evening of the third I went to the Navy Ministry to see Vice Minister Kobayashi and had a talk with him on various matters. The new Navy Minister was absent from the Ministry, paying formal courtesy calls on the Imperial Princes.

Since I had a message for Admiral Okada I called on him about five o'clock and conveyed the following message: "I returned from Okitsu just yesterday. Prince Saionji listened carefully for an hour as I conveyed Your Excellency's account of the circumstances concerning the selection of the new Navy Minister. Finally, he gave me this message for you: 'Very well. I understand. Tell Admiral Okada that considerations of national defense are important, of course; but I expect him to exert himself even more for our country from a wider viewpoint, both directly and indirectly.' "

Admiral Okada was pleased that the matter had been disposed of so speedily and without any trouble.

On the evening of the fourth Vice Admiral Ōsumi returned to

Tokyo. After I talked with him by phone, he joined me for dinner at my house. During dinner I learned about the following circumstances from him.

"Although I was urged by both Navy Minister Takarabe and Fleet Admiral Tōgō to accept the post, there are still so many senior to me in the service that I thought this was not the time for me to step forward, and I held to my refusal to do so. Admiral Abo, in accepting this post, will never deliberately cause trouble for the Government nor engage in foolish schemes along with the so-called die-hard elements. Both Kobayashi and I think we can be sure of that. In the end it may well prove the best way to restrain the activities of the ex-Chief of the Naval Staff, Katō."

I then met with the Minister of the Imperial Household and the Lord Keeper of the Privy Seal and outlined fully the developments up to this time. For the time being, it seemed to me, all was well.

On the morning of the sixth I visited the former Navy Minister Takarabe. He said to me:

"My resignation will help toward the success of the next disarmament conference. From one point of view I may seem to be irresponsible; yet in the present situation it is best for me to resign.

"There is another matter I have already discussed with the Lord Keeper of the Privy Seal some time ago, but I wish you would convey it to Prince Saionji himself and request his earnest consideration of it. For an Imperial Prince to take a responsible public post implies that he must inevitably exercise the authority of that post. No harm may come from this if all goes well. But if his actions and words are determined by interfering officious attendants around him, the results will be good neither for that Prince himself nor for the Imperial institution. In England there are honorary offices—posts which have no actual authority—attendant upon the King, such as the *'Personal Aide-de-Camp,'* for members of the royal family who are admirals or field marshals. It seems to me such a system would be better for the Japanese Imperial family."

In closing our conversation I said, "Considering seriously the great efforts that Your Excellency has exerted for so long a period and your sacrifices for the nation, it is most regrettable that you should have felt forced to resign; in fact, there's no reason for it. But I know how fatigued you must be and I hope you'll be able to enjoy a long deserved rest now that you've decided on this course." And with these remarks I returned home.

That evening I called on the Prime Minister in Kamakura

and went on to Okitsu directly from there. When I saw the Prince the following morning and apologized for not having come to report immediately on the day when the change in the Navy Ministry was accomplished, the Prince said, "Well, when you came recently with the report from Admiral Okada I knew this would be the inevitable result though I made no comment on it then. Nor was I very anxious over the outcome."

I then went on to review all that had transpired on this matter up to the present and I told him what Railways Minister Egi had had to say:

"The Seiyūkai had hoped to make it difficult for the government to find a successor to Takarabe and thus, if this move worked, to force the Cabinet out of office. Under this threat, then, the government has moved with lightning speed in the appointment of a new Minister. We have also obtained from Abo, the new Minister, fullest assurance of unprejudiced impartial performance of his new duties."

Then there was the story I had heard from Admiral Takarabe. On the very day he resigned from the post of Minister, Admiral Katō, the former Chief of the Naval General Staff, had come to his office in the Navy Ministry and pled tearfully with Takarabe, saying:

"I am deeply sorry that I have behaved up to now in such an improper way as to cause you embarrassment. Please forgive me for what I've done up to now. Let us return again to that goodwill that has been between us in the past forty years. I need your help and guidance yet again."

So Takarabe extending his hand in friendship said, "Of course, that goes without saying. But there is just one word of counsel which I hope you will heed. You must absolutely stop all contact with politicians of low class and scheming minds. This is a matter I hope you'll take to heart, especially now." To this Katō replied, "I shall never again see such persons. In fact, I have already been careful to break this practice."

To my recounting of this episode, the Prince remarked, "After all, his tearfulness—which he's indulged in on occasion before, hasn't he?—is one of Admiral Katō's tricks." And the Prince went on to say, "Admiral Abo, the new Minister, seems to be well-liked; even the press criticism is not bad. It seems to have worked out quite well. I am glad that the change was accomplished so skillfully and speedily. We've moved one step further along."

When I returned to Tokyo I met with the Prime Minister and

let him know that Prince Saionji was quite satisfied and relieved about the situation.

Since the attitude of some of the Privy Councillors toward the London Treaty clearly evidenced some kind of political motivation, there was increasingly open discussion of Privy Council reform. Many among the Councillors feel a deep uneasiness in their hearts at the present condition of the Privy Council wherein a group of three or four Councillors seem to hold the Council in their control, a circumstance quite contrary to the Council's original nature. Yet since they are all aged men, they have tolerated this situation lest there be commotion within the Council. Since this treaty was referred to the Privy Council, four men—the President, the Vice President, Councillor Itō, and Chief Secretary Futagami—have carried on more or less open political maneuvering; and of these the President is nothing more than a puppet of Itō and Hiranuma. The President has no prestige and it is this lack of prestige which has given rise to very sharp criticism. Especially is it said that there is no precedent at all in the past for the President to call on the Prime Minister and, taking his cue in this instance from Hiranuma or Itō, to try to obtain a copy of the formal reply of the Supreme War Council. There is considerable question of the very propriety of his making such a request at all. Whether it be the act itself or the motive behind it, there is general condemnation of it as imprudent and rash in the President of the Privy Council.

Of course there has long been much discussion of Privy Council reform. Men like Privy Councillor Okada have been saying, "By all means we want to set our hands to revising the Privy Council rules of procedure and to work gradually toward more basic reform."[1]

For nearly a month after the London Treaty had been referred to the Council, it had been impossible even for members of the Council to know what was the nature of the Throne's request for Council advice or anything of its contents. This might be disposed of by saying that preliminary investigation was necessary. A month was thus wasted with assertions that the government had been careless or that mistakes had been made in translation; yet in fact there were no such serious mistakes at all, beyond a misplaced comma or period. It was simply an exaggeration calculated to put

---

[1] [Okada Ryōhei (1864-1934), elder brother of the Imperial Household Minister, Dr. Ikki, has already been reported as critical of the present Council leadership (above, p. 209 ff.). After the ratification of the London treaty he spearheaded a move to reform Council procedures from within, a move which Kuratomi and others fairly effectively blocked. Cf. Colegrove, "The Japanese Privy Council," *Am. Pol. Sci. Rev.*, XXV (1931), 881-905.]

the blame on the government for the delay for which the Privy
Council itself was responsible. This excuse was concocted wholly by
Futagami, the Chief Secretary, and by Councillors Hiranuma and
Itō. And it came to my attention that those of long experience in
the Privy Council secretariat were themselves much upset by such
trickery. In this context it was natural for Privy Councillor Okada
to say:

"First of all there should have been a meeting of the full
Council for a first reading of the matter at hand. Whenever a matter has been referred to the Council by the Emperor, the whole
membership of the Council ought to be informed fully of its contents. Then comes the time for the preparations by the Privy Council to deliberate with thorough care and responsibility."

While such revision of the Privy Council procedures may involve a number of other items, it is clearly the first problem and the
Cabinet must set in motion the official procedure for such revision
by obtaining an Imperial ordinance. Since Councillor Okada is
thought to be very close to the Minseitō, there are those who may be
dubious, feeling that such a proposal for revision of the regulations
is an attempt to change the Council from within by connivance with
the Government. If only such reform proposals are made after full
preparation so that doubts may not arise and after the whole Council membership has become quite cognizant of the logic of such
regulations, then without strange conjectures, indeed with the willing acceptance of the majority, the plan may well be carried out.
But as the situation is at present, I feel that it is a very risky possibility.

On this matter I saw Prince Saionji in Okitsu on October 12
and returned after reviewing the situation with him.

Some time earlier he had had this to say to me:

"I want to be sure that Takarabe is allowed to retain all the
official dignities of his former position. I have a deep sympathy for
the very great efforts that he has put forth up to this time. Actually,
of course, he wanted to resign immediately upon his return to
Japan after having served as a delegate to the London Conference
and had spoken of this intent to Railways Minister Egi. Egi, and
others too, had begged him not to step aside till after ratification
had been completed. Furthermore, when he reported formally to
the Emperor upon his return, His Majesty had, on his own initiative, asked him, 'Please do all you can to have the treaty approved
by the Privy Council.' These words moved him deeply and led him
to change his mind about resignation; and despite his difficult position he has worked for this result. In view of what he has done it is

only fitting that he be given the formal honors of his former official rank. After all Admiral Takarabe has been Minister of the Navy five times[2]—or is it three times?—and readily merits having such honors allowed him."

As a matter of fact Vice Minister Kobayashi had previously raised this question with me and I had taken it up with the Prime Minister and I mentioned this to Prince Saionji. The Prince agreed, readily enough, for these very reasons and urged that it be so arranged. Yet, there was some doubt and question of how it could be possible to bestow this honor on a person who, as a member of the Supreme War Council, is still in an official position. Fortunately, however, these doubts came to naught when on the eleventh it was announced that the former Navy Minister Takarabe was formally granted permission to retain the privileges and status of his former position.[3]

> *The Problem of the Supplementary Program—*
> *The Declaration by the Chief of the Naval*
> *General Staff after the Grand Fleet Maneu-*
> *vers—Admiral Katō's Statement—An*
> *Editorial from the* Tōkyō Nichi Nichi Shimbun
> *The Prospects for the Supplementary Program*
> *The Position of the Chief of the Naval*
> *General Staff—The Prime Minister's At-*
> *titude—The Composure Shown by*
> *British and French Political Figures.*

On October 22 I met the Finance Minister [Inoue Junnosuke].[4] He said, "On the matter of the Navy's supplementary pro-

---

[2] [Harada is not suggesting any senile forgetfulness or uncertainty on the part of the old prince, but rather reflecting Saionji's lifelong skill and habit in speaking of or to others on their own terms. In counting cabinets *politically*, Takarabe had indeed been Navy Minister under five Prime Ministers; but seen from the *professional* viewpoint of an officer (a viewpoint General Ugaki also took), he had had three "tours of duty" in the ministry; for he had thrice continued from one cabinet to its successor: under Katō Tomosaburō and Yamamoto Gombei, then under Katō Kōmei and Wakatsuki, and finally under Hamaguchi.]

[3] [*Zenkan reigū* (the courtesies of former official position) was a rather unusual accolade bestowed by the Court upon a retiring official who thereupon held personal right to the court status which he had hitherto enjoyed only *ex officio*. Saionji himself enjoyed *zenkan reigū* as a former Prime Minister, in addition to his formal rank as a Prince. Given the highly stylized forms of expression permitted the Throne, this was perhaps as overt a sign of approval as the Court could give to Takarabe.]

[4] [Inoue Junnosuke (1869-1932), though he has scarcely appeared in Harada's narrative up to this point, was one of the strong men in the Minseitō cab-

gram, we shall undoubtedly work out some suitable compromise with the Naval Ministry. On this point you needn't be concerned. Next year's budget shows a revenue drastically reduced; by as much as 150 million yen. To provide even the normal operating budgets for each department has been a most perplexing matter, but somehow it must be completed. And I am confident it can be completed."

I understood that since the budget would be completed by the Finance Ministry on the twenty-second, it was expected that the Vice Minister of the Navy would be called in to see it on the next day. Hence I called on Vice Minister Kobayashi on the morning of the following day, the twenty-fourth. He said,

"The Navy appropriation has been reduced far below our expectations. With an allocation like this the Navy can move neither hand nor foot."

Just at this point the Chief of the Navy Technical Department[5] happened to come in. He complained bitterly,

"The total labor force which is presently employed by the Navy is in round numbers 45,000 men. This is the total force employed in all our arsenals. According to what has been decided now by the Finance Ministry, 15,000 of them will have to be discharged. The Navy will be responsible for this large number of unemployed. There will be almost no work next year to be sub-contracted to private enterprise. Even ship repair will be scarcely possible."

I understood that the Vice Minister of the Navy would leave that evening or the next for Kobe to show the Finance Ministry's draft budget proposals to the Navy Minister.

Inoue

---

inets of both Hamaguchi and Wakatsuki. He typified the big-business wing of the party, as Hamaguchi and Wakatsuki its bureaucracy-derived elements and Adachi reflected earlier party organization. His early affiliations had been with the Mitsui. He became President of the Bank of Japan in 1919, Finance Minister in the second Yamamoto cabinet (1923), and for a second time President of the Bank of Japan in 1927. He returned to the Finance Ministry under Hamaguchi. A skilled financier and economist in the old liberal tradition, he had been critical of fiscal policies since World War I, and in face of the onsetting depression sought stalwartly to apply the classic recipe of retrenchment, deflation, balanced budgets, and free gold movements. This position, as much as liberal political principle, made him one of the strongest opponents, with Shidehara, of military claims and ventures, including the Manchurian invasion the following year. After the collapse of the Second Wakatsuki cabinet, caused by Adachi's courting common front with the Seiyūkai and the military, Inoue became Chairman of the Minseitō Elections Committee. Shortly after, on February 9, 1932, he was assassinated by a member of the *Ketsumeidan* (Blood Brotherhood League). Cf. George Cyril Allen, *A Short Economic History of Modern Japan* (London: George Allen & Unwin Ltd., 1946), chap. vi, *passim*; William W. Lockwood, *The Economic Development of Japan: Growth and Structural Change, 1868-1938* (Princeton: Princeton University Press, 1954), pp. 63-64; Aoki, I, 337-38.]

[5] [Vice Admiral Fujita Hisanori (b. 1880), commandant of the Yokosuka Naval Arsenal; subsequently full Admiral and Supreme War Councillor.]

It was just at this time that the Navy's Grand Fleet maneuvers were concluded, and the fleet was at anchor off Kishiwada. Thus it was on the twenty-fifth, at the conclusion of these fleet exercises, that the Chief of the Naval General Staff, Taniguchi, issued a general statement which said in part:

"I may not, of course discuss the results of these fleet maneuvers. I believe, without a shadow of doubt, however, that we have garnered more valuable results than from any previous maneuvers, large or small. Even so I cannot help wishing we might be able to have many times the strength and manpower that we have today, and I cannot dispel the regret that we could not let the public witness maneuvers like these."

Katō, the former Chief of the Naval General Staff, also talked with newsmen,

"It is dangerous for rank outsiders to argue about naval armaments. The Navy's supplemental program is the absolute minimum.

"On this matter of disarmament we persist in our original belief. Armaments never have the waging of war as their objective. But each country must possess them so that the very existence of the state may not be endangered. The strength allowed us under this London Treaty, unless the supplemental program is established fully, will be a most serious matter for the rise or fall of the state. Especially in view of the Government's response to the Throne that it would take all necessary measures to insure national defense once the treaty was ratified, I feel that we must look forward to the fulfillment of our national defense plans through complete realization of the Navy's supplementary program. Talk of resolving our national defense needs through political solutions is an extremely dangerous layman's notion and it makes me shudder for the consequences it may have."

Thus he persists, both directly and indirectly, in attacking the ratification of the treaty. It's another point demonstrating the continuation of political activity and scheming on the part of the Navy. It was about this time that an editorial in the newspaper *Tōkyō Nichi Nichi* contained a statement to this effect: "Nothing can be more dangerous than a military man's solutions in politics. Look at the recent collapse of Germany!" It took grave exception to Admiral Katō's harsh words. This seemed to me a sentiment with which all might well agree.

On the evening of the twenty-ninth because the ratification of the treaty was completed, Mr. Wakatsuki gave a quite private dinner party at the Shinkiraku restaurant in the Tsukiji district for his Cabinet colleagues, especially those who had been concerned with the treaty. I, too, had the honor to be invited. I planned to go to Okitsu directly from there. Thus I called on the Prime Minister on the morning of that day.

"I can't understand this Navy situation," the Prime Minister told me. "The Chief of the Naval General Staff, for instance, has been telling the newspapers, 'We'll fight to the finish to fulfill the terms of the Supreme War Council's reply to the Throne.' Admiral Katō also is using very harsh language. This is most regrettable. Still we must cooperate with them as far as possible, and then I think we can bring an end to this business. The present day, so filled with financial crisis, is troublesome enough, but I want to know the Navy situation, too. In this circumstance, then, I'd like to have a message from Prince Saionji go to Admiral Okada and his group to exert themselves to bring this problem to a safe conclusion. I shall be grateful if you can arrange this when you next go down to Okitsu."

I planned to see Admiral Okada that same evening to inquire into several matters. I had thought it would also be well to visit the Navy Minister and the Chief of the Naval General Staff. But in the present case, because of this delicate situation, it seemed better for one in my position not to visit and make inquiries too frequently in these quarters. Fortunately, however, I was to have lunch that day at the Tokyo Club with Vice Admiral Nomura and Rear Admiral Terashima and I could then make certain inquiries about the situation in Naval General Staff circles. Vice Admiral Nomura seemed to have a clear understanding of the problem. "In the present financial crisis," he said, "it is not good for the Navy to talk of what it cannot know. At any rate there must be some conclusion on this matter."

Later I met with the Railways Minister at his office and noted his deep anxiety when he said, "The supplementary program must, somehow, be put through. I'm sure it can be done. Still it's going to be a difficult problem." Then I talked with the Finance Minister who said, "Of course it can be done and it shall be done."

Then, as I had planned earlier, I called on Admiral Okada at his private residence.

"I, for one, think you should not worry," he said. "Ultimately it will work out. I believe it must work out. But it can be quite difficult, for it is not a problem to be settled just between the Navy Minister and the Finance Minister. I think that they must finally call upon the Prime Minister for his decision."

I asked him if it were true that Chief of the Naval General Staff Taniguchi had said he would fight to the end to see that the terms of the Supreme War Council's reply to the Throne are fulfilled. "Well," he said, "it may be true. Actually, that he speaks like this, now that he holds the post of Chief of Naval General Staff, is not an expression of his personal views, but he was obliged to explain the contents of the reply by using figures. In other words, the reason why the so-called seniors of the service—the Fleet Admiral and the War Councillors—had accepted this form of the reply to the Throne was because he had enumerated precise figures and had said, 'We shall hold to such and such a program.' That is, its approval was tantamount to stipulating certain conditions. Hence, if the figures that he thus presented are not realized, Taniguchi's position will be undermined. Surely neither Taniguchi nor Abo will be in the least moved by Katō's words or his maneuvers. Yet when Katō and his faction work on the admirals and the Fleet Admiral there is little that Taniguchi can do to counter Katō. It is this relationship, I am convinced, that is the cause of the trouble. On the other hand Katō himself is a tool of the reservist groups and of those who are seeking to undermine the Cabinet. It goes without saying that they use this problem simply as a weapon in partisan political dispute. Naturally Admiral Abo is determined to bring the matter to an end. Of the more than half-billion yen now demanded by the Navy, by no means was all of it stipulated in the reply. Thus, if it's handled skillfully, let them have, say, 100 million. Then, later, I imagine another 30 or 40 million could be found through careful manipulation. In the first place the Navy Ministry can cut some 40 to 60 million yen in administrative costs and thus come to the Finance Ministry for the remainder. But a further 50-60 million yen may be more difficult to negotiate. The Finance Ministry may recognize sincerely the claims, principles and policies of the Navy; but in this time of financial stringency, whatever it may expect to accomplish in the future, it can do nothing but expect that the Navy will endure the present situation. I'm sure, however, that the Navy will be greatly put out if it does not receive at least enough so that Taniguchi may save face. In the last analysis, I think the problem can be settled. Of course, minor troubles cannot be avoided."

And he went further to ask me to deliver his assurances to the Prince, so that he might not be worried.

When I later went to the Shinkiraku, I discovered that Admiral Okada, too, had been invited by Mr. Wakatsuki. At the Shinkiraku I had the Prime Minister called aside to another room, without attracting the attention of others. He was pleased to have me relate in some detail my earlier conversation with Admiral Okada. Then he said to me,

"I'll be grateful if you can have a message from the Prince to Admiral Okada that his good offices in this situation will be much appreciated. In the present crisis many among the general public have come forward with various suggestions: that the financial world be saved by issuing bonds and stocks; or that unemployment bonds be set up. Whichever step may be taken, the basic problem is that the government must boldly effect a reduction in taxation now. We're going to insist that a reduction of close to 200 million yen must be made. At the very least it must be by some 150 or 160 million yen.

"Please take my greetings to the Prince. Tell him that since I've missed the chance to see him recently I hope to have the opportunity to call on him in the near future."

I left the party at nine o'clock and went to Okitsu. There I met with the Prince the next morning—the thirtieth—and reported in detail. The Prince queried,

"So I'm to send another message to Okada. What shall I say? It would be much more convenient if the Prime Minister himself were to keep in closer touch with Okada on ordinary occasions, instead of calling on him only when some problem arises. This is one of Prime Minister Hamaguchi's faults; or perhaps it's one of his strong points."

I remarked that in its context Hamaguchi's request was natural enough. "He knew that I had seen Okada yesterday because of your deep concern; and I've just given you the gist of Okada's remarks. Now I can take to Okada, as from you, a message something like this: 'I can well understand the situation from your message. In the days ahead also, I hope you will exert yourself fully, should any trouble arise, to bring it to a safe conclusion for the good of the country.' Might this not do?"

"Yes, that is all right. When you've returned, give Admiral Okada my greetings and convey a message along those lines. But for the Navy Minister and Prime Minister to meet and not to touch on matters of budget, or to hesitate even to talk on the matter of the supplementary program—it's as if the Prime Minister and his cabinet colleagues were like France and Germany! This is surely a parlous situation. At the very least they have to learn to get along with each other more easily. Why, it should be perfectly all right for the Prime Minister, if necessity arises, even to go outside his cabinet for discussions with the Supreme War Councillor or any others."

To which I couldn't help rejoining, "But if, as Prime Minister, he were to call on Admiral Okada too frequently, might it not be unwise in that it might well damage the services which Okada can provide as a mediator?" Our talk concluded with the Prince asking me to convey his greetings to the Prime Minister.

Later we were talking of various matters and I mentioned reading something about Balfour[6] the other day. "What a popular man he had been among political figures of recent times! When, as Prime Minister, he was explaining the budget before Parliament and mistakenly read certain figures, it caused him no great concern. Noticing that he had made such an error, he dismissed the matter simply by saying, 'In reading these figures I've made an error in the units involved. The 50 million should be 500 million. My figures may be off a place or two, but I'm sure you gentlemen will be certain that there is no mistake in my principles and policies.' Even members of the opposition joined in the laughter, did not tax him for his errors, and the measure was passed. An atmosphere like this shows the composure of both those who attack and those who are attacked, at the same time that it shows Balfour's personality."

"Yes," said the Prince. "I agree with you. I knew Balfour myself, and he was a fine man. In France, too, once when Gambetta[7] was in his prime as president of the Chamber of Deputies, the party opposing him held the Government and the Minister of Finance made a mistake in his figures so that the opposition, that is, Gambetta's party, raised a clamor against him. But Gambetta arose, and mentioning a figure of some 30 million francs said, 'This is the figure on which he has made a mistake, is it not? However poor we may be, we can meet this figure.' And with admonition to his own partisans, the affair was ended in a round of applause. We should indeed be envious of such an atmosphere as this."

---

[6] [Arthur James Balfour's career in British politics was contemporary with Saionji's active period in Japanese politics: Prime Minister in 1902-05, subsequently First Lord of the Admirality, Foreign Secretary in Lloyd George's war cabinet, and head of the British delegation to the Washington Conference. Balfour died in 1930.]

[7] [Leon Gambetta (1838-82), vigorous French republican leader in opposition to the Second Empire, was a principal figure in shaping the Third Republic's constitution in his position as president of the Chamber of Deputies.]

Then citing examples from the Japanese Diet and Privy Council, such as the fuss made about commas and periods by Chief Secretary Futagami in connection with the London Treaty, he said, "What a shame, what a shame!"

From Shizuoka I took the special express at noon for Tokyo. The following day I saw the Prime Minister and reported in detail. And on the morning of the following day, I called on Admiral Okada to convey the Prince's message.

Lack of Sympathy—Key Points for the
Prince's Consideration—Admiral Okada's
Views—Negotiations with the Navy—
Prince Saionji's Concern about the Future
of the Military Departments.

I met with the Prime Minister, conveying the Prince's greetings and reporting that his words of counsel to Admiral Okada, asked for by the Prime Minister, would of course be transmitted. In fact I intended to give such a message to Admiral Okada in person on the morrow.

Then I called on Vice Minister Yoshida, at the Ministry of Foreign Affairs. "At that party at the Shinkiraku on the twenty-ninth," he said, "Wakatsuki should have been advised to seat Admiral Okada next to or at least closer to the Prime Minister. He should have been treated more politely, and the Prime Minister and other cabinet ministers should have been more careful in exchanging toasts with him. In present circumstances it might have helped to soothe ruffled feelings and had a better psychological effect all 'round. Surely, at a time like that—how shall I say it?—whether from a lack of human feeling or from inattentiveness, it was a good opportunity missed."

With this observation I quite agreed. Often the present cabinet members seem to be remiss in such niceties.

Later I saw Admiral Okada. "I have been with the Prince," I said, "and have just come from speaking to him about the general situation as Your Excellency had commented on it. He understands quite well what you had to say. The Prince would not only have me convey to you his greetings but also express to you his hope that you may continue to exert your talents, both directly and indirectly, so this important issue may be concluded with the least difficulty."

Okada replied, "I'll do my best to keep it to a hundred million yen. But if I'm expected to cut it below such a figure, I'm afraid it's hopeless."

To this I said, "The Prince is not, in general, concerned with stipulating some precise amount. He asks only that your own best efforts be addressed to working out an acceptable solution because of the serious nature of present political circumstances. In short, the Prince's view is that no better or more ideal cabinet can result from a political change at this time. The alternatives to the present cabinet are not heartening. As Your Excellency has already said, the situation in the Seiyūkai now is far from satisfactory. A middle-of-the-road, non-party cabinet *(chūkan naikaku)* would probably also be undesirable. This counsel, of course, is meant only for Your Excellency's ears, the better to understand the ramifications of the present issues."

Okada agreed, "Certainly today the Seiyūkai is in a parlous state and a non-party cabinet would be no solution. Until the Seiyūkai can pull itself together into a better and a more effective organization, I'm sure that a political change now would not be of any advantage to the country.

"Even so," he continued, "if this matter of the supplementary program is not settled soon, every day's delay may produce wider repercussions and involve other groups. Should men like Fleet Admiral Tōgō become involved, it could be most troublesome. It could cause a worse disturbance than the imbroglio with the Privy Council. These talks—between the Chief of the Naval General Staff and the Navy Minister, between the government and the Navy (that is, between the Cabinet and the Navy Ministry)—should be concluded without a day's delay. Then they can say to Tōgō and Katō and the other Supreme War Councillors, 'We've reached such and such a conclusion!' This would be the best procedure, wouldn't it? As it stands today, the London treaty, though still a serious issue for the government, has already been approved, so that the government ought not to boggle at 30 or 40 million yen in the budget."

It seems some articles in the Sunday evening papers have just come to the attention of Admiral Okada's circle: articles scurrilously written asserting that Ambassador Castle has used one and a half to two million yen to buy up Japanese press and government officials, that Shidehara is America's foreign minister, that Hamaguchi has betrayed his country. It was said that such propaganda has greatly roused men like Fleet Admiral Tōgō. I couldn't help thinking to myself what a fool he must be if he gives credence to such rumors; but of course I listened to these stories without comment.

Admiral Okada, in other words, had intimated that he would exert his best efforts to effect the result desired. So I went on to say, "My own view is that the Government wants to stop at a sum of about 300 million yen, and it does not want to provoke any clamor for, say, 400 million." The Admiral had many other things to say with which I expressed agreement. Finally I took my leave of him with a parting injunction that I was hopeful of his bringing about the best results.

I had expected to see the Prime Minister that evening, but he had a meeting of the Committee on Electoral Reform at eight-thirty, so I did not call upon him. A telephoned message, however, came from him asking that I see him at nine o'clock. Calling on him then, I related what Okada had had to say. He asked me to convey the same information to the Finance Minister.

I planned to see this minister in the morning; but, instead, he preferred to come to my house. Thus I waited till Finance Minister Inoue dropped by about eleven o'clock. Then I repeated to him what Okada had said. And I added, "To cut out 100 million yen will be very difficult. Extremely so, he says. Perhaps he's using a certain amount of diplomacy—suggesting a bargain of some sort with us. The heart of the problem would seem to be Vice Minister Kobayashi. Abo has become Navy Minister, apparently, chiefly because under him the work of the Ministry will be actually done by Kobayashi; whereas the appointment of Ōsumi, a man who handles his own responsibilities and would have handled his duties himself, would have left the Vice Minister Kobayashi to accomplish nothing. Hence I know that he is doing his best to solve this problem. Thus, too, it's probably best we concentrate on what can be done and through Kobayashi."

I had already passed on these views to Railways Minister Egi; and he, in turn, had carried on earnest discussions with Vice Minister Kobayashi though it was a very ticklish problem. The Government as such, from its own standpoint, is confronted with the necessity of lightening the burdens of the people; and consequently expects the Navy to be willing to accept a cut of 30 to 40 million yen. The London Treaty, over which the Navy had caused so much difficulty, has now been satisfactorily concluded. Perhaps this issue, too, Egi seemed to say, may soon be ended. The Finance Minister himself has said, "At least I must push it quickly, for I want to transmit the whole proposal to the Navy in the next day or two."

I left for Okitsu on the night of the second, and reported in detail to the Prince, including my latest talk with Admiral Okada. He commented, "This seems very good indeed. But of course it would be quite improper for you to say to any of them than Saionji made mention of specific sums, such as a hundred million yen, or some other figure." And to this I replied, "Of course you, as Prince, would not undertake to make such specific recommendations. And this I gave them plainly to understand. Admiral Okada knows full well that you had not mentioned any precise figures."

Saionji continued, "Of course I want to hear no one talking in terms of 400 millions. Such are the ways of human nature that if it is not put as 300 and so many thousands it will have a bad effect on people. It will be harmful, too, if it is not handled in such a way that the people are not further alienated from the military establishment."

"Yes," I said, "a situation like that in postwar Germany would be very bad, wouldn't it?"

"But the Germans have a strong sense of discipline and thus it did not lead to disturbances shaking the whole state. But if things come to such a pass in Japan, the people are likely to turn communistic. This is quite different from the revolution in Germany. It's to be hoped that our military departments are kept from provoking and stimulating just such a response.

"Properly speaking, in coping with the long standing high-handed and unreasonable actions by the Navy and such groups, those who profess to be constitutional politicians under our modern constitutional regime ought to eschew mere partisan opposition to each other. Rather, they should collaborate against such militarists' moves as threaten constitutionalism itself. For one party now to try to use the military can be dangerous in the extreme. In fact, it causes me the deepest concern.

"Recently I've received some of the reports of the American Senate Foreign Relations Committee. Normally, on the precedent of past experience, one might say that the American Senate's deficiencies in understanding diplomacy are not to be equaled elsewhere. Even in Europe it is usual to disregard it. Diplomats and those who are at all familiar with diplomacy do not concern themselves with it. Those who spend good money in Japan to circulate these committee reports as if they were the final word on the matter are themselves not well-versed in world diplomacy. It's unfortunate that so many are in fact so ignorant."

The Government now turned its efforts to working out the most satisfactory possible solution to the question of the supplemental program. When the Finance Minister saw the colossal sum of 508 million yen proposed by the Navy Ministry, he said in astonishment, "Why, this is outrageous!" The Finance Minister himself, as he had said once visiting me at my home, was trying both to conclude this matter and at the same time to avoid confrontation directly by anyone representing the Navy's position. At the same time, the Chief of the Naval General Staff on his part was stubbornly holding his ground. Thus, recently, Railways Minister Egi and Vice Minister Kobayashi have been meeting secretly to try to work out a solution. These efforts they still continue; but the Navy refuses to consider anything under 398,600,000 yen, and the negotiations seem deadlocked. To counter the Finance Minister's reduction by 15 per cent, the Navy claimed it could not reduce by more than 5 per cent but proposed to delay airplane construction by about one year. In spite of this confusion, the discussion proceeded without interference from others, from the Supreme War Council or from Fleet Admiral Tōgō.

Since I was going down to Okitsu on the evening of the seventh I met with the Prime Minister and with the Finance and Railway Ministers as well. They all three insisted they were bending all efforts to the solution of the task. The Prime Minister said, "The Government must somehow effect a reduction in taxation. A reduction of less than 150 million yen will scarcely do. But I want to make it at least that amount. When you meet men in the Navy who may inquire about this matter, please say that a sum less than this will be quite ineffective. It's not just the case that a solution be agreed upon; rather, the Government absolutely cannot accept a reduction of less than 150 million."

I reached Shizuoka about midnight. As I was leaving Tokyo, some newsmen had come to me at the Shimbashi station. "This is going to be a difficult matter," they said. "Just now, after a conference between the Chief of the Naval General Staff and the Navy

Minister, the Chief of the Naval General Staff said to us with great stubbornness, 'I shall not budge an inch!' " And the reporters implied in their comments to me that there had been a complete change in the situation. Hence it was with some concern that, when I reached Shizuoka, I phoned to Vice Minister Kobayashi at his official residence from the Daitōkan sometime past midnight to ask him about this.

"There were reports of a drastic change in the situation just before I left the city. What seems to be the matter? I hope everything's all right." And to this he replied, "Nothing new. It will work out all right."

I outlined the situation to Prince Saionji when I saw him the next morning. I suggested that though the Chief of the Naval General Staff's very strong and stubborn attitude may be written up in tomorrow's newspapers, we can—according to Vice Minister Kobayashi—expect an eventual satisfactory conclusion. From the Government's side, both the Railways Minister and the Finance Minister are hard at work on it and I'm sure they will succeed. Of course the general budget is yet open and I imagine they will do something about this, too. I had another item to relate:

"Just after the train passed Kōzu yesterday evening the Chief of the Army General Staff, who seemed to be on his way to the Grand Maneuvers, came into my car. His conversation was vehement, and perhaps a little drunk, as he said, 'I've just come from seeing War Minister Ugaki.[8] His health's much better. He should be around again at the end of the month. It'll be a bad business if he isn't. The Government is still sticking to the "no-borrowing" policy it proclaimed at the Diet session. It seems it's cutting the budget with the excuse that the political parties must not lose face. It's certainly putting the screws on the Army, bleeding it. Morale can't be improved in these circumstances. After all, a national defense plan should be decided once for all. But if it's to be changed by each succeeding political party that sets up a cabinet—then the future is going to see some mighty serious consequences of this sort of thing. I wish that Prince Saionji would give some thought to the evils of the political parties. Of course I'm sure that in his venerable wisdom Prince Saionji is quite aware of this situation without re-

---

[8] [General Kanaya, the Chief of Staff, was a leading member of the Ugaki team or "clique," through whom the proposed "military reorganization" was to be accomplished. He was also a fellow classmate and known as a boon companion of the War Minister. In Japanese a "boon companion" is, literally, a "drinking friend (nomitomodachi)." See Itō Masanori, *Gumbatsu kōbōshi,* [*Rise and Fall of Army Cliques*] (3 vols., Tōkyō: Bungei Shunjūsha, 1958) II, 143.]

minders from such as I. Still, this is indeed a most difficult problem. Of course, in my present position I can make no comments like this in public; and I keep absolutely close-mouthed on any matter touching on politics, but what's going to come of all this 'curtailment' and 'retrenchment?' If the country's whole fate is to be miscalculated because of the Government's adherence to a single policy statement in the Diet, there'll eventually be neither country nor anything else left.'

"I told him, 'This fiscal policy must not be looked on simply as stubborn adherence to a position once taken at a Diet session; nor is it simply a matter of sentiment, of face-saving. If I were to find a way to summarize it, I'd suggest it's like the surgical diagnoses of two doctors in an appendicitis case. One may insist that removal would be harmful; that he can only provide the necessary fundamental treatment if the appendix is not removed. The other may as stoutly believe that it must be removed as soon as possible. These two views may be alike founded on the faith and life-long study of the two doctors. Each believes that only by accepting his method can the patient be saved. Thus from a financial expert's viewpoint, to relieve the present financial crisis, to end its basic sickness, there's nothing but a strict retrenchment policy. Thus they would urge retrenchment, and at the same time they would float no loans. Actually the situation is quite analogous to the story of the two doctors; and I believe the situation is not what it has appeared to you.' This is the substance of what I said to him."

The Prince said, "Well that's that. What a bothersome lot these military men can be. Somehow, of course, the supplemental program will be worked out; but I wish they'd do it quickly. Naturally there must be a suitable reduction of taxes. Well then, once again; take my greetings when you return."

It was the evening of the eighth when I returned to Tokyo. The budget problem, by all accounts, was expected to come up for decision at the Cabinet meeting called for the ninth, but matters had not yet reached that stage. There seemed to be much confusion; and thus I called on Egi at his home that evening.

"No," he said, "Your impression is not quite right. A rough settlement has been worked out. Hence the supplemental program, too, will be wound up. On the matter of the general budget, because they're working on it so assiduously, I'm sure it will ultimately be worked out. In fact the Finance and Navy Ministers are to meet tonight. Since they are going to phone me the results of their conference, why not wait up so that you can make your

Kanaya

report to Okitsu, when they've reached their agreement, without waiting for the Cabinet meeting. The sooner word of this reaches the Prince the better."

Then something occurred which surprised me. I first heard of it when the Prime Minister called me in on the next morning. He said,

"I had thought that the Army would cause no trouble, but it has become quite difficult. I've had to call in Acting War Minister Abe as well as the Finance and Navy Ministers. I've seen the Army's budget for the first time, considered it from several standpoints, and have consulted these men about it. Again and again, I tried to work it out with subtractions here, additions there. The Finance Minister and the War Minister are continuing their direct negotiations on it still.

"As for the supplemental plan, action has been deferred, but I believe it finally can be settled without affecting the Navy's principles and policies. The reduction in the general budget demanded by the Finance Ministry for fiscal 1931 comes to 160 million yen. Of this more than half—some 85 million—is to come from the Army and Navy budgets. The sum to be cut from the Navy budget is 54 million; and the Navy's trying to limit its reduction to 41 million. For the Army a reduction of 31 million yen has been planned, but the Army now wants to hold this to 25 million, leaving some 6,470,000 which has become a problem. In sum, of the 85,800,000 to be taken out of the military budgets, the services accept 66 million. Negotiations are thus now under way on the remaining 19 million; and I should have a phone call from Inoue about it sometime this evening. Stand by until then, and I'll notify you of the results. I'd then appreciate your taking word of them to Okitsu as early as possible tomorrow morning."

Though I waited till past twelve o'clock, there was no phone call. Then Egi called, "Let's postpone it till tomorrow, since it's past midnight." I asked that he rouse me, even if it were in the middle of the night. "Otherwise, I'll not be able to take the early morning train." Since there had been no calls, I took the initiative and phoned the Finance Minister at his official residence about twelve-thirty.

Inoue said, "We've finally settled it. The supplemental program calls for 374 million yen; the tax reduction will be 135 million. To accomplish this, items which will total 10 million have been postponed to each of the years 1937 and 1938; and this the Navy has accepted. On the general budget the Navy accepts a further reduction of 4 million. This leaves 9 million yen which the Navy wants to have restored somehow. For its part the Army is not willing to accept the remaining 6,470,000 as a cut in its general budget and I've decided to accede to its wishes. Since it will take some little time to incorporate these modifications in the general budget, the Cabinet meeting to consider the budget will probably be held on the afternoon of the eleventh. As far as the supplemental program is concerned, the Navy Minister has accepted it, and the Chief of the Naval General Staff has had to give his assent also. It's quite regrettable that the anticipated tax reduction was not fully reached; but it cannot be helped. In reporting on these matters please give my greetings to the Prince."

Some thirty or forty minutes later Egi telephoned and repeated what Inoue had already told me.

At six o'clock on the morning of the tenth, I took the train for Okitsu and arrived there at eleven o'clock. The Prince was highly pleased. "This is fine," he said, "It's really splendid." I pointed out, "The Army's extra 6 million yen in the general budget will be obtained from German reparations; and revenues from tobacco sales can be allotted to meet the Navy's 9 million."

The Prince smiled and said, "Well, I thought it might turn out like this. Not bad, not bad. Not only is this a drastic reduction, but the gold embargo is settled, the London Treaty concluded, the budget, tax reduction, and the supplemental plan—all are successfully concluded. Saionji is very happy for what this means to this country. Please tell Hamaguchi how I appreciate the work he has done towards these goals. My regards to him. And tell Egi and especially Inoue that Saionji particularly appreciates their devoted efforts."

Back in Tokyo by the 1:40 express. There are yet discernable voices of discontent among military and naval men. But with the London Treaty, which had earlier been a problem, now settled, and with the supplemental program and tax reduction now put through, the confused relations with the militarists are somewhat mollified. The whole London Treaty problem has come to a happy end.

CHAPTER IX

From the Attack
on Prime Minister Hamaguchi
to the Promulgation of the Treaty

The Attack on the Prime Minister—
Prince Saionji's Admonitions—Ioki
and the Aikokusha—Foreign Minister
Shidehara Assumes the Post of Prime
Minister pro tem—The Egi and Adachi
Factions Pitted against Each Other.

On November 13, I attended the wedding reception of a relative. Since the Prime Minister was to leave the next day for the Grand Maneuvers to be held near Okayama, I made a point of calling at his official residence about eight-thirty on my way back from the reception and we talked together for an hour. He was scheduled to call on the Prince on the morning of the twenty-second.

"The time has come," he said, "for a fundamental administrative and fiscal reorganization. It will be useless unless done honestly and thoroughly, and this I am determined to try. And a military reform, too, however embarrassing it may be for the War Minister, must be carried out. Be this as it may, I must be off to the maneuvers tomorrow."

I took leave of the Prime Minister sometime after nine o'clock; and in parting I urged him to take good care of himself. Recently it has been reported that some one has been trailing both the Prime Minister and the Lord Keeper of the Privy Seal, and I hoped this did not bode ill for them.

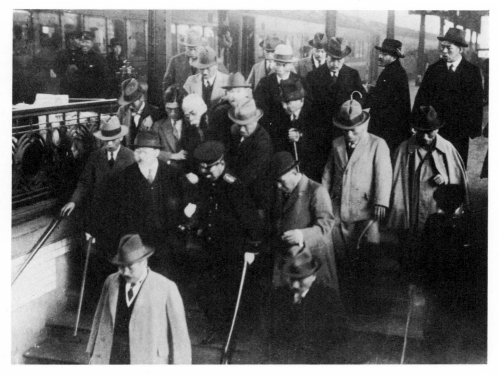

Prime Minister Hamaguchi (hatless) being carried from the Tokyo Station platform just after the attempted assassination, November 14, 1930. Baron Shidehara appears third from the right in the top rank.

The following morning I had occasion to call on Prince Konoe about nine o'clock. While we were talking together, about nine-thirty, there was a phone call from Shidehara's secretary: "There's just been a message from the Prime Minister's secretary. Just as the Prime Minister was on the point of leaving Tokyo Station, some ruffian[1] shot him with a pistol. His condition is quite serious."

---

[1] [The would-be assassin was a twenty-three-year-old member of the Aikokusha (Patriot's Society), named Sagoya Tomeo. Wearing a cotton striped *haori*—a swaggering costume once the mark of a *samurai* and widely affected by youthful bullies in this period—Sagoya was easily overpowered by the police and detectives accompanying the Prime Minister and hauled off for investigation and trial. Aoki, *Historical Prelude to the Pacific War*, I, 101-3.

Immediately I reported this by phone to the Prince in Okitsu and then went promptly to the Station Master's office to inquire into Hamaguchi's condition. The place was in such a commotion that I soon left after noting the situation there. Again I phoned the Prince: "I can come down to Okitsu either by the train tonight, or immediately if it seems urgent to you that I do so. Shall I wait to get a fuller picture of the situation, or come immediately?" The Prince's reply was that I should come at once.

I then retraced my steps to Tokyo Station and there met Railways Minister Egi. "Since the Prince has asked me to come at once," I told him, "I'm going down on the one o'clock express."

"Please tell the Prince we'll do everything possible to calm the public mind and to straighten things out. Don't let him become too anxious and worried. You've seen for yourself what the situation is, so you can tell the Prince about it fully." After making necessary arrangements with Kido, the chief secretary to the Lord Privy Seal,[2] I left for Okitsu on the one o'clock train, arrived at Shizuoka at four, and proceeded forthwith to Okitsu for an hour's conversation with the Prince. He was greatly shocked.

"First of all," he said, "what we must be most attentive to, in a matter of this kind, is to prevent the public from assuming that a political change will result from the mischance that has befallen the Prime Minister. To avert this, when Hara[3] was also attacked at the Tokyo Station by an assassin, I had the then Minister of Finance—Takahashi—go immediately to see Prince Yamagata; and with the latter's consent he was invested with the office as Prime Minister pro tem.[4] Since under circumstances like this it is also

---

[Shidehara, who chanced to be at the station that same morning to bid adieu to Hirota Koki who was off to his new post as Ambassador to Russia, sped to the stricken Hamaguchi and got him to the Tokyo University Hospital. A close old friend of Hamaguchi from school-boy days together in Osaka, Shidehara has left a poignant account of this episode. Shidehara, *Diplomacy Through Fifty Years*, p. 127f.

[Hamaguchi never recovered from the wound. He was to resume his role as Prime Minister before the end of the Fifty-ninth Diet session next spring, appearing on the floor of the House on March 10, 1931. But after the end of that session he returned to the hospital on April 4, resigned with his whole cabinet on April 13; and died the following August 26 before the Manchurian invasion revealed the complete failure of the political and economic programs he had lived for. Cf. Harada, II, 438-42.]

[2] [Harada's close friend, Marquis Kido Koichi, had just assumed this court post on October 28. (See above, chap. iii, n. 30.)]

[3] Prime Minister Hara had been struck down by a dagger-wielding youth on November 4, 1921.

[4] [Takahashi Korekiyo, then a viscount and member of the House of

important for the Justice Minister to be quite firm, I want you
to be on the alert on this score too. My next point may be like
counsel to children, yet it is essential, as far as possible in this
emergency, for the party to avoid any such confusion as may result
from squabbles for power within the party. This is something to
which all should also be attentive. Of course, this counsel of mine
must not seem to be conspicuous meddling. But I want you to
convey the impression that I am speaking thus in all earnestness."

I pointed out to the Prince that Hamaguchi's assailant was
a member of the Aikokusha,[5] a right-wing organization, and that
he was tied up with Iwata Ainosuke, the henchman of Ogawa[6]
the former Railways Minister. There's talk of various reasons for
this action—the treaty, the depression, and the like; but the fact
remains it is sheer gangsterism. The Prince commented,

"Well, when the public is treated to the spectacle of admirals
and vice-admirals, and similar presumably well-informed persons,
issuing statements that 'the supreme command has been contemned' or that 'the London Treaty is against the national interest,' of course such statements are an incitement to young

Peers, was thus made the successor Prime Minister so that the assassination
would not effect a "political change." His cabinet survived only till the following June. This succession maneuver was clearly Saionji's doing; but he here
recalls his deference to old Yamagata Aritomo (1838-1922), the Chōshū clans-
man who rose to be Prince and Field Marshal, Prime Minister, and Privy
Council President and till his last the most powerful *genrō*. Imamura Takeo,
Hyōden Takahashi Korekiyo [*A Critical Biography of Takahashi Korekiyo*]
(Tōkyō: Jiji Tsūshinsha, 1948), p. 103.]

[5] The Aikokusha (Patriots' Society), taking the name of an early Meiji
era association, had been founded in 1928 by Iwata and others with the objective
of studying, discussing, and fostering a more aggressive ideology and policy
toward Asia.

[It was but one of many such groups with which Iwata was connected,
following earlier association with the Taishūsha, the Yūzonsha, *et al.* He was
particularly associated with "direct action" groups and those affected by Kita's
"coup d'état" theories (cf. O. Tanin and E. Yohan, *Voenno-fashistskoye
dvizhenie v Yaponii* [Moscow, 1933], used in the English edition titled *Militarism and Fascism in Japan* [London: Martin Lawrence, 1934], *passim*). He
was the type commanding a gangster following whose services were bought
from time to time on the home front by the less scrupulous politicians of both
major parties (above, chap. i, n. 21). Although this linking of Iwata with Ogawa
may suggest direct Seiyūkai complicity in Hamaguchi's murder, I am unaware
of other more probative evidence.]

[6] [Ogawa Heikichi (1869-1942), involved in corruption scandals as Railways Minister in the Tanaka cabinet (1927-29), was associated with several
right-wing groups (Shiraki, *Nihon seitō shi*, pp. 55-58; Tiedemann, "The
Hamaguchi Cabinet," chap. iii). Ogawa was tried and subsequently imprisoned
on bribery charges. In his youth he had been involved with the elder Prince
Konoe's continental schemes.]

ignoramuses. I hope very careful attention will be paid to such points as this."

Since I was able to catch the super-express, the "Tsubame," out of Numazu at seven o'clock I was able to be back in Tokyo by nine o'clock. Later that evening I had Kido, the chief secretary to the Lord Keeper of the Privy Seal, come to meet me at Prince Konoe's house and passed on to him Prince Saionji's various words of counsel and advice. In talking with Konoe then, he was reminded that he had met recently with Ioki Ryōzō. Ioki had told him, "Things will go on from this point till something really big breaks next February or March." Ioki, a leader of the Seikyōsha[7] and managing editor of *Nihon oyobi Nihonjin (Japan and the Japanese)*, is in other words a prominent figure in right-wing organizations. He is a holdover from the group of "China *rōnin*" with whom the late Prince Konoe was wont to associate and thus is accustomed to frequenting the Konoe establishment. On an earlier occasion a few days before Prime Minister Hara was assassinated, Ioki had said, "Within the next day or two Hara will be attacked." Since a few days later Hara was in fact struck down at the Tokyo Station, there is considerable reason to be disturbed by Ioki's reports; the more so since members of the Genyōsha[8] are said to have been recently in secret communication with him. At any event it's another aspect of today's crisis.

The next morning I called on Ohara, the Vice Minister of Justice, at the Justice Ministry, to ask about the causes behind this most recent crime. I related these various elements and urged him, "I'd like you to be especially attentive to this whole issue. Especially and particularly should you be thoroughgoing so that

---

[7] [Cf. prior mention by Harada of Ioki and his affiliations: above, chap. i, n. 21.]

[8] [The Genyōsha, with Tōyama Mitsuru among its original founders in 1881, had certain roots in the unsuccessful Satsuma Rebellion and urged continental expansion as its prime objective. It established the main current from which stemmed such later nationalist and expansionist societies as the Kokuryūkai (The Amur Society) and later numerous progeny among extreme right-wing groups. Cf. E. Herbert Norman, "The Genyōsha, A Study in the Origins of Japanese Imperialism," *Pacific Affairs*, XVII (1934), 261-84; Kinoshita, *Nihon fuasshizumu-shi*, I, *passim*; Colegrove, *Militarism in Japan*; Scalapino, *Democracy and the Party Movement in Pre-War Japan*, especially chap. ix.]

[Part of the Genyōsha's activity had consisted in dispatching the so-called "China *rōnin*" and "continental *rōnin*," filibusterers of many roles, to fish in revolutionary waters of China, Manchuria, Mongolia, and even further fields. Marius B. Jansen, in *The Japanese and Sun Yat-sen*, has given an effective study of such *rōnin* who involved themselves in the Chinese revolution.]

there may be no recurrence of such villainous acts, harmful to the whole nation, by so-called right-wing groups."

Ohara remarked, "This particular fellow is a henchman of Iwata Ainosuke, and I understand he was going about making fervent speeches when the London Treaty was under discussion. Iwata is on quite intimate terms with Ogawa, the former Railways Minister. In fact he accompanied Ogawa when he was on trial, as can be shown by pictures which appeared in the press at the time. Men like this are extremely troublesome. A thorough investigation is under way. Sooner or later it must be cleared up."[9]

I understood, incidentally, that Ogawa had recently visited Konoe to say he felt sure it was Suzuki who had caused his arrest to keep him from a chance to become president of the Seiyūkai. I would gather from this, and from the comments which the Vice Minister had made about Ogawa that the Vice Minister belongs to the Hiranuma-Suzuki clique; that is, to the anti-Ogawa faction; and by like token that Ogawa is anti-Suzuki.[10]

The Vice Minister went on to say: "I understand that members of the Aikokusha have been meeting with such men as Admiral Katō. Certainly it is undeniable that Admiral Katō's arguments have done much to stimulate them."

Afterwards I told this story to Navy Vice Minister Kobayashi. I pointed out to him that if Admiral Katō had in fact had such relationship either direct or indirect, or if it were a fact that he had prompted and stimulated this group, then his is indeed a most serious responsibility. To this Kobayashi agreed, "If there's the slightest indication that this may be so, then some very drastic steps must be taken."

In mid-morning the Cabinet decided to have Foreign Min-

---

[9] [Ohara Naoshi (b. 1877), whether from following Harada's promptings here reported, his sense of duty, or other higher authority, was sufficiently strenuous in the prosecution of the case against Sagoya that this was understood to be the principal reason the Army refused to sanction his inclusion as Justice Minister in the Hirota cabinet organized in 1936 (Colegrove, *Militarism in Japan*, p. 25). He had meanwhile been Justice Minister in the Okada cabinet that was ended by the February Twenty-Sixth Incident (1936).]

[10] [On Suzuki Kisaburō, see above, p. 239. Suzuki's own patent ambition to head the Seiyūkai was fulfilled after the assassination of Inukai in the May Fifteenth Incident, 1932. By that date, however, Saionji was prepared to break his practice of recommending, upon the death in office of a party Prime Minister, that his party successor follow him in organizing the successor government. While other factors entered into the choice of Admiral Viscount Saitō to follow the assassinated Inukai, the blatant factionalism in the Seiyūkai and Suzuki's chauvinism clearly affected Saionji's recommendation. Cf. Harada, II, 272-337.]

ister Shidehara act as Prime Minister pro tem pending Hamaguchi's recovery; and by two-fifteen Imperial sanction had been given to this arrangement. It was Railways Minister Egi who had informed me of this Cabinet decision with the request that I inform the Prince of what had been done. Thus I was able to report immediately in some detail to the Prince by telephone, and further to plan to leave Tokyo that evening and reach Okitsu the next morning—the sixteenth.

Anent his pro tem post Shidehara had said, "If the Prime Minister should be unable to attend the session of the Diet, I shall not be able to undertake all the continuing details of parliamentary business. That is, I have undertaken to handle certain administrative matters on an interim basis in the present emergency, but it would be embarrassing to be saddled with the task of serving concurrently for the Prime Minister in a political sense. When I accepted this *ad interim* responsibility, it was on condition that I do so only until the Diet session. Now, within Minseitō circles there are various proposals in case the Prime Minister should be unable to attend: Adachi, the Home Minister, might become Prime Minister pro tem; or if not Adachi, then Ugaki would be acceptable; still others would have Wakatsuki resume the post. That is, these quite differing movements are cropping up here and there.[11] For instance, the chief secretary of the Minseitō has come to me with this to say:

" 'Neither Egi nor Adachi can settle this situation. To those who have come to me with questions I've replied in general terms—without naming any names—that we must have a man who can

---

[11] [While perhaps less riven than the Seiyūkai at this time the Minseitō's internal factional character was especially exhibited when Hamaguchi was incapacitated. The sharp rivalry between an Egi faction and an Adachi faction called on the services of a kind of "council of elders" for the party—a device cognate with so many other types of response to crisis in the Japanese milieu, and evoked a readiness to seek a "transcendent" solution. Note, in the next several pages, the reference to such seniors as Yamamoto Tatsuo and Sengoku Mitsugu; the decision to accept Shidehara, a non-party man, as Prime Minister pro tem; the appeal to many party men in the possibility of drafting Ugaki, also a non-party figure, to head both party and ministry. The final resolution, after Hamaguchi's resignation the next spring, to recall Wakatsuki from retirement again, to be party president and, in consequence, Prime Minister, can be seen as evidencing the bureaucratic elements' ability to win against partymen such as Adachi without in fact removing discords. The removal from behind the scenes of such canny managers as Egi and Sengoku (by illness and death) and the sharpening dissidence of Adachi must have contributed to the indecision and "lack of courage" with which Wakatsuki can be charged after the Manchurian invasion less than a year later. Cf. Shidehara, pp. 127-45; Wakatsuki, *Kōfuan kaikōroku*, pp. 367-87.]

meet the existing situation, be he Minseitō party member or not; that in order to get to the bottom of the contemporary crises, no set limitations should be stipulated, for in fact an outsider may prove to be the real solution. In brief, the right man must be held in high public esteem, must have the self-confidence to be able to tackle administrative and fiscal as well as military reforms, must have the courage to solve also the problem of the Privy Council and yet stand in the good graces of the House of Peers. All the better if a person of these qualifications can be found within the party, but a non-party member should be acceptable, too.' " And Shidehara went on to say,

"It seemed to me he was quite evidently pointing toward General Ugaki."

Shidehara

Members of Adachi's group are prone to see Railways Minister Egi standing behind Shidehara. Egi manipulates the real power, they say, while Shidehara is nothing more than a puppet. That is, Shidehara may be titular acting Prime Minister, but in substance it is Egi who is Prime Minister. Considered from this point of view, a number of people would seem to begrudge Egi his power. For instance, in the initial Cabinet discussions about making Shidehara Prime Minister pro tem, Adachi expressed this opposition in saying, "Let's not rush to make an *ad interim* appointment. Wouldn't it be better to put off such a decision till more is known of Hamaguchi's condition in the days ahead?" Of the same view was Communications Minister Koizumi. In this circumstance, then, both Tawara, the Commerce and Industry Minister, and Watanabe, the Justice Minister, also urged postponement of establishing the interim post. Egi, however, insisted, "In a case like this, it is most urgent to appoint an acting Prime Minister. All sorts of routine administrative business and even memorials presented to the Throne require the signature or counter-signature of the Prime Minister before they may be approved. There's no time to be lost. For the conduct of even the slightest governmental business, the sooner the better." Thus Egi, a man widely experienced in administrative affairs, employed his persuasion against any loss of time in making a selection; whereas Home Minister Adachi, comparatively inexperienced in such affairs, not only saw no reason for haste, but also was inclined to be more or less wary of Egi. Many like Prince Saionji were pleased that a decision on the appointment of an acting Prime Minister was reached so speedily. I went to Okitsu to review these circumstances for the Prince, and to inform him of Hamaguchi's condition.

"Let's hope the Prime Minister recovers," he said. "In this emergency, it is well that Shidehara was decided on so speedily. If it should turn out that Hamaguchi may not have recovered sufficiently to attend the Diet session, it would be well to elicit the views of such elders in the party as Baron Yamamoto Tatsuo[12] on who might be chosen.

Sometime earlier a message had come to me from Egi. "Tell the old Prince," he thus asked, "that despite talk of an Egi faction and an Adachi faction within the party, this is quite untrue. Tell him that he may rest assured Egi will do his best to keep the party united." When I had conveyed this message to the Prince, he said,

"In giving my regards to Egi, please tell him I'm especially anxious to avoid any unnecessary confusion at this juncture. Take my greetings to the others as well. Shidehara has been good enough to send me a telegram. Please express my appreciation to him."

As I was on the point of leaving, the Prince remarked, "By the way, if the Government is not quite careful in handling Ugaki, if he would resign and leave the Cabinet, the aftermath could be extremely troublesome." And I rejoined, "What shall I say then, if I encounter him, for he's likely to question me?"

"Just tell him," the Prince answered, "that Saionji is expecting him to work assiduously on behalf of the Government."

The Right-Wingers and the Justice Minister
—The Prime Minister's Condition and the
Question of Raising Ugaki to this Post—
The Prospects for Foreign Minister Shidehara
—The Attitude of Ohara, the Vice Minister
of Justice—The Question of the Minseitō
Presidency—Rumors on the Succession to the
Presidency.

On my return to Tokyo I met with both the Railways Minister and the Foreign Minister. Then, curious about the results of investigation of Hamaguchi's assailant, I called at the Justice Ministry to talk with the Vice Minister. Since he was out, I talked

---

[12] [Baron Yamamoto Tatsuo (1856-1947), currently a Minseitō "counsellor *(komon)*," was a bureaucrat turned politician like Hamaguchi, Wakatsuki, *et al.*, at the beginning of the Taishō era. He had been President of the Bank of Japan, Finance Minister in the second Saionji cabinet, Agriculture Minister in the first Yamamoto cabinet (as a member of the Seiyūkai), was associated with the Seiyū Hontō party, and thus entered the Minseitō. He was later to serve as Home Minister in the "transcendent" Saitō cabinet.]

with Sasaki, the Chief Secretary, who had no notable new developments to report. It seemed to me that while the courts are rigorous
in inquiring into left-wing activities, as far as right-wing activities
are concerned the courts are not only lenient but seem intentionally
inclined to be more or less protective. This is undoubtedly due to
the influence of Hiranuma, the Vice President of the Privy Council,
and of those like him contemptuous of political parties who say,
"For a crime like this to happen today must be ascribed to the evils
inherent in government by political parties. It is the growing evil of
party politics which drives young men to such crimes." When they
make assertions like this, I'm impressed that they may think this is
just the case, the perfect trigger, so to speak, to turn the people to
curse and condemn all party politics. I felt it confirmed more clearly
that their past attitudes yet animate them. Moreover, the criminal
in this case is affiliated with the Kokuhonsha. The facts, further,
are that he had been staying in the home of an influential member
of the Kokuhonsha, that he had learned indirectly of Admiral
Katō's indignation, that the pistol which he used in his assault on
Hamaguchi belonged to a certain Aikokusha member named
Matsuki and had been lent to him, and that he had spent the night
before his crime in a drunken carouse with a number of friends.
These are all facts.[13] Where the money came from we can well

---

[13] [Aoki reproduces further facts which equip the assassin with a characteristic *sōshi* delinquent background (I, 101-3): Sagoya, whose family roots
were in the Nagasaki area, had been born in Manchuria (in Ta-la-tzu, Holung-
hsien) whence the family moved to Korea where he received only an elementary
education. A runaway at fifteen, he held a variety of short-term jobs in the
waterfront and dock areas of Fukuoka, Kobe, and Yokohama, where he was not
well-liked by his fellows. After a further year in Manchuria he shipped off to
Singapore where he became a typesetter for and found lodging at the headquarters of a paper called *Nanyō oyobi Nihonjin* (*The South Seas and the
Japanese*) for about a year. In October, 1928 he returned to Japan, sought out
certain "patriotic society" persons in the capital, was billeted by a succession of
them until in mid-July, 1930, he moved to a small hostelry maintained by and
serving as headquarters of the Aikokusha. He had been on the police blotter
for two charges of physical assault (apparently involving imbroglios with fellow
sōshi) and was on probation at the time of his attack on Hamaguchi. His character was noted as "highly impressionable" and "easily moved to emotion."
[His trial, delayed after the fashion of such matters in Japan, did not
occur till well after popular patriotic passions had been exacerbated by the
Manchurian invasion and the later more dramatic terrorist attacks against symbols of the old order. At his trial Uzawa Sōmei (above, chap. ii, n. 40) dwelt on
the issue of "contempt for the supreme command" which Hamaguchi had
allegedly exhibited and defended the crime on grounds of patriotic intent.
(Uzawa was to step forward as civilian counsel at the court-martial of Lt. Col.
Aizawa for the murder of General Nagata in 1935, and again to make the most
of this "supreme command" argument.) Sagoya appears to have been released in

imagine. When a case like this is investigated thoroughly, it invariably develops that someone is behind it all. Thus, there must be some influence in the courts which can prevent a thorough investigation. Originally, the members of the Hiranuma-founded Kokuhonsha,[14] when not military men, were procurators or officials of the Justice Ministry. It is undeniable that the inclination prevails among this group to see only the deficiencies of political parties, without examining their basic significance, their *raison d'être*. It can be understood in the present case, then, what must be the sentiments of judges and other Justice officials who move in such an atmosphere.

While reflecting on these things I went again on the nineteenth to Okitsu and spoke of the general situation to the Prince.

"Though I believe that Hamaguchi will have made a remarkable recovery by the time of the Diet's session, I doubt if he will actually be able to attend the session. Just before coming down to see you now I met with Baron Yamamoto and raised with him the question of who should take over Hamaguchi's duties if he is unable to attend the Diet sessions. 'Well,' Yamamoto said, 'There's Adachi, and Wakatsuki, and Ugaki, for each of whom there is some clamor. But to me this now seems an improper question. Prime Minister Hamaguchi is making a good recovery, and I am confident he will be able to attend the sessions. At present, then, we can only work on the assumption that he will be able to attend. There may be various sorts of divisive activity, but I'll do my best to quell them. Tell the old Prince, then, to take heart; for I am not one to throw the party into confusion.' "

Continuing my review for the Prince, I went on to raise the further question, "If in the last analysis, Hamaguchi cannot attend the Diet session, how would it be to propose General Ugaki, before the Diet, to be acting Prime Minister? If he should leave the Cabinet out of a sense of grievance, wouldn't the military establishment welcome this development and make of it the pretext for establishing an interim cabinet of Hiranuma partisans or of right-

---

consequence of the general amnesty proclaimed on February 11, 1934, following the birth of a Crown Prince the preceding December. He has been extremely active in the post-war rightist movement (Morris, *Post-war Nationalism*, pp. 339-44, 449). See also Young, *Imperial Japan*, pp. 59-60, 197; Byas, *Government by Assassination*, pp. 99, 107f; Yanaga, *Japan Since Perry*, pp. 514-15.]

[14] Kokuhonsha (National Foundation Society) was founded in 1924 to strengthen the national foundation, reviving the essence of the national polity [*kokutai*] with Hiranuma as president. Its membership included many notable figures from the bureaucracy, the military establishment, and from industry.

wing reactionary groups? This could have grave future consequences. Perhaps in these circumstances, if Ugaki can be appeased,
he may be able to effect a military reorganization and replace both
the President and Vice President of the Privy Council as well. I
imagine that Ugaki is the best man to do both these jobs. In other
words, if Hamaguchi cannot attend the Diet session, don't you
think it might be best to have Ugaki serve in this capacity vis-à-vis
the Diet?"

To this the Prince rejoined, "There do seem to be some in the
Minseitō who think this an excellent idea. If what you say is
true, there may be something to your argument."

I went on to say, "Shidehara would never accept the job. Besides, he's much too valuable a person, so that if his career is not
tarnished, it may be better as you have often remarked before to
have him become in the future an adviser to the Throne or serve
in the Privy Council."

The Prince responded, "It may not be possible in Japan; but
surely in Western countries a man of Shidehara's qualifications
would become a sort of elder statesman in diplomacy so that even
though he might hold no office the diplomatic corps in Tokyo,
having long associated with him, would continue to pay him
respect, and at the same time the Foreign Ministry could continue
to consult with him, lest our diplomacy go off on strange tangents.
For the welfare of our nation I believe this might be of great importance. Yet I doubt if this could be done in Japan. It's not that we
should imitate the role of Thiers in France. I remember how there
were always the carriages of foreign ambassadors and ministers
before his house, which was always a lively throng-filled place."

Then he concluded, "Give my greetings to them all in
Tokyo."

When I told him what I had found out of the plans to curb
rightist activities, the Prince was very much in accord with them.
On returning to Tokyo I met with Egi and with the Foreign Minister as well. When I spoke with Egi of the attitude of the courts, he
said, "That can't be! Why not have a chat with Kanayama, the pro-
curator?"

About this time there were reports that the Prime Minister's
condition was improving daily so that there were hopes that he
might recover for the Diet session.

On the morrow I met with Shidehara, the acting Prime Minister. He said to me, "That talk you heard the other day about
certain Justice Ministry officials has also come to the attention of

the Chief Secretary of the Cabinet and it seems he took it up with the Attorney General. I therefore called the Vice Minister of Justice to my office and told him, in the presence of the Chief Secretary, 'There is a tendency among Justice officials to give cover to rightists, even in this case to let certain high figures escape implication. Thoroughgoing measures are taken against leftists but lenience is shown toward rightists. This is extremely unfair.'

"The Justice Vice Minister became angry. 'I told Harada the other day,' he said, 'that we are quite thorough with rightists and I assured him we are carrying out the investigation with strict justice and fairness. This attitude of his toward Justice officials is contemptuous and utterly unpardonable!'

"Thus," Shidehara continued, "he'll have it in for you when next you meet him."

"If that's the case then," I said, "I'll look him up now." With this I took my leave of Shidehara.

I had taken the occasion the other day to speak with Shidehara about the Justice Ministry officials' reputed attitude toward rightists because I thought it might be useful data in his new role as acting Prime Minister. I couldn't help being somewhat annoyed that he would call in the Vice Minister of Justice to speak of the matter using my name. It indicates how much more administratively or bureaucratically minded rather than politically minded he is. Hence, since it might bode ill in the future if I did not do something about the Vice Minister, I phoned him immediately to arrange to see him. He said that I should come at once. When I entered his office at the Justice Ministry, he greeted me, saying, "The fact of the matter is I've been anxious to see you, and I've phoned you unsuccessfully several times."

I then explained to him the aforementioned circumstances. "Frankly," I told him, "I went to Shidehara the other day to tell him why I had sought reassurances from you. Although you had already given me such assurance as I sought on the matter, when he talked with you he must have forgotten that the question I had raised with you had been settled; and thus he took the matter up with you anew. This he quite understands now. But I'm told you are quite angry with me; yet with the facts of the matter as they are, I hope you'll understand and not harbor it against me."

The Vice Minister readily understood. "Henceforth," he suggested, "so that mistakes may be avoided I will see you whenever you wish. I want you to come directly to me." And I assured him that I would call on him whenever there might be misunderstanding. He reiterated, as I took my leave of him, "The Justice officials are doing their best to be eminently fair, and I trust you will bear this in mind."

On the next day the Lord Privy Seal returned from his tour accompanying the Emperor; and since it had been some time since I had talked with him, I called on him at Takanawa. I spoke with him about the recent condition of the stricken Hamaguchi and reviewed the various maneuvers that were under way on the assumption that Hamaguchi might not be well enough to attend the Diet session. At the same time I spoke in some detail about the Prince's views, although I had had Kido previously convey them to him.

"Put succinctly," I said, "there is apprehension that General Ugaki's personal value is so highly overrated that it may somehow cause grave disturbances in the world of affairs. If he were to leave the cabinet out of some sense of grievance, it might, on the one hand, serve to unite the military services to make common cause; and, on the other hand, a foolish public might be taken in by the right-wing organizations' claims to be all-powerful, and opinion could thus be manipulated. If this should happen, it could pave the way for that alleged antithesis between the military services and parliamentary politics to become a reality. Then the proponents of non-party cabinets with their notions about 'Imperial absolutism' may seize the chance to smash the pattern of politics by political parties.[15] That is why it is absolutely essential to keep General Ugaki satisfied to remain in the present cabinet and at the same time to get him to effect some sort of military reorganization. The task, thus, is not only to keep him from being used by Hiranuma's rightist faction; but even more, to utilize General Ugaki to crush Hiranuma and bring about a reformation of the Privy Council. In these circumstances, then, should Hamaguchi be unable to resume his post, does not the logic of the situation suggest the necessity of making Ugaki temporarily president of the Minseitō and thus Prime Minister? As for Home Minister Adachi, he quite lacks the caliber to be Prime Minister. Foreign Minister Shidehara, if by chance he would accept party leadership, would require approval

Saionji

---

[15] [Ugaki may have seemed to be, up to this point, a relatively reliable Saionji-type of liberal, readily open to a word of counsel from the old Prince and ready to do his bidding. Here, however, we are reminded that he was just another ambitious piece among the many to be used carefully but realistically on Saionji's political chessboard. Harada's dialectically-expressed prognosis seems an astutely prescient forecast both of the "March plot" of 1931 and of Japan's whole plight in the ensuing decade.]

of Iwasaki. Furthermore, it is clear that he is frankly indifferent and utterly without ambition to take over the post."

Continuing my report to Count Makino, I related the comments made to me recently by Sengoku, the South Manchurian Railway president.[16] Sengoku had said, "In the first place three men seem likely candidates:—Shidehara, Ugaki, and Yamamoto Tatsuo. Of these Baron Yamamoto has the more suitable party background although he is personally so cold and aloof that he would garner little popular support. Even if he were to accept, he would perhaps stipulate unwelcome conditions to his acceptance. For these reasons, then, Yamamoto will not do."

Sengoku had also said, "Even if Hamaguchi is unable to participate in the Diet session that is forthcoming, why shouldn't Shidehara continue as acting Prime Minister? The members of political parties have no right to stipulate that this post must be filled only from their own group, from within the ranks of party members. Perhaps they should look to themselves and their inadequacies for reasons why such an issue as this arises."

All this I related to the Lord Keeper of the Privy Seal. The fact that I had gone to see Sengoku before meeting with Makino had resulted from a suggestion of the Prince, who had raised the question of what Sengoku's views in this present situation might be.

Subsequently I went to Okitsu to report in some detail to the Prince, whose only comment was, "Well, we must wait and see what develops."

When I returned from seeing the Prince, I was aware of a plethora of rumors among newsmen and political analysts: that Prince Saionji considered Adachi unsatisfactory, or Ugaki unsuitable as a military man, or Wakatsuki as acceptable; that Harada had let slip this or that bit of data about who said what to whom. All of this rumor-mongering I found quite distasteful and embarrassing. Yet I suppose such cases as the present one always give rise to unfounded reports. Still, I had to face a query from a close friend of Adachi, from his home district, who sought me out to ask, "What's this all

---

[16] [Sengoku Mitsugu (1857-1931), a Tosa man who became a Mitsubishi *bantō* (manager) in the Meiji period, is a good example of the business-man-in-politics figure from Taishō times on. He had been skilful and influential in building the coalition *Kenseikai*, the party formation which preceded and became the main element in the Minseitō. He had been Railways Minister in cabinets of Katō Kōmei. He was currently President of the South Manchurian Railway, an appointment by Hamaguchi in 1929 which had been widely heralded because of Sengoku's reputation for probity and economic common sense. Cf. Shidehara, p. 170; John E. Turner, "The Kenseikai: Leader vs. Party Liberal," *Far Eastern Quarterly*, XI 1952), 317-34.]

about? If Adachi does not enjoy the confidence of Prince Saionji, why wasn't the movement to have him become party president stopped at the very beginning? What are we to expect?"

To this I could only reply, "Prince Saionji is not minded heedlessly to intervene in a matter of this kind, or to intervene against anyone whom a party wishes to elevate to its presidency. At any rate in the present situation there is no reason for him to participate one way or another in the matter."

When he went on to press me for my personal view in the matter, I said, "That's all very well, but you must understand that my personal opinion wouldn't necessarily reflect Prince Saionji's view, so perhaps it's best for me to say nothing to a question like this."

A number of just such fabrications are current nowadays and are the cause of much embarrassment—and not only from my own point of view. The least I could do in this particular instance was to meet with both Home Minister Adachi and War Minister Ugaki and I told each of them the following:

"Many of the rumors and false reports now current may be as annoying to you as some of them are highly distressing to me. Perhaps you have heard of them too; but as you well know, Prince Saionji would not countenance some of the remarks that are being attributed to him. And of course I could never jeopardize my position by indulging in the talk that has been attributed to me, and I have in fact said nothing. I am sure you will understand, in full candor, that all this talk is quite outside my ken. As long as you yourself do so understand, it doesn't really matter what they may say about me."

And to this explanation both Adachi and Ugaki in turn assured me they were well aware of the facts and that I had no cause for concern.

> *The State of the Prime Minister's Health*
> *—Vice Foreign Minister Yoshida Voices*
> *his Concern—The Chientao Problem and*
> *the Seiyūkai—The Foreign Minister*
> *versus Mori—The Problem of Choosing a*
> *Successor to Imamura as Imperial Aide-de-*
> *Camp—The Proclamation of the London*
> *Treaty.*

In spite of the gradual improvement in Prime Minister Hamaguchi's condition, rumors to the contrary continue to be spread.

When I gave a farewell party on December 4 for Arita[17] and Matsunaga at the Hōryu, Mori of the Seiyūkai was among those present. He took the occasion to call me aside.

"I hear that Hamaguchi is much worse," he said. "The bullet wound continues to suppurate and its proper treatment is extremely difficult because of his diabetes. Furthermore, since he was shot he has grown fearful, has suffered a nervous collapse, and cannot take adequate nourishment. It's doubtful, I'm told, that he can live out the month. This sounds extremely bad."

"But," I protested, "I've heard nothing at all like this. Might it not be just another of these wild rumors?" I immediately checked on the story and found it was a complete fabrication.

As we talked Mori had also said to me, "When the president of the Seiyūkai recently returned to town I told him I had thought of calling on Prince Saionji. Since he in fact instructed me to do so, would you be good enough to phone to Okitsu to find out when it might be convenient for me to go down?" When I inquired as he requested, the answer came that the eighth would be a suitable date; and thus it was arranged.

Earlier Vice Foreign Minister Yoshida had expressed deep concern for the fact that on foreign affairs the Seiyūkai interpretation so frequently and widely deviated from the facts. He thus took the trouble to call on me personally. "Before Mori goes down to see Prince Saionji," he asked, "I hope you'll have a chance to forewarn the Prince so that he may counsel the Seiyūkai through Mori to take a more responsible and serious attitude on foreign affairs." What troubled Yoshida most was his fear that Japan's diplomatic position would be sadly weakened when, as political controversy sharpens, issues of foreign affairs are made weapons of internal political struggle. Even at present, issues not infrequently arise having most unfortunate repercussions in our conduct of foreign affairs. If only problems of this sort did not arise! To take an example, during the recent issue at Chientao the Government-General in Korea proclaimed its intention to maintain peace and order at Chientao,[18]

---

[17] [Arita Hachirō was the newly appointed Minister to Australia; and Matsunaga newly appointed as Minister to the Netherlands.]

[18] [The Chientao district of Manchuria, immediately north of the Korean frontier, was largely settled by Korean refugees from their Japanese-controlled homeland. In this setting there were recurrent, almost constant, episodes, more numerous than the textbooks record, of violence involving the Chinese authorities, the Japanese consular police, and the Korean émigrés. The incident to which Yoshida here probably refers was the alleged wounding of Japanese consular police by Chinese military police on October 6, 1930. Cf. the numerous

even to the point of employing troops to do so. The Foreign Ministry, on the other hand, had announced that the use of troops was to be avoided at all costs. The two views seemed diametrically opposed. And finally it was the Foreign Ministry which had its way and the issue was settled without the dispatch of a single soldier. Since the Chinese evinced a notable spirit of cooperation, the result was eminently satisfactory. And yet, during the time of the controversy, Seiyūkai partisans sought to quiz the Foreign Minister for details. When he learned from Mori that four or five leading Seiyūkai men felt they must see the Foreign Minister, Yoshida had told Mori:

Yoshida

"Now that this issue has at last, after much effort, been smoothed out, if it becomes known that the Seiyūkai is questioning the Government's position and this inquiry is reported in the press, it can only have extremely unfortunate results in our diplomatic position. From the standpoint of national policy there would be nothing to gain, and everything to lose in reopening the matter now. I hope they will show a national rather than a partisan attitude. If it's a question of information alone, it should be sufficient for you as the General Secretary to call on the Foreign Minister. Whether the Minister will be able to see them or not is up to him to indicate. Please be good enough to wait a while."

Having said this to Mori, Yoshida went and explained the situation to Shidehara. He added, "I believe it would be well for you to talk with Mori." But Shidehara replied, "To talk with men like Mori produces no understanding. Since it would be a waste of time, I do not want to see him." To this Yoshida rejoined, "It may be quite annoying for you, but if you were to take the trouble to see him, the whole matter might be cleared up; whereas if you refuse, who can tell what complications might not arise."

Meanwhile Mori sought out Yoshida again and Yoshida told him, "The Minister cannot meet with them, but I shall be glad to, as his deputy." But Mori said, "You know I'm here as a representative of my party. It's no child's errand I've come on. I can't go back saying everything is satisfactory. I want your answer in writing." So Yoshida went to Shidehara. "The Seiyūkai now wants a written

---

special studies by Foreign Ministry staff, such as *Kantō ni okeru futei Senjindan no jōkyō* [*The Condition of Recalcitrant Korean Groups in Chientao*], 1920 (LC Microfilm Collection, SP 131); *Kantō mondai chōsho* [*A Research Study of Chientao Problems*], a survey made in 1931 (*ibid.*, SP 236); and the section of the huge *Gaimushō keisatsushi* [*A History of the Foreign Office Police*] dealing with this area: *Kantō Konshun chiho* [*The Chientao and Hun-ch'un Areas*], *1910-1938* (*ibid.*, SP 205-5).]

statement of our handling of the Chientao affair. What do we do now?"

Shidehara replied, "If we give a statement to the Seiyūkai, we'll be similarly badgered by each of the parties, and by the Privy Council and the House of Peers as well. If we give in to one, we must give in to all. Rather than be troubled thus, it's best we not let it start."

Yoshida, even more troubled, said to Mori, "The Minister is not at all pleased at your request, but I hope you'll be patient just a little longer."

It was at this point that Yoshida came to me. "Whatever may be said for it, Shidehara's attitude is making a bad matter worse. Isn't there something that can be done about it? . . ."

Once before, I had reported to the Prince at Okitsu that Shidehara was reluctant to meet with Mori. The Prince pointed out, "I recall that there was once some issue or other with the United States. Shidehara took great pains to meet with and explain the matter in detail to Mori or some such opposition politicians. He was somehow doublecrossed—his confidences were betrayed and turned around into an attack upon him and he was greatly distressed. The more so, as I recall it, when the effect of it reached countries abroad. Perhaps after bitter experiences of this kind it's too much to expect Shidehara to meet with Mori again."

I had passed this along to Yoshida suggesting that he perhaps should check with Shidehara to see if some such past experience was back of his present reluctance. And with this I let the matter drop.

Certainly the Seiyūkai's current attitude on foreign affairs is quite absurd, and those in the know seem worried about it. For example to hear them campaigning while the London Treaty was under discussion one would think that they expected an American attack to come the next day. Also, with some members of the Navy's Yōyōkai, together with some from the House of Peers, a part of the Seiyūkai is said to have organized an Ikankai—a Society of Regret—to hold commemorative meetings to deplore the conclusion of the London Treaty.

With respect to the recent need to choose a successor to Vice Admiral Imamura, the Imperial Naval Aide-de-Camp, the Naval General Staff had planned to designate a naval officer who had spearheaded the opposition to treaty ratification. I understand, however, that Admiral Suzuki, the Grand Chamberlain, knew enough about the man to raise objection to the appointment and asked the Navy to reconsider. Thus the designation of Imamura's successor yet remains to be made. This is just another matter arising in the aftermath of conclusion of the treaty, to which I'm sure the forthcoming session of the Diet must give most careful attention.

Finally the long delayed ratification of the London Naval Treaty by the Irish Free State was concluded with the deposit of its instrument of ratification with the Foreign Office in London on December 31, 1930. Thus the treaty which had so long been an issue was at last put into effect in governing the relations of the three states—Japan, Britain, and the United States. Occurring as it did at the time of the traditional year-end holidays in Japan, the various governmental offices were closed. The official report of Ireland's ratification reached the Foreign Office on the morning of the thirty-first, and the officer on duty immediately initiated the steps for the official proclamation of the treaty. Then early on New Year's Day, 1931, Ambassador Matsudaira's cable brought word that ratification was now completed. On the same day the Treaty was officially proclaimed through publication in a special edition of *Kampō*, the *Official Gazette*.

Appendices

Principal Officials and
Members of Official Bodies

A. The Hamaguchi Cabinet
July 2, 1929-April 14, 1931[1]

Office	Name	Period in Office
Prime Minister	Hamaguchi Yūkō	July 2, 1929—Apr. 14, 1931
(Ad interim)	Shidehara Kijūrō	Nov. 15, 1930—Mar. 9, 1931
Foreign Minister	Shidehara Kijūrō	July 2, 1929—Dec. 13, 1931
Home Minister	Adachi Kenzō	July 2, 1929—Dec. 13, 1931
Finance Minister	Inoue Junnosuke	July 2, 1929—Dec. 13, 1931
War Minister	Ugaki Kazushige	July 2, 1929—Apr. 14, 1931
(Ad interim)	Abe Nobuyuki	July 16, 1930—Dec. 10, 1930
Navy Minister	Takarabe Takeshi	July 2, 1929—Oct. 3, 1930
(Acting Navy Minister)	Hamaguchi Yūkō	Nov. 26, 1929—May 19, 1930
	Abo Kiyokazu	Oct. 3, 1930—Dec. 13, 1931
Justice Minister	Watanabe Chifuyu	July 2, 1929—Dec. 13, 1931
Education Minister	Kobashi Itta	July 2, 1929—Nov. 29, 1929
	Tanaka Ryūzō	Nov. 29, 1929—Dec. 13, 1931
Agriculture and Forestry Minister	Machida Chūji	July 2, 1929—Dec. 13, 1931
Commerce and Industry Minister	Tawara Magoichi	July 2, 1929—Apr. 14, 1931
Communications Minister	Koizumi Matajirō	July 2, 1929—Dec. 13, 1931
Railways Minister	Egi Yoku	July 2, 1929—Sep. 10, 1931

---

[1] Dates later than April 14, 1931 indicate retention in office under the succeeding second Wakatsuki cabinet.

Overseas Minister	Matsuda Genji	July 2, 1929–Apr. 14, 1931
Chief Cabinet Secretary	Suzuki Fujiya	July 2, 1929–Apr. 13, 1931
Director, Legislative Bureau	Kawasaki Takukichi	July 3, 1929–July 14, 1931

B. *Principal Officers of the Imperial Court in 1930*

Lord Keeper of the Privy Seal	Makino Nobuaki
Private Secretary to the Lord Keeper	Okabe Nagakabe (until October 28, 1930)
	Kido Kōichi (after October 28, 1930
Minister of the Imperial Household	Ikki Kitokurō
Vice Minister of the Imperial Household	Sekiya Teisaburō
Grand Chamberlain	Suzuki Kantarō (after January 25, 1930)
Chief Aide-de-Camp	Nara Takeji
President of the Privy Council	Kuratomi Yusaburō
Vice President of the Privy Council	Hiranuma Kiichirō
Chief Secretary of the Privy Council	Futagami Hyōji

C. *The Privy Councillors, as of July 1, 1930*

President	Kuratomi Yusaburō
Vice President	Hiranuma Kiichirō
Imperial Princes	Yasuhito, Prince Chichibu
	Nobuhito, Prince Takamatsu
	Kotohito, Prince Kan'in

Councillors:

Itō Miyoji[1]	Sakurai Jōji
Kuki Ryūichi	Den Kenjirō[2]
Kaneko Kentarō[2]	Arai Kentarō[2]
Kubota Yuzuru[2]	Kawai Misao[2]
Tomii Masanori	Ishihara Kenzō
Ishikura Tadanori	Kamada Eikichi
Yamakawa Kenjirō[2]	Suzuki Kantarō
Kuroda Nagashige[2]	Ishii Kikujirō
Furuichi Koi	Mizumachi Kesaroku[2]
Matsumuro Itasu	Okada Ryōhei
Egi Chiyuki	Fukuda Masatarō

[1] Chairman of the subcommittee on the London Treaty.
[2] Members of the subcommittee on the London Treaty.

D.   Principal Army and Navy Officials in 1930

Chief of the General Staff	Kanaya Hanzō (after February 19, 1930)
Vice Chief of the General Staff	Okamoto Renichirō (until December 22, 1930) Ninomiya Harushige (after December 22, 1930)
War Minister	Ugaki Kazushige (Abe Nobuyuki, *ad interim,* June 16 to December 10)
Vice Minister of War	Abe Nobuyuki (until August 1, 1930) Sugiyama Gen (after August 1, 1930)
Chief of the Naval General Staff	Katō Kanji (until June 11) Taniguchi Naozane (after June 11)
Vice Chief of the Naval General Staff	Suetsugu Nobumasa (until June 10) Nagano Osami (after June 10)
Navy Minister	Takarabe Takeshi (until October 3) Abo Kiyokazu (after October 3)
Vice Minister of Navy	Yamanashi Katsunoshin (until June 10) Kobayashi Seizō (after June 10)

E.   The Board of Field Marshals and Fleet Admirals

Field Marshal	Oku Yasugata
Fleet Admiral	Tōgō Heihachirō
Field Marshal	Prince Kan'in Kotohito
Field Marshal	Uehara Yusaka

F.   The Supreme War Councillors, as of July 1, 1930

Admiral Prince Fushimi Hiroyasu
General Prince Nashimoto Morimasa
Admiral Okada Keisuke
General Shirakawa Yoshinori
General Mutō Nobuyoshi
General Inoue Ikutarō
Admiral Katō Kanji
Admiral Abo Kiyokazu
General Suzuki Takao

**Laws and Ordinances
Cited or Referred to
in the Harada Text**

A. Extracts from the Meiji Constitution,
Promulgated February 11, 1889

. . . .

Article XI.   The Emperor has the supreme command of the Army and Navy.

Article XII.   The Emperor determines the organization and peace standing of the Army and Navy.

Article XIII.   The Emperor declares war, makes peace, and concludes treaties.

. . . .

Article LV.   The respective Ministers of State shall give their advice to the Emperor, and be responsible for it.

All laws, Imperial Ordinances and Imperial Rescripts of whatever kind, that relate to the affairs of the state, require the countersignature of a Minister of State.

Article LVI.   The Privy Councillors shall, in accordance with the provisions for the organization of the Privy Council, deliberate upon important matters of State, when they have been consulted by the Emperor.

. . . .

B. Imperial Ordinance on the Organization
of the Cabinet

*Imperial Ordinance No. 135, December 24, 1889,
as amended by Imperial Ordinance No. 7 of 1907*

Article I.   The Cabinet is composed of the various Ministers of State.

Article II. The Prime Minister stands at the head of the Ministers of State, reports affairs of State to the Sovereign, and in compliance with Imperial instructions, has general control over the various branches of the administration.

Article III. The Prime Minister, should an occasion seem sufficiently important to demand such a course, has competence to suspend dispositions made or orders issued by any branch of the administration, pending Imperial sanction.

Article IV. The Prime Minister is empowered to issue Cabinet Ordinances on the authority of his office, or by special delegation.

Article IV-2. The Prime Minister directs and supervises the Superintendent-General of the Metropolitan Police, the Governor of Hokkaido, and the Prefectural governors with respect to matters in their jurisdiction. If he judges that their orders or dispositions are in contravention of regulations, harmful to public interest, or violative of their competence, he may suspend or repeal such orders and dispositions.

Article V. The following matters shall be submitted for deliberation by the Cabinet:

1. Drafts of laws, estimates, and accounts.

2. Treaties and important international questions.

3. Imperial ordinances concerning administrative organization or the execution of regulations and laws.

4. Jurisdictional disputes among departments.

5. Petitions from the people which may be handed down from the throne or submitted by the Diet.

6. Expenditures apart from the budget.

7. Appointments, promotions, and removals of officials of *chokunin*[1] rank and of local governors.

---

[1] The Japanese civil service was divided into two major groups: the higher officials (*kōtō-kan*) and the junior officials (*hannin-kan*). *Kōtō-kan* included, in turn, two groups: the *chokunin-kan*, directly involving Imperial sanction, and the *sōnin-kan*. Of the *chokunin-kan* the highest were personally appointed by the Emperor and were thus known as *shinnin-kan* (personally appointed officials). Below these stood the "ordinary" *chokunin-kan* (and in practice this term was used for this latter group alone) who were direct but not personal Imperial appointees, and comprised grades I and II of the *kōtō-kan* ranks.

Below the *chokunin-kan* stood the *sōnin-kan*, officials appointed with Imperial approval. These *sōnin-kan* held grades III—IX of the *Kōtō-kan* rank.

In contrast to this status complexity for the higher officials, *hannin-kan* were simply divided into classes I through IV.

Schematically this might be shown as follows:

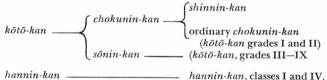

In addition, other matters within the domain of the business of the departments, involving questions of high policy of the administration as a whole, shall be submitted for deliberation by the Cabinet.

Article VI.   Each Minister of a department is competent, at his discretion, to submit any matter whatsoever for the Cabinet's consideration through the Prime Minister.

Article VII.   Matters concerning military secrets and command which are reported to the Throne, except when submitted to the Cabinet by direction of the Emperor, shall be reported to the Prime Minister by the Minister of War and the Minister of Navy.

Article VIII.   Should the Prime Minister be prevented from discharging his functions, another Minister of State may be temporarily ordered to take charge of such functions.

Article IX.   Should any Minister of State be prevented from discharging his functions, another Minister of State may temporarily act for him or be ordered to take charge of such functions.

Article X.   In addition to the Ministers of the several departments, by special Imperial consideration, other persons may be authorized to sit in the Cabinet as Ministers of State.

C.   Imperial Household Ordinance on the Organization of the Office of the Lord Keeper of the Privy Seal

Imperial Household Ordinance No. 4, November 1, 1907, as amended by Imperial Household Ordinances No. 5 and No. 24 of 1910; No. 3 of 1914; and No. 3 of 1917

Article I.   The Office of the Lord Keeper of the Privy Seal shall have custody of the Imperial Seal and of the Great Seal of State, and shall take charge of such documents as Imperial edicts, rescripts and other documents.

Article II.   The Lord Keeper of the Privy Seal shall be personally appointed by the Emperor, shall daily attend upon his Majesty, and shall supervise the Office of the Lord Keeper of the Privy Seal.

Article III.   On matters relating to the grant of honors and the bestowal of decoration upon officials, to their promotion and demotion, the Lord Keeper of the Privy Seal shall give notice to the Minister of the Imperial Household.

Article IV.   The Office of the Lord Keeper of the Privy Seal shall have the following personnel: a chief private secretary, private secretaries, and subordinate officials.

(Continuation of footnote 1 from page 299)

Cf. Harold S. Quigley, *Japanese Government and Politics: An Introductory Study* (New York: The Century Co., 1932), pp. 142-59; Leonard D. White (ed.), *The Civil Service in the Modern State* (Chicago: The University of Chicago Press, 1930), pp. 513-55.

Article V.   The Chief Private Secretary shall be of *chokunin* rank and shall be put in charge of all documents.

Article VI.   There shall be two Private Secretaries, of *sōnin* rank. The routine duties of the office shall be apportioned between them.

Article VII.   Subordinate officials, of *hannin* rank, shall be assigned appropriate duties.

Supplementary Provision

From and after January 1, 1908, this ordinance shall revoke and supplant Order No. 68 of the Great Council of State, of 1885 and Imperial Household Ministry Order No. 23 of 1890.

D.   *Imperial Ordinance on the Organization of the Privy Council*

Imperial Ordinance No. 22, April 30, 1888, as
amended by the following Imperial Ordinances:
No. 216, of 1890; No. 120, of 1893; No. 117,
of 1903; No. 184, of 1909; No. 137, of 1913;
and No. 355, of 1918

Chapter I. *Organization*

I. The Privy Council shall be the place at which it will be the Emperor's pleasure to attend and there hold consultation on important matters of state.

II. The Privy Council shall be composed of a President, a Vice President, twenty-four Councillors, a chief secretary and secretaries. The number of secretaries shall be fixed at three.

III. The President, Vice President, and Councillors of the Privy Council shall be personally appointed by the Emperor, i.e., of *shinnin* rank. The Chief Secretary shall be of *chokunin* rank. The secretaries shall be of *sōnin* rank.

IV. No one who has not reached the fortieth year of his age shall be eligible to be appointed President, Vice President, or a Councillor of the Privy Council.

V. There shall be one Private Secretary to the President of the Privy Council who shall be of *sonin* rank.

Chapter II. *Functions*

VI. The Privy Council shall hold deliberations and present its opinions to the Emperor of his decision on the under-mentioned matters:

1. Matters which are within its competence under the Imperial House Law.

2. Drafts of amendments of the Constitution and of laws appertaining thereto.

3. Proclamation of martial law as provided for in Article XIV of the Constitution; and Imperial Ordinances as provided for in Articles VIII and LXX of the Constitution; and other Imperial Ordinances prescribing penal regulations.

4. Treaties and agreements with foreign states.

5. Matters concerning organization of the Privy Council and of the regulations for the conduct of business of the Privy Council.

6. Matters other than those mentioned above which may be especially referred to the Privy Council for advice.

VII. (Deleted).

VIII. The Privy Council, although it is the Emperor's highest resort of counsel on administrative and legislative matters, shall not interfere with the executive.

Chapter III. *Deliberations and Business*

IX. The deliberations of the Privy Council cannot be opened unless ten or more Privy Councillors are present.

X. The deliberations of the Privy Council shall be presided over by the President. When the President is prevented from doing so by unavoidable circumstances, the Vice President shall preside; and in case the Vice President is also prevented one of the Privy Councillors, according to their order to precedence, shall preside.

XI. The Ministers of State shall be entitled by virtue of their office to sit in the Privy Council as Councillors, and shall have the right to vote. The Ministers of State may send their representatives to the deliberations of the Council, with the right to speak and offer explanation; but such representatives shall not have the right to vote.

XII. Debates in the Privy Council shall be decided by a majority of the members present. In case of an equal division of votes the presiding officer shall have the deciding vote.

XIII. The President shall have the supreme control of all the business of the Privy Council and shall sign every official document proceeding from the Council.

The Vice President shall assist the President in the discharge of his duties.

XIV. The Chief Secretary shall manage all ordinary business of the Privy Council, under the direction of the President, shall countersign every public document issuing from the Privy Council, shall investigate matters to be submitted to deliberation, shall prepare reports, and shall have a seat in the assembly during deliberations that he may offer needed explanations, but he shall not have the power to vote.

The Secretaries shall take minutes of the proceedings, and shall assist the Chief Secretary in the discharge of his duties. When the Chief Secretary is prevented from discharging his duties, one of the Secretaries shall represent him therein.

In the minutes referred to in the preceding paragraph, there shall be mentioned the names of those present at the proceedings, the essential points of the matters discussed, of the questions propounded and the replies thereto, and of the decisions reached.

XIV-2. The Private Secretary of the President shall take charge of affairs of the President's secretariat.

XV. Except in special cases, no deliberation can be opened unless reports of any investigation that may have been ordered have been prepared and forwarded to each member of the Privy Council with the documents necessary for due deliberation.

The agenda for discussion and reports are to be previously forwarded to the Ministers of State.

Regulations for the Conduct of Privy Council Business

I. The Privy Council shall formulate its opinions on matters submitted to its deliberation by order of the Emperor.

II. The Privy Council cannot receive petitions, representations, or other communications from the Imperial Diet, from either House of the same, from any government office, or from any of His Majesty's private subjects whatever.

III. The Privy Council shall have official connection with the Cabinet and with the Ministers of State only, and officially shall not communicate or have any connection whatever with any other governmental offices, with the Imperial Diet, or with any of His Majesty's private subjects.

IV. The President shall cause the Chief Secretary to investigate matters submitted to the Privy Council, and also to prepare reports on matters to be submitted to its deliberations.

In case the President deems it necessary he may undertake himself to prepare the above-mentioned reports, or he may appoint one or more of the Privy Councillors for the purpose.

V. Reports of investigations shall be forwarded to the President by the persons charged with the preparation thereof.

In cases requiring expedition such reports may be made orally. In these cases the essential points of the matter reported on shall be briefly stated in the record herein referred to in Article VIII.

VI. The President may fix the period within which reports of investigation shall be made. The reports shall be prepared with as much dispatch as possible, and no procrastination is allowable.

The Cabinet may, in matters of urgent importance, address communications of that nature to the Privy Council, and may also fix the time of deliberation thereon.

VII. Copies of reports of investigations, together with copies of accompanying papers, shall be forwarded to each one of the members of the Privy Council at least three days prior to the opening of deliberations on the matters in question.

VIII. A record shall be kept in chronological order of the deliberations held. The matters to be so recorded are:

1. The nature of the matters deliberated upon.

2. The date of the forwarding of papers priod to the opening of deliberations.

3. The date of actual deliberation, and so forth.

An agenda, similar in form to the records mentioned in the preceding paragraph shall be prepared on the items to be submitted for deliberation. The said agenda shall be forwarded to each Councillor three days prior to the opening of deliberations thereon. The forwarding of said agenda shall also be regarded as an order to attend at the deliberations in question.

IX. The time of the deliberations of the Privy Council shall be fixed by the President. The Ministers of State, however, may request that the time be changed.

X. The deliberations of the Privy Council shall be conducted by the President or the Vice President in conformity with the following rules:

The President shall have the Chief Secretary state briefly the nature of the matter at hand. Thereupon members present shall be free to engage in debate on the subject, but none of them shall speak without having first obtained the permission of the President. The President shall also be free to participate in the debate. When the debate has been concluded, the President shall state the question and take the vote thereon.

The President shall declare the result of the vote.

XI. When a debate on any matter mentioned on the agenda has not been concluded in one day, it may be continued at another meeting, in which case the foregoing formalities need not be repeated.

XII. The opinions of the Privy Council's deliberations, by result of the vote cast, shall be recorded by the Chief Secretary or the Secretaries and submitted to the President. To this written statement of opinion there shall be appended the reasons that conduced to it; and, in case of highly important matters, a memorandum of the essential points of debate shall accompany it.

Members present who entertain opposing opinions may request the recording of their votes, and of the reasons for their opinion, in the record of the debates, in documents stating the reasons for the Council's opinion, or in the memorandum of the essential points of debate.

XIII.. The opinion mentioned in the proceeding article shall be presented to the Emperor, and at the same time a copy thereof shall be forwarded to the Prime Minister.

XIV. The records of the debates of the Privy Council shall be signed by the President and the Chief Secretary, or secretaries present, to attest to their accuracy.

E. On the Matter of the Attendance
of Imperial Princes
at Sessions of the Privy Council

*Imperial Message to Princes of the Blood,
May 18, 1888*

Being desirous, since reaching our majority, to obtain the assistance of the Imperial Princes in important affairs of state, we hereby empower them to attend in the deliberations of Our Privy Council.

F. Imperial Ordinance on the Supreme Council

Imperial Ordinance No. 294, December 28, 1903

I. The Supreme War Council shall be under the direct Imperial command and shall give answer in response to inquiries respecting military affairs of importance.

II. Upon reference of matters for deliberation the Supreme War Council shall meet and tender its advice to the throne.

III. The Supreme War Council shall have a Chairman, Councillors, a secretary-general, and a secretary.

IV. The following shall be Supreme War Councillors:

> Field Marshals and Admirals of the Fleet.
> The Minister of War.
> The Minister of Navy.
> The Chief of the General Staff.
> The Chief of the Naval General Staff.

Such general officers of the Army and flag officers of the Navy as may be especially appointed to be Supreme War Councillors.

V. The Chairman of the Supreme War Council shall be the highest ranking and senior member among the Supreme War Councillors.

VI. When necessary, a general officer holding an important position may be appointed councillor *pro tempore* and may attend Council meetings. However, he shall be deemed relieved of this appointment when the proceedings are closed on the matter in which he is connected.

VII. Matters relating to both the Army and the Navy require the joint examination of plans therefore, and the maintenance of mutual coordination in the primary interest of national defense and strategy.

VIII. With regard to matters that are not of common concern to the Army and Navy together, the Army Councillors alone, or the Navy Councillors alone, may meet for deliberation.

IX. In cases of emergency, the chairman may proffer advice in response to inquiry without deliberation by the Council.

X. The Secretary-General may be the Chief Aide-de-Camp to His Majesty or another officer of general or flag rank and shall have general charge of the ordinary affairs of the Supreme War Council.

The Secretary shall be chosen from among the Imperial Aides-de-Camp or from officers of field or senior rank, and shall assist the Secretary-general in his duties.

XI. To each Imperially appointed Supreme War Councillor shall be assigned as adjutant an officer of field or company grade or of senior or junior rank.

Supplementary Provision

The previous Regulations for the Supreme War Councillors are hereby rescinded [i.e., those previous to December 28, 1903].

G. Imperial Military Ordinance on the General Staff

Imperial Military Ordinance No. 15,
December 19, 1908

I. The General Staff shall take charge of matters of national defense and strategy.

II. The Chief of the General Staff shall be personally appointed by the Emperor from the ranks of general or lieutenant general. He shall have direct access to the Emperor on military matters; shall formulate plans with respect to national defense and strategy, and shall supervise the General Staff Office.

III. The Chief of the General Staff shall supervise the officers assigned to the General Staff, and be responsible for their training. He shall have jurisdiction over the Army General Staff College and of the Land Surveying Department.

IV. The Vice Chief of the General Staff shall assist the Chief of Staff and shall have general charge of the business of the Staff Office.

V. The heads of the various departments of the General Staff, under orders of the Chief of Staff, shall superintend the section heads and their subordinates and control their main duties.

VI. The form of organization of the General Staff shall be set forth in separate stipulations.

VII. Regulations on the period of service in the General Staff shall be prescribed by the Chief of Staff.

H.   *Imperial Military Ordinance on the Naval General Staff*

Imperial Military Ordinance (Navy) No. 7,
August 25, 1914; as amended by No. 8,
of 1916, and by No. 2, of 1918

1. The Naval General Staff shall take charge of matters of national defense and strategy.

II. There shall be a Chief of the Naval General Staff.

The Chief of the Naval General Staff shall have direct access to the Emperor on military matters, and shall direct the activities of the Naval General Staff.

The Chief of the Naval General Staff shall be personally appointed by the Emperor.

III. The Chief of the Naval General Staff shall participate in planning matters related to national defense and strategy; following Imperial decision he shall transmit them to the Ministry of Navy. In time of war, however, when the Imperial Headquarters has not been established, matters relating to operations shall be transmitted by the Chief of the Naval General Staff.

IV. There shall be a Vice Chief of the Naval General Staff to assist the Chief of the Naval General Staff, and he shall superintend Staff business.

V. There shall be a Secretary in the Naval General Staff office who shall manage its general affairs.

VI. There shall be Staff Officers assigned to the following matters:

1. Training and operational planning; the disposition, readiness, movement, and commissioning of ships.

2. The organization of fleets, the assignment of forces, the rules of maneuvers, transport communications, exercises, and inspection.

3. The selection and determination of militarily essential places as naval bases, naval stations, defended harbors; and the defensive preparation thereof.

4. Intelligence, translation, and editing.

VII. Suitable commissioned officers of the naval service shall be assigned to the Naval General Staff, under the orders of the Chief of the Naval General Staff.

VIII. Naval officers assigned to Japanese embassies and legations abroad as attachés or as assistant attachés shall be under the jurisdiction of the Chief of the Naval General Staff.

IX. In addition to the personnel stipulated in the foregoing articles, there shall be chief yeomen, chief carpenters, carpenters, yeomen, civilian clerks, and technicians[1] under the orders of the various senior officers.

---

[1]These Japanese ratings are given in approximate English equivalents, rather than in literal translation.

London Treaty Documents Cited or Referred to in the Harada Text

A. Extracts from the "Treaty for the Limitation and Reduction of Naval Armament, Signed at London, Aprill 22, 1930"[1]

.   .   .   .

Part III

Article 16

1. The completed tonnage in the cruiser, destroyer and submarine categories which is not to be exceeded on the 31st December, 1936, is given in the following table:

Category	United States	British Commonwealth of Nations	Japan
Cruiser:			
(a) with guns of more than 6.1 inch (155 mm.) caliber	180,000 tons (182,880 metric tons)	146,800 (149,149)	108,400 (110,134)
(b) with guns of 6.1 inch (155 mm.) caliber or less	143,500 (145,796)	192,200 (195,275)	100,450 (102,057)
Destroyers	150,000 (152,400)	150,000 (152,400)	105,500 (107,188)
Submarines	52,700 (53,543)	52,700 (53,543)	52,700 (53,543)

[1] (Text as in *Papers Relating to the Foreign Relations of the United States, 1930* (Washington: Government Printing Office, 1945), Vol. I, pp. 107-25.)

2. Vessels which cause the total tonnage in any category to exceed the figure given in the preceding table shall be disposed of gradually during the period ending on the 31st December, 1936.

3. The maximum number of cruisers of sub-category (a) shall be as follows: for the United States, eighteen; for the British Commonwealth of Nations, fifteen; for Japan, twelve.

Article 17

A transfer not exceeding 10 per cent of the allowed total tonnage of the category or sub-category into which the transfer is to be made shall be permitted between cruisers of sub-category (b) and destroyers.

Article 18

The United States contemplates the completion by 1935 of fifteen cruisers of sub-category (a) of an aggregate tonnage of 150,000 tons (152,400 metric tons). For each of the remaining cruisers of sub-category (a) which it is entitled to construct, the United States may elect to substitute 15,166 tons (15,409 metric tons) of cruisers of sub-category (b). In case the United States will construct one or more of such three remaining cruisers of sub-category (a), the sixteenth unit will not be laid down before 1933 and will not be completed before 1936; the seventeenth unit will not be laid down before 1934 and will not be completed before 1937; the eighteenth unit will not be laid down before 1935 and will not be completed before 1938.

. . . .

Part V

Article 23

The present Treaty shall remain in force until the 31st December, 1936, subject to the following exceptions:

(1) Part IV shall remain in force without limit of time;

(2) the provisions of Articles 3, 4 and 5, and of Article 11 and Annex II to Part II, so far as they relate to aircraft carriers, shall remain in force for the same period as the Washington Treaty.

Unless the High Contracting Parties should agree otherwise by reason of a more general agreement limiting naval armaments to which they all become parties, they shall meet in conference in 1935 to frame a new treaty to replace and to carry out the purposes of the present Treaty, it being understood that none of the provisions of the present Treaty shall prejudice the attitude of any of the High Contracting Parties at the conference agreed to.

B. A Chart Comparing the American and Japanese Proposals on Auxiliary Ship Tonnage[1]

	American Proposal February 5, 1930			Japanese Counter Proposal February 12, 1930			Compromise March 13, 1930		
	U. S.	JAPAN	%	U. S.	JAPAN	%	U. S.	JAPAN	%
Heavy Cruisers	180,000 (150,000)	108,400	60.2 (72.3)	150,000 (180,000)	108,400 (126,000)	72.3 (70.0)	180,000	108,400	60.2
Light Cruisers	147,000 (189,000)	90,255	61.5 (47.7)	189,000 (147,000)	107,755 (81,700)	57.0 (55.6)	143,500	100,450	70.0
Destroyers	200,000	120,000	60.0	150,000	105,000	70.0	150,000	105,500	70.3
Submarines	60,000	40,000	66.7	81,000	77,900	96.2	52,700	52,700	100.0
TOTAL	587,000 (599,000)	358,655	61.1 (59.9)	570.000 (558,000)	399,055 (390,600)	70.0 (70.3)	526,200	367,050	69.7

Figures enclosed in parentheses indicate alternative Japanese proposals.

U. S. to lay down one 8-inch 10,000 ton cruiser each year 1933, 1934, 1935.

[1]Derived from Itō Masanori, *Kokubo-shi* (*History of National Defense*), Vol. IV (*Gendai Nihon Bummei-shi* [*History of Modern Japanese Civilization*] (Tōkyō: Tōkyō Keizai Shimpōsha, 1941). More detailed tables on the decreases or augmentation of strength provided by the terms of the treaty may be found in *Rondon ikken* (LC Microfilm Collection, S 2.12.0.0.1), pp. 820-26.

C. The Navy Supplemental Program, as Adopted
by the Cabinet, November 11, 1930[1]

Ship construction (6-year program, 1931-36):

1. Cruiser, destroyer, and submarine replacement	¥227,080,000	
2. Construction in unlimited categories	20,000,000	¥247,080,000

Aviation replacement and expansion:

1. Activation of 14 Airgroups (8-year program, 1931-38).	¥ 46,340,000	
2. Maintenance of same (7-year program, 1932-38)	45,510,000	
3. Maintenance of carrier-plane units	6,000,000	
4. Experimental aviation construction	4,250,000	¥102,100,000

Miscellaneous replenishment:

1. Modernization, reconstruction of capital ships and auxiliaries (in addition to balance of ¥23,000,000 from previous appropriation), 1931-36	¥ 20,000,000	
2. Increase in special ship repair fund	5,000,000	
3. Costs incidental to maintenance of ship performance, improvement of training, and adjunct technical skills	19,950,000	¥ 44,950,000
		¥394,130,000

Ship Construction under the Supplemental Program:

1. Cruisers (6-inch 8,500 ton)	4 ships
2. Destroyers	9 ships
3. Submarines	12 ships
4. Vessels of other, unlimited categories	2 ships

Sources of Funds for this Navy Supplemental Program:

From the balance in the ¥508,000,000 ship construction fund, appropriated for 1931-36.	¥374,000,000
From other sources, appropriated for 1937-39.	¥ 20,000,000

There is, thus, a saving of ¥134 million from the ¥508 million appropriation to be allocated for tax reduction.

---

[1] Based on reports published in the *Tōkyō Asahi Shimbun*, November 10-12, 1930.

Bibliography

I. The Text

The basic element for a work of translation is, of course, the text itself. I have used the published Japanese edition:

Harada Kumao. *Saionji kō to seikyoku (Prince Saionji and the Political Situation)*. 9 vols. Tōkyō: Iwanami Shoten, 1950-56.

I have compared this text and my translation of it with that prepared for the use of the International Military Tribunal for the Far East which bears the following imprint data:

GHQ, Far East Command, Military Intelligence Service, General Staff, Civil Intelligence Section. *Special Report: Saionji-Harada Memoirs*. Place and date of issue not given.

In this originally "confidential" publication, there are three major parts: the "Diary," comprising Harada's dictations from July 31, 1931, through November 21, 1940; and two "Supplements" to include the memoirs of earlier dictation date. Both of the "Supplements" are derived from the materials published together in Volume I of the Iwanami edition. The "Diary" is thus the equivalent of Volumes II through VIII of the Iwanami edition.

The Army version was not "de-classified" for public use until my major undertaking had been done from the Iwanami text. It is now available in the Library of Congress microfilm collection that is basically taken from the Japanese Ministry of Foreign Affairs archives, of which—of course—it is not a part. In this microfilm collection the whole version is identified by the classification symbol, SP 161, in the subgroup denominated as "Special Studies."

I have not had access to the microfilmed copy of the original manuscript by Harada's secretary from which both ultimately derive.

II. Archival Materials

A. International Military Tribunal for the Far East. "Proceedings" and "Exhibits." Manuscript (mimeographed) collections.

These have been consulted in the imperfect sets in the Law Library, the Library of Congress; the Center for Japanese Studies, University of Michigan; and the Library of the Detroit Bar Association. (A portion of the

312

relevant materials available at these proceedings has been included in the collection identified next below.)

Japanese specialists will find it useful to consult:

Mori Kyōzō. *Kyokutō kokusai gunji saiban kiroku: mokuroku oyobi sakuin (Catalog and Index of the International Military Tribunal for the Far East)*. Tokyo, 1953.

And a useful guide to the "Proceedings" is available in:

Dull, Paul S. and Michael Takaaki Umemura. *The Tokyo Trials: A Functional Index to the Proceedings of the International Military Tribunal for the Far East*. Center for Japanese Studies, Occasional Papers, No. 6. Ann Arbor: University of Michigan Press, 1957.

B. Library of Congress. Microfilmed collection of archives from the Japanese Ministry of Foreign Affairs, Tokyo, Japan, 1868-1945, [and other documents].

A most essential guide to this entire microfilm collection has been published:

Uyehara, Cecil H., and Edwin G. Beal. *Checklist of Archives in the Japanese Ministry of Foreign Affairs, Tokyo, Japan, 1868-1945, Microfilmed for the Library of Congress, 1949-1951*. Washington: Photoduplication Service, Library of Congress, 1954.

The principal pertinent sub-groups within this whole collection, with their location symbols bracketed after their titles, include the following:

Japan, Ministry of Foreign Affairs. *Rondon kaigun kaigi ikken*. (Documents Relating to the London Naval Conference). [S 2.12.0.0. (1-35)]

————. *1930-nen Rondon jōyaku setsumeisho . . . kisō suii chōsho*. (Explanatory Documents Relating to the London Naval Treaty of 1930, and a Research Paper on the Drafting Thereof). June 1930. [SP 209]

————. *1930-nen Rondon kaigun jōyaku setsumeisho*. (Explanatory Documents Relating to the London Naval Treaty of 1930). 1930. [SP 110]

————. *1930-nen Rondon kaigun jōyaku, 1922-nen Washington kaigun jōyaku kankei jōbun taishō*. (A Comparison of the Provisions of the London Naval Treaty of 1930 and the Washington Naval Treaty of 1922). [SP 211]

————. *Rondon kaigun kaigi teikoku zenken fukumeisho oyobi hōkokusho*. (Report of the Japanese Plenipotentiaries to the London Naval Conference). June, 1930. [SP 227]

————. Documents preserved by [Japanese] Embassy in London. *Gumbi shukusho* (Disarmament). [UD 55-(1-3)]

International Prosecution Section, GHQ, SCAP. A Selection of Documents Analysed [for Use at the International Military Tribunal for the Far East]. [IMT (1-682)]

III. Japanese Works Consulted

Andō Norikata (Tokki) *Saionji Kimmochi*. Tōkyō: Hakuyōsha, 1938.
————. *Saionji kō to Kōnan sensei (Prince Saionji and Mr. Konan [Naitō Torajirō])*. Tōkyō: Genkai Shobō, 1936.

Ando Tokki. *Tōan-kō eifū (Mementoes of Prince Tōan Saionji).* Tōkyō: Shinmi Shoin, 1937.

Aoki Tokuzō. *Taiheiyō sensō zenshi (The Historical Prelude to the Pacific War).* 6 vols. Tōkyō: Sekai Heiwa Kensetsu Kyōkai, 1950-51.

Arima Yoriyasu. *Yūjin Konoe (My Friend Konoe).* Tōkyō: Kōbundō, 1952.

Asahi Shimbun Seijikeizaibu (ed.). *Kaigun Shukushō no hanashi (On Naval Disarmament).* Tōkyō: Asahi shimbunsha, 1930.

Baba Tsunegō. *Gendai jimbutsu hyōron (Contemporary Personalities).* Tōkyō: Chūō Kōronsha, 1930.

———. *Gikai seijiron (A Critique of Parliamentary Politics).* Tōkyō: Chūō Koronsha, 1933.

———. *Seikai jimbutsu fūkei (Men on the Political Scene).* Tōkyō: Chūō Kōronsha, 1931.

Fukai Eigo. *Sūmitsu-in jūyō giji oboegaki (Private Notes of Important Proceedings in the Privy Council).* Tōkyō: Iwanami Shoten, 1953.

Gendai Nihon shi kenkyū (Studies in Contemporary Japanese History). Tōkyō: Iwanami Shoten, 1938.

Hara Keiichirō (ed.). *Hara Takashi nikki (The Diary of Hara Takashi).* 10 vols. Tōkyō: Kengensha 1950-51.

Harada Kumao. "Ni-niroku jiken-jōsobu no ugoki (The February Twenty-Sixth Incident—Changes in the Elite)," *Sekai,* No. 50 (February, 1950), 92-102.

———. "Fuasshizumu no rōka—Gojūgo jiken (The Signal for Fascism—the May 15th Incident)," *Sekai,* No. 49 (January, 1950), 59-69.

Hashimoto Saneaya. "Saionji-kō no omoide (Reminiscences of Prince Saionji)," *Kokoro,* June-August, 1950; September-November, 1954.

Hattori Shisō. *Zettaishugi-ron (Essays on Absolutism).* Tōkyō: Getsuyō Shobō, 1948.

Hayashi Shigeru. *Kindai Nihon no shisōkatachi (Political Thinkers of Modern Japan).* Tōkyō: Iwanami Shinsho, 1958.

Hirano Yoshitarō. *Nihon shihonshugi shakai no kikō (The Mechanisms of Japanese Capitalist Society).* Tōkyō: Iwanami Shoten, 1934.

Imamura Takeo. *Hyōden Takahashi Korekiyo (A Critical Biography of Takahashi Korekiyo).* Tōkyō: Jiji Tsūshinsha, 1948.

Imanaka Tsugimarō. *Nihon seiji shi taikō (An Outline of Japanese Political History).* Tōkyō: Iwanami Shoten, 1936.

Inukai Tsuyoshi. *Bokudō hiwa (Secret Life of Bokudō [Inukai Tsuyoshi]).* Tōkyō: Mainichi Shimbunsha, 1950.

Itō Masanori. *Gunbatsu kōbōshi (Rise and Fall of Army Cliques).* 3 vols. Tōkyō: Bungei Shinjū Shinsha, 1958.

———. *Kokubō shi (A History of National Defense).* (Gendai Nihon bummei shi [Contemporary Japanese Civilization], Vol. IV.) Tōkyō: Tōyō Keizai Shimpōsha, 1941.

Iwabuchi Tatsuo. *Gendai Nihon seijiron (A Discussion of Modern Japanese Politics).* Tōkyō: Chūō Kōronsha, 1941.

————. *Jūshin-ron (Senior Statesmen)*. Tōkyō: Takayama Shoin, 1941.

(Japan, Ministry of Foreign Affairs.) *Shusen shiroku (Historical Records of the Termination of the War)*. Tōkyō: Shimbun gekkansha, 1952.

————. *Nihon gaikō nenpyō narabi shuyo bunsho (Chronology and Main Documents of Japanese Foreign Policy)*. 2 Vols. Tōkyō: Nihon Kokusai Rengo Kyōkai, 1955.

Kada Tadaomi. *Kindai Nihon shakai seiritsu shi (A History of the Development of Modern Japanese Society)*. Tōkyō: Bungei Shunjūsha, 1949.

Kada Tetsuji. *Nihon kokkashugi no hattatsu (The Development of Japanese Nationalism)*. Tōkyō: Keiō Shobō, 1938.

Kimura Ki. *Saionji Kimmochi*. Tōkyō: Shomotsu Tembōkai, 1933.

————. *Saionji Kimmochi den. (A Biography of Saionji Kimmochi)*. Tōkyō: Denki Kankō Kai, 1937.

————. *Saionji Kimmochi*. Tōkyō: Sara Shobō, 1948.

————. *Saionji Kimmochi jiden*. Tōkyō: Kōdansha, 1949.

————. *Saionji Kimmochi*. Tōkyō: Jiji Tsūshinsha, 1958.

Kinoshita Hanji. *Nihon fuasshizumu shi (A History of Japanese Fascism)*. 3 vols. Tōkyō: Iwanami Shoten, 1949.

Kiyosawa Kiyoshi. *Gaikō shi (A Diplomatic History). Gendai Nihon bummei shi [Contemporary Japanese Civilization]*, Vol. III.) Tōkyō: Keizai Shimpōsha, 1941.

Koizumi Sakutarō, (Shansin). *Zuihitsu Saionji-kō*. Tōkyō: Iwanami Shoten, 1939.

Konoe Fumimaro. *Heiwa e no dōryoku (Efforts Toward Peace)*. Tōkyō: Nihon Dempō Tsūshinsha, 1946.

————. *Ushinawareshi seiji (The Policy that Failed)*. Tōkyō: Asahi Shimbunsha, n.d.

Kuroita Katsumi. *Kōtei Kokushi no kenkyū (A Study of Japanese History—Revised)*. 4 vols. Tōkyō: Iwanami Shoten, 1931-36.

Makino Nobuaki. *Kaikoroku (Memoirs)*. Tōkyō: Bungei Shunjū Shinsha, 1948.

Maruyama Kunio. *Gendai Nihon gaikō shi (Modern Japanese Diplomatic History)*. (*Nihon gendai shi zensho [A Complete Series on Recent Japanese History]*, Vol. VII.) Tōkyō: Mikasa Shobō, 1941.

Maruyama Masao. *Gendai seiji no shisō to kōdō (Thought and Behavior in Modern Japanese Politics)*. 2 Vols. Tōkyō: Miraisha, 1958. (See partial English translation listed below.)

Minobe Tatsukichi. *Gendai kensei hyōron (A Discussion of the Present Constitution)*. Tōkyō: Iwanami Shoten, 1930.

————. *Gikai seiji no kentō (A Study of Parliamentary Politics)*. Tōkyō: Hyōronsha, 1934.

————. *Kempō to seitō (The Constitution and the Political Parties)*. Tōkyō: Hyōronsha, 1934.

Naikaku kambō kirokuka (Cabinet Secretariat, Records Section). *Genkō hōrei shūran (Compilation of Laws and Ordinances in Force)*. Tōkyō, 1907.

Bibliography

Nihon kokusai seiji gakki (Japan Association of International Relations); general editor, Tsunoda Jun. *Taiheiyō sensō e no michi: Kaisen gaikōchi (The Road to the Pacific War: A Diplomatic History).* 7 vols. Tōkyō: Asahi Shimbunsha, 1962-63.

Oka Yoshitake. *Kindai Nihon no seijika (Modern Japanese Statesmen).* Tōkyō: Bungei Shunjū Shinsha, 1960.

Okada Keisuke. *Okada Keisuke kaikōroku (Memoirs of Okada Keisuke).* Tōkyō: Mainichi Shimbunsha, 1950.

Osatake Takeshi. *Nihon kensei shi taikō (A Summary of Japanese Constitutional History).* 2 vols. Tōkyō: Hyōronsha, 1938-39.

Rekishigaku Kenkyū Kai. *Taiheiyō sensō shi (A History of the Pacific War).* 4 vols. Tōkyō: Tōyō Keizai Shimpōsha, 1953-54.

Rōyama Masamichi. *Seiji shi (Political History). (Gendai Nihon bummei shi [Contemporary Japanese Civilization],* Vol. II.) Tōkyō: Tōyō Keizai Shimpōsha, 1940.

Saionji Kinkazu. "Harada no Kuma-san," *Bungei Shunjū,* No. 16 (1953), 184-89.

Shidehara Kijūrō. *Gaikō gojūnen (Diplomacy Through Fifty Years).* Tōkyō: Yomiuri Shimbunsha, 1951.

Shigemitsu Mamoru. *Shōwa no dōran (Upheavals of the Showa Era).* 2 vols. Tōkyō: Chūō Kōronsha, 1952.

Shiraki Masayuki. *Nihon seitō shi—Shōwa hen (A History of Japanese Political Parties—Showa Era).* Tōkyō: Chūō Koronsha, 1949.

Shirayanagi Shūko. *Saionji Kimmochi den (A Biography of Saionji Kimmochi).* Tōkyō: Hyōronsha, 1929.

Takekoshi Yosaburō. *Tōan kō (A Biography of Prince Tōan [Saionji]).* Tōkyō: Sōbunkaku, 1930.

Takigawa Masajirō. *Nihon shakai shi (A History of Japanese Society).* Tōkyō: Tōkō Shoin, 1940.

Tanaka Kōtarō. *Saionji Kimmochi den.* Tōkyō: Kaizōsha, 1932.

Tanaka Sōgorō. *Nihon fuasshizumu no genryū (Origins of Japanese Fascism).* Tōkyō: Hakuyōsha, 1949.

Togasaka Masanari. *Dantai sōran (A Compendium of Organizations):* 2nd ed. Tōkyō: Dai Nihon Teikoku Sangyō Sōrenmei Dantai Kenkyūjo, 1934.

Toyama Shigeki. *Meiji ishin (The Meiji Restoration).* Tōkyō: Iwanami Shoten.

Ugaki Kazushige. *Shōrai seidan (Old Man's Talk 'Midst Sighing Pines).* Tōkyō: Bungei Shunjū Shinsha, 1951.

———. *Ugaki nikki (The Ugaki Diary).* Tōkyō: Asahi Shimbunsha, 1954.

Wakatsuki Reijirō. *Kofuan Kaikoroku (Memoirs of Kofuan [Wakatsuki]).* Tōkyō: Yomiuri Shimbunsha, 1950.

Yabe Teiji. *Konoe Fumimaro.* 2 vols. Tōkyō: Kōbundō, 1952.

Yoshino Sakuzō. *Seiji oyobi seijishi kenkyū (Studies in Politics and Political History).* Tōkyō: Iwanami Shoten, 1936.

IV. Other Works

Allen, George Cyril. *A Short Economic History of Japan*. London: G. Allen and Unwin, 1946.

———. *Japan, the Hungry Guest*. New York: Dutton, 1938.

———. *Japanese Industry: Its Recent Development and Present Condition*. New York: Institute of Pacific Relations, 1940.

Atkinson, James David. "The London Naval Conference of 1930." unpublished Ph.D. dissertation, Georgetown University, 1949.

Bailey, Jackson H. "Prince Saionji: A Study in Modern Japanese Political Leadership," unpublished Ph.D. dissertation, Harvard University, 1959.

———. "Prince Saionji and the Popular Rights Movement," *Journal of Asian Studies*, XXI (1961), 49-63.

———. "Prince Saionji and the Taisho Political Crisis," in Sidney Devere Brown (ed.), *Studies on Asia, 1962*. Lincoln: University of Nebraska Press, 1962. Pp. 39-57.

Benedict, Ruth Fulton. *The Chrysanthemum and The Sword*. Boston: Houghton Mifflin Co., 1946.

Borton, Hugh (ed.). *Japan*. Ithaca, N.Y.: Cornell University Press, 1951.

———. *Japan Since 1931, Its Social and Political Development*. New York: Institute of Pacific Relations, International Secretariat, 1940.

———. *Japan's Modern Century*. New York: The Ronald Press, 1955.

Brown, Delmer M. "Recent Japanese Political and Historical Materials," *American Political Science Review*, XLIII (December, 1949), 1010-17.

Butow, Robert J. C. *Japan's Decision to Surrender*. Stanford: Stanford University Press, 1954.

———. *Tojo and the Coming of the War*. Princeton: Princeton University Press, 1961.

Byas, Hugh. *Government by Assassination*. New York: Alfred A. Knopf, 1942.

Colegrove, Kenneth. *Militarism in Japan*. Boston: World Peace Foundation, 1936.

———. "The Japanese Cabinet," *American Political Science Review*, XXX (1936), 903-23.

———. "The Japanese Constitution," *American Political Science Review*, XXXI, (1937), 1027-49.

———. "The Japanese Emperor," *American Political Science Review*, XXVI (1932), 642-59, 828-45.

———. "The Japanese Foreign Office," *American Journal of International Law*, XXX (1936), 585-613.

———. "The Japanese Privy Council," *American Political Science Review*, XXV (1931), 589-604, 881-905.

———. "The Powers and Functions of the Japanese Diet," *American Political Science Review*, XXVII (1933), 885-98; XXVIII (1934), 23-39.

———. "The Treaty-making Power in Japan," *American Journal of International Law*, XXV (1931), 270-297.

Conroy, Hilary. *The Japanese Seizure of Korea, 1869-1910: A Study of Realism and Idealism in International Relations*. Philadelphia: University of Pennsylvania Press, 1960.

Crowley, James B. *Japan's Quest for Autonomy: National Security and Foreign Policy, 1921-1938*. Princeton: Princeton University Press, 1966.

———. "From Closed Door to Empire: The Formation of the Meiji Military Establishment," in Silberman and Harootunian (eds.), *Modern Japanese Leadership*, 261-287.

———. "Japanese Army Factionalism in the 1930's," *Journal of Asian Studies*, XXI (1962), 309-326.

Dawes, Charles Gates. *Journal as Ambassador to Great Britain*. New York: The Macmillan Co., 1939.

Deakin, F. W. and G. R. Storry. *The Case of Richard Sorge*. New York: Harper and Row, 1966.

Dull, Paul S. "The Assassination of Chang Tso-lin," *The Far Eastern Quarterly*, XV (1952), 453-63.

Embree, John F. *The Japanese Nation, A Social Survey*. New York: Farrar and Rinehart, Inc., 1945.

Fahs, Charles Burton. "Political Groups in the Japanese House of Peers," *American Political Science Review*, XXXIV (1940), 898-919.

———. *Government in Japan, Recent Trends in Scope and Operation*. New York: Institute of Pacific Relations, International Secretariat, 1940.

Fairbank, John K., Edwin O. Reischauer, and Albert M. Craig. *A History of East Asian Civilization*. Vol. II: *East Asia—The Modern Transformation*. Boston: Houghton Mifflin Co., 1965.

Falk, Edwin A. *From Perry to Pearl Harbor—The Struggle for Supremacy in the Pacific*. Garden City, New York: Doubleday, Doran and Co., 1943.

———. *Togo and the Rise of Japanese Sea Power*. New York: Doubleday, Doran and Co., 1936.

Feis, Herbert. *The Road to Pearl Harbor: The Coming of the War Between the United States and Japan*. Princeton: Princeton University Press, 1950.

Fifield, Russell H. *Woodrow Wilson and the Far East: The Diplomacy of the Shantung Question*. New York: Thomas Y. Crowell Co., 1952.

Foreign Affairs Association of Japan. *The Japan Year Book, 1943-44*. Tokyo, 1943.

Fujisawa R. *The Recent Aims and Political Development of Japan*. New Haven: Yale University Press, 1923.

Great Britain, Foreign Office. *Documents on the London Naval Conference*. London: H. M. Stationer's Office, 1930.

Grew, Joseph Clark, *Ten Years in Japan*. New York: Simon and Shuster, 1944.

———. *Turbulent Era: A Diplomatic Record of Forty Years, 1904-1945*. Edited by Walter Johnson. 2 vols. Boston: Houghton Mifflin Co., 1952.

Griswold, A. Whitney. *The Far Eastern Policy of the United States.* New York: Harcourt, Brace and Co., 1938.

Gubbins, J. H. *The Making of Modern Japan.* London: Seely, Service and Co., Ltd., 1922.

Hackett, Roger. "The Military—Japan," in Ward and Rustow (eds.), *Political Modernization in Japan and Turkey,* 328-351.

———. "Yamagata and the Taisho Crisis, 1912-1913," in Sidney Devere Brown (ed.), *Studies on Asia, 1962.* Lincoln: University of Nebraska Press, 1962 Pp. 21-38.

Hall, John Whitney and Richard K. Beardsley (eds.). *Twelve Doors To Japan.* New York: McGraw-Hill Book Co., 1965.

Hall, John Whitney. *Japanese History: A Guide to Japanese Reference and Research Materials.* Center for Japanese Studies, Bibliographical Series, No. 4. Ann Arbor, Michigan: University of Michigan Press, 1954.

Hall, Robert. *Education for a New Japan.* New Haven: Yale University Press, 1949.

Holtom, Daniel C. *Modern Japan and Shinto Nationalism.* Chicago: The University of Chicago Press, 1943.

———. *The Political Philosophy of Modern Shinto.* Transactions of the Asiatic Society of Japan, Vol. XLIX, Part II. Tokyo: Keio University Press, 1922.

———. *The National Faith of Japan: A Study of Modern Shinto.* London: Kegan Paul, Trench, Trubner and Co., 1938.

Horwitz, Solis. *The Tokyo Trial.* "International Conciliation," No. 465. New York: Carnegie Endowment for International Peace, 1950.

Howland, Charles Prentice (ed.). *A Survey of American Foreign Relations, 1930.* New Haven: Yale University Press, 1931.

Ike, Nobutake. *The Beginnings of Political Democracy in Japan.* Baltimore: The Johns Hopkins University Press, 1950.

———. *Japanese Politics.* New York: Alfred A. Knopf, 1957.

Iriye, Akira. *After Imperialism: The Search for a New Order in the Far East, 1921-1931.* Cambridge: Harvard University Press, 1965.

Ishii, Ryoichi. *Population Pressure and Economic Life in Japan.* London: P. S. King and Son, Ltd., 1937.

Iwasaki, Uichi. *Working Forces in Japanese Politics.* New York: Columbia University Press, 1921.

Jansen, Marius B. (ed.). *Changing Japanese Attitudes Toward Modernization.* Princeton: Princeton University Press, 1965.

———. *The Japanese and Sun Yat-sen.* Cambridge: Harvard University Press, 1954.

———. "Oi Kentaro: Radicalism and Chauvinism," *The Far Eastern Quarterly,* XI (1952), 305-16.

Kitazawa, Naokichi. *The Government of Japan.* Princeton: Princeton University Press, 1929.

Kodama, Yoshio. *I Was Defeated*. Tokyo: Robt. Booth and Taro Fukuda, Pub., 1951.

League of Nations. *Report of the Commission of Enquiry*. Doc. C. 663.M.320, 1932, VII (Geneva: League of Nations, 1932). [The Lytton Report.]

Lewis, Sir Willmot, *et al. The London Naval Conference*. New York: Foreign Policy Association, 1929.

Lockwood, William W. *The Economic Development of Japan: Growth and Structural Change, 1868-1938*. Princeton: Princeton University Press, 1954.

Maki, John McGilvrey. *Japanese Militarism, Its Cause and Cure*. New York: Alfred A. Knopf, 1945.

McLaren, Walter Wallace (ed.). *Japanese Government Documents, 1867-89*. Transactions of the Asiatic Society of Japan, Vol. XLII, Part I. Tokyo, 1914.

———. *A Political History of Japan During the Meiji Era, 1867-1912*. New York: Charles Scribner's Sons, 1916.

Maruyama, Masao. *Thought and Behaviour in Modern Japanese Politics*. London: Oxford University Press, 1963.

Maxon, Yale Candee. *Control of Japanese Foreign Policy*. Berkeley: University of California Press, 1957.

Mayo, Marlene J. "Rationality in the Meiji Restoration: The Iwakura Embassy," in Silberman and Harootunian (eds.). *Modern Japanese Leadership*, 323-370.

———. "The Iwakura Mission to the United States and Europe, 1871-1873," in *Researches in the Social Sciences on Japan*, No. 6, Columbia University, East Asian Institute Studies, 1959, 28-47.

Merton, Robert King (ed.). *Reader in Bureaucracy*. Glencoe, Illinois: The Free Press, 1952.

Miller, Frank O. *Minobe Tatsukichi: Interpreter of Constitutionalism in Japan*. Berkeley: University of California Press, 1965.

Morley, James William. "Checklist of Seized Japanese Records in the National Archives," *The Far Eastern Quarterly*, IX (1950), 306-33.

Morris, I[van] I. *Nationalism and the Right Wing in Japan: A Study of Postwar Trends*. London: Oxford University Press, 1960.

Morris, Ivan. *The World of the Shining Prince: Court Life in Ancient Japan*. New York: Alfred A. Knopf, 1964.

Morse, Hosea Ballou, and Harley Farnsworth MacNair. *Far Eastern International Relations*. Boston: Houghton Mifflin Co., 1931.

Moulton, Harold Glenn. *Japan, an Economic and Financial Appraisal*. Washington: The Brookings Institution, 1931.

Myers, William Starr. *The Foreign Policy of Herbert C. Hoover*. New York: Charles Scribner's Sons, 1940.

Nagai, Micho. "Herbert Spencer in Early Meiji Japan," *The Far Eastern Quarterly*, XIV (1954), 55-64.

Nakano, Tomio. *The Ordinance Power of the Japanese Emperor*. Baltimore: The Johns Hopkins University Press, 1923.

Norman, E. Herbert. "The Feudal Background of Japanese Politics." Secretariat Paper No. 9 for the Ninth Conference of the Institute of Pacific Relations; New York, 1945.

————. "The Genyosha, A Study in the Origins of Japanese Imperialism," *Pacific Affairs*, XVII (1944), 261-84.

————. *Japan's Emergence as a Modern State: Political and Economic Problems of the Meiji Period*. New York: Institute of Pacific Relations, International Secretariat, 1940.

Oka, Takashi. "Saionji and the Manchurian Crisis." Papers on China from the Regional Studies Seminars, VIII, Committee on International and Regional Studies, Harvard University, 1954.

Omura, Bunji. *The Last Genro: Prince Saionji, The Man Who Westernized Japan*. Philadelphia: J. B. Lippincott Co., 1938.

Orchard, John E. *Japan's Economic Position. The Progress of Industrialization*. New York: McGraw-Hill Book Co., 1930.

Pearson, Drew, and Constantine Brown. *The American Diplomatic Game*. New York: Doubleday, Doran and Co., 1935.

Pittau, Joseph. *Political Thought in Early Meiji Japan*. Cambridge: Harvard University Press, 1967.

Quigley, Harold S. *Far Eastern War, 1937-1941*. Boston: World Peace Foundation, 1942.

————. *Japanese Government and Politics: An Introductory Study*. New York: The Century Company, 1932.

Read, Conyers. "Recent United States and British Publication on the London Naval Conference of 1930," *American Historical Review*, LIV (1949), 307-14.

Reed, John Paul. "Kokutai: A Study of Certain Sacred and Secular Aspects of Japanese Nationalism." Unpublished doctoral dissertation, Department of Sociology, The University of Chicago, 1940.

Reischauer, Edwin O. *Japan Past and Present*. 3d ed., rev.; New York: Alfred A. Knopf, 1964.

————. *The United States and Japan*. 3d ed.; Cambridge: Harvard University Press, 1965.

Reischauer, Robert Karl. *Japan, Government—Politics*. New York: The Ronald Press, 1939.

Sansom, Sir George B. *A History of Japan*. 3 Vols. Stanford: Stanford University Press, 1958-1963.

————. *Japan, A Short Cultural History*. New York: D. Appleton, Century Co., 1943.

————. *The Western World and Japan: A Study in the Interaction of European and Asiatic Cultures*. New York: Alfred A. Knopf, 1950.

Scalapino, Robert A. *Democracy and the Party Movement in Pre-war Japan: The Failure of the First Attempt*. Berkeley: University of California Press, 1953.

Schumpeter, Elizabeth B. (ed.). *The Industrialization of Japan and Manchukuo, 1930-1940*. New York: Macmillan, 1940.

Shaw, Roger. "The London Naval Conference of 1930." Unpublished doctoral dissertation, Department of History, Fordham University, 1946.

Silberman, Bernard S. and H. D. Harootunian (eds.). *Modern Japanese Leadership: Transition and Change.* Tucson: University of Arizona Press, 1966.

Statler, Oliver. *Japanese Inn.* New York: Random House, 1961.

Stimson, Henry L. *The Far Eastern Crisis.* New York: Harper and Brothers, 1936.

————, and MacGeorge Bundy. *On Active Service in Peace and War.* New York: Harper and Brothers, 1948.

Storry, Richard. *The Double Patriots: A Study of Japanese Nationalism.* London: Chatto and Windus, 1957.

————. "Konoye Fumimaro, 'Last of the Fujiwara'," *St. Anthony's Papers, No. 7: Far Eastern Affairs, No. 2,* G. F. Hudson (ed.). London: Chatto and Windus, Ltd., 1960.

Takekoshi, Yosaburo. *Economic Aspects of the History of the Civilization of Japan.* 3 vols. New York: The Macmillan Co., 1930.

————. *Prince Saionji.* Translated by Kozaki Nariaki. Kyoto: Retsumeikan University, 1933.

Takeuchi, Tatsuji. *War and Diplomacy in the Japanese Empire.* New York: Doubleday, Doran and Co., 1935.

Tanin, O. and E. Yohan. *Militarism and Fascism in Japan.* London: Martin Lawrence Ltd., 1935.

Tate, Merze. *The United States and Armaments.* Cambridge: Harvard University Press, 1948.

Tiedemann, Arthur E. "The Hamaguchi Cabinet: First Phase July 1929—February 1930: A Study in Japanese Parliamentary Government," unpublished Ph.D. dissertation, History Department, Columbia University, 1959.

Totten, George O. (ed.). *Democracy in Prewar Japan: Groundwork or Façade?* Boston: D. C. Heath and Co., 1965.

Tsunoda, Ryusaku, and others (eds.). *Sources of the Japanese Tradition.* New York: Columbia University Press, 1958.

Turner, John E. "The Kenseikai: Leader vs. Party Liberal." *The Far Eastern Quarterly,* XV (1953), 317-34.

U. S. State Department. *Proceedings of the London Naval Conference of 1930 and Supplementary Documents.* Washington: Government Printing Office, 1931.

U. S. State Department. *Papers Relating to the Foreign Relations of the United States, 1930.* Vol. I. Washington: Government Printing Office, 1945.

Wald, Royal. "The Young Officers' Movement in Japan, 1925-1937: Ideology and Actions." Unpublished dissertation, University of California, 1949.

Ward, Robert E. *Japanese Political Science: A Guide.* Center for Japanese Studies, Bibliographical Series, No. 1. Rev. ed.; Ann Arbor: University of Michigan Press, 1961.

————, and Dankwart A. Rustow (eds.). *Political Modernization in Japan and Turkey.* Princeton: Princeton University Press, 1964.

Wheeler-Bennett, J. W. *Disarmament and Security Since Locarno, 1925-1931.* London, 1932.

White, Leonard D. (ed.). *The Civil Service in the Modern State.* Chicago: University of Chicago Press, 1930.

Wildes, Harry Emerson. *Japan in Crisis.* New York: Macmillan Co., 1934.

Williams, Benjamin H. *The United States and Disarmament.* New York: McGraw-Hill Book Co., 1931.

Woodward, E. L., and Rohan Butler (eds.). *Documents on British Foreign Policy, 1919-1939.* Second Series, Vol. I. London: H. M. Stationer's Office, 1946.

Yamagiwa, Joseph K. "Language as an Expression of Japanese Culture," in Hall and Beardsley, *Twelve Doors to Japan,* 186-221.

————. *The Modern Japanese Written Language.* Ann Arbor: Edwards Brothers, 1942.

Yanaga, Chitoshi. *Japan Since Perry.* New York: McGraw-Hill Book Co., 1949.

Yoshihashi, Takehiko. *Conspiracy at Mukden: The Rise of the Japanese Military.* New Haven: Yale University Press, 1963.

Young, Arthur Morgan. *Imperial Japan, 1926-1938.* New York: William Morrow and Company, 1938.

————. *Japan in Recent Times, 1912-1916.* New York: William Morrow and Company, 1929.

V. Biographical Aids

Apart from sources otherwise noted, biographical data for the annotations have been derived variously from the following standard reference works:

Dai jimei jiten. 1954 ed.

Jinji kōshinroku. 1932 ed.

Nihon Shinshiroku. 1931 ed.

Taishū jinjiroku. 1932 ed.

Who's Who in Japan. 1931 ed.

Index

Page numbers in italic type indicate the pages on which photographic illustrations appear. A list of all illustrations appears on page 330.

ILLUSTRATIONS

THE SAIONJI-HARADA MEMOIRS

*Baron Harada Kumao was political secretary to Prince Saionji
Kimmochi for fourteen years before the Prince's death in 1940. Harada
kept a faithful record of the ideas, comments, and activities of Prince
Saionji, who was not only the last of the* genrō *(Elder Statesmen) but
also Japan's leading "liberal."*
In Fragile Victory, *Thomas Francis Mayer-Oakes, a teacher of
history, Wayne State University, translates that part of
Harada's record which details the 1930 power struggle in Japan over
ratification of the London Naval Treaty.*

*The manuscript was prepared for publication by Barbara Woodward
and Ralph Busick. The book was designed by Richard Kinney. The type
face for the text is Linotype Baskerville, originally cut by John Baskerville
in the mid-18th Century. The display face is Mistral
designed by Roger Excoffon in 1953.
The book is printed on S. D. Warren's Olde Style Antique and
bound in Columbia Mills' Bayside Vellum.
Manufactured in the United States of America.*

Sea of Japan

Pacific Ocean

Mt. Fuji

Gotemba

Gōra

Odawar

K

Lake
Hakone

Suruga Bay

Numazu

Atami

Okitsu

Miho

Izu Peninsula